DANIEL SHAYS'S
Honorable
Rebellion

DANIEL SHAYS'S Honorable Rebellion

❧ *An American Story* ❧

DANIEL BULLEN

WESTHOLME
Yardley

To Uncle Dick & Terry, since before the beginning

Westholme Publishing, LLC
904 Edgewood Road
Yardley, Pennsylvania 19067
Visit our Web site at www.westholmepublishing.com

ISBN: 978-1-59416-365-4
Also available as an eBook.

Printed in the United States of America.

"Can history produce an instance of a rebellion so honourably conducted? . . . God forbid we should ever be twenty years without such a rebellion."—Thomas Jefferson, November 13, 1787

"These things never happened; they always are."—Sallust

Contents

Illustrations

MAPS

ILLUSTRATIONS

(Gallery follows page 156)

Timeline

1747   Daniel Shays born, second child of six, first son, on Saddle Hill farm in Hopkinton, Massachusetts, to Patrick Shea and Margaret Dempsey.

1748   June 16: Abigail Gilbert born in Brookfield, daughter of Sergeant Jonathan Gilbert; Orphaned in 1760.

1766   The "Great Rebellion" against the feudal land barons in Duchess Country, New York.

1766   Green Mountain Boys oppose New York real estate speculators' claims to the Wentworth Grants in what is now Vermont.

1767   South Carolina Regulators impose law and order in the absence of government authority or support.

1771   North Carolina Regulators organize resistance to unjust local authorities; North Carolina Governor Tryon leads an army to suppress them; a shootout at Alamance Creek (May 16) kills nine on each side; Regulators are arrested and seven are executed later.

1772   September: Daniel Shays marries Abigail Gilbert; with his dowry, Shays buys sixty-eight acres in Shutesbury, then an additional six acres in 1773.

1773   January: First son born, Daniel Jr.

1774   Farmers in all the Massachusetts towns west of Boston defy the Crown's Massachusetts Government Act, and assert local control by forcing the king's agents to resign their commissions or flee, making Massachusetts functionally independent two years before the Declaration of Independence.

       Shays's daughter Lucy born

1775   April 19: Confrontations at Lexington and Concord push Massachusetts to a state of war.

       Shays marches to Boston after Lexington, enlists in Reuben Dickinson's regiment; recognized for bravery at the Battle of Bunker Hill.

1776   July 4: The thirteen colonies declare their independence from Great Britain.

       Shays's daughter Hannah Margaret born.

1777   Vermont is established as an independent republic.

       Shays promoted to commissioned rank of captain while recruiting along the Hudson River.

1777   Shays serves at the battles of Ticonderoga (July, colonial defeat) and
        Saratoga (September–October, victory), where the Continental army de-
        feats British General John Burgoyne, turning the tide of the war by making
        French support possible.

1779   July 16: Battle of Stony Point on the Hudson River; Shays is among the
        colonials who dislodge the British from a fortified hill on the Hudson,
        ending their attempt to divide New York and New England.

        Redcoats sail south in December, ending the northern war; many Massa-
        chusetts regiments return home.

1780   John Hancock elected the first governor of Massachusetts; Massachusetts
        barely ratifies the aristocratic state constitution drafted by James Bowdoin,
        John Adams, and Samuel Adams.

        October 14: Shays honorably discharged in Newark, New Jersey.

1781   October 19: British surrender at Yorktown.

1782   March 9: Shays selected to lead Pelham's committee of safety as one of the
        four heads of the local militia.

        April–August: Reverend Samuel Ely leads widespread protests in Massa-
        chusetts against taxes that were levied to fund lump sum payments to re-
        tired officers for five years' pay.

1783   March: Collapse of the "Newburgh Conspiracy," in which Continental
        Army officers threatened a coup if they were not paid their bonuses; retired
        officers led by Henry Knox establish the Society of the Cincinnati, which
        continues to lobby for privileges for officers; critics say they are trying to
        create an American aristocracy.

1783   September 3: Treaty of Paris formally ends the Revolution, granting Amer-
        ica its independence.

1784   January: British ministers pass Navigation Acts closing the West Indies
        to American shipping, precipitating a financial crisis in all thirteen states.

1785   May: James Bowdoin elected governor, passes austerity measures, raises
        taxes.

1785   September: The federal government sends demands to the states for pay-
        ment on the war debt.

1786   March: Massachusetts levies £29,000 pounds of direct specie taxes, 70 per-
        cent of which will repay government creditors at full value on depreciated
        bonds and soldiers' notes; Massachusetts towns petition for reforms.

        April–May: Rhode Island's Country party defeats the Mercantile Party,
        enacts economic reforms including printing paper money; farmers in
        Maryland and Pennsylvania stage protests and win concessions from their

states' governments to depreciate debts and issue paper money; Governor Bowdoin settles claims against his lands in Maine, selling off hundred acre plots at nominal prices, but still refuses to resolve the deepening crisis.

June: Farmers in Bristol County, Massachusetts, try but fail to stop their county court from meeting to hear suits for debt and foreclosure.

July 18: The General Court ignores the people's petitions and adjourns without issuing reforms, precipitating emergency meetings in Pelham and other western Massachusetts hill towns.

August 22–25: Delegates from fifty Hampshire County towns discuss remedies at the Hatfield Convention. Shays declines the invitation to lead the Regulators in their first protests in Northampton.

August 29: 1,500 Massachusetts Regulators under Luke Day close the Northampton Court of Common Pleas without violence.

September 2: Governor Bowdoin issues a proclamation stating that the nonviolent protestors have introduced "riot, anarchy, and confusion" into the state, and asserts that the protests will lead to "absolute despotism."

September 5–13: Hundreds of Regulators close regional foreclosure courts in Worcester, Concord, Taunton, and Great Barrington. In Great Barrington, Justice William Whiting asks the militia to show their loyalties: 800 of the 1,000 militiamen take the people's side of the road.

September 19: Worcester Supreme Judicial Court issues arrest warrants for protest leaders.

September 21: New Hampshire Governor Sullivan suppresses protests in Exeter in a showdown that comes to be known as the Paper Money Riot.

September 25–27: Shays recruited to lead the Regulators, assumes responsibility for 2,000 men, and keeps the peace while closing the Springfield Supreme Judicial Court without violence; judges cancel their Berkshire session as well.

September 27: Governor Bowdoin convenes an emergency session of the Massachusetts General Court; legislators pass a law that threatens consequences for militiamen who refuse to muster against protestors, but make only minimal adjustments to economic policy; Bowdoin and Henry Knox ask for federal troops.

Late September: Bowdoin sends 2,000 troops to Taunton, where the court is opened without disruption.

October: Samuel Adams drafts a Riot Act to suppress the protests.

October 23: A note circulates through Massachusetts over Shays's name, asking towns to be organized with officers and ammunition.

October 24: General Court passes the Militia Act, which threatens court martial or death for militiamen who refuse to serve.

October 28: General Court passes the Riot Act, which forbids all gatherings of more than twelve armed persons; allows sheriffs to kill rioters; seizes protestors' lands, tenements, goods, and chattel for the commonwealth, and threatens imprisonment for six–twelve months with thirty-nine lashes every three months.

October 31: Regulators in Windham, Vermont, close their court.

Late October: Congress approves $530,000 requisition to garrison 1,340 federal troops in Springfield, Massachusetts; delegates in every state but Virginia deny this request; no army troops are sent to Springfield.

Early November: General Court passes an Indemnity Act, offering pardons for previous demonstrations; legislature suspends the writ of habeas corpus, and makes it illegal to spread false reports to the prejudice of government.

Mid November: Shays leads 350 picked men to Rutland, where they establish a base of operations in the barracks that housed the army British General John Burgoyne had surrendered at Saratoga in 1777.

November 21: Shays, Adam Wheeler, and Abraham Gale close the Worcester Court of General Sessions without violence.

November 26: Concord court opens, thoroughly protected by militia.

November 28: Job Shattuck arrested, crippled while resisting arrest; John Hapsgood also injured; arresting constable Aaron Brown's potash works burned.

Early December: Grafton County, New Hampshire, courthouse burned to the ground; Groton, Massachusetts, courthouse burned.

December 5: Shays and his 350 men close the Worcester court again, without violence.

December 26: Shays, Luke Day, and Thomas Grover and 300 men close the Springfield court, again without violence.

1787   Early January: Bowdoin collects subscriptions from wealthy merchants and speculators; raises £6,000 to fund a private army of 4,400 men.

January 10: Bowdoin's proclamation names ringleaders for arrest.

January 18: General William Shepard occupies the Springfield arsenal.

January 19: 2,200 Regulators convene in Pelham, West Springfield, and Chicopee; Bowdoin's private army of about 3,000 men marches from Boston in a snowstorm.

January 25: Shepard repels Shays's approach to the Springfield arsenal with cannon fire that kills four and wounds twenty.

January 27: Benjamin Lincoln arrives in Springfield at 3:30 p.m.; Shepard routs Luke Day out of West Springfield and pursues his men north to Northampton; Shays and Eli Parsons retreat toward East Amherst; in South Hadley, snipers kill two regulators; Lincoln sets up camp in Hadley.

January 28: Regulators retreat farther, from East Amherst to Pelham.

January 29–February 2: A period of severe cold keeps both forces in their camps; Lincoln refuses to negotiate a truce or pardons; the General Court denies the Regulators' petitions for pardon.

February 3: 1,100 of Shays's men move to Petersham with Lincoln in pursuit.

February 4: Lincoln marches his 3,000 men thirty miles overnight to surprise 1,100 Regulators in Petersham; Shays flees to Vermont with 300 followers.

February 7: Shays and followers arrive in Bennington, Vermont; Luke and Elijah Day and others arrive over the next week.

February 9: Bowdoin offers a £150 reward for Shays, £100 each for Adam Wheeler, Day, and Parsons.

February 16: Samuel Buffington and twenty horsemen are turned back in Brattleboro, Vermont, by Shays supporters; Massachusetts General Court passes the Disqualification Act, which bars rebels from voting or serving as jurors, from town or state government, or from the professions of innkeeper, schoolmaster, or retailer of liquors for three years.

February 21: The *Worcester Centinel* reports that Abigail Shays and her brother were seen passing through Northampton with her property and children, on their way west to join her husband in exile.

February 25: Shays in Quebec with Wheeler, Sylvanus Billings, William Conkey, Nehemiah Hines, Mr. Cornell, and Daniel Gray, to request asylum from Lord Dorchester, after having failed to secure asylum from Vermont Governor Thomas Chittenden in Williston.

February 26–27: Hamlin's raid, marauding, ends in skirmish in Sheffield.

Late February: Shays returns to Arlington, Vermont; ten of Shays's creditors file suit against his property in Pelham.

Late March: Trials begin in Great Barrington; judges sentence six Hampshire County men to death, six in Berkshire County, one in Worcester, one in Concord.

April 1: Massachusetts elections; Voters elect John Hancock in a 2 to 1 landslide; when Hancock takes office in June, his new government will reform the tax structures, restore suffrage to disqualified protestors, and cancel the death sentences, in addition to lowering taxes and releasing debtors from jail; Hancock cancels the bounty on Shays, Day, and Parsons, but he cannot repeal the arrest warrants or pardon them.

Spring: Daniel Shays and his followers build a settlement high up in the hills of Sandgate, Vermont.

May 24: Scheduled hangings are delayed a month because of threats.

May 25: Constitutional Convention begins in Philadelphia.

June 21: Jason Parmenter and Henry McCullough scheduled to be hung; they are pardoned on the gallows in front of a large, tense crowd.

July 24: Hampshire County Court divides Shays's property into ten lots to satisfy creditors, including former Regulators.

1788   February: United States Constitution ratified, over the objection of western Massachusetts' delegates.

Spring: Shays and his family moves from Sandgate to a house that still stands on the south side of Arlington on the road to Bennington.

June 25: Shays and Parsons receive a full pardon.

1795   June: Shays and his family move from Arlington to Rensselaerville, New York.

1799   Abigail dies; Shays living in Scoharie, New York.

1815   April: In Sparta, New York, Daniel Shays marries Rhoda Havens, a widow and tavernkeeper.

1825   Shays dies in Sparta, New York, leaving his property to his son Gilbert and assigning David Conkey administrator of his estate.

Preface

I FOUND THIS STORY ON THE SIDE OF THE ROAD and took it home with me. Literally, this book started when I saw a "Daniel Shays Highway" road sign northbound on Massachusetts Route 202, between Pelham and Shutesbury. When I came home and looked up this Daniel Shays fellow, I found a story that had basically been discarded to the care of an inaccurate legend. I read and read, and soon I started to suspect that I might be able to give the story a home in a narrative that would respect the human experience at its heart.

I found this story in summer 2012. I was still fairly new to western Massachusetts, and I adopted this story for my own sake as much as for the story's. I was a recent transplant from the Hudson River valley—I grew up in the New York suburbs, went upstate to college and down to the city for graduate school. The Connecticut River valley and its culture were still foreign territory for me, so the protests of 1786-1787 became a framework for getting to know my new home. I visited all the local libraries for their Shays books. I visited Pelham, where I encountered knowledgeable and generous historical society members who had organized a Shays bicentennial in 1986. I visited the Springfield Armory National Historic Site, where rangers were preserving artifacts from the day four men were killed by cannon fire there in 1787. I drove to Brookfield, where Daniel Shays met his wife while he was a laborer on her father's farm, and to the hills of Sandgate, Vermont, where Shays and his family started from scratch in exile after having been hounded out of Massachusetts.

I looked at the hills through the eyes of families who had got their food and clothing from the fields and woodlots, people who had worked on each other's farms for years before the men ever marched through knee-deep snow to stop the courts. I looked for continuities in the landscape and in the seasons, and in books like Eric Sloane's *Almanack and Weather Forecaster* or Tom Wessels's *Reading the Forested Landscape*. In the Porter-Phelps Museum in Hadley, I saw a gorgeous golden cloud of unspun flax for the first time and learned something about Daniel Shays's people, who were great cultivators of flax and producers of linen. I visited the Shays family's Pelham home site and saw their view of the mountains. I attended historical reenactments and a lecture at the Cambridge, New York, historical society, on the New York-Vermont border, describing excavations at the Shays' Settlement in Sandgate. I used the story as a pretense to phone up my godfather, Uncle Richard, a master builder, to get him talking about historical building techniques and to learn what it would have taken for one hundred men to clear the woods and build a blockhouse using 1787 tools.

I learned about the region and the country from the conflict known— also inaccurately—as King Philip's War (also driven by powerful officials abusing their power)—to the river-powered mills and machine tool shops where parts were famously standardized in the manufacture of guns. I found echoes of the protests in other histories, including the so-called "Great Rebellion" on the Hudson in 1766 and in the North Carolina Regulation in 1771, and then in the hundreds of strikes and resistance movements Howard Zinn describes in *The People's History of the United States*. The history did not seem to be repeating itself, exactly, but flaring up from time to time in a long-running condition that had never stopped.

Even as I was researching and drafting, protests were in the headlines again. The country was reeling from the economic crash brought on by criminal real estate speculation and fraud. Regular people were losing their homes. The government had bailed out the big banks but refused to prosecute bankers. Occupy Wall Street had recently been driven out of the Financial District by riot police after building a movement around the rallying cry, "We are the 99%," and two populist presidential candidates were promising to give common Americans a voice against the powerful, wealthy, and deeply entrenched interests that had captured the government.

While I was searching through the books and the landscape for the people who had experienced this historical moment here in western Massachusetts to learn something about this landscape and this history—as the place

that might shape me, a place where I might contribute something of mine—
I thought that the best way to enter this ongoing history would be to bring
the Regulators' story to life as I could see it having been lived—as it was
still being lived—by long-suffering, peace-loving, proud, tenacious, and dignified Americans.

As clearly as I thought I could see the living experience in the history
books and in the headlines, I was hampered in the telling by a historical
record that had been warped by two hundred years of misrepresentations.
Key records were either missing (because ordinary people did not write long
letters for posterity) or else they were filled with contradictions—even for
some of the pivotal moments.

I settled on a firm rule: where facts existed, either in the primary sources
or in the research, I would neither ignore nor alter them. The story would
remain nonfiction, because reality deserves to be described on its own terms.
But at the same time, I refused to let the absence of documentation sap the
living experience from the narrative. There are plenty of things we can know
without records. You don't have to live in New England for long to know
that the lilacs give way to peonies at the end of May, or that afternoon thunderstorms yield to clear, fine Septemberish evenings in late summer. You
shouldn't need detailed records to know that when powerful men use the
mechanism of the state's laws to benefit themselves at the people's expense,
they will then use their authority to demonize their opposition, portraying
them as an existential threat to the state, in order to polarize the debate, to
isolate their critics, and to keep the rest of the populace on the sideline.

This affected how I weighted the sources to tell the story. For instance,
when the government issued arrest warrants on January 10 for Daniel Shays
and other leaders, Shays called his men together on January 19, 1787, in
Pelham. Historians have always asserted that Shays was planning to seize
the Springfield arsenal and wage war against the state—but the men only
marched to Springfield five days later, when the government's army was on
the verge of arriving. How do we explain his crucial delay?

To tell the story, you have to decide how to resolve these contradictions,
and to do that, you have to decide for yourself who these people really were.
I worked from a portrait that was less drunken rabble-rouser or discontented
farmers (as Shays and his people were characterized at the time) and more
mutual aid society—regular people who organized networks within their
communities and risked their lives and property to regulate their affairs
when their elected leaders turned their backs on them. Surely there are risks

involved in telling a people's history like this, but there are also risks in letting a history slip away simply because regular people did not submit detailed paperwork to the archives.

It's been nine years since I found this story. It will only be two-and-a-half more generations before I can really call this region my home, but telling this story felt like a good start toward understanding the spirit that lives in this place. I hope that what I have brought to the narrative will help you see the decent, dignified, and restrained Americans I got to know through my reading and my travels, a proud people who banded together to get through an experience that is not really all that different from some of the challenges we face today.

Introduction

I N SUMMER 1786, a postwar economic crisis roiled the new United States of America. In all the states, cash was in short supply, prices were skyrocketing, and debts were compounded by court fees. Regular people were losing their property or moldering in debtor's prison, or else they were fleeing to the frontiers. In the Commonwealth of Massachusetts, the crisis was also political. Farmers in Hampshire, Worcester, Middlesex, Berkshire, and Bristol Counties posted petitions to Boston by the dozen, begging for reforms and relief, but Governor James Bowdoin claimed that the state's authority depended on repaying the state's war debts in full.

When the people of Massachusetts could not get reforms after more than a year of petitioning, they organized protests to close the courts where judges would hear suits for debt. By late September, thousands of farmers had stopped seven courts, from Taunton in the east to Great Barrington in the west: five foreclosure courts and two of the criminal courts that might have issued arrest warrants for protest leaders.

When politicians swung into action in October, they did not advocate for the relief measures governments had issued in Pennsylvania, Maryland, and other states where protests had erupted in response to similar conditions. Instead, they passed a Riot Act and strengthened the state's militia to threaten the protestors. Boston resident Henry Knox, the famous Revolutionary War artillery officer, wrote to Mount Vernon, begging George Washington to act. His ominous October 28 letter said that "12 or 15,000 desperate and unprincipled men" were staging "a formidable rebellion against reason, the principle of all government, and the very name of liberty." He said protests would lead to "all the horror of faction and civil war" and to "an arbitrary and capricious armed tyranny."[1] In a separate letter to Congress in Philadelphia, Knox begged for resources to suppress what he branded "Shays' Rebellion," for he claimed that the statewide protests were led by one man: Captain Daniel Shays, a thirty-nine-year-old retired Revolutionary War officer who was intent on overthrowing the state, and seizing and redistributing rich men's wealth. At no point did the government swing into action to repel an actual force of more than 10,000 armed men, but two weeks later, Knox's account had its desired effect. Washington wrote to James Madison—not to say he would use his considerable authority to ask Bowdoin to reform the policies that tormented his people but to say that he would come back from retirement to lead a constitutional convention that would strengthen the federal government against internal disturbances.

With this gesture, Washington was subscribing to a view that was widespread among nationalist elitists like Alexander Hamilton and Bowdoin: that the country needed a strong federal government to counter the dangerous farmers who would replace order and good government with "natural law," where mobs would commandeer the wealth of the country and rule by brute force.[2] Without a word about the fiscal policies that had antagonized the people of Massachusetts, Washington said in a letter that the crisis proved that "mankind when left to themselves are unfit for their own government."[3]

By May 1787, delegates convened the Constitutional Convention, and by September 1787, a draft of a new constitution was circulating among the states. Less than a year later, it was ratified, creating the federal government America has been known for ever since. To this day, this account of "Shays's Rebellion" as "the unrest that led to the Constitution" is a mainstay in school curricula, and is it widely accepted in constitutional histories, even though Knox's account was almost entirely inaccurate, even to the point of slander against the people.

When you look at events from the ground, where people experienced them, it is clear that the protests were never a rebellion. The people's protests were all in line with a long English tradition of theatrical direct action. They staged more than a dozen protests over five months, without a single act of violence. The farmers never made any attempt to overthrow or supplant their government. They repeatedly disavowed any such desire in their letters. By the time they took action, they had sent scores of petitions to Boston over a year and a half, begging for reforms to the openly unjust policies that threatened their property and liberties. But even when reforms made it out of the House of Representatives, they were suppressed by Bowdoin and the merchant elites who held power in the Senate, who drove the farmers to desperation by ignoring their concerns.

These farmers were also not a mob of disaffected riffraff but proud, cash-poor farmers, many of whom were distinguished veterans of the Revolution. Thirty were commissioned officers, three were members of the elite officers' Society of the Cincinnati, and their ranks contained numerous state repre-sentatives. Their campaign enjoyed broad support among the towns' militias, who shared their sufferings and either joined or refused to suppress them. They were tolerated well by government men, who did not disperse them but once in twelve protests. Nor did the farmers return fire when four of their men were shot down by government cannon. They simply fled to cries of "murder, murder."

By calling the Massachusetts protests a "rebellion" in his letters to fellow leaders, Knox was condescendingly branding the crisis as a dangerous but doomed enterprise, destined to be suppressed before it was absorbed into the growing nation—but he was wrong here as well. The people of Massa-chusetts were not defeated. Two months after Shays's men scattered before the government's guns, his people won a landslide electoral victory that led to reforms of all the economic policies that had driven them into the court-yards in August and September.

We are used to saying that history is written by the victors, but in this case, the people of Massachusetts won a decisive victory that brought re-forms, and yet the Massachusetts history standards still call for teaching "Shays's Rebellion" as "the armed uprising that gave us the US Constitu-tion." In the mythology of America, it seems to be easier to believe the story that the American people could not be trusted to govern themselves than the story that keeps also trying to be told: that sometimes regular people have to band together to protect themselves from the government and from the rich men who use its laws and economic policies to serve their interests at the people's expense.

It was not easy to gather the facts that would let me tell the story of the crisis from the perspective of the people who experienced it. The historical record itself was tilted against the farmers. The voices of men in govern-ment had been preserved in detail, for prominent men were always writing for posterity, describing their role in forging the new nation. Common people's letters were not as well preserved, so when historians looked for their statements, they tended to cherry-pick the most inflammatory statements from anonymous editorials to portray the people in the most threatening light.

The living history was not just hindered by missing records. It had also been obscured at the time by government officials who used righteous-sounding rhetoric to hide inflammatory policies and actions. The government repeatedly stoked the people's outrage with flagrantly unjust economic policies—which explicitly benefitted the rich at the farmers' expense—even as government officials held forth about the virtues of honoring contracts and repaying borrowed money. The government's monetary policy filled the debtors' prisons with distinguished men, but the governor said that his legislators did not experience the sufferings the people described. He then claimed that the people had brought the crisis on themselves by luxurious spending. Most provocatively, the government suspended habeas corpus and passed a Riot Act that would seize protestors' land. The government even went so far as to authorize its agents to murder protestors—and then called the people rebels and anarchists when they organized resistance to these baldly tyrannical measures.

The myth of an unruly populace was so effective in obscuring the people's victory that historians have largely failed to describe the degree to which the people's discontent was a direct product of their government's actions. Most historians have steered around the complex details of the eighteenth-century currency, voting, and law-enforcement policies that had already antagonized the people before the fiscal policy finally brought them into the streets. They have largely overlooked the submissive letters and the fawning petitions the people's committees sent to Boston, and the people's oft-repeated commitment to nonviolence. Likewise have they ignored the people's restraint, defining the movement instead by outrageous claims in anonymous editorials, or by the outbursts of uncoordinated violence that erupted in the months after Shays and his officers and three hundred men had been driven out of the state as refugees.

In the 1786 protests, American mythmakers had an opportunity to celebrate the dignity, pride, and restraint of their freedom-defending countrymen. Instead, we have inherited this other story, about elites saving the nation from ruffians, a story that feeds the perennial narrative that poor people and small landowners need to be subdued by force when they become politically active, with the fear-mongering caricature that their protests will jeopardize order and good government—or worse, threaten private property.

The facts about the people's 1786 protest campaign have all been in the public record for years. This book does not present new archival scholarship, with major new revelations about people or events. It simply tells the story that was hidden beneath "Shays' Rebellion," Knox's tidy and grossly inaccurate title. I offer "Daniel Shays's Honorable Rebellion" as a bridge that leads away from that story by gesturing toward the spirit of this prolonged, nonviolent, and victorious campaign. The title comes from Jefferson himself, who asked if the world had ever seen "a rebellion so honourably conducted," then said that the country should have such a rebellion every twenty years, advancing the view, popular at the time, that the true source of all political authority and power lay with the people and that popular demonstrations would ensure that a government remained responsive to the people.[4] Even George Washington said at the time that he had never seen such an "innocent insurrection."[5]

But "Daniel Shays's Honorable Rebellion" still does not revise Knox's narrative enough. A more objectively accurate title would name the crisis at its origins, with something more like "Governor Bowdoin's counter-revolutionary panic."[6] For the Massachusetts government was not the victim of its citizens' petulance or greed so much as it was caught in a crisis of its own creation. James Bowdoin and the merchant elites' hard-line positions on taxation and fiscal policy and representation and court fees created a self-fulfilling prophecy of opposition, which was meant to justify a demonstration of force that would bolster the government's authority. To judge by Bowdoin's landslide defeat in April elections, these were all losing tactics, although they did serve the larger purpose of clarifying the need for a constitution. Not a few of the country's elites were openly hoping for mayhem, to bolster the case for a stronger federal government.

I offer these explanations only for context, and to break the ice of an old story, to bring the reality to the surface. *Daniel Shays's Honorable Rebellion* is a narrative history. It draws on deep and far-ranging research into the times, people, and events, but it does not advance academic claims about post-Revolutionary or constitutional history or political philosophy, and it does not take a historian's detached stance. It tells the story from the people's perspective, allowing them to speak in their own voices as much as possible, as the crisis unfolded week to week, and Daniel Shays and the dozens of other leaders and the thousands of men and their families were forced to make hard decisions, up to the point of risking their lives, in order to protect what was important to them. I offer this narrative to professional historians and general readers alike, in hopes that it will scour away a tarnishing, misleading myth and remind us of our proud American tradition of solidarity and resistance in the face of unjust authority.

DANIEL SHAYS'S
Honorable
Rebellion

Prelude

January 25, 1787

P AST SNOWY FIELDS AND DRIFTED WOODLOTS, the column of twelve
hundred men poured down from the western Massachusetts hills in a
river of snow-flecked coats and faces red with cold.[1] Their orderly lines bris-
tled with muskets and clubs and flags on staffs, as the men's feet churned
the snow in time with marching songs that issued from rattling drums and
piercing pipes.[2]

The music brought farmers and their families to the roadside. Women
and children thrust their heads out of windows, their breath steaming into
the cold January afternoon light. Men stepped out of their barns without
coats to witness the spectacle of farmers marching to town to protest the
taxes and court fees that had been driving them out of their homes.

This was the third time in five months that families on the road to
Springfield had witnessed this same procession. Twice before—in September and then again a month ago, the day after Christmas—the farmers had
surrounded the courts to keep judges from hearing suits for debt and foreclosure, and also from issuing warrants to confiscate livestock and land.

For the past five months, as protestors throughout Massachusetts had
closed courts from Concord outside of Boston to Great Barrington on the
other side of the Berkshires, cash-poor farmers in all the states up and down
the Atlantic coast had followed the news of these protests in the newspapers.
Bankers in New York and merchants in Philadelphia and South Carolina
had scoured the reports from Massachusetts to see whether the farmers who
had thrown off British rule would still refuse to be governed, or whether

their protests would force Governor James Bowdoin to issue reforms. In their taverns and in the barns where they did their winter's work together, Americans speculated whether Bowdoin was going to suppress the people's protests with force and tyrannize them as the British had done in their time.

Now when the families along the road to Springfield heard military music and marching boots, some of them expected to see the common-wealth's infantry, the cavalry and draft horses sledding howitzers and cannon, the sledges loaded with ammunition and supplies.[3] For the papers had reported that Bowdoin was sending General Benjamin Lincoln west with an army of three thousand men charged with imposing order on his unsettled state.[4]

The drums did not belong to the army. It was the farmers who had waded down, through knee-deep snow, from hill towns thirty or forty miles away.[5] They were marching to the federal arsenal, where the American government maintained barracks and stockpiles of salt beef and fish, casks of flour and corn, in addition to thousands of muskets and cannon, gunpowder, ammunition, and bayonets.

Farmers along the roadside shouted encouragements for the battle that must be inevitable now, but Shays's men and their officers answered from within their lines that they were not marching to Springfield to start a war. They said they were going to keep the arsenal's weapons from falling into Lincoln's hands. They were going to take control of the weapons themselves, and once they could balance their force against Lincoln's, they meant to draw out the peace while they negotiated reforms.[6]

Not all the men pledged themselves to peace, though. Some raised their voices to say that they would never allow their leaders to be arrested, and some cried out that they would rather die in battle than at the gallows. Others warned the bystanders that the great men in Boston would take their land and property if they did not rise and protect them.

From windows along the road to Springfield, farmers and their families craned their necks, trying to gauge the farmers' mood by getting a glimpse of their leader, Captain Daniel Shays from Pelham. All the government proclamations and merchants' editorials blamed him for the disturbances and called the people Shaysites.

In reality, dozens of men from various towns had signed the people's proclamations. When asked, they consistently refused to say that any one man led them.[7] Frequently they had called themselves Regulators, joining a long tradition of common people banding together to regulate their government and administer justice in their region—even if it meant opposing men in power.[8]

So many of the thousands of men had served in the war together that any number of officers could have led the protests, but it was Captain Shays who rode near the head of the column on a white horse that distinguished him from his officers.

Proud and erect in his Continental army uniform, he handled his reins with a pistol in one hand and a sword in the other.[9] Almost as soon as the townspeople could identify him in the column, though, he was carried along on the tide of hats and muskets, and bystanders had to gauge his temperament by the appearance and the discipline of his men.

Many of Shays's men wore their uniforms from the war, but many wore suits of homespun linen or wool their wives or mothers had woven with their own hands. They had dyed them with chestnut or indigo, with hickory or squash. They took their colors from so many roots, barks, and berries that the men hardly looked like an army. Only one in four of them had a musket, and only one in ten of these had a bayonet.[10] The rest carried clubs, or else they were not armed at all, but they swung their cold hands to the uneven rhythms of forging through deep snow. Some wore leather gaiters, but many had marched from Colrain or Worcester with only heavy, homespun woolen hose.[11]

Still, they did not lag or straggle for the cold. They moved as one body, following each other, each town's contingents beneath their flags, in one long column that snaked along the border of fields, farms, and woodlots toward whatever negotiations waited for them in Springfield.

When the stream of flags and hats and swinging arms retreated—when the whistling flutes and thudding drums faded off into the distance and cows could be heard again, lowing across the snowy fields—the people along the road to Springfield returned to whatever work the procession had interrupted.

Whether these farmers hoped in their hearts that the people would arm themselves and renew the war against nobles in Boston, or whether they hoped that the government would crush this impudent insurrection—however they hoped the conflict would be settled, the cold kept them quick between barns and houses, and they measured their chores against the deepening chill as the thin January sun sank toward the snow-covered hills.

When Shays and his men finally came in sight of the arsenal buildings clustered at the top of the hill overlooking the Connecticut River, they found that Westfield General William Shepard had deployed a thousand men in lines across the road in front of the grounds.[12]

Shays and his men could see their bristling muskets from a distance, but this did not slow their approach. Soon they were close enough to see that Shepard's men had also sledded cannon out to face the road, but even once this was clear, Shays still refused to order a halt.[13] He did not pause to assess Shepard's defenses or wait for his scouts to tell him where his men might breach Shepard's lines with the fewest casualties.[14] He did not order his men to deploy for battle or tell them to pause while he sent envoys ahead under a white flag to negotiate for the grounds. For the past five months, he and his men had petitioned for reforms at the courts. They had kept the peace. Thousands of them had camped close to hundreds of government men without incident. Shays was not about to tarnish his people's reputation by commencing hostilities now.

On the white horse that had been lent to him for the occasion, Shays urged his men forward, as if he were simply impatient, after riding the eight cold miles from Ludlow, to warm himself at the hearths in the arsenal barracks.[15]

Shepard did not wait for Shays's men to come close enough to start negotiations for the arsenal's stockpiles of weapons and provisions. As soon as the farmers' lines came within range, he ordered his artillerymen to fire.

The men who worked the cannon had served alongside Shays's farmers in the war. Shepard himself knew Shays and his officers, and many of the armed men in his lines recognized their fathers and brothers within the approaching ranks, but Shepard gave the order, and his soldiers did not disobey him. They touched the smoldering wicks to the cannon, which bucked and belched fire and shook the air as the grapeshot flew out.[16]

Puffs of smoke rose from the cannon. Men in the front lines of the approaching column lowered their heads to brace for the impact, but the guns were aimed high, and the first two shots whistled past.[17] When the sharp percussion hit them a moment later they shuddered, but it was only for the sound. The stunned men realized they had not been shot. Some of the mounted officers were frightened off of their horses, but the others hunched together—they even picked up their pace, as if they might cross those last hundred yards in one rush.[18]

Still Daniel Shays did not order a halt. His men advanced as one body, bound to their cause as close as if they were married and each man could take refuge in the others as they approached their fate together.

As they pressed ahead, men in the front lines watched Shepard's men swab out the steaming cannon barrels to cool them and load new powder and canisters of grapeshot.

Again the guns coughed hot smoke into the cold air. But before the heavy reverberation of cannon shots reached them, men in the front lines were stopped in their tracks as grapeshot—as iron balls bigger than thumb knuckles—ripped through their chests, arms, and faces, spattering men behind them with blood, cloth, and bone.

The sound of wounded men's cries turned the forward platoons inside-out.[19] Shays ordered his men to continue forward, and the danger of battle rose in his throat, but even as the breath that gave then repeated the order dissolved in the cold, his column melted around him.[20] If his men thought they would commandeer the weapons in the arsenal to protect themselves from the governor's army, they were not going to fight through grapeshot and muskets to claim them.

Driven by instincts deeper than justice, each man obeyed his panic. The men in the front lines doubled back, but with snow drifted deep at the roadside, the men behind them had nowhere to go to get out of the way. They shouted and cursed at the men who had turned to push past them, but then the sharp blast and echoes of cannon—then the wounded men's cries of agony hit them, and they turned as well.

The column that had acted as one body a minute ago was shattered, and nothing Shays said could turn his men back into fire. The column that stretched up the road flooded back on itself, till finally the men in the rear caught the charge of revulsion. All twelve hundred farmers sprinted fleet as they could through the knee-deep snow, and the officers wheeled their horses around to follow.

The cannon's thunder had not even finished echoing back from hills across the river, but Shays's men's solidarity and opposition to government were already relics of an old world they had left behind.[21]

The men in the rear with Daniel Shays—men who had only a minute ago formed the forward-most rank—had not answered the cannon fire with anything stronger than cries of "murder, murder."[22]

Soon enough, they realized that the men protecting the arsenal had not left their posts to charge out and cut them to pieces in the narrow, snow-lined road.

Even after they had run far enough in the first rush and slowed their pace, Shays and his officers did not pause to regroup or consider different approaches. Their terrified men, desperate to get away from the swirling flames at the arsenal gate, simply dropped their arms, abandoned their wounded, and left their dead in the road as they turned back toward their homes.

In a panic, they put a half a mile, a mile, then two miles between themselves and the grounds where they might have seized arms and become an army.[23]

They fled past the houses where families had watched them march into town half an hour ago. Now those same men and women came out to witness their chaotic retreat, to spit in the snow and curse the wealthy merchants whose militia had betrayed their countrymen with cannon fire.

The evening's first shadows absorbed Daniel Shays and his twelve hundred men as they ran away from Springfield. When they finally slowed their pace and stopped tripping on each other's heels—when their blood stopped throbbing behind their eyes and they could finally understand their situation—most of the men knew in their guts that if they refused to fight, they could probably escape without punishment. For Governor Bowdoin's proclamations had offered pardons for men who would divorce themselves from this body and vow not to join further protests.[24] If they and the other foot soldiers swore an oath of allegiance to the commonwealth, they could return to their homes unmolested. They would still have to suffer the government's taxes and the courts' bailiffs seizing their livestock and land—they would have to choke down the injustice of government troops in their towns, but elections were slated for April. They would only have to wait the two months until they could try for reforms at the ballot.

Following his men in retreat, Shays would not be able to follow his men home. He might have lost his authority when his men turned away from the cannon, but General Lincoln would pursue him as the one man who represented the people—not just these men in the road but the dozens of communities who had hosted them and provisioned them through five months of organized protests. The people throughout the whole countryside had come to be known as Shaysites, and now he and a few other men would have to pay for the people's sin of rebellion.

Even if the people did win reforms through diplomacy or through the ballot in April—even if those reforms ultimately proved that their cause had been just in their countrymen's eyes—he had still led armed men against the courts. He would have to be arrested and punished, or driven out of the commonwealth, before the government could say that justice had been served.

As Shays's twelve hundred Regulators settled into the long, slow rhythm of retreat, they remained in their column. Even as dusk deepened over their heads, they did not take advantage of the shadows along the roadside to slink away to their farms. They were bound in solidarity—they would not abandon Shays or their other leaders. They resumed their orderly lines and put one foot in front of the other. They moved as a single body again, marching back as one people toward food and beds eight miles away, in Ludlow, where sympathetic families had hosted them last night.[25]

The houses came farther and farther apart as they left Springfield behind. They marched between snow-covered fields, and more and more stars pierced the gloaming. The windows at the roadside glowed yellow with lamp and candlelight, but as appealing as those lights were, the men did not stop to warm themselves. Nor were they so desperate that they broke into houses to stoke their resentments with violence or looted rum. Even when they marched past the homes of the wealthy men who had just defended the arsenal against them, they did not stop to vent their rage by plundering. In defeat as in protest, they retreated as one disciplined body.[26]

As the column of men snaked along fields and snowy streams in retreat, the darkness descended and deepened, and lights from houses sparkled across the hills. The night wind was cold in the men's eyes, the slushy snow cold in their soggy boots. Any redeeming beauty in the familiar landscape was poisoned by their betrayal and defeat and by the cold miles they still had to cover.

In two or three more hours of dark marching, Shays and his men would arrive back in Ludlow. After only a few hours' sleep, the false dawn would show in the sky. By the time the winter dawn itself broke frigid and pale, Shays and his officers would have to say what they would do before General Lincoln's army arrived, tomorrow or the day after tomorrow.

Everyone in the region was waiting to hear whether they would dissolve their force and abandon their cause—or would Shays make another attempt on the arsenal grounds? Perhaps they would hear that he had stationed men behind stone walls to aggravate Lincoln's army and slow his approach with unexpected gunfire, while he rallied more troops and prepared to renew the revolution.

For now, Shays and his men continued to march. With the scent of blood sharp in their noses—with the sound of cannon fire and their panicked neighbors' cries still ringing in their frozen ears—they forged ahead into the dark.

Whatever they thought they might still have to suffer, they stayed in their lines and let themselves be carried by their marching songs deep into the purple-blue night. Deep into their cold defeat, they covered the eight miles back to the houses and barns of Ludlow, where their people had taken them in and even now were waiting to give them refuge.

Chapter One

The Crisis Begins

I N JANUARY 1784, Daniel Shays had only been back from the war for a little more than four years. He had just filled his storerooms with the
pumpkins and squash, the carrots and onions and wheat and corn of his
third harvest in Pelham. His wife, Abigail, was spinning and weaving linen
and lace through her third winter of peace. Their son, Daniel Junior, and
daughters Lucy and Hannah, at eleven, nine, and seven, were studying
through their third winter at the Pelham school. Shays and his wife were
looking forward to a time when the little ones, Polly and Gilbert, at three
and one, would be old enough to contribute as well. But whatever plans
Daniel and Abigail Shays were making for their family that January, everything was disrupted when their new country was plunged into economic
crisis.[1]

The Treaty of Paris had formalized the colonies' independence from
England in September 1783, but in January 1784, the British ministers in
Parliament decided to punish their renegade subjects by striking a blow at
their trade.[2] They argued that the colonists who had waged a war to free
themselves from their country had lost the privilege of trading in its ports,
so they had passed Navigation Acts that closed the West Indies wharves to
American shipping.[3]

By spring 1784, Shays and his neighbors in the rolling hills along the
Swift River went to their taverns to learn from the newspapers tacked to
the walls that the aristocratic families who owned the commonwealth's industry, shipping, and trade were suffering steep declines in their income

from sales abroad.[4] From their Beacon Hill mansions and their offices over-looking the quays of Boston, the Bradfords and Winthrops, Philipses and Masons, the Faneuils and Phelpses, Breecks, Tyngs and Winslows—the shipping magnates whose trade reached every corner of the Atlantic Ocean—could not send their captains instructions to sell their cargoes of lumber and salt fish and beef in alternate ports.[5] The Baltic states exported the same raw materials, and shipments to Spain and the Mediterranean risked being seized or held for ransom by Barbary pirates, for along with the privilege of trade in English ports, the American captains had also lost the English navy's protection.[6]

With nowhere to export its produce, the new country watched its economy slow to a trickle as more and more ships sat idle at their moorings. Not just merchants but shipbuilders, sailmakers, rope makers, and chandlers were crippled as trade contracted.[7]

The inland farmers like Daniel Shays were not immediately affected by this contraction. They tended their livestock and crops and worked the land, but their independence, far from the coast on rocky subsistence farms, did not protect them for long.

The merchant elites in Boston had ties to all of New England's commerce. Their sales abroad were only one leg of their trade.[8] They balanced their exports by importing English manufactured goods for sale to the inland farms, and the British Navigation Acts had not done anything to stop the flow of English goods into American ports. Coastal merchants kept stocking their warehouses with nails, glass, and medicine that would help the interior settlements expand.[9] They stocked their shelves with dresses and coats, shoes and vests, the porcelain, wallpaper, or English wool that would remind the rustic Americans of civilized life in Europe.

The merchants had to make regular payments to English exporters for the wholesale goods they had imported in large quantities at the end of the war.[10] They had bought these goods largely on credit. They had not bought from the French, who offered goods at better prices, because the French demanded a larger percentage of a purchase up front in cash.[11] But now that merchants were starting to lose their income from sales abroad, they did not have cash to keep up with their regular payments to their suppliers.

American merchants asked their English trade partners if they could make their payments in paper money, but paper did not get its value from commodities and therefore lost its value over time. The merchants' request to devalue their debts shook their creditors' confidence. They thought the

Americans were trying to steal from them by paying their debts in depreci-ated money that was cheaper than the real value of what they had bor-rowed.[12]

As soon as English financiers saw signs that the Americans might not be able to pay what they owed, they refused to accept paper money and in-sisted on payment in hard coin that had been issued by banks whose money was backed by silver or land and therefore held its value.

This demand threatened to bankrupt even the wealthiest merchants. Hard coin was in short supply in the newly liberated colonies, but the Treaty of Paris explicitly respected trade agreements, so international law would take the European exporters' side when their lawyers presented unpaid bills to the courts and asked judges for warrants to seize merchants' property.[13]

From their offices in the narrow streets of Boston and New Haven, coastal merchants paid what they could, but soon their sales abroad were barely covering 10 percent of their payments. Scrambling to stave off bank-ruptcy, they sat down with their ledger books to see where they had loaned money so they could start to call in their loans. They turned to their dis-tributors and the inland retailers to whom they had advanced goods on credit, and their lawyers sent letters demanding payment with the same de-mands they themselves had faced: they would have to pay in coin.[14]

The inland retailers' customers were not used to paying for goods in coin. They normally paid in produce or paper money, so the shopkeepers who stocked the merchants' imported goods only did about a quarter of their business in cash; the rest was in produce or barter.[15] But that was not the coastal merchants' problem. Someone would have to pay. They would not allow themselves to be threatened with court proceedings if they still had the power to raise funds by making that threat in turn.

From their rocky hills, the inland farmers of Massachusetts might have looked down with satisfaction as the coastal merchants and businessmen fought for scraps in the courts. They might have said, as some wrote in ed-itorials, that the merchants should "shut up their shops and get their living by following the plough," for farming was "the last temptation for fraud and lying."[16] But the farmers could not feel satisfaction because they too were bound to the struggling merchants in chains of credit and debts. Soon enough the contraction pinched them as well.

By the time farmers were planting their crops in spring 1784, merchants and shopkeepers in the river towns had been receiving letters from their suppliers on the coast. These merchants were known as the River Gods, the handful of early settlers whose families controlled the major businesses, as well as the towns' business, in the commercial towns on the Connecticut River in Hampshire County and the Housatonic in Berkshire.[17] Even these aristocratic families had been visited by the importers' agents demanding payment and threatening to take their accounts to the courts.

Soon the farmers in Daniel Shays's region were starting to open letters from shopkeepers in Brookfield and Worcester, in Springfield, Northampton and Greenfield, in Pittsfield and Great Barrington, demanding they settle accounts. The shopkeepers, like the merchants, faced demands for payment, and they too sat down with their accountants to tally the funds they could raise if they called in their outstanding loans.

The shopkeepers and the farmers had worked together as partners for years, financing the farms' expansion into the uncut forests and hills. But that did not stop the men in the mercantile towns from passing along the same threat the merchants had made: if the farmers could not pay in coin, they would petition the commonwealth for authority to seize their property and land.

People in farming communities lived close to the land, satisfying as many needs as they could from their forests and fields, but it was not uncommon for families to carry small debts through the seasons, then pay the merchants with their harvests of wheat or corn, carrots or pumpkins or squash.[18] They would pay with lumber cut from their forests or with their winters' production of linen or lace, or shingles they would cut, brooms they would tie in their barns in the cold.

By summer 1784, the local merchants could not wait for farmers to load their carts with their harvests and bring them to town in spring. They sent letters demanding payment, but when the farmers opened those letters, they did not have anyone else to turn to, to raise funds to pay their debts. In their tight-knit communities, farmers traded their labor freely, working their fields, timbering their woods in teams. The future itself was a currency they traded back and forth freely. The families trusted that they would each work for the others in turn, paying their debts in work, even as they indebted themselves to their neighbors.

As more and more merchants demanded payment, and as payments shipped hard coin out of the country, hard coin was in such high demand that the value of every commodity started to plummet: soon farmers would need to bring ten or twenty or fifty times as much wheat or corn, timber or linen to market, to pay the same value in coin.[19] And that was only if they could find someone to trade hard coin for their goods, for wealthier farmers who held specie money were more and more reluctant to let it out of their hands, for its value would likely be higher tomorrow.

With hard coin scarce and inflation driving prices out of reach, the farmers who had fought a war for their liberty were helpless to pay what they owed. In Pelham, Daniel Shays had not been embarrassed by demands for money, but he and his neighbors in farming communities the length of the commonwealth stopped spending money on anything but necessities. They had always trusted their self-reliance and their distance from commercial centers to carry them through hard times. They knew how to return to traditional crafts, to replace manufactured goods by spending the tedious hours in making clothes and candles, foraging in their forests for their medicines, teas, and dyes.[20] Economizing could not save them from debts they had already contracted to pay, though. Soon they were starting to toss and turn through the summer nights, tallying their obligations against their farms' produce, calculating how much longer they could hold out before their creditors took their debts to the courts.

As the bottom fell out of the new country's economy, dockets in Massachusetts courts filled with suits for debt. Regional courts met in market towns, where wealthy magistrates added fees to the sums the debtors were obligated to pay.[21] In the widely hated courts, debtors were also held responsible for paying the cost of drawing up and serving writs, entering actions, and recording judgments.[22] This added £2 to £3 of court fees to over £6, a steep increase in a country where laborers had only been paid £15 for a year's labor before the crisis.[23]

Once the courts were involved, the people's debts mounted to the point where they abandoned any hope of paying. Their lives and property were held in their creditors' hands. Merchants could not afford to be forgiving, though, so when farmers could not come up with hard coin, they took their claims to the courts, where judges issued warrants that authorized them to seize the farmers' livestock and land for payment. If debtors did not have the money to pay, they could take a humiliating oath of insolvency, publicly declaring that they were incapable of meeting their obligations.[24] If a creditor thought that a debtor was only refusing to pay a debt out of pride or stubbornness, he would pay for the commonwealth to keep the man in debtors' prison in hopes that the cramped, four-foot-tall cells plus the humiliation and the labor his family lost on their farm would motivate relatives to sell off valuable property or borrow money from neighbors to raise funds and redeem them from prison.[25]

Soon the farmers of Pelham, and farmers and artisans in other farm towns were squeezed by demands for payment. By summer 1784, they were all working relentlessly to pay their own debts and volunteering on farms where families were missing the labor of men who had been taken to debtors' prison.

Working together under the hot summer sun, the people of Massachusetts broiled in their resentment of lawyers, of legislators, of public servants whose salaries they were sure were bankrupting them. A tide of rumors inflated Massachusetts's first governor John Hancock's £1,100 yearly salary to as much as £60,000, and the veterans who had stayed in the war to watch the British flag struck at Yorktown wondered whether they had really freed themselves from lords.[26]

In the summer evenings, when Daniel Shays rode a half-mile downhill from his house to meet his neighbors at William and Rebecca Conkey's Tavern on the west branch of the Swift River, advertisements in the newspapers tacked to the walls invited them to auctions where the courts were selling their neighbors' livestock and farms—auctions where rich men who still had hard coin were buying up farms at steep discounts and renting the farms back to the families who had homesteaded them.[27] No amount of beer or brandy could wash away the fear that the people were being brought under lordships again, as their ancestors had lived in England.[28]

If men turned their eyes toward the state for relief, the papers told them the Commonwealth of Massachusetts was not in any position to help them. During the Revolution, the government had borrowed huge amounts of money from French and Dutch financiers, and also from wealthy Boston merchants, to arm and provision ninety-two thousand men in thirty-eight regiments.[29] These loans had driven the commonwealth's debts from £100,000 before the war to £1.5 million now,[30] a staggering sum for a state whose impost and excise taxes only brought in about £60,000 a year.[31]

Even if Massachusetts's trade were not collapsing on account of the Navigation Acts, the commonwealth would still have been challenged to pay these debts. Its rocky farms did not generate much wealth in taxes, for the British Parliament had always prevented the colonies from developing their industries in order to protect British manufacturers' monopolies on trade in colonial markets. The loss of income had reduced the commonwealth's tax receipts to a trickle at the same time that its creditors were demanding to be paid. Inland merchants were losing sleep as they wondered how they would pay their debts, and powerful men in Boston were tossing and turning as well, for fear that the commonwealth might default on its debts and lose its credit. What would their hard-won liberty be worth if the commonwealth could not generate enough wealth to meet its obligations? In the newspapers, editorials fretted that without good credit, the state's creditors would help themselves to its assets or territories—or that the state would not be able to "defend their liberties and property in case of an invasion."[32]

The fear of collapse drove the crisis deeper, for the commonwealth's most influential businessmen stood to lose fortunes if the treasury could not repay the huge sums they had invested in the war—with the interest they had been promised. Soon powerful factions of merchants and financiers started scrambling to protect their interests and minimize their losses, at each other's expense if necessary.

Through their senators in the upper chamber of the General Court, the commonwealth's wealthiest businessmen suggested that the government should raise funds to pay its war debts by levying new taxes, but Hancock said the state had already demanded enough in the war, and he refused.[33] Hancock was one of the commonwealth's wealthiest men, but he had always courted the common people's favor, and he valued his popularity too highly to turn them against him with taxes. He proposed to stimulate the commonwealth's economy by issuing paper money.[34] This would make debts easier to pay, but the merchant elites would not agree to a policy that would simultaneously cost them money and increase Hancock's popularity.

Through summer into fall 1784, the crisis spiraled deeper as the factions battled. Hancock proposed that the state should write down its debts, like delegates had done in the nation's capital in New York, forcing some of the federal government's creditors to settle for as little as six pennies on the pound, a fortieth of their debts' value. Virginia's legislature had told some of its creditors that the state could not afford to pay more than a thousandth of its debts' worth, but the heads of Boston commercial houses would not allow their senators to agree to pay anything less than full value.[35] For farmers who followed the government's discussions in the papers, the General Court's debate over payment revealed the degree to which the commonwealth was dominated by influential men, for none of the economic reforms passed in the lower house—an issue of paper money, or a tender law that would let farmers pay debts in produce—stood any chance of surviving in the Senate.

From their inland towns, the farmers grudged the fact that the state's debts were not even legitimate debts any longer. The bonds had long ago been abandoned by the original bondholders.[36] They had sold the securities at discounted rates when they needed cash. Exchanges had sprung up, and the prices of these securities were published widely.[37] Speculators traded these notes, gambling their money on the hope that the commonwealth would one day be able to pay the notes plus the compounding 6 percent interest.[38] Everyone knew that whoever held these bonds would collect windfall profits—with effective interest of 20 or 30 percent—if they were ever paid in full.[39] One contributor complained about the speculators' inflated returns, writing that even "the simplest peasant sees that FIVE is less than TWENTY."[40] Another asked whether "the substance of the people [must] be sold at [auction] to redeem securities which did not cost the possessors one sixth part of the nominal value."[41]

Through summer and fall 1784, the papers were full of the crisis. On September 7, 1784, the *Hampshire Herald* reported that "the war has impoverished [the people], as well as brought a debt on the State. Their farms, buildings, clothes and furniture were all out of repair. They were in debt to one another and in debt to the soldiers they had hired. The crops for two or three years past have been cut short. From these and other causes, the most prudent people are deeply embarrassed."[42]

In editorials, farmers called for depreciation of debts, challenging wealthy men to "sacrifice the profits of the trade on the altar of liberty" as they had made their own sacrifices. Some complained that they were treated as "traitors, incendiaries, vile creatures" and that they were "threatened with prosecutions for daring to inquire into the present gross mismanagement of our rulers."[43] Merchants answered with editorials that argued for the importance of honoring contracts to the letter. They fretted that cash-strapped farmers might demand "a total abolition of debts both public and private and even a general distribution of property."[44] They prescribed "temperance, frugality and industry" as the solution to the crisis.[45]

Through all of this, the legislature lay deadlocked, helping no one. Hancock could only muster the political will to instruct his tax collectors not to press his citizens for taxes. This saved the people money and it preserved his popularity, but it also deprived the commonwealth of funds, compounding the crisis and exposing him to attacks from the wealthy merchants.

Through autumn 1784 into winter 1785, the question of taxes and debts and the economy was limited to the newspapers' editorial pages: no one pushed the crisis to the point of confrontation. The farmers did not summon their neighbors to mob the courts or to tar and feather the judges or merchants who tormented them. For that first year of the economic crisis, the people of Massachusetts were willing to be patient and even to suffer their losses while their new country got on its feet, even though the people had a rich tradition of extralegal action when the state's protections were not strong enough to shield people from injustice.[46]

By the end of winter 1785, farmers and merchants alike hoped that April elections would bring a solution, one way or another. That winter, Hancock announced his bid for reelection. He was challenged by wealthy merchant James Bowdoin II, who had run against Hancock before, in the commonwealth's first elections in 1780. At fifty-eight years old, Bowdoin had already enjoyed a successful career overseeing the vast commercial and real estate empire he had inherited from his father, a Huguenot merchant and land speculator who had been known as the wealthiest man in Boston before he died in 1747, handing his land and his business to his sons.[47]

Bowdoin had bolstered his place in the commonwealth's aristocracy by marrying his college roommate's sister, Elizabeth Erving—daughter of John Erving, who sat on the colony's governing council—then set about expanding his father's holdings.[48] With properties ranging from a large plot along the Kennebec River in Maine to farms, homes, warehouses, ironworks, and businesses from Cape Cod west to the Upper Housatonic (as the Berkshires were called when his father commissioned towns there), his interests stretched the length of the state, and the people of Massachusetts had watched them expand year to year.[49]

Massachusetts had grown as Bowdoin's father and Bowdoin himself and other speculators had commissioned surveyors to inventory the country, then paid to build roads, bridges, and mills, risking their money on settlements that might always collapse because of poor crops or mismanagement. They recruited settlers to work the land and improve it, and they reserved choice plots for themselves, to live in or else to sell to the next round of settlers after the first families had improved the land, raising its value.[50] They had invested in legal proceedings to answer competing landlords' claims, to keep the land free of squatters, or to evict or prosecute debtors, all tasks for which Bowdoin had retained attorney John Adams's services.[51]

Before the crisis, the citizens of Massachusetts had claimed men like Bowdoin with pride, for in addition to financing the country's expansion, they were advancing the new nation's standing in science and industry. In 1780, James Bowdoin had founded the American Academy of Arts, joining with men trained at Harvard and Yale, at Oxford and Cambridge and universities in Germany and France to improve the country with new techniques for rotating crops or preserving fruit; with new understandings of propagation in livestock, of pollination in plants; with scientific journals that published the results of experiments in electricity and optics, and with expeditions like the one Bowdoin financed to Newfoundland, to make observations when Venus's path crossed the sun in the 1760s.[52]

James Bowdoin and the men who passed through his parlors—he and Ben Franklin and the other American and European scientists with whom he carried on correspondence—could see America's future taking shape before their eyes. Bowdoin and his colleagues were going to improve the folk customs and superstitions their citizens followed, feeding the narrative that first the Natives' ancient ways and now the farmers' folk customs were being shouldered aside by light and progress, law and reason, civilization and industry.[53]

Bowdoin was not alone in resenting Hancock for currying favor with the people, and he appealed to the other merchant elites who were losing money during the postwar struggles. Through January and February 1785, he made his campaign a referendum on Hancock's management of the commonwealth's finances, and his campaign proclamations argued that Hancock's leniency on taxes was a luxury the state could not afford.[54] He assured Massachusetts's creditors and financiers that he had the business sense and courage to balance the commonwealth's accounts by making the necessary sacrifices. He proposed new taxes, as well as a fiscal policy based on hard coin instead of paper money. He also proposed to enforce strict collection and foreclosure laws that would insulate merchants from bankruptcy, and he promised to veto any measures that would prevent them from seizing farmers' assets as payment.[55]

In their taverns nestled in the snow-covered hills that winter, the farmers of Massachusetts read Bowdoin's proposals with dread, for many of them knew that they would lose their farms if his policies became law. They read Hancock's proposals for paper money, tender laws, and depreciation of debts, and they hoped that the election would give him a mandate to reform the commonwealth's fiscal policies.[56]

Bowdoin's and Hancock's supporters battled back and forth in editorials, struggling to win the hearts of the commonwealth's voters. As elections approached, prominent merchants got tired of losing money and threw their support behind Bowdoin. Hancock tried to bring the merchants in line by threatening to withdraw his name from the ballot, but his threat did not inspire any compromises. A month before voters went to the polls, Hancock stepped down as governor, claiming his diet of rich meats and fish had made his gout too painful to perform his official duties.[57] His lieutenant governor, Thomas Cushing, took over, but Cushing lacked Hancock's charisma and could not assemble a winning coalition.[58]

After the votes were certified, James Bowdoin had not won a majority of the popular vote, so the election was decided in the legislature, where the House voted for Cushing 134 to 89. When it forwarded this result to the Senate, though, legislators in the Commonwealth's more aristocratic upper chamber overrode them, voting for Bowdoin 18 to 10.[59]

When Bowdoin was sworn in as governor on June 2, 1785, importers and financiers on the coast, big merchants in local commercial centers, and lawyers in the regional courts celebrated his victory, for now they could expect to get relief.[60] The lesser merchants and farmers groaned at this news. They knew that they were going to have to break their backs getting money out of rocky fields and forests. In the rural taverns, some men who resented the government's taxes started to grumble that their revolution against powerful men had not gone far enough.[61] They said that they might need to fight another war to keep the rich men in government from using steep taxes as tools to push them off their land and claim it for themselves.

Chapter Two

The Commonwealth
Compounds the Problem

I N EARLY SUMMER 1785, even as meadows finally turned green and the dark soil in the fields was dotted with long rows of new sprouts, Daniel Shays and his neighbors in Pelham—farmers from Cape Cod to Pittsfield—prepared to endure the ordeal. Soon after Bowdoin took office in June, the newspapers tacked to the tavern walls announced that the legislature had voted to repay the commonwealth's £1.5 million federal war debt—plus £250,000 due to officers and sailors, and £1.3 million of state debt—in full, in four annual payments.[1] The General Court planned to raise the money to pay these debts by levying steep new taxes, which burdened the farmers disproportionately. The merchant elites, who owned the commonwealth's shipping and ran its largest, most profitable businesses, were only taxed to pay 10 percent of the funds.[2] The common farmers were going to have to pay the remaining 90 percent, which raised their taxes to rates four or five times higher than any taxes they had paid under the British.[3]

Gathered around the newspapers in the taverns, they complained that the governor's proclamation included the insulting claim that the "principal source of [the commonwealth's] difficulties" was the people's "habits of luxury" and their taste for imported rum—ignoring the government's and speculators' role in the crisis by blaming the people's vices. The farmers laughed and called the rich men hypocrites, for the wealth of Bowdoin's luxurious furnishings had been widely reported throughout the state. Everyone had heard about the enormous mirror he had imported for his parlor, which cost £13, almost as much as a laborer would get for a full year's work. Another mirror, worth £10, reflected his guests' fashionable, imported French silks and English velvets, which the farmers could never afford. The rest of the house was furnished with Wilton and Turkish carpets, French furniture, Japanned—we would say lacquered—chests and drawers, chairs and tables of tropical mahogany, and chairs imported from England. The governor's guests were served from fine silver by servants and ate from imported porcelain. An expensive thermometer and barometer, and scientific instruments for experiments in electricity and in optics for telescopes, were also prominently displayed. Bowdoin further flaunted his wealth by maintaining private carriages—two chariots, a chaise, and a sleigh—with pairs of black horses whenever possible. It was a luxury only twenty-two other men in Massachusetts could afford (including his father-in-law and brother-in-law) while his economic program exempted families of his class from taxes and turned to the cash-strapped people, in the heart of an economic crisis, to raise the necessary funds.[4]

When the governor called the people irresponsible spendthrifts and told them that they would have to cut back on their spending, the taverns and woodlots were filled with loud protests and furious axes, and Daniel Shays and the landowners of Pelham spent long evenings worrying over the question of how they would keep their communities together if even more of their leading men were hauled to debtors' prison or if speculators bought up more of their farms cheap at auction.

The news of this new tax burden felt heavier yet when Shays and his fellow veterans learned that the commonwealth was also going to pay full value for the promissory notes with which they and their fellow veterans had been paid for their service during the war.

In the beginning of the war, the state had paid its soldiers in paper money that was worthless almost as soon as it was printed.[5] Later, the state had eased the soldiers' discontent by paying them in promissory notes that would be redeemed at some future date. When the war ended, those notes were likewise practically worthless, since no one believed that the commonwealth would be able to pay them, so Shays and many of Massachusetts's ninety-two thousand veterans had sold their notes to speculators and financiers.[6] Some of the men who had cash to offer in exchange for these notes were the very generals who had led their lines in battle. They risked their own money in order to give men cash for their service, but they would not pay more than 10 to 15 percent of the notes' face value.[7] Veterans leaving the army calculated that cash in hand would buy more supplies than worthless paper, so they swallowed their losses and took the cash to restart the farms that had languished while they were away. One war-weary soldier explained in an editorial that he and his fellow veterans merely wanted to "procure decent clothing and money sufficient to enable them to pass with decency through the country and to appear something like themselves when they arrived among their friends."[8]

Whatever money Shays and the Massachusetts veterans had gotten for their service when they came home in 1780 had long ago been spent on seeds, livestock, and tools. For the past five years, though, whenever they struggled to come up with money to buy supplies or pay their debts, they were haunted by the shadow of the notes they had abandoned, for those notes had continued to circulate all that time. As with the state's bonds, rich men and speculators had been buying them on exchanges at prices that rose or fell according to rumors that the commonwealth might or might not finally redeem them.

They were not simply waiting on rumors, though. Many of the bondholders had gotten themselves into the government, where they could influence the state's policy on bond payment.[9] Men who kept track of the rates on these exchanges told their neighbors that by the time Bowdoin came into office, thirty-five legislators held 40 percent of the notes. It was not a secret that some of these men in government had acquired the notes by giving away large tracts of prime government land—keeping the notes for themselves. Bowdoin had collected notes worth almost £3,300,[10] a sum that would allow him to buy up almost fifty farms if he paid the price farmers had paid: £70 for a hundred acres of fields, woodlots, and meadows. Now, though, with prices collapsing, who could say how many farms that sum could buy at auction?[11]

The farmers of Massachusetts were galled by news that legislators in other states had written down the value of their soldiers' notes precisely because the soldiers themselves no longer held them.[12] Other states had settled their notes in paper money. They would not insult the veterans by paying the value of their war pay to speculators, for many financiers had not fought and had probably bought their notes for pennies on the pound.

In their taverns, Massachusetts's veterans raged at the fact that the merchant elites who held the notes now planned to enrich themselves at their expense, allocating all £60,000 of the state's tax income to pay interest on the bondholders' notes.[13] Bitterly they complained that Bowdoin's campaign rhetoric of fiscal responsibility and patriotic sacrifice was going to benefit a "self-created nobility" at their expense.[14] As one farmer put it in an editorial, Bowdoin and his rich friends were using their authority to "accumulate fortunes by the general distress."[15]

The people of Massachusetts took this news and their indignation to their fields, to their looms, to their workrooms. They took it to church and prayed for strength to bear their anger about the fact that even in the depths of an economic crisis, they were being forced to pay taxes in pounds to give speculators the full amount of notes they themselves had parted with for shillings.

Nevertheless, it was not long after Bowdoin took office that Massachusetts's towns' clerks got orders to assess their townsmen's houses and barns, furniture, and livestock so the commonwealth could levy taxes according to its new, steep schedule, which the people would have to pay in coin.

The people were going to have to pay back taxes as well, for Bowdoin's accountants published reports that Governor Hancock's irresponsible policy of neglecting tax collection had cost the commonwealth £279,000, less than one-fifth the cost of the war if Bowdoin could collect it now.[16]

To men who remembered the times before the Revolution, Bowdoin's insistence on collecting back taxes reeked of hypocrisy. It was common knowledge that Samuel Adams, one of Bowdoin's chief advisers, had earned his reputation as a friend of liberty by using his role as one of the king's tax collectors as a platform from which to mount opposition to the Crown's authority.[17] He refused to press his countrymen for taxes, and he was personally sued by the king's administrators for the £8,000 he should have collected.[18] The rebels' victory canceled Adams's debt, but now he helped pass laws that made tax collectors personally responsible for the sums they were assigned to collect, and he joined the governor in insisting that farmers should honor their legitimate obligations and repay the statesmen and financiers who had provided them with their freedom.[19]

In the towns where farmers read Bowdoin and other merchants' editorials justifying these taxes, the older men and women felt a sickening sense of recognition: they had heard this same rhetoric twenty years ago, when Parliament tried to levy taxes after Prime Minister William Pitt had borrowed huge sums to conduct the French and Indian War as part of the Seven Years' War that took place in theaters from Europe to India.[20] At the time, John Hancock and James Bowdoin and Samuel Adams had organized legal challenges to Parliament, objecting that British ministers were losing their claims to legitimacy by making demands on their subjects without their consent.

When the Crown ignored their complaints, these same men had organized delegates in the other colonies and agitated for independence in an attempt to purify their government and ensure their rights.[21] For years leading up to the war, Adams had argued for righteous opposition to Britain's unjust treatment of its colonists, but now that he held a prominent place in a government that gave people representation, his editorials treated opposition to the state as treason.[22] In editorials, Adams and Bowdoin and the merchants of Boston ignored the fact that steep property requirements had kept common farmers from voting. They ignored the fact that the Senate dominated by wealthy men's representatives had consistently voted down any reforms that came out of the House of Representatives. They argued that popular opposition to government policies would threaten to supplant the popular will that had been expressed in elections.[23]

To the farmers of Massachusetts, it was clear that their new republican government was hiding their oppressive taxes behind the language of patriotism and fiscal responsibility, the same way the Crown had done when it had levied crippling taxes before the war. Now, as before, the people were in danger of losing their property if they could not pay, and if they resisted, they risked being cast as threats to the republic.[24] But the people were not calling for revolution—not yet. As early as September 7, 1784, the editors of the *Hampshire Herald* asked, suggestively, "is there not danger that the powers of Government, stretch'd beyond a certain tone, will burst asunder?"[25]

The elected officers of Pelham, many of whom were veterans, knew in advance that the governor's program of taxes would fail. These men served on the committees that appointed the town's tax assessors, and they reported that Pelham did not have enough coin in circulation to pay what the government demanded.[26]

These prosperous men and their ancestors had farmed the best plots of their towns' rocky hills since their families started to trickle into the region in 1738, then founded the town in 1743. Unlike some of their poorer neighbors, they could afford to wait for Bowdoin's plans to fail. They trusted that the governor would have to write down the state's debts in the end. But not everyone in Pelham could afford to wait for relief. In the face of this added burden of taxes, families were starting to leave the state. They harvested what they could or sold their crops still in the fields. Many families sold their farms for as little as a tenth of their value.[27] They packed their clothing in trunks and loaded their tools in carts. They harnessed their horses and livestock and rode off to new towns in western New York or as far west as the unsettled territories of Ohio. They rode north to the independent republic of Vermont, which had not yet joined the union and bore no obligation to repay America's war debts.[28]

The country they had established through five years of war might already be subjecting them to the same unjust demands the British had made, but the continent itself stretched far beyond their coastal state's borders. There was still plenty of open country where they could live in the freedom they had fought for.[29]

Daniel Shays and his wife and five children did not give up their farm in Pelham, even though they could have gone north to live near two of Shays's sisters in Barnard, Vermont, northwest of White River Junction.[30] Many of the men who had fought at Shays's side had been drawn to Vermont after the war, and now they were sending him news of available plots. They could have gone to western Vermont to live near his wife Abigail's brother, Jonathan, in Bennington, in southwestern Vermont, where he and his wife, Hannah Converse, and their five children were farming.[31] Another of Shays's sisters, Polly, lived with her family just across the border in Salem, New York, and she invited him there as well, but Shays had reasons to stay where he was.

Shays did not have family in Pelham when he moved there, but the town had been founded by his father's Scots-Irish people, Lowland Scots who had followed James I to Ulster in 1603,[32] before the English landlords raised their rents and pushed them out to the colonies in the early 1700s. The Scots-Irish farmers had tried to settle in Boston and then in Worcester, but they were driven west by Puritans who disapproved of their Presbyterian insistence on knowing religious truths at first hand instead of trusting wisdom received from ministers.[33] They settled in the hills around the Connecticut River valley, where they were known for their hardy, sometimes ornery self-reliance, and their expertise in making their clothes, tools, and furniture themselves.[34]

Shays had farmed in the rocky hill town of Shutesbury before the war, but after he had been promoted to captain—a commissioned rank that promised a life-long pension at the time—he had exercised his officer's privilege of furlough and left his men camped with General Rufus Putnam in Albany in winter 1778. He went home to visit his family and arranged to trade his Shutesbury farm for one that reflected his new status, with a well-placed house in a hollow above the west branch of the Swift River.[35]

Ever since Shays had moved to Pelham after he returned from the war in 1780, he had planted his crops in the rich soil of a wet meadow on either side of a stream and grazed his livestock in long woods uphill behind the house to the east. From a cliff top just west of the hollow, he commanded expansive views of the river valley below, where he could watch the traffic in the roads west and south to Amherst and Belchertown, and see the weather coming before it blew in. From this perch, he tracked the progress on distant farms, and at the end of each day, he and his family marveled as the lapping ridges turned blue then translucent then purple and black beneath the afternoon sky and the flare of sunset.

The old Johnson place, with its long vista, was a big step up for the son of an indentured servant who had paid for his passage from Ireland with years of his labor. But the house in Pelham also had the advantage of being only a day's ride from his in-laws in Brookfield on the Quaboag River. Shays's wife's people were Puritans from the English midlands who had started on the Connecticut coast in the 1640s, then moved up the river to Hartford, then Springfield before they founded the town of Brookfield in 1688. Her great-grandfather Thomas Gilbert had built Gilbert's Fort there in 1691, when Brookfield was still frontier after the war with Metacom and Weetamoo.[36] For the last hundred years, Gilberts had cycled in and out of Springfield and Brookfield's elected offices.[37]

Daniel Shays had met his wife when he worked on Captain Daniel Gilbert's Brookfield farm as a hired hand. As the first male child of laborers, Daniel Shays had hired out his labor from an early age. By the time he came to the Gilberts' farm, he had distinguished himself enough to command pay of £16 a year in a region where the normal rate for laborers was £15.[38]

Shays was twenty-five when he met Abigail Gilbert, who was not Captain Gilbert's daughter by birth. Gilbert had taken her in after her father, Jonathan Gilbert, died in the French and Indian War, then her mother and one brother had died in 1760. Captain Gilbert did not stand in the way of his laborer's suit for his adopted daughter's hand. In fact, he performed the rites to marry them in the kitchen of his house in September 1772. He blessed their marriage with a significant dowry, raising Shays into the ranks of gentlemen farmers, for that is how Shays's name appeared in the tax rolls in Shutesbury, where he bought his first farm and started his family in 1773.

Shays's success proved his father-in-law's faith in him, and he built on it with his own distinguished record. He rose through the ranks of the Continental army in the war, earning promotions through bravery in the Battle at Bunker Hill and then again at Ticonderoga in 1777, where the colonists surrendered the fort to British General John Burgoyne. He demonstrated bravery again under General Horatio Gates, when the Americans redeemed their loss by turning Burgoyne's flank at Saratoga one month later and taking the larger British force captive.[39]

In 1777, near West Point on the Hudson River, Shays was promoted to the commissioned rank of captain in Colonel Rufus Putnam's 5th Regiment of the Massachusetts line, a rank that promised a life-long half-pay pension.[40] He was promoted from below, for twenty men he recruited had recognized his qualities and refused to enlist unless he led them.[41] Shays improved his prospects further by joining the fraternity of Freemasons, a secret society that saw the Revolution as an opportunity to replace Old World hierarchies with a new society based on talent and merit instead of birth.[42]

The British fort at Stony Point was not strategically meaningful, although the rebel victory there did halt the redcoats' creeping advance north toward West Point.[43] More importantly, it humiliated the redcoats on the verge of winter, causing British General Henry Clinton to board his New York and Rhode Island soldiers on ships and sail them to South Carolina, effectively ending the northern war.

After this battle, no less a personage than the Marquis de Lafayette, a fellow Mason, rewarded Shays and other officers with gifts of gold-handled ceremonial swords. With these gifts, the marquis was helping General George Washington build an aristocratic officer corps out of the farmers who had been fighting professional British soldiers in homespun linen shirts and woolen coats.[44] For Shays, though, the sword was less a distinction than a sign that he had climbed to a status he could not maintain. Shortly after he left the war in 1780, he sold the sword to pay a debt. Like all the other soldiers, he had not been paid for his service, except in the worthless notes, and he already had a serviceable weapon of his own. He could not afford to join the officers who wore fine uniforms and kept servants and horses.[45]

In certain circles, the sale of the sword tarnished Shays's reputation. To the other officers who had bought their commissions and ran their companies' business from commandeered houses or comfortable tents, the sale of the sword was conduct unbecoming an officer. Some of them went so far as

to threaten court-martial, but Shays was never ultimately sanctioned by anything stronger than muttered disapproval.[46] To the hundreds of men Shays
commanded, the sword was a relic of the Old World the farmers were fighting to free themselves from. By selling it, he showed his men that he had
not allowed his promotions to pull him away from his people.

The talk did not hinder Shays's career. Two years after he returned from
the war, in 1782, the leaders of Pelham trusted him to serve as one of the
four heads of the town's militia.[47] Now, in 1785, as the steep new taxes were
reaching Pelham from Boston, he was thirty-eight. He enjoyed his community's trust and lived in a good farm high on a hillside with his high-born
wife and five children. He was not going to let the crisis strip him of his
gains and force him to start anew elsewhere, like a new man without a history or a people.

Settled now in their hollow, in a community close to family, Shays and
his wife bore their debts and never packed up their things to start over anywhere else. They could afford to weather Bowdoin's taxes and court fees
longer than others, but their neighbors and the men in Shays's militia were
not free from the humiliation of debtor's prison or the fear of foreclosure.[48]

When Shays's militia finished their weekly maneuvers in the Pelham
meeting house green, his men sought him out in Conkey's Tavern on the
Swift River between the meeting house on West Hill and Shays's house in
its hollow on East Hill opposite. The men came to Shays as someone who
had started in poverty and understood their sufferings. They told him their
troubles and asked him why they had fought to establish their natural rights,
which obligated them to treat unjust laws with contempt—even to change
their government if it oppressed them—only to let their government oppress
them with excessive taxes, the same as the British had done, to sit back as
rich men bought up their confiscated farms at auction.

The men invoked their long history of standing against injustice and
governing themselves.[49] They remembered back to summer 1774, when the
Crown had voided the colony's charter and installed agents to govern all the
commonwealth's town meetings as punishment for the destruction of tea in
Boston Harbor.[50] In Pelham and in every town from outside of Boston to
Great Barrington in the west, the people had forced the king's agents to resign their posts, or else they banished them to Boston. Two years before the
Declaration of Independence, the farmers of Massachusetts had obstructed
the king's courts and governed themselves through town meetings and
county conventions, passing laws, levying taxes, and working with other

towns to arrange for their common defense.[51] With this precedent in their minds, the farmers clamored to march to the courts as they had done before the war, to interrupt unjust authority and demand that the government's laws respect the people.

The farmers of Pelham did not even have to reach back to the time before the war to find a precedent for taking action against a court. They pointed to protests as recent as spring 1782, when a preacher named Samuel Ely and hundreds of farmers had been outraged by an aristocratic constitution that did not give regular people a voice when the government levied taxes on common farmers in order to give commissioned officers lump sums for five years' pay.[52] Ely and his supporters had marched to Northampton to close the Hampshire County Court of Common Pleas to keep the judges from hearing foreclosure cases and suits for debt.[53] They submitted demands for reforms to the 1780 constitution, which gave wealthy eastern merchants disproportionate power over the commonwealth.[54]

Now Shays's men offered to take clubs from their woodpiles, the same as Ely's men had done, to menace the judges and demand reforms,[55] but Shays and the other militia leaders remembered the crisis as well, and they reminded their townsmen that government men had arrested Ely, and the people never won reforms. Even after Ely's supporters rescued him from prison, causing the state to seize others in his place, Ely had not stayed in Massachusetts to fight for his cause. He fled to Vermont, and the government kept his supporters in jail for months after his flight, using the hostages as leverage to keep the protests from sparking a wider insurgency. Between the government's threats of further arrests and the farmers' threats against the courts and law enforcement, the western counties had been convulsed with alarms and the danger of riots for months—all to no end.[56]

When Pelham men could not elicit sympathy from Shays and the other militia leaders, they took their concerns to Colonel John Powers, Captain William Conkey, Dr. Nehemiah Hines, and the other officers who conducted Pelham's business, but these men could not encourage them either. The leading men's farms were swamped with debts and burdened with taxes as well, but they urged their neighbors not to stir up a country that had suffered so many losses in five years of war.

In Pelham and in all the farm towns of Massachusetts, soldiers and veterans and town officials and leading landowners urged their people to resign themselves to their losses, the same as they might resign themselves when hailstones and blight, when floods and drought ruined their crops, or when wives died in childbirth, or children died of disease. They told them to wait for elections, when they could win reforms through legitimate channels, but the outraged farmers argued that it would still be two years before they could challenge the governor's taxes at the polls. If the commonwealth's economic policies were not reformed soon, there would not be anything left for the bailiffs to seize. By April 1787, rich men would own the whole country.

Whatever words the leading men found to contain their neighbors' outrage, the pressure of taxes and debts and the outrage of nonrepresentation did not relent through spring 1785. Bowdoin's austerity policies were still just beginning to take effect. No one could see yet how the crisis was going to end. They could only see it getting worse, because the commonwealth was going to have to make interest payments to Dutch financiers in February 1786. Anyone who followed the news from Boston knew that the funds in the treasury would not be sufficient to pay the debts as well as the state's incidental charges.[57]

As the months progressed through the fall, the people's sufferings spread so widely that more and more land-owning veterans joined the calls for action. In angry editorials, some said that they should march to Boston in uniform, with fife and drums, to show their countrymen that Governor Bowdoin and his advisers were betraying the regular people who had established the commonwealth's liberty with their courage, with their own blood and their kinsmen's.

In the heated discussions that dominated the taverns, Colonel Powers and Captains Conkey, Shays, and Daniel Gray contained the angry talk. What had the people themselves done to improve their conditions, they wanted to know. Most of the towns west of Boston had not even sent representatives to sit in the General Court when Bowdoin's policies were being debated and passed.[58] Even if they claimed that it was poverty that kept them from sending delegates, the people could not complain if they had not bothered to advocate for their interests.[59] They said if the people were determined to act, they should draft petitions to beg for relief through constitutional channels or recruit representatives to run in the next elections. Bluntly, they painted the picture of how things would go if men mobbed the court. Prominent men in the market towns would treat them as outlaws. Northampton Justice of the Peace Joseph Hawley, or Amherst's Solomon Boltwood or Oliver Cowles, or Westfield's General William Shepard or Colrain's Hugh McClellan would summon their townsmen and deputize their fellow veterans to hunt down the men who led the mobs, and they would arrest them or shoot them or hound them out of the commonwealth, as they had arrested Ely and driven him out.

In crowded taverns, they warned that if any one of them tore up judges' or bailiffs' fences, or cut down their orchards, all the rest would feel the punishment. If one man so much as threw a stone through a merchant's or lawyer's windows, the papers would say they were proving the scurrilous rumor that Americans were a lesser people who lived in a lawless wilderness, rude mobs who could only be governed by force.[60]

Angry men laughed at this ominous picture. Who would arrest them, when they themselves were the commonwealth's militia and they had served alongside the men who made up the market towns' militias? Many of their friends in the towns shared their sufferings. No one expected their countrymen to suppress their resistance to such flagrantly unjust taxes. They dismissed the fears as inflammatory propaganda and wagered that the militiamen would rather join their lines than turn against them.

Why, they demanded to know, should their towns' militias hold weekly maneuvers, if not to protect their property from bailiffs who rode to their houses with warrants from Bowdoin's courts?[61] Young men who had been children when columns of soldiers and distant artillery rattled lamps on the walls joined the argument, offering to march to the courts and finish the revolution their fathers had started.

Shays and the other officers who led their towns militias had seen to the needs of hundreds of men in camps during the war. They answered their bellicose townsmen by asking them how they planned to wage the war that would start if they closed the courts. Where did they plan to get credit to purchase guns and ammunition, flour and beef, to sustain their opposition when nobles in Boston fielded troops to suppress them? How would they pay for tents, bandages, and carts, and for drivers to haul their supplies when they had to move their camps to evade the government's army? Would they dispatch envoys to Europe to ask for help from the same French and Dutch financiers who had helped put James Bowdoin and John and Samuel Adams in power—financiers whose loans Bowdoin's government could not even repay?

They reminded their struggling townsmen that even though they themselves had dodged redcoats' musket balls, their contributions were tiny compared to the sacrifices the merchants had made, committing treason in speaking against the Crown, risking their own fortunes to finance a rebel army. Farmers who had seen the statehouse and Faneuil Hall for themselves reminded their neighbors that their liberty was an aftereffect of the wealth that flowed through those offices and through the ports from which their own exports were shipped to the Indies. They described the salt tang of the wharves and the forests of masts that darkened the sky, the ships and their crews from London and Amsterdam, from the Azores and Senegal, Rio, and Havana, and from around Cape Horn in the Pacific.[62] If merchants suffered, the farmers would have to make sacrifices and live from their fields until the merchants could prosper again.

Some went so far as to claim that their neighbors only envied the merchants' wealth and power and said that if they really wanted to level the social classes, perhaps they would like to give their own farms to freed blacks, who had only been liberated from slavery in 1783, in Massachusetts, or to enslaved Africans in New York.[63]

Still the angry laborers, landowners, and veterans refused to submit to Bowdoin's taxes. They invoked their people's long tradition of standing up for justice. They drew out the long debates by telling the story of the three hundred men in the Pennsylvania line who improved their conditions by taking action at the end of 1780.[64] Camped in the cold in Jockey Hollow, New Jersey, they had been suffering for lack of boots, blankets, and food. They had not been paid and so could not buy provisions. On the first day of January 1781, after their enlistments expired with the last stroke of midnight, they finally lost their patience and marched out of camp. When their officers called them deserters and called their departure a mutiny, the men refused to reenlist and return to camp without reenlistment bonuses.

Boastfully, the men described how the officers would not dare to shoot or arrest the enlisted men, but they took their concerns to their superior officers and arranged for the men to be paid. In the end, the men returned to camp, where they suffered the same as before, but the farmers said they suffered as free men, not subjects. Even if the pay they received was worthless, they had extracted a concession from their leaders and did not serve under compulsion.

Conkey, Gray, Shays, and the other officers of Pelham heard this story sadly, and they answered by recalling what had happened three weeks later, when soldiers in the New Jersey line tried to improve their own horrid conditions. They too had marched out of their camps in Pompton Lakes, but this time, George Washington did not authorize his officers to negotiate. The new country's finances had not allowed him to pay his men—he could not afford to give them bonuses now, or to buy the supplies that would improve their conditions. Nor could Washington afford to let his defenses soften, so he made a demonstration of force that would be as visible to the British as to the colonists themselves. He ordered South Carolinian General Robert Howe to march a battalion from Boston to New Jersey—a six-day forced march on snowy roads—to drive the men back to their posts.[65]

Pelham's yeomen farmers, who owned their own land and ran their own towns, listened with shame to this story of how the New Jersey soldiers were treated by their own countrymen. For when Howe's men found the men the government called deserters in the road, cold and hungry in their rags, Howe ordered his soldiers to surround them. He did not pause to negotiate terms by which they would return to camp. He arrested the sergeants who led what he called the mutiny.

With shame, Pelham's farmers heard how Howe's officers picked twelve men from their ranks, gave them muskets, then forced them, at bayonet point, to load their weapons, then raise and aim them, and shoot their leaders dead. In the silence that filled the taverns after the recollection of these authorized murders, the farmers' anger was dulled and also hardened. It was true that the common soldiers formed the spine of the commonwealth's army, but until they could count on their officers' support, they would not have the strength of arms to demand reforms to Bowdoin's unjust taxes.

Night after night, in taverns throughout Massachusetts, through the increasing heat of summer 1785, the people mined their history and told their stories back and forth, debating what could be done. They drank together and sang their marching and fighting songs from the Revolution and from the French and Indian War before that, and the ballads they still remembered from their ancestors' lives in the Old World a hundred years ago and more.

When at last they stepped out of the taverns into the damp, cool nights, when they walked along the fields in moonlight and made their way through their orchards back to their houses, they still did not make mischief. Outraged as they were, they were not lawless men who would tear down judges' fences or plunder merchants' warehouses or shops, to tax them, in their way, for profiting by the people's misery. They kept the peace and lived by the law, but the constant strain of their debts and their calculations tormented their sleep, and their resentments were sharp when they woke and started each day's toil at dawn.

On Sundays, when the people of Massachusetts filed into the hard pews of their churches, ministers everywhere west of Boston echoed the leading citizens' warnings.[66] In the Congregationalist churches, where the Puritans arrived and were seated in order of status—least members first, to form an audience for the River Gods and the leading merchants, as they proceeded to their prominent seats—ministers reminded their parishioners that they were bound by the state's laws the same as by higher laws and proclaimed that protests would violate God's holy writ.[67] Opposition to government was the devil's work, they said, and it would only bring grief to their families and communities.[68] All the length of Massachusetts, ministers who were typically paid in coin reminded the farmers that the God who created the soil and seeds, the livestock and game in the woods, had a plan that included the men in power. They said the Bible commanded the people to make "payment of taxes as well as debts" and instructed them to "render to Caesar the things that are Caesar's."[69] If the ministers still felt anger rising hot from the pews, they soothed it with the promise that the people's sufferings would all be redeemed if they bore them with patient piety and used their trials to testify to the mysteries of God's grace.[70]

These sermons did nothing to resolve the injustice that plagued their people's farms, but when the congregants rose from their benches and sang their hymns, they submitted their voices to their people's one common voice. They offered their prayers to the heavens. Speaking now as one people in song, they could feel in their vibrating bones that they were held in traditions that were so much larger than themselves that it was pointless to fear. Finally, they relinquished their irritation, bowed their heads in prayer, and submitted themselves to their lot.

Whatever peace the farmers found in their churches, their outrage over the government's unjust taxes was waiting for them when they stepped out into the sweltering late-summer afternoons. The independent-minded Scots-Irish farmers of Pelham were used to determining for themselves what was right and wrong, and they had cycled through a number of temporary pastors, unable to settle on one whose voice and authority they would submit to.[71] Their ministers' warnings against direct action did not settle the issue, but as they tramped home through the patchwork of fields and woodlots, they refused to allow injustice its regular season.[72] The governor's will was not simply a plague of locusts, sent from God, that they should suffer it in silence.

Walking home through the summer heat, past fields where they had all worked together—through fields that were now full of the corn and wheat and oats that would have to see their families and livestock through winter— they demanded to know why they should surrender their property if they were indeed the equals of men in government. Why should they watch their land be seized when merchants in Boston hardly lived by these same laws and were not being asked to give up their land and property for the general good?

When the pumpkins and squash were fat on the vine and the crisp nights threatened frost at the end of the summer, the farmers of Massachusetts harvested the crops that had survived the heat, rainstorms, and pests. Through long days of hard toil, they filled carts with produce. They cut the last hay and oats and hauled their corn to the mill, but the torment of Bowdoin's policies did not relent. The courts continued to meet, and even after the farmers had put up their harvests and started preparing their farms for winter, the seizures and imprisonments for debt continued unopposed.

Angry men continued to press for action, but Daniel Shays and the prominent men who led Pelham's militia never did agree to organize formal protests to close the courts. Now that their harvests were stored in their cellars and piled in corners of bedrooms, they were vulnerable to any force the government might send against them. They refused to be ruined by risking their wealth in protests.

Fall slid toward winter, and now they came in from the fields and made their houses ready for winter work. Over their hearths, husbands assured their wives that they would survive this crisis the same way they had survived the shortages and the inflation during the war and the years that led to it. They would make do with teas and medicines out of their meadows, and dyes from bark and roots. Maple sugar would get them through the winter instead of refined sugar from the Indies.[73] Their beer and brandy would take the place of imported rum, and they would make their clothes of homemade linen instead of English wool, by the light of candles they made from bayberry wax, with milkweed floss wicks instead of store-bought.

For long, snowbound days, men carted their wives and daughters to their friends' and neighbors' families' houses where they cleaned, spun, and wove the flax into linen in large parties, or else they took their broadaxes out to their woodlots or worked in their barns splitting shingles or tying rushes into brooms they would sell in the spring.

When they rode their sleighs or tramped the snowy roads to their taverns, the newspapers tacked to the walls there told them that families in other states were enduring the same trials, as all the new American states groaned for the loss of income from Indies trade. In other states too, the merchant elites had passed laws like Bowdoin and Adams had passed, hoping to minimize their losses by taxing common farmers.

By January 1786, petitions were starting to flow toward Boston. One petition signed by sixty men in Greenwich, in the hills between the three branches of the Swift River, argued to "your honors" in the General Court that during the late war the people had "spared no pains, but freely granted all the aid and assistance of every kind that our civel fathers required of us" but that now "unless something takes place more favourable to the people, in a little time att least one half of our inhabitants will become bankrupt."

The men complained that "sutes att law are very numerous and the attorneys in our oppinion are very extravigent and oppressive in their demands. When we compute the taxes laid upon us the five preceding years: the state and county, town and class taxes, the amount is equil to what our farms will rent for." They begged for an issue of paper money to make the debts lighter to bear and pointed out that as more of the people were confined to jail for their debts, others were fleeing the state, a combination of trends that must be bad for the commonwealth.[74]

As the farmers cautiously drew down their stores through winter, they heard news from travelers from up and down the coast, and from far into the inland hills, that common people in other states were also starting to talk about risking their safety by protesting at their courts.[75]

Soon enough, winter's snows started to mix with sleet and rain. By the time songbirds returned to the hedges and peepers started chirping from vernal pools in spring 1786, news reached Massachusetts that farmers in Maryland and Pennsylvania had banded together to protest their states' unjust taxes. They had occupied courtyards and barricaded the courts to prevent the judges from entertaining suits for foreclosure and debt. In Maryland they had gone so far as to organize boycotts of sales of seized livestock at auction.[76]

The protests had not been suppressed. The courts were not forced open by the militias. No shots had been fired, no one had been arrested. No blood had been spilled. In the end, the states' legislatures passed tender laws and issued paper money so people would not be forced off their land.[77]

In Massachusetts, though, men who waited for news of reforms waited in vain. Instead of reforms, they learned that their troubles were compounded in March 1786, when the government issued £29,000 of direct specie taxes, which were designed to take more money from the people and pay the face value of the government bonds that had been trading at as little as a sixth of their value.[78] On June 6, the editors of the *Hampshire Herald* warned that the debt burden would ultimately be relieved "only by the subversion of our present political establishment, under some ambitious spirit, with the *vox populi vox Dei* in his mouth."[79]

This news brought men back to Shays and the other elected officers in Pelham, clamoring to protest their conditions, but Shays and the others who had spent the winter advocating restraint pointed to news from Rhode Island, where their southern neighbors had used constitutional methods to throw off the burden of debts and inflation. In April elections, after campaigning with the slogan "To Relieve the Distressed," Rhode Island's Country Party won a majority of the legislature, turning the Mercantile Party out of power.[80] As soon as they were sworn in, its elected members issued reforms, depreciating the state's debts and printing £100,000 in paper money.[81] When Rhode Island merchants refused to accept the paper money, the new ruling party took them to court. When wealthy judges found for the merchants, the farmers' party dismissed the judges, replacing them with men who would uphold the people's law.[82] In the end, the merchants' warehouses were forced open. The merchants suffered losses, but paper money and produce were accepted as official currency, and the common people were no longer bankrupted by their debts.

Massachusetts merchants' editorials denounced the reforms in "Rogue's Island," and they prophesied that these policies would bring the state to ruin. Even as other states issued reforms, the leaders in Massachusetts doubled down in defense of their currency policies and taxes.[83] Rhode Island remained an exception, for the ruling parties in Connecticut and New Hampshire did not retreat from their strict austerity measures either.

The farmers of Massachusetts did learn from Maine that Governor Bowdoin was capable of leniency. That spring, he compromised with his tenants on the Kennebec River, settling claims against the lands his father had left him by selling off hundred-acre plots at nominal prices.[84] But Bowdoin did not signal any willingness to redistribute the unjust taxes that tortured his citizens. Still he refused to ease the farmers' burdens by letting them pay their debts in produce or paper money.

In spring 1786, the farmers of Massachusetts planted the new year's crops, and the courts continued to seize their livestock and property. Their oxen, woodlots, and farms were still being bought up at auction by rich men who got them at steeply discounted prices. In many auctions, there were not enough buyers to keep prices up with competitive bidding, and farmers watched the wealth of their counties concentrated in just a few men's hands.

Farmers were still being taken to debtor's prison in record numbers. Even distinguished veterans of the colony's wars and leading landowners were joining their region's laborers and subsistence farmers in the common-wealth's dank, four-foot-tall cellars, suffering the jailors' contempt alongside murderers, rapists, and criminals. In the past, a debtor would typically spend a week or two behind bars, but now they were stranded for months, and still their towns' leaders refused to agree to take action against the courts.[85]

As spring turned to summer 1786, the people started to plead their case in the newspapers that were read by farmers and businessmen, by lawyers and drovers, by legislators and financiers in taverns and in offices and in neighboring states and eventually in English taverns as well.

In the *Hampshire Herald*, they complained about having come home from war only to have been "loaded with class-rates, lawsuits and . . . pulled and hauled by sheriffs, constables and collectors"[86] who then sold their land "for about one-third of its value, our cattle about half."[87] They complained that the tax collectors were seizing and selling "cattle and other property belong-ing not merely to the poorer people, but to substantial farmers."[88] One com-plained that "I have been obliged to pay and nobody will pay me,"[89] another that "money had flown away, and neither the farmer nor the mechanic could find means to procure it."[90]

In the *Worcester Centinel* they boasted they got their living "by hard labor—not by a pension" like government appointees, or by "monopoliz-ing," like the influential merchants. "Husbandry is as honest a calling as any in the world," their letters proclaimed, "the last temptation for fraud and lying."[91] They said they all knew that "nineteen parts of twenty of the public securities were possessed by merchants and opulent gentlemen in the capital, and other maritime towns," who are "accumulating fortunes by the general distress."[92] The country would flourish faster, they said, if there were "fewer white shirts and more frocks," if more merchants would "shut up their shops and get their living by following the plough."[93] Veterans re-counted the sufferings they had endured in the war, while their "creditors and legislators," they said, "sauntered at home, enjoying the smiles of for-tune, wallowing in affluence, and fattening in the ease of sunshine and prosperity."[94]

In the *Massachusetts Gazette*, they said that the heavy burden of taxes threatened to turn them into "a miserable, cruel-hearted and wicked people." They urged each other to "rise up and put a stop to it—and have no more courts, nor sheriffs, nor collectors, nor lawyers."[95]

The farmers did not always sign these letters with their own names. They signed themselves "Ploughman" or "Plough Jogger," "Rusticus," "Honestus," or "Public Faith," or they signed with their towns' names, to speak for their neighbors.[96] Some of the learned farmers signed with the names of Roman populists like Tiberius Gracchus, to tell their readers that there was a long, proud history of farmers standing together in opposition to urban rulers.[97]

In the offices and parlors where wealthy local merchants like Northampton's Joseph Hawley or Amherst's Ebenezer Mattoon or Oliver Cowls read these letters, the farmers' opinions sounded like mobs obstructing the commonwealth's business at the courts, menacing and robbing respectable people, looting stores and houses, leveling the wealth of the country to common, democratic squalor.

Filled with these dreadful visions, the merchants responded with inflammatory letters of their own, reminding their countrymen that their government had borrowed enormous sums to fund the war. With proud, Puritanical condescension—ignoring the reality that the war bonds were being traded among speculators—they chided the people for thinking they could avoid paying, and they accused the farmers of being "luxurious in their diet, idle and profligate in their manners, encouragers of foreign manufacturers."[98]

They lectured that contracts were the sacred ground their new country had to be founded on, and they prophesied dire consequences if contracts were not respected. They said the country would return to natural law if debts were abolished: no one's possessions would be safe from the threat of mob violence.[99] "What industrious man," one retailer wanted to know, "can live while his property is at the mercy of knaves and thieves?" Another predicted that if the people had their way, "private property will lie wholly at the mercy of the most idle, vicious and disorderly set of men in the community."[100]

In ominous letters, the wealthy businessmen warned their countrymen that the war had unleashed democratic hordes who would never agree to be ruled, even by fellow veterans and statesmen.[101] Their letters said that "monarchy is better than the tyranny of the mob."[102] Crowds of angry farmers, one general wrote, would "overturn the very foundations of our government and constitution, and on their ruins exert the unprincipled and lawless domination of one man."[103]

Merchants' editorials said they hoped Bowdoin would exert himself to keep the lazy and degenerate element of the commonwealth from stifling their new nation in the crib by taking to arms. In many letters, merchants mocked the people by signing satirical letters as "Amos Spendthrift," "Tom Seldomsober," or "Simon Dreadwork."[104]

To Shays and the other leaders of Pelham, these letters sounded like manacles clicking shut, pinching their wrists. The merchants' letters recalled the smell of musty prisons to their nostrils, and the cold indifference of bailiffs who executed foreclosures, moving families' things into the yard while parents cursed and their children cried.

From May into June 1786, common soldiers and wealthy financiers each claimed that they alone had won their nation its independence, and each side accused the other of betraying their sacred sacrifices. Division between the farmers and the mercantile interests was so deep that newspapers printed the Boston merchants' accusation that the farmers were acting as instruments of "British Emissaries" who wanted to overthrow the government.[105]

At the counters of their taverns, farmers pounded their fists in fury at the effrontery of this claim, and they fretted that people who lived in towns might not know enough to see through this inflammatory ruse. Plenty of families in the farm towns had proven their patriotism by sending their men to the war. Amherst and Pelham, Colrain and Montague had sent larger proportions of their men than mercantile towns on the rivers or the coast, where wealthier men could afford to hire substitutes to serve in their stead. Many farmers bore scars from the battles, and they complained that the merchants had not also demonstrated their patriotism by fighting at their sides. Governor Bowdoin himself had spent the war years with rich merchant friends in Middleborough, south of Boston, claiming that ill health kept him from fighting.[106]

Choking on the irony of this accusation, the farmers recalled the governor's swearing in the previous summer, when Bowdoin had been required to take a special oath to explicitly disavow loyalty to England.[107] Legislators had seen conflicts of interest in his daughter's marriage to the man who was serving as British consul general to the United States in New York, and in the years his son, James III, had spent in school at Cambridge and Oxford, and then in business in London.[108]

With the accusation of foreign influence in the air, the farmers' debates in the taverns developed a thick fog of distrust and disdain. Scoff though they might at the irony of the merchants' accusations, the farmers were still powerless to win reforms from a legislature that voted down every proposal for paper money or tender laws.[109] In the end, they could only follow their ministers' advice and work as hard as they could to carry their people through to better times.

By the time the farmers' seeds had taken root and apple blossoms filled the orchards in spring 1786, Pelham's Colonel Powers and Captains Conkey and Hines and prominent landowners in farm towns throughout the commonwealth began to seek each other out to see what could be done.[110] They could no longer battle the rising tide of suits for debt in their hills, or the strong winds of men's complaints.

Hot in the fields, cool in the dusky barns, sticky in the summer dining rooms where they talked, they finally agreed they should organize formal town meetings to bring their people together and consider their options. The men who proposed these first meetings were wealthy enough to vote in the commonwealth's elections. They had served as selectmen and councillors, surveyors and inspectors, tithing men and clerks.[111] Many had served in the wars and retired from the commissioned ranks of captain or even colonel. Some had served as their towns' representatives in the legislature, but the economic pressure was so widespread that rank and status no longer protected anyone from the torments of taxes and court fees, of skyrocketing debts and of plummeting values for produce. The people's anger was increasing to the point that the wealthier men started to fear that their townsmen might turn on them if they thought they were standing in the way of reforms.

The leading men of the towns met privately throughout May and June, for these were men who already had a long tradition of taking affairs into their own hands and administering their towns' business in the absence and sometimes in defiance of administrators from Boston or from London.[112] They set agendas for meetings and publicized the times and locations when they would convene their towns' legal government bodies and seek relief officially.

When the appointed days came, the farmers in one town after another put down their tools and left their work to their older children and hired hands, and they set out on footpaths through orchards and fields sweet with lilacs and grasses. Winding their way through land they had all worked together, they followed the roads to the taverns and town meeting halls. On horseback, afoot, and in carts, through clouds of biting insects, down from their long hills alongside tumbling streams, the people of western Massachusetts arrived at their meeting places as one people.

Simply by showing up at these meeting places, the farmers in towns from Concord west to Great Barrington, from Taunton north to Colrain were saying their days had been dogged by calculations and dread and injustice for so long that they were desperate and in need of relief.[113]

They pressed through the doorways together, filling the galleries of their churches and meeting houses, cramming into taverns whose windows were all thrown open against the heat. The right to speak and vote in these meetings was not reserved for landowners, or men who had ascended to ranks above common laborers or poor farmers. In most of the towns west of Boston, all adult men were authorized to speak and vote in town meetings.[114] The prominent landowners whose fathers had settled the hill towns had decided that in their new democracy, their townsmen should be able to vote regardless of how much property they owned.[115]

Before the war, the Crown's government in Boston had tried to limit the power of local assemblies and to assert centralized control, but this challenge fueled the people's resentment about the Crown's steep taxes and precipitated the movement to throw off the king's authority—and protect the towns' rights—starting in 1774.[116] After the revolution, though, the leading men in Boston had felt the same fear of the people's local governments and moved to restrain the people's influence in the commonwealth. Across the border in Vermont, all adult men could vote, but the 1780 constitution John and Samuel Adams and James Bowdoin had written denied the vote to any men whose land and property were worth less than £60, which raised the qualification from £40 before the war.[117] Even if the men could vote, their towns' representatives were relegated to a lower house in the legislature: their proposals were balanced by a Senate of merchant elites who would have to show that they were each worth at least £600.[118] A man could not run for governor unless his accountant could demonstrate that he was worth at least £1,000. These were some of the provisions Samuel Ely's hundreds of men had tried to reform in 1782, defying the constitution's provision forbidding any changes for fifteen years.[119]

As men filed into their meeting houses in summer 1786, the strength of their numbers emboldened them to talk about using this crisis as an opportunity to demand more than just an end to the taxes and currency crisis: some of the men were already starting to whisper about changing the constitution to give smaller landowners more of a voice in government.[120]

In each town's meeting place, men crammed together, their strident voices growing louder and louder till finally someone tapped a glass with a knife or banged a gavel and called the assemblies to order. One or two men were vested with the authority to speak for the rest, and the others in their silence allowed themselves to be spoken for.

The moderators started their meetings as they had always started town meetings: by proposing that they would hereby form themselves into a legal and constitutional convention in defiance of the merchants and government men whose editorials had doubted whether town meetings were even legal under the state's new constitution—some of whom had even gone so far as to claim that they represented a treasonous usurpation of the commonwealth's authority.[121] But now as the men assented, they formed themselves into an official body, authorized by the democratic principles they had fought and won a war for. Moderators opened the floor to hear the people's grievances, and farmers with anger throbbing in scars from the war and in the nicks and blisters of their work stepped forward and poured out their outrage. With voices that cracked with indignation, they described the children, the aging parents displaced by foreclosures, the old women whose sickbeds had been seized from underneath them.[122] How was this different from British rule, they demanded, with rich men using the courts and warrants as thin pretexts for theft, and financiers and speculators taking everything they had worked for?

Angry men asked their neighbors to raise their hands if they had been sued or imprisoned for debt. In most of the farm towns west of Boston, one out of three raised their hands.[123] The cloud of indignation only grew thicker as the forest of forearms confirmed what they had all heard.

Sweltering in their meeting houses, the farmers renewed the arguments they had been having for months in their fields and in their taverns. The towns' leaders finally saw that the people could not be expected to restrain themselves indefinitely. They still refused to sanction action against the courts, but they offered to draft formal petitions begging Bowdoin for reforms. Men who were still impatient for action predicted that Bowdoin would never back down. They prophesied that they would still have to march to the courts, as the farmers had done in Maryland and Pennsylvania, to take the law into their own hands, but they agreed to let the process of petitioning play out as a first step.

In Pelham, Benjamin Bonney, in Montague, Thomas Grover, in New Braintree, Francis Stone, in Groton, Job Shattuck took up their pens and distilled their townsmen's anger into formal lists of requests. Farmers with dark earth marking the nicks and cuts on their hands urged their well-schooled townsmen not to lower themselves by using nobles' flowery, formal language. Straight-talking men begged them to call things what they were, in plain speech, but the men whose fingers were dark with ink stains said that they weren't rude peasants. They refused to expose their townsmen's uncouth country brogues to ridicule in Boston. They wrote that they had no intention of "subverting government, and throw[ing] all things into a state of confusion" and "sincerely deprecate[d] the consequences of anarchy." They reassured their leaders in Boston that they were "induced by the ties of friendship, and by the stronger laws which religion inculcates, of doing as we would be done by."[124]

"If your Honours will be so kind," one such note pleaded, "as to consider the great Scarcity of Cash, we have not the least Doubt but that your Honours upon a serious Consideration will join us in Sentiment."[125]

In town after town, the farmers drafted similar petitions. They begged the legislature to issue paper money.[126] Formally, they requested the right to pay their debts and taxes in goods and produce, and they asked for reforms to the fees with which courts and lawyers compounded the debts merchants brought to the courts. In these petitions, the constitutionally authorized gatherings of veterans and landowners explicitly and repeatedly disavowed any ambition to replace the commonwealth's constitution or to establish rival governments. They vowed not to meet in unlawful assemblies or to take direct action until they heard an official response from Boston.[127]

When at last the scribes read the final drafts aloud, the sentiments were acceptable to enough men that they voted to approve the towns' petitions. All the length and width of Massachusetts, from Sheffield in the Taconic mountains along the New York border to Taunton south of Boston, from Longmeadow south of Springfield on the Connecticut River to Bernardston and Athol nestled in the northern hills, the farmers of Massachusetts entrusted themselves to the statements contained in their towns' official letters. They voted to forward copies to local printers and papers so the whole countryside should understand their intentions.

Finally, the men filed out of the stifling buildings, back into the night, where the first fireflies were blinking up into the treetops, and they walked home along the meadows and fields heavy with growing crops, relieved that they were finally doing something to protect themselves from the government.

Through May and June 1786, while the Massachusetts legislature held session in Boston, the farm towns throughout the commonwealth posted petitions by the dozen, begging the General Court for an issue of paper money and suspension of debts and tax-collection efforts.[128] The petitions that traveled to Boston were sent on a swirl of excitement and expectation that further actions would be inevitable if the government did not offer reforms.

In the middle of June, news reached Pelham that farmers in Bristol County had tried but failed to stop their county court from meeting to hear suits for debt and foreclosure.[129] In early July, eight towns in Bristol County called for a statewide convention centered on reducing the state's expenses by eliminating the Senate and on making government appointees dependent on the people for their salaries.[130]

While the people waited for news from Boston, the crops took hold in the fields. The sun had a bite of warmth in it now, and the last sprays of white-and-purple lilac turned sour and overripe. Tiger lilies shed their fiery petals for leathery seed pods, and finally the fields filled with sprouts and grasses, and blue flax blossoms started to sway in the breezes. Day to day, wheat, oats, and corn stretched their stalks, potato vines spread in the fields, and squashes' and pumpkins' wide yellow flowers peeked out from underneath leaves that shadowed the soil and held a cool moisture through days of strengthening sun. When the farmers paused in their work, their growing produce filled them with a pride they could claim as wealth in the face of the debts measured in money.

Governor Bowdoin had not responded to their petitions by the time the summer sun reached the solstice and took its first tiny steps toward the equinox in autumn. The heat continued to build. Through long days of work, teams of men with brute force in their shoulders and subtle knowledge in their hands traveled farm to farm in circuits, mowing each farm's hay, harvesting wheat and oats, cutting the flax stalks as whole communities together. These were the dusty afternoons for which they had brewed their beer, cider, and brandy, their dandelion wine. With precisely these long days' hard work in their minds, they had spent their long evenings last winter whittling wood into ax handles, making flails and scythes, rakes and pitchforks, mauls and hatchets, all the tools they could make out of wood, to fit with the saw blades and ax-heads, the knife blades and chisels they had bought from merchants.[131]

As far up and down the Swift River valley as they could see from their hillside, Daniel and Abigail Shays showed their five children a living people on farms just like theirs, storing up their goods in advance of winter. At thirteen years old, their first son, Daniel Junior, was starting to put his shoulders to the farm's work. At eleven and nine, their daughters Lucy and Hannah were making their mother's work lighter as well. Even little Gilbert, at six, and their youngest daughter Polly, at three, studied their parents' stories, listening closely for clues and instructions about how they ought to behave to be part of their community.[132]

All through the frontier hills, in the ritual repetition of every task, Daniel and Abigail Shays and the farmers of Massachusetts showed their children the thousand ways in which their people were married to the land. Through their days' long rhythms, they described the details of each animal's care, and the uses every seed, grass, and herb, every bark, husk, and nut could be put to, for medicines, baskets, and dyes. They described the conditions of the climate and the time of year appropriate for each chore, fitting their children into the seasons and age-old customs their people had carried on, no matter the value of currency or the burden of taxes.

Throughout their labors, they told the stories of why their people had come from Scotland or Ulster or England to farm here on these rough hills. They explained as best they could why they had fought for their freedom from England. When their children asked them how their nation was different from the Old World they had left behind, they stared off into the western hills, or up the long-running rivers. They tested the rhetoric of liberty and rights against the current injustices, which even the children could recognize. They tried to say words that were true about their American opportunities, but they had to explain what they could about the conflict that had followed them here from the Old World, between their people and the men in offices on the coast whose lawyers could quote chapter and verse of the statutes that would let them seize this land.

Day after day, the farmers of Massachusetts waited to see how the men in Boston would respond to their petitions, but day after day, no news came. Even as they waited to see how their governor and their legislators would respond to their petitions, they promised their children that they had not suffered through five years of war only to come home and surrender their rights and property to wealthy men again. They would not consent to be peasants on land they themselves had broken to the plow.

Chapter Three

The Farmers Organize
Their First Protest

F INALLY, ON JULY 18, a week after the full moon, when farmers had been
putting up tools and livestock by moonlight long past sunset, riders
brought reports up the post road from Boston. It was not the news the people had hoped to hear. The General Court had adjourned without address-
ing the scourge of foreclosures. It had not revised the courts' fees. It had not
issued paper money or passed a tender law. It had not made any concession
whatsoever to their countrymen's sufferings.[1]

All through Massachusetts, young men raced their horses past orchards
heavy with droning insects and fields where clouds of pollen swirled over
their heads, looking for their neighbors to tell this news. Their neighbors
spat in the dirt when they heard that men with fortunes from imports and
exports and income from rents had retreated to their estates for the rest of
the summer. They had refused to hear the people's concerns and would not
return to Boston to consider the commonwealth's problems again till January
next year.

Now that the General Court had adjourned, the last week of August
stood like a threat at the end of the growing season. Courts of Common
Pleas would meet in Hampshire and Worcester, Middlesex, Bristol, and
Berkshire Counties. The farmers of Massachusetts knew that they or their
neighbors would have to stand before the judges without any protections
from powerful men on the coast. They would lose their farms unless they

gave up the better part of their harvests to pay to keep them. There was not enough wealth in the towns that prosperous farmers could afford to save their townsmen's property from the gavel. Even the farmers who could afford to stay on their land cringed to think that their neighbors' farms would be bought up at auction, parcel by discounted parcel, by wealthy landlords who would not have any interest in keeping their people's communities together.

From Leicester, west of Worcester, farmers heard that townsmen had entered into a mutual protection society whose members pledged to attend the auctions where their property was being sold to urge creditors to accept fair terms for settlement. In other towns, farmers formed similar pacts, preparing to represent the highest laws, themselves, even in the face of state authority if need be.[2]

As the news spread through Massachusetts, the leading men of the farm towns convened emergency meetings. In Groton northwest of Boston, Job Shattuck called his people together. In Holden, west of there, Isaac Chenery collected his neighbors together to see how they might respond to the government's insult. In Pelham, Captains Daniel Gray and Nehemiah Hines sent runners to summon the other town officers. In Amherst, Moses and Nathan Dickinson dispatched riders, and in Montague, State Representatives Moses Harvey and Thomas Grover.

In Bernardston, north of Montague on the border with Vermont, Agrippa Wells convened his men, and in Colrain, Hezekia Smith, John Clark, and John Anderson. In Whately, Oliver Graves and Rufus Wells, in Egremont, Ephraim Fitch, in Alford on Massachusetts's border with New York, John Hurlburt put out the call, and in West Springfield, the Day and Ely families sent messengers to tell their neighbors where and when to meet. Like a wave that ran the length of the commonwealth, the farmers and veterans came together in emergency meetings. They could not afford to answer the General Court's inaction with inaction of their own.

Once again, the farmers from Rehoboth in the east to Sheffield in the west crammed into rooms that were stuffy with indignation and outrage. Again, they hushed when their towns' leaders called for a formal vote to make their conventions constitutional by the commonwealth's laws.

When they opened the floor to debate again, the men who renewed their call for organized opposition to the courts would only submit to dignified restraint if their townsmen promised to do more than petition. Their towns' leaders offered to coordinate with officials in other towns to see whether their requests for reform might carry more weight if the towns submitted them in unison. There was still a month before the first court would meet in Northampton, more than enough time to draft a joint petition and beg for reforms together.

When the meetings finally dispersed and the men headed home in the muggy, late-July nights, Daniel Shays and the officers of Pelham and officers in towns the length of Massachusetts stayed late, assigning committees to write to other towns' leaders to see how far each towns' men were willing to go to protect their land.

By the time Governor Bowdoin celebrated his sixtieth birthday on August 7, 1786, young men in the hills had been jockeying with each other for the chance to race their horses from town to town with invitations and letters arranging the details for a meeting at Colonel Seth Murray's house in Hatfield, north of Northampton.[3] From Monday, August twenty-second, to Thursday the twenty-fifth—four days before the Northampton Court of Common Pleas was scheduled to open on Tuesday the twenty-ninth—the towns of Hampshire County were going to see what they could do as a region.

For weeks leading up to the twenty-second, the gentlemen farmers in all the western towns spent their evenings nominating their neighbors to serve as delegates. Through the hot nights of sterile lightning, they followed parliamentary rules of order to say what their delegates would and would not be authorized to agree to in all their names.

The convention was scheduled to start on the day when the moon aligned with the sun and did not appear in the sky. From week to week through the heart of the growing season, yeoman farmers and laborers from Longmeadow to Groton watched the moon grow thinner and closer to sunrise each morning, counting down to the day when the towns' delegates would decide as one body how to protect their farms in the face of their government's indifference and hostility.

Finally, on Monday, August 21, representatives rode to Hatfield on its plain in a bend of the Connecticut River. Daniel Shays did not join Pelham's delegates, Colonel John Powers and Captains William Conkey and Daniel Gray, as well as farmers Benjamin Bonney, Caleb Keith, and Mathew Clark.[4] In Hatfield, these men were joined by farmers and veterans from Shutesbury, from Enfield and Greenwich on the Swift River, from Montague and Turner's Falls and Greenfield upriver from Shelburne Falls on the Deerfield River, from Colrain and Charlemont in the hills, from Ashfield and Chesterfield, and from Worthington in the foothills to the Berkshires.

Fifty towns in all sent delegates to Hatfield. Hatfield and West Springfield's representatives, John Hastings and Benjamin Ely, joined the gathering, and William Pynchon, from Springfield's first family, contributed an aristocratic gravity to the discussions, although by this point, the sufferings were so widespread that even the leading families shared their neighbors' pains. Everyone was desperate for relief and furious to have been put in this position by their leaders.[5]

In the evening after their first day of deliberations, the moon returned as a sliver over the western hills at sunset. Day to day it ripened with the convention's deliberations. In the afternoons, the muggy heat built thunderheads over the delegates' fields where their relatives and neighbors kept up the work in their absence, dreading the hail or rain or locusts that might ruin all their efforts. When the clouds built and darkened then broke in lighting and rain, the winds blew cold and clear for a short time before the heat built its pressurized stillness over the hills again. In the evenings, the katydids, which had started to croak their call and response at dusk, compounded each other's voices until they made a numbing din that filled the people's ears with a constant and inescapable pressure that lasted into the night.

In Pelham, Shays and his neighbors laid down their heads those three nights knowing that their troubles were being addressed, that their region's leading men were crafting proposals to resolve the crisis before it consumed their crops.

Finally, on Friday night and Saturday morning, the delegates trickled back from Hatfield. Pelham's Caleb Keith, Mathew Clark, and Captain Daniel Gray called their townsmen together to say what their convention had resolved and to read the letter they had signed and sent to Governor Bowdoin in Boston.

With one voice, fifty towns listed the "unnecessary burdens now lying upon the people." In twenty-five articles, they renewed the same requests each individual town had made in petitions all summer.[6] They called for a revision of the commonwealth's constitution, which made it too easy for wealthy merchants to disregard the common people's concerns.

They asked the government to issue "a bank of paper money, subject to depreciation," as other states had done, since there was a shortage of coin.

They asked the legislature to pass a tender law "to remedy the mischiefs arising from the scarcity of money."

They begged the government to revise the schedule of court fees and the taxes that "operate unequally between the polls and estates and between landed and mercantile interests."

They even went so far as to propose that the commonwealth move its capital inland at least as far as Worcester so the western towns would not be so heavily burdened by the expense of sending representatives to its sessions. Their final resolve was to forward their list of resolutions to printers in Springfield so the whole countryside could read the people's reasonable and constitutionally authorized requests, and Thomas Grover of Montague summarized the letter in an editorial to the *Hampshire Herald*.[7]

The delegates in Hatfield had concluded their petition by pledging to "abstain from all mobs or unlawful assemblies until a constitutional method of redress could be obtained," but this point of their letter did not speak for all of the men in their towns.[8] For Shays and other men who had stayed home had spent their evenings laying contingency plans: to take direct action if the joint petition still failed to win reforms.

In the evenings, they had met to consider whom they might send to Northampton to obstruct the court, if it came to that. They considered the veterans who had fought beside them, from their own towns and neighboring towns, and they corresponded with town officials to see which towns would join them. Not all did. Some towns hesitated to commit men to a protest against an elected government, and they urged their neighbors to wait for elections in April. Others dismissed the unhappy farmers' concerns as the talk of young, restless, or irresponsible men, and they refused to join a panic that would convulse the commonwealth for months, as Ely's protests had done.[9]

Nevertheless, after three weeks of correspondence and negotiation, when the leaders in Hampshire County towns had tallied their neighbors' feelings, they counted more than forty-five towns that were willing to send more than twenty men to the court, including five towns that promised to send more than one hundred men, and twelve towns that pledge more than fifty, while scores of additional towns had pledged up to twenty men each.[10]

Each town's militiamen had been bound by years of fighting the British and the French and Indians before them, but now that the farmers of Hampshire County were staging a unified protest, they considered which of the militia leaders could be trusted to lead a dignified protest and keep the peace at the court.

Overleaf: "The State of Massachusetts" by Samuel Lewis. Published in Philadelphia by Mathew Carey, 1795. The map shows the commercial towns, founded in the mid-1600s near the Connecticut and Housatonic Rivers, that hosted the courts, and the Regulator towns in the hills to the west, which were typically settled in the mid-1700s. (*Boston Public Library, Norman B. Leventhal Map Center*)

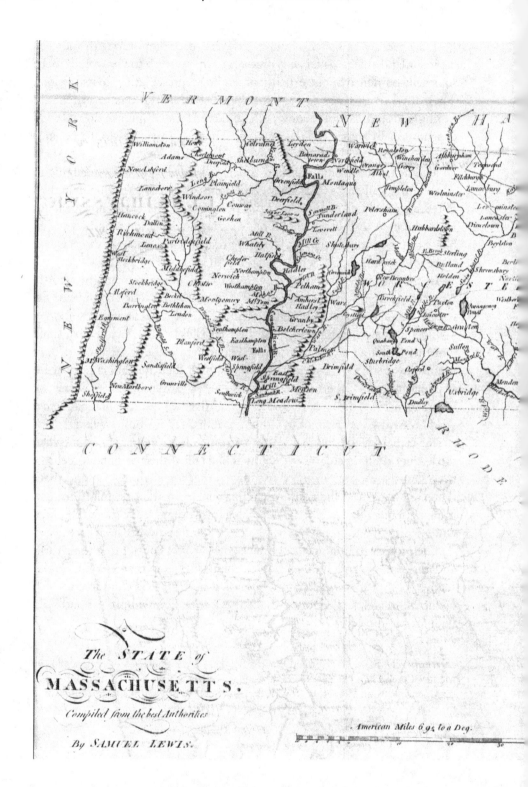

The STATE of
MASSACHUSETTS.
Compiled from the best Authorities
By SAMUEL LEWIS.

American Miles 69½ to a Deg.

So many people were suffering under the commonwealth's unjust taxes that almost any common farmer could have expressed the people's complaints. So many men had served in the war that almost any of the towns' militiamen could have led a joint demonstration. But of all the towns in Hampshire County, it was Pelham whose men took the lead in planning the protest. The hardy Scots-Irish farmers were known for their tight-knit communities, living close to nature and God's strict laws. They had proved this reputation for fierce independence and self-reliance by harassing Hatfield Tories before the war, then sending large numbers of men to fight the British. Now they took the first place in organizing resistance to the injustices coming from Boston.[11]

Pelham's prominent place was partly bolstered by geography, for the town was situated as a gateway to the other Scots-Irish hill towns. Pelham's East and West Hills, on either side of the Swift River's western branch, were perched on north-south ridgelines that connected the post road south of Pelham to the other Scots-Irish hill towns of New Salem, Shutesbury, and Montague, Greenfield, and Colrain. From Conkey's Tavern on the river or from the meeting house on West Hill, the farmers of Pelham could take the news from the post road and pass it along with instructions to the towns like Montague and Colrain, where hostility to Boston's central authority and unjust taxes also ran deep.

By the time the Pelham delegates returned from Hatfield and reported on their petition, Shays and the other militia leaders in Pelham and towns throughout Hampshire County had determined that there was danger in letting the government open its courts if the people's petitions were not respected. In their delegates' absence, they had loosely organized bodies of men who were waiting to hear instructions about staging a protest at the next court.

There were only four days till the court was scheduled to open in Northampton. The farmers did not have much time to wait for an answer to their petition. They would have to put men in the roads in advance of the twenty-ninth. The men debated back and forth, and when it was time to decide, they concluded that they would be neglecting their interests if they continued to wait patiently for relief.

The influential men of Pelham conferred with Shays and the other militia leaders, who confirmed that the infrastructure for a protest was all in place. They had identified leaders among them, and men who had pledged to obey their orders. Other towns had organized their men, and promised to send disciplined units that could both show their strength and exercise restraint.

Some towns had declined to back the petitions they had sent to Boston by sending militiamen now, but enough towns had volunteered men that the people could make a dignified protest.[12]

Pelham's Colonel Powers and Captains Conkey and Gray had each led at least a company during the war, but when they considered who should command the hundreds of men from all the towns together, they turned to thirty-nine-year-old gentleman farmer Captain Daniel Shays, who had worked his way up from laborer to commissioned officer and commanded respect from men of every rank. For the past four years, Shays had led the men and boys of Pelham through maneuvers in the green beside the meeting house on West Hill, but when Powers, Conkey, and Gray asked Shays to take the first position at the protest, Shays declined.[13] He offered to work with his townsmen to organize the march, but he would not risk his authority or his safety leading so many men.

When Shays declined, Powers, Conkey, and Grey turned to a former selectman, Deacon John Thompson, a civic leader instead of a soldier, to lead their men to Northampton. All weekend in advance of the court date on Tuesday the twenty-ninth, Shays and Thompson rode through Pelham with their fellow officers. House to house, they recruited trustworthy men who could follow orders and resist the temptation of violence. They assured their neighbors that they were not sending a mob to the court. They were going to march to Northampton in orderly lines, with fife and drum and military discipline, with so many organized men that Northampton Sheriff Elisha Porter would not dare arrest them or turn them away and force the court open. They solicited provisions from influential landowners who declined to lead or participate but were willing to offer supplies. They asked men who were staying home to help on the farms where men would be gone for five days, spreading the cost of their protests as widely as possible among the community.

Not all the towns sent men, though. In Granville west of West Springfield, in Heath and Rowe near Colrain—in Goshen, which bordered the towns of Ashfield and Whately, which sent large numbers of men—officials refused to join the protest.[14] They had posted petitions to Boston begging for fiscal relief, but now they argued against opposing their own elected government. These neutral towns did not condemn the protest or send men to suppress it, they only kept their men from joining either the protestors from the hill towns or the government men from the towns on the flat lands near the rivers.

In Pelham, Shays and Thompson, and in Colrain, West Springfield, and the other hill towns, fellow officers went house to house, building support for their plan. Of the men who agreed to join the protest, two out of three had been sued for debts, but the crisis affected people of every station, from laborers to yeoman farmers to gentlemen farmers and leading local landowners.[15]

As they rode along the borders of fields they had passed countless times in five years of work since the war, they never stopped watching the sky for signs of weather that might threaten their crops on the eve of the harvest. But now they were also looking ahead to Tuesday's courtyard, where hundreds of men would confront each other with the runaway inflation and unpaid bills and the government's unjust policies and their neighbors' losses and more than a year's inflammatory editorials between them. In the future they saw there, they tried to picture how large a force Sheriff Porter might be able to gather. They debated among themselves whether Porter would ask General Shepard to reinforce him with wealthy merchants and clerks from the Springfield militia. They tried to estimate how many of Shepard's militiamen might answer the call to march against their countrymen and how many might refuse.

Through Pelham and Prescott east of Pelham, messengers were always overtaking them in the road with letters from towns farther off, from leaders who pledged men or support or asked for guidance. All weekend, Shays and the leading men of Pelham answered their countrymen's questions, and all their instructions were calculated to ensure that their men had force enough to close the court, to restrain their angry elements, and to defend themselves if the protests came to blows.

On Monday morning, August 28, dozens of men and their families from Pelham and Prescott and Shutesbury met on the green in front of the Pelham meeting house on West Hill. They milled about in the fine Septemberish weather, with the first trees turning scarlet and auburn and gold in the nights' cooler breezes.

The men would march to Northampton and camp in town. Unless they heard that men in Boston had passed reforms, they would muster under Captain Luke Day of West Springfield and close the court tomorrow. They came in uniforms, if they had them, though many wore coats of homespun cloth their wives and mothers had made with their own hands and dyed from their fields and forests with beech or walnuts, barks and berries, indigo and squash. Only about a quarter were armed with muskets, to show they were veterans.[16] Many brought clubs from their woods, to show the people of Northampton they were prepared to defend their rights and to show their discipline by keeping their arms at their shoulders.

As their numbers swelled, Shays and the other town officers made their way through the crowd, distributing sprigs of hemlock for the men to wear in their hatbands.[17] In the war, they had worn sprigs of pine, but now they would be known by hemlock, a useful tree that made the same gray-green hush over evergreen laurels and ferns in everyone's woods. They would not wear sprigs of laurel since they were not intent on victory in battle or the poetry that would commemorate an epic struggle. They only wanted freedom to live on the land their people had settled.

Finally in the warm, humid, late-August Monday morning, with hemlock in everyone's hatbands and all the thick scents of ripe summer rich in their nostrils, Thompson and Shays's officers called their men out of the crowd of wives and children who had come to see them off. Seventy farmers arranged themselves in lines beneath flags their wives had woven and dyed from their own flax and stitched with their own hands.

On Thompson's order, the musicians struck up their marching tunes, and a column of seventy men set out in lines eight abreast. They crested the short rise west of the meeting house, then descended the hill out of sight toward Amherst. Soon enough, the sound of their fifes and drums died away, and then the creak of saddle leather, as men mounted their horses to return to their fields. From the meeting house lawn, Shays and the other officers listened to the quiet of the fields and the hum of August insects before they retreated into the meeting house and wrote to leaders in other towns, letting them know that their men were on the march.

Eventually they too returned to their homes and their work, but all day they tracked Thompson's progress. They all knew the roads, they knew how long it would take the men to march up the hill through Amherst, where they would join former Amherst selectman Captain Joel Billings and his men, then continue down to the floodplains of Hadley. No one expected the wealthy farmers of Hadley to leave their rich fields to join Thompson and Billings's ranks, but Shays and his neighbors worked through the afternoon, guessing about what time the ferrymen would be poling their townsmen across the Connecticut River and into Northampton. As the sun slanted down in the afternoon, they expected their force to have merged with other farmers who had spent the day marching from Hatfield, Whately, and Ashfield, from Greenfield and hill towns as far north as Colrain and Charlemont, as far west as Worthington.

When Shays and his neighbors finished their work for the day they were still envisioning the sights their townsmen must be seeing as each of the other towns' militias arrived under their flags. They reminisced about the men they knew, who had probably gone to Northampton from other towns. They calculated, as best they could, what it must feel like to march in columns and set up their tents again as in the war, but now with the question of justice at issue again and the risk of arrest, the possibility of violence in tomorrow's humid summer dawn.

They told each other stories about Captain Day of West Springfield, the leader who would give orders to Thompson and Billings and all the other towns' officers. Pelham men who knew Day from the war described him as a distinguished officer who had earned the respect of his men and stayed in the army till the final victory at Yorktown.[18] They said that he was the kind of man whom Sheriff Porter and the Northampton merchants were likely to respect, for men in Day's family had served in the city of Springfield's leading offices for decades.[19]

Captain Day had not held political office himself, but he had been well positioned to enter the new American aristocracy after the war. He had donated one month's pay to join the exclusive Society of the Cincinnati, which had lobbied for life-long half-pay pensions for commissioned officers and their sons. Day had banked on this promised income when he came home from war and borrowed money to start his farm again, but when the Atlantic trade collapsed and chains of debt pulled tight all across the region, his creditors' demands for hard coin found him short of cash. Then he lost any hope of a pension when the Congress in Philadelphia voted down the Society of the Cincinnati's proposal: they refused to create an aristocracy of retired commissioned officers.

Without this expected income, Day could not keep up with his creditors' threatening letters and suits for debt. Finally, they lost patience with his failure to pay. They took him to court, and the judges committed him to debtor's prison for half of July, all of August, and half of September 1785, while his family failed to raise funds to free him.[20]

When the hundreds of Hampshire County farmers joined his lines and followed his orders in Northampton tomorrow morning, his presence at the head of their column—along with two other Cincinnati members and thirty other officers from the Continental army—would tell the wealthy men in Boston that the people who suffered under the commonwealth's taxes were not poor rabble but dignified veterans and aristocratic landowners from the region's leading farms.

All day Tuesday, Shays and the other officers who had stayed behind in Pelham worked their farms. Men who remembered spring 1782 described the day when Samuel Ely's hundreds of angry farmers had marched into Northampton to protest the constitution. They worried that Sheriff Porter would rally influential Northampton merchants and make a show of force by capturing Day the same way the government men had arrested Ely in '82.

At the end of the day, they gathered at Conkey's Tavern to wait for news. It was only at dusk that the first riders brought reports. They said Day had marched into town with five hundred men in disciplined lines, under flags that represented towns up and down the Connecticut River valley.

When they reached the court they surrounded it and silenced their fifes and drums. Captain Day ascended the courthouse steps to keep any judges, lawyers, or businessmen from entering. He had stood at the top of these same courthouse steps four years ago to protect the court from Ely's protestors, but now he was there to press for some of the same reforms Ely had demanded.[21]

Messengers reported that soon after Day's men arrived, Sheriff Porter marched into town with hundreds of men to balance Day's hundreds. Porter's men wore paper in their hatbands, to stand for contracts and law against the people's hemlock.[22] Porter halted his men and demanded that Day retreat from the courthouse steps, but Day refused. He said that he and his men would not allow the government to conduct its business until the legislature had answered the people's petition from Hatfield.

Day's challenge hung in the air, but Porter did not command his men to dislodge Day and his men. Instead, they surrounded the men occupying the court and waited for an opportunity to escort the judges in. The morning sun climbed the sky and dried the last dew from the Northampton green as the bodies of men regarded each other across the courthouse square. Men on both sides carried muskets, but neither side's leaders challenged the other by giving orders to load them or fix bayonets.

The judges and bailiffs huddled in Captain Samuel Clark's Tavern nearby with the merchants who had brought their business to the court.[23] They calculated the people's mood, trying to reckon the chances that their cases might be heard, and worried about what would happen to them if they could not recover enough money from the farmers to make their own payments.

As the heat of the late-August day began to build, farmers and militiamen trickled in and joined the respective lines. By the middle of the day, the farmers' numbers had swelled to fifteen hundred, much larger than

Porter's force, but the sheriff never summoned General Shepard's militia from Springfield for help dispersing the protestors.[24] Finally, Porter invited Day and his officers to parley, but even when the officers from both sides met face to face, they could not agree to terms by which the farmers would let the judges convene the court.

When negotiations reached an impasse, Day asked for permission to parade his men in the courtyard. Porter allowed it, provided he could parade his men in turn. The men on opposite sides of the courtyard had served together in both the French and Indian War and the Revolution. They had stood together in battles starting at Bunker Hill, and they had campaigned together the length of Lake Champlain, as far north as Quebec, and then on the Hudson River.[25] Some had stayed with Captain Day till the final battle in Virginia.

Under Porter's critical gaze, Day commanded his fifes and drums to begin, and he called the commands to wheel and turn his men in formations they had practiced in town greens these years since the war. Here in front of the Northampton courthouse, their maneuvers were not quite a fighting display but a reprimand to the people whose laws oppressed them. Their homespun clothing, their rough manners and calloused hands, their dignified restraint beneath the book-taught merchants' and lawyers' eyes showed agents of law how to act as men of one community together, as if their solidarity and discipline gave a lesson in how to be American.

They paraded for Porter's men's benefit and also for the Northampton townspeople, who had barricaded themselves in their houses and drawn their shutters, the same as when Ely brought his men in '82.[26] But the heat was too thick to close themselves in entirely, so even if they only cracked windows that faced away from the street, they could still hear the day's proceedings. As closely as they listened, though, they never heard the sound of shots or the cries of distress they might have heard if the sheriff's men had tried to disperse Day's men and take the courtyard. All they heard was the people's rattling drums and Day and his officers barking orders, crisp and distinct, answered by the sound of the farmers' boots all in unison, telling the townspeople that they were not a lawless mob.[27]

Finally, Day's men finished parading and resumed their posts around the courthouse, and then the people of Northampton listened as Porter's men started their drums and flutes and made the same demonstration of order and discipline to show their countrymen how the men of the law conducted themselves.

In Conkey's Tavern, the messengers back from Northampton reported that after each side had paraded, they both resumed their positions without any struggle. Porter escorted the judges out of Clark's Tavern in their wigs and gowns, but he did not try to clear a path through the crowd of farmers to escort them into the courthouse. In the end, he turned them around, and they retreated to Clark's Tavern.[28]

To resolve the standoff, the judges received a six-man delegation, among them Dr. Hines from Prescott and Joel Billings from Amherst. These men submitted a request to the court to not let more land or livestock be seized till the "resolves of the convention of this county can have an opportunity of having their grievances redressed by the General Court." The judges answered that they did not have any authority to provide the relief the people asked for. Without relief, the farmers' representatives refused to withdraw.

Merchants and lawyers begged Porter to arrest the people's impudent leaders and make a forceful display of the government's authority, but the sheriff refused to inflame the people with arrests. In the end, the judges wrote in their books that they adjourned *sine die*, Latin for "without the day." They agreed not to convene their court again until after the farmers had brought in the last of their flour corn in late November.[29]

When Billings and Hines and the rest of the farmers' delegates brought this news out to the courtyard, the farmers sent up a cheer. Their unjust sufferings and their proud and dignified restraint had bought them three months' relief. They had paid for this delay without men on either side spilling blood.

The government's men under Porter withdrew, and the fifteen hundred farmers formed their lines, each town's men beneath their flags, to make the march back home. One after another, their officers started their fifes and drums, and Deacon Thompson and Joel Billings led their Pelham and Amherst men back toward the ferry.

The messengers who had whipped their horses back across the eleven miles from Hadley and up to Pelham reported that their men had crossed and started back home without any disturbance from farmers who had taken the government's side against them.

At Conkey's Tavern, Shays and his neighbors rejoiced at this report. More than a thousand men had joined their people's organized protest. The townspeople had not joined the government men who opposed them. The court had been closed without a struggle.

All evening, as Shays and the men of Pelham finished their work and put their livestock and farms to bed, they waited to hear the sound of their drums and the sound of families cheering their men from the roadside as they came home through the muggy chorus of katydids and crickets.

Any satisfaction the people felt in the towns of Hampshire County was only tempered by the knowledge that Springfield and Northampton lawyers rode home from Northampton in outrage. The merchants and distributors who returned to Enfield and Hartford were going to have to tell their creditors that they could not pay them, and their creditors would hardly discount their debts to reflect the value of the farmers' proud displays.

So even as farmers settled to sleep in Pelham and in all the towns that sent men to Northampton, they knew that the merchants would wake up tomorrow and send their own petitions to Boston, complaining that Sheriff Porter had abandoned the law by respecting the people's demands, insisting that Governor Bowdoin assert his authority by arresting the men who stopped the court.

Chapter Four

A Middle Path

A S THE NEWSPAPERS STARTED TO FIGHT the war over what had happened, the editors of the *Hampshire Herald* stated plainly in their August 29 edition that "the principal source of the present disquietude seems to be the late appropriation of the revenue arising from the excise" and impost taxes, referring to the £29,000 levied in March. They suggested that "a different mode of paying the interest . . . might restore tranquility."[1] A bystander wrote the next day in the same paper that the people had conducted themselves "from first to last, with less insolence and violence, and with more sobriety and good order, than is commonly to be expected in such a large and promiscuous assembly, collected in so illegal a manner, and for so unwarrantable a purpose."[2]

Nevertheless, on Saturday, September 2, four days after the Hampshire County Court of Common Pleas was closed, the people of Massachusetts came in from their fields to the taverns to read that Governor Bowdoin had issued a proclamation denouncing the protest.[3] He said that the people's protest was an attempt to "subvert all law and government and introduce riot, anarchy and confusion, which would probably terminate in absolute despotism, consequently destroying the fairest prospects of political happiness that any people was ever favored with."[4]

The protesting farmers were not his only audience for this statement.[5] He spoke for the governors of twelve other states, and for Vermont's Governor Thomas Chittenden and for all the powerful men who were watching to see if the people who had started the Revolution were even now breeding another rebellion.

Bowdoin uttered these words for the benefit of British ministers who doubted that the restive Americans would really be able to govern themselves now that the masses had had a taste of self-determination.

Bowdoin made this proclamation to answer Canadian Governor Sir Guy Carleton, Lord Dorchester, in Quebec, who had prophesied at the end of the war that the Americans would beg for protection soon enough, even from their own people.[6]

Bowdoin spoke these words for the sake of newspapers in England, which were waiting to trumpet the fact that degenerate colonists could not manage their own affairs in the absence of redcoats to force the law upon them.[7]

Most of all, Bowdoin was speaking to Boston's wealthy merchants, who had financed the war from their own pockets and needed to know that their bonds would be paid without interruption from farmers. Bowdoin's own income of £1,000 a year depended on regular fulfillment of contracts and payment of rents, and his words assured the state's creditors that the courts would continue to meet and that there would be money to satisfy contracts.[8] That if there was not money, the courts would see that the people sacrificed property that could be turned into money, and that if there was not property, the government would keep the men themselves in prison until their families paid. His words also assured them that any man who stood in the way of the courts would answer to the state.

Bowdoin did not make these threats explicitly but by refusing to grant that the people had any legitimate complaints. By claiming instead that the people had broken the law, he was clearly laying the groundwork to justify his actions if the commonwealth tried to make them pay with their bodies, or with blood, if necessary.

To the wealthy families of Massachusetts, whose sons were studying chemistry, husbandry, metallurgy, and engineering in Europe—to the wealthy families who laughed at the farmers' crude folk traditions and superstitions—the warnings implied in Bowdoin's proclamation were deeply reassuring, though some of the men who had served in the war and now held positions in government knew that the proud, self-governing people were not likely to wilt beneath the governor's implied threats.

In their town halls and in their taverns, the farmers of Massachusetts were hardly encouraged by Bowdoin's proclamation. When the governor called their peaceful demonstration a riot—when he called their negotiations with judges anarchy, or the local militias' solidarity with their protest a kind of confusion—they knew well enough the long history that was threatening to repeat itself.[9]

The Scots-Irish farmers who had settled Pelham and Colrain and Montague had heard this scornful language before, from the British lords who had used contempt and threats to justify seizing their lands for almost two hundred years. The flush of defensive indignation had run in their blood since their Lowland Scots ancestors had followed James I to Ulster in 1603. They had fought alongside the British to drive out the Irish kings and establish plantations in Irish forests, but as soon as their people had increased the value of their land, the British landlords drove up their rents, disregarding their claims as they forced them to flee to the colonies starting in 1718.[10] The Scots-Irish settlers came as indentured servants or else they paid for their passage and purchased land with whatever savings they brought. But the Boston Puritans had not let them settle within their towns. They had driven them west toward the frontier around the margins of Worcester, and even after they had started new settlements there, landlords had raised their rents again, and Puritans burned down their Presbyterian church, and they were forced to surrender their improvements once more and take their carts farther west into the hills.[11]

When the Scots-Irish farmers had finally set up their towns in the uncut forests of Pelham, starting in 1738, then founded the town in 1743, they had hoped they were starting again for the last time, too far from Boston to suffer for merchants and landlords' threats or violence. They had sent men north to fight the French and Indians, and they had sent men to fight the redcoats, and those men returned in triumph, asserting their country's independence, claiming their land for themselves after years of displacement and sacrifices. Nonetheless, here came Bowdoin's taxes and now his threats, pursuing them into the hills, threatening to force them west again if they could not raise money to pay.

To the farmers who had served on the Hudson River during the Revolution, Bowdoin's proclamation resembled the language New York's Governor Sir Henry Moore had used to justify sending the colony's troops against the farmers of Dutchess County between the Hudson River and Connecticut's western border twenty years ago. Tenant farmers there had organized protests against the Livingstons, Philipses, Van Rensselears, and Van Cortlandts, feudal land barons who had been raising their rents, forcing them off the estates into unclaimed lands. When the farmers claimed those lands and improved them, the landlords sent bailiffs to seize the land and their improvements. When the farmers gathered in crowds to prevent evictions, and ultimately to stop the courts that authorized them, Governor Moore dismissed their claims to the lands they had improved. He called the people squatters and outlaws and labeled their nonviolent resistance "the Great Rebellion" to justify sending redcoats north from Manhattan and south from Albany to break up their protests and arrest the farmers' leaders.[12]

Daniel Shays and other Massachusetts men who had served in the Hudson Highlands during the war had heard the story firsthand from the Dutchess County farmers who knew William Prendergast, William Finch, and Samuel Munroe, the men who had been arrested as scapegoats and sentenced to death so that Governor Moore could make a display of the state's authority and assert the powerful lords' right to claim land the people had settled.[13]

Massachusetts men remembered the troubles that started in Vermont the same year as the troubles in Dutchess County, although the troubles to their north had not ended with defeat or executions. At the same time that Moore was sending his redcoats to put down the protests in Dutchess County, New York officials in Albany and Lake George were calling Ethan and Ira Allen and their Green Mountain Boys squatters and outlaws for resisting New Yorkers' claims to land in the region between New York and New Hampshire that would become Vermont.[14]

The farmers who stood with the Allen brothers had legally chartered their towns in New Hampshire when Governor John Wentworth's land grants opened Vermont to settlement. But New York land speculators had claimed the same land in New York courts, and they refused to recognize Wentworth's grants. In 1766, they took their titles to New York courts, and the judges sent bailiffs and sheriffs to force farmers off their farms and seize their improvements.

For years of tense confrontations with bailiffs and protests at the courts, the Green Mountain Boys kept the New York surveyors from stealing their people's land, and Ethan Allen made a name for himself with his flamboyant gestures. When New York Attorney General John Kemp placed a £150 bounty on his head, Allen endeared himself to the common people by publishing a letter placing a £5 bounty on Kemp's.[15] In the end, the Allens escaped the fate that had cost the three Dutchess County farmers their lives. In 1777, when the colonies were deep in their war to free themselves from the Crown, the Allens and other leading men of Vermont declared themselves an independent republic and started to govern their rocky hills as a republic where all men could vote.

So now when Massachusetts farmers heard Bowdoin's language echoing New York state's threats against honest farmers, they knew that the Revolution was not the only recent precedent for local resistance leading to justice and independence.

The Massachusetts farmers could not ignore the fact that Bowdoin's proclamation echoed the sentiments they had heard from British officials in the years leading up to the Revolution, when they called the colonists rioters and traitors. All up and down the Atlantic coast, the colonists had heard their royal governors insult them when they organized opposition to the taxes the Crown had levied after the Seven Years' War, which the British had fought in Europe, in America, and on battlefields as far away as India.

Prime Minister William Pitt had turned the tide of that war by borrowing huge sums from London financiers, who needed to be paid back with interest.[16] The Crown had turned to its colonists, whose industries had been kept in check, to raise these funds. When the colonists objected that they had not been represented when ministers in Parliament obligated Britain to pay these funds—nor when ministers levied their crushing taxes—the Crown called them traitors and criminals and passed the Coercive Acts to force them into submission.[17]

Again, this precedent gave the people of Massachusetts hope, for the farmers remembered clearly how the towns of Massachusetts had forced the Crown's administrators to either resign their posts or flee to Boston. They had governed themselves in town meetings and county conventions, collecting taxes, enforcing their laws, and living in freedom from 1774, one year before Lexington, two years before Thomas Jefferson had written the Declaration of Independence.[18]

With this proud legacy of self-determination in their minds, the men in Pelham and men in towns the length of Massachusetts heard Bowdoin's accusations and condemnations as a challenge to the liberties they had won during the war. They wondered whether they would have to renew their enlistments and work together to free themselves at last from the ruling nobles.

Men in Massachusetts had heard the language in reports from other states, where farmers were fighting similar fiscal policies even now. As recently as this spring, Massachusetts farmers had heard reports from the Wyoming Valley of the Susquehanna River, in Pennsylvania near the New

York border, where judges and land speculators had been using this same vocabulary of legitimate contracts and illegitimate opposition to justify using force against the people.[19] Like the Vermonters, the settlers in Pennsylvania had already legally chartered their towns in Connecticut land offices, but Pennsylvania landlords made contrary claims in the local courts.[20] When the local judges authorized bailiffs to remove the settlers if they could not pay for their own land at the landlords' inflated prices, the farmers armed themselves in self-defense, the same as Ethan and Ira Allen had done in Vermont.

Just this April, Ethan Allen had traveled to Pennsylvania to consult with the farmers. The authorities in Pennsylvania knew Allen's reputation and dreaded the publicity he would bring to the farmers' cause, so they pressed the speculators to drop their claims and end the conflict.

In the shadow of this victory—plus the Rhode Islanders' recent victory in elections, and victories and reforms farmers had won in Maryland and Pennsylvania—the people of Massachusetts were not intimidated when their governor condemned them as rebels and anarchists. They had already shown the world that they would stand together and throw off unjust laws and govern themselves. It was a legacy they could be proud of before all the world, and they knew how to fight if their government forced them to defend the liberties they had won.

Bowdoin's proclamation elicited strong responses from around the commonwealth. The people of Boston circulated a letter to the towns, invoking the "mutual ties of friendship and affection" and the "blood of brethren shed to obtain our freedom," asking the farmers to seek "redress of grievances . . . in a Constitutional and orderly way," and they pledged themselves "to join our exertions with yours in the same way, to obtain redress of such as do really exist."[21] But the people of Boston did not have sway with elites in the General Court, and farmers in all the counties west of the city heard their prayer for civility as a call for capitulation, since constitutional methods had failed them in July, when the General Court had adjourned without hearing their concerns.

In all the other counties west of Boston, farmers and townspeople prepared their responses as well. From September 2 to 13, foreclosure courts were slated to open in Worcester; in Taunton south of Boston in Bristol County; in Concord in Middlesex County; and in Great Barrington in Berkshire. Each of these courts would pose the same question: would the people abandon their protests under Bowdoin's threats? How far would they go to defend the rights they had fought a war for?

In each of the counties, landowners, veterans, and small merchants read Bowdoin's proclamation and blew the conch shells or trumpets or rang the church bells that called their townsmen together.[22] They explained the danger they faced, and they weighed their loyalties and obligations against their fears and possible losses. When they took their constitutional votes, towns in all the counties west of Boston resolved to stand beside their countrymen in Hampshire County.

Three days after Bowdoin published his proclamation, on September 5, messengers raced to Pelham with news that the chief justice of the Worcester County Court had arrived at his courthouse to find it surrounded by hundreds of men in uniform, many of whom were armed, who refused to allow him or anyone into the courthouse.

Artemas Ward had served as commander in chief of New England's militia for a year before George Washington took over, and now he was the speaker of the Massachusetts House of Representatives. He had led six thousand men to close the Worcester court in September 1774, but now he was confronted by his own citizens' bayonets.[23] He ordered Worcester Sheriff William Greenleaf, to summon General Jonathan Warner's militia, but too many men in the militia were veterans who knew the protesting farmers and shared their concerns. When they heard the town's bell ringing the alarm, they refused to join their general in the courtyard to force the governor's laws on their neighbors and fellow veterans. When Sheriff Greenleaf's messengers sought them individually, they did not refuse outright, but they made excuses or dragged their feet and never arrived in the courtyard.[24]

When Ward finally realized that help would not be coming, he gave the hundreds of protestors a lesson in courage by making his way toward the courthouse steps to challenge them alone. The farmers presented bayonets to prevent him, but Ward pressed his robe against their blades till finally the silence was broken by the sound of his silk robe ripping.[25]

The men stepped aside, and Ward ascended the courthouse steps. In a voice all the men could hear, he demanded to know who was in charge and what were their demands.[26] Adam Wheeler, a man in his fifties, came forward. Like so many others a veteran of wars against both the British and the French and Indians, Wheeler had been cited for acts of conspicuous bravery as early in the Revolution as the colonists' skirmish at Concord.[27]

Now Wheeler climbed the courthouse steps and told Justice Ward that he himself was not in charge. He said that no one was, but he offered to speak for the others and proceeded to tell Ward the same thing Luke Day and the men in Northampton had told Sheriff Porter: that they wanted relief from foreclosures and courts' fees.[28] He said that the number of suits for debt was double the total of the previous two years, and that there were three debtors in prison for every criminal, a tenfold increase from two years ago.[29] He reminded the judge that his people had made polite requests in petitions authorized by constitutional town meetings—petitions Bowdoin's ministers had ignored. Wheeler said that they could not allow the courts to convene till the General Court addressed their grievances.

Ward did not yield. He lectured the men on the vanity and folly of their ideas. When it started to rain, he lectured them still.[30] He berated the dignified farmers, but they let him speak without shouting him down or ever laying hands on him—though some did call for tarring him and covering him with feathers, as they had tarred and feathered agents of the Crown before the war.

Ward's lecture failed to disperse the sodden protestors. Nor did he soften Wheeler's resolve when he warned him that obstructing the court was an act of treason that would end at the gallows.[31] When the men still refused to admit anyone to the courthouse, Ward retreated to Patch's Tavern, where he and the other judges convened their court, but only as a formality, and only for long enough to agree to adjourn till November 21.[32]

When the farmers heard that their judges too had entered *sine die* in their books, they sent up a cheer. Most dispersed, but some men needed to see for themselves that the judges who had surrendered the day would not then meet at night.[33] They kept watch till after the almost-full moon passed its zenith.

By the time the judges departed from Patch's Tavern, they had not conducted any business for the merchants whose accounts still demanded payment, and those merchants and businessmen and Artemas Ward himself joined the merchants of Hampshire County in posting petitions and letters to Boston, begging the governor to help them enforce the law.

As in Northampton, though, the merchants and judges could not advertise the people's violence by waving any bloody shirts in editorials, to rally an outraged populace against the men they described as disordered rabble. They could not accuse the people of insurrection. For in all the time that the farmers had held the courtyard till the judges adjourned the court, neither side's men had raised a fist or lowered a loaded musket against the others. In the reports that rippled out from Worcester in letters that evening, everyone had to admit that the people had made a dignified, peaceful protest, although some letters departed from the truth and started the rumor that thousands of drunken farmers, even tens of thousands of uncouth rabble, had rioted in the streets.

Whatever letters or pleas Bowdoin sent to the other towns in the next six days did not prevent the same scene from playing out in Concord, a mere twenty miles from Bowdoin's seat of authority in Boston, where farmers prevented the Middlesex County Court of Common Pleas from opening on September 11. That evening, the farmers in Pelham learned that the judges and merchants had arrived at the courthouse that morning to find one of Groton's leading veterans camped on the courthouse grounds with former selectman Job Shattuck and three hundred men.[34]

Like Luke Day and Adam Wheeler, Shattuck had distinguished himself in his military service, and he had endeared himself to his townsmen in 1781 by intervening when bailiffs were seizing a neighbor's cattle.[35] Shattuck had been arrested then, but now he stood with his beleaguered neighbors again. He had organized committees in advance, one to restrain and discipline the men, another to negotiate with the judges and sheriffs.[36]

Again, as in Worcester, the Concord sheriff summoned his militia, but the Concord militia likewise refused to muster. Without a guard, the judges and sheriff were powerless to hold court. They tallied the number of armed men, then withdrew to Jones' Tavern, where Shattuck presented them with a letter that said "the voice of the people of this county" had determined that "the court shall not enter this courthouse until such time as the people shall have redress of the grievances they labor under at present."[37]

As in Northampton and Worcester, the judges only convened the court among themselves, and only long enough to adjourn court till November 27.

Once again, the people had kept the commonwealth from helping merchants collect their debts. Again no blood had been spilled.

The next day, the farmers of Hampshire County rejoiced again when they heard news from Bristol County, in Taunton south of Boston. The regional court session there had been clouded with danger ever since Chief Justice and former Major General David Cobb had boldly claimed that he would sit as judge or die in his boots as general.[38]

When the appointed day came, he found his court opposed in spite of his threats. His militia had mustered, but not in numbers large enough to disperse the protestors.[39] Like Artemas Ward in Worcester, he refused to risk a struggle for fear of the consequences if the state should give the people bloody shirts to wave as evidence of Bowdoin's tyranny.

For the fourth time in two weeks, the farmers of Hampshire County heard that judges had adjourned a court without a fight. Again, merchants were delayed in their suits for debts. Again, no blood had been spilled.

Luke Day and Deacon Thompson and Daniel Shays and the fifteen hundred farmers who had returned to their work in the Swift and Quaboag and Connecticut River valleys celebrated for a second time that same day when messengers brought news east from Berkshire County that the fifth and final foreclosure court west of Boston had been closed in a stunning victory for the people.[40]

The Berkshire County farmers had surrounded their court in the morning, but Sheriff Caleb Hyde and General John Paterson mustered a thousand militiamen who marched into town to force the court open.[41] For a moment it looked like Berkshire County would stem the tide of opposition, but one of the court's own judges, Justice William Whiting, stopped Paterson on his approach and asked his militiamen to indicate their loyalties by stepping to one side or the other of the road.

General Paterson had distinguished himself at the rebel victory at Saratoga, where he commanded five regiments under General Horatio Gates, but now when Justice Whiting put his question to them, eight hundred of Paterson's thousand men stepped to the people's side of the road. This gesture ended the government's opposition. The two hundred men who stood beside their general did not make any attempt to enforce the commonwealth's laws. Their townsmen had shown with their bodies that the people's ideas about justice were more convincing than the government's. Nor did the people abuse their lopsided advantage to pillage the shops or the wealthy families' homes.[42] Officers kept men in order, and the only ones arrested that day had been taken into custody by the farmers: two Pittsfield men had gotten drunk, and their townsmen pulled them aside to keep them from sparking a general lawlessness.[43]

Betrayed by their militia—and now by one of their own colleagues—the judges gave up any hope of opening court. Whiting invited the people's leaders to meet at his home, where they drafted a statement asking the judges not to meet again until legislators in Boston had reformed the taxes and court fees. Whiting and two of the other three justices signed. Only Justice Jahleel Woodbridge refused. Theodore Sedgwick accused Whiting of sedition in private correspondence, then forwarded Whiting's tract and their correspondence to Bowdoin, denouncing his colleagues and complaining about the consequences if debts were not paid and if the people prevented the courts from enforcing the law.[44]

In five towns in two weeks, the people had struck the court days from the calendar. No clubs had been swung, no shots had been fired, no windows had been broken. No blood had been spilled. No one had been arrested except by the people's own officers. The people had even been joined by armed and organized men who had seen justice on the people's side of the road. Even some of the judges had taken their side.

Like birds calling their mates, the veteran farmers of Massachusetts called from one town, "We are the people and we will bear inequality but we will not bear injustice," and from their neighboring counties' court towns, the same cry returned in answer the length of the commonwealth.

The days went by and news of their protests spread up and down the Atlantic coast. Inland farmers in other states, who had been struggling through the same crises of war debts and collapsing markets, cheered their kinsmen in Massachusetts. The people who had won reforms by closing their own states' courts, these last two years—in New Jersey and Pennsylvania, in Virginia and South Carolina—were comforted by news that their fellow Americans were still protecting their liberties. All the length of the new nation's coast, and far into the hills, the common people were glad to see that American farmers still refused to back down when powerful men tried to use unjust laws, then threats, to steal their land.

The rumors that spread through the country, though, increased the numbers of protestors and fanned the flames of anxiety by describing scenes of violence and looting, or scenes of violent oppression by government men. The leading landowners and businessmen who had stepped in to set up a government in the absence of British administrators worried that the authority they had won through revolution might not survive this current of popular opposition to elected leaders' laws.

After this round of protests, the editorials tacked to the walls of Massachusetts's taverns started to be signed by men who called themselves "Regulators." They were not calling themselves "descendants of the Sons of Liberty." They did not call themselves rebels, or impugn Governor Bowdoin's loyalty by calling themselves patriots.

In calling themselves Regulators, they revived a name farmers had used in North Carolina fifteen years ago, before the war, when corrupt judges, bailiffs, and sheriffs in inland towns had taken advantage of farmers' lack of hard currency and their distance from the authorities on the coast. They had used force and the pretext of law to steal from the farmers and then to suppress their protests.[45] Over three years of demonstrations that escalated as the colony's royal governor, William Tryon and his government hardened their stance, the North Carolinians had banded together to regulate their own country, and now the men of Massachusetts renewed their proud cry for justice and self-determination.[46]

The older men and women who remembered the Regulators' story hoped that this tribute would redeem the North Carolinian Regulators' experiences, rather than repeat them. For in 1771, the North Carolinian farmers who had banded together beneath that name had not succeeded in their campaign for justice. When young men asked why the letters were signed by Regulators, they were told the story of the tense months when the North Carolinians marched to the courts to protest their treatment. They were told that Tryon had been inflamed by exaggerated accounts of the people's belligerence, and he had marched an army west from the coast to assert his royal authority.[47] When they heard that an army was coming, the Regulators gathered a force of two thousand men to defend themselves.

Tryon's forces found them in an encampment south of Burlington on Alamance Creek on May 16.[48] They surrounded the protestors while Tryon and his officers started to negotiate with their leaders. When discussions foundered, Tryon, in a fit of pique, shot and killed one of the people's envoys, Robert Thompson.[49] This murder caused both sides to open fire. When the smoke cleared, the Regulators had seized and then been driven away from the government's cannon, and nine men on each side lay dead. Tryon's forces rushed in to make arrests. Seven more men were executed later. These sixteen martyred men had fueled the North Carolinians' desire for independence. They had redeemed them when they joined the other colonies in throwing off British rule, but even in the light of the Massachusetts farmers' recent victories, the North Carolinian protestors' deaths reminded them that they might lose their lives if they challenged their government's authority. The liberties they had won in the war might have to be asserted and defended again and again.

If the Massachusetts farmers feared violence in the government's rhetoric and in their precedents, they bolstered each other with the rhetoric that had inspired them through the war. Great Barrington's Justice William Whiting, the judge who had halted Paterson's militia, published a pamphlet called *Some Brief Remarks on the Present State of Publick Affairs*.[50] With the authority of his office, he asserted that the politicians and financiers in Boston were a pack of "overgrown Plunderers" who were "tyrannizing over the people, whom they have impoverish'd and rendered incapable of resistance."

He called on the people not to forget the Declaration of Independence, where Thomas Jefferson had claimed for all the world to hear that Americans did not just have a right—he said they had an "indispensable duty . . . to exert themselves, and persevere in their exertions" until they can remove the "baneful injustice and inequality" that torments them.[51]

Educated men in the farm towns noted that the judge had published his pamphlet under the name of the Roman populist Tiberius Gracchus, rooting his authority in a farmer famous for his resistance to oppressive urban government almost two thousand years ago.[52]

When riders carried copies of Whiting's pamphlet from town to town, they also spread the prejudicial fact the judge had also put in circulation: that his colleague, Justice Sedgwick, had used the court's steep fee schedule to expropriate more than £1,000 from the people.[53]

If the men of Massachusetts felt a sense of justice expanding in their chests when they heard Whiting defend their rights and appeal to their countrymen's patriotism, those hopes froze in their blood when they read the letter Samuel Adams published two days after the court closing in Great Barrington.

In the *Worcester Centinel*, Adams claimed that "in monarchies, the crime of treason and rebellion may admit of being pardoned or lightly punished, but the man who dares rebel against the laws of a republic ought to suffer death."[54] Adams was not simply speaking in his own name when he said this, either. Everyone knew that he had been one of the chief architects of the Revolution, asserting the colonists' rights in opposing the Crown's illegitimate authority. But now that he was serving as one of Governor Bowdoin's principal advisers, he spoke to defend his duly elected government from the people. His assertion had been endorsed by the applause of hundreds of wealthy merchants when he made it before an emergency meeting Bowdoin had convened in Faneuil Hall.[55]

As ominous as Adams's letter was—as tense as the farmers were, as they worked through the next few days—the letter from Boston was not followed by news of arrests or new repressive measures.

The days of rain that had soaked Artemas Ward in Worcester and Job Shattuck in Concord had chased out the muggy haze of the last heavy days of summer. The skies were crystalline, glorious after months of sticky heat as the people returned to the work of bringing in their harvests. No one brought news that armies were marching from Boston to press the people into submission. The people and merchants only continued to argue back and forth in letters to their local papers, each side predicting the end of their liberties and the collapse of the state.

There was only a week till the equinox, now. The nights were turning crisp for sleeping again. Morning dew was thick on fields, and fog lay thick on the valleys until the sun rose high enough that the maples and oaks emerged red and orange from the mist. All the length of their valleys and up to the highest hilltops, the trees turned scarlet and gold, and the air was thick with the smell of their crisp decay, and also with the smells of the people's cooking, as they brought in their harvests.

In these golden mornings—free from the threat of bailiffs, now—the farmers took their turbulent hearts to their fields. In long days of careful labor, they dug up bulging potatoes and beets and carrots and turnips caked with soil. In teams, they rooted under broad leaves, cutting squash and pumpkins from their vines. They pulled up onions and garlic by their long stems. They took ladders into their orchards, combing through apple and pear trees, stacking their fruit in one barrel after another. With sharp scythes, they cut their milk corn, leaving the flour corn to brown in the fields, tassels limp, stripped by rain and sun, while the ears dried on the stalk, waiting till October when they would husk them and cart the kernels to the mills.

Free from the strain of listening for bailiffs' horses, the people piled their produce into carts. They drove the carts home with their horses or oxen to interrupt the women and children in their work of piling up clouds of golden flax fibers they would spin, weave, and dye through winter. All together, they unloaded their cargoes into their cellars and storerooms and even into the spare corners of their bedrooms. The farms were busy dawn to dusk, as neighbors worked side by side to bring in their produce from orchards and fields. When the men's backs were sore from loading and unloading produce, they proceeded in teams to the houses, where the women and children were taking turns pressing apples for cider and brandy.

Safe from the courts till November, the farmers of Massachusetts inventoried the cellars and storerooms, measuring their harvests against the demands the winter months would make. Whatever they had harvested would have to last them till May or June, when they would be able to plant again. They calculated the rates of exchange for hard coin, reckoning which necessities they could afford, figuring which debts they should pay first and which to bear.

As September marched toward October, the cooling and lengthening nights led the farmers and their wives up into their eaves and attics to haul out the trunks full of blankets and coats, the sweaters and mittens they had stored away at the end of winter. If moths had gotten into their clothing, or clothes no longer fit the children, they estimated how much wool they would have to reserve for their own use from the bolts of cloth they thought they would be able to sell or trade.

However long they estimated their harvests would last them, though— whatever they thought they might buy with their surplus—they knew that their produce would not be safe until Governor Bowdoin had settled the crisis of debts and reformed the taxes that threatened them. From towns on the coast to the Berkshire hills, where the fall was already in full swing, the farmers waited anxiously to hear that their peaceful protests had given the governor reason to ask less of them in taxes. If he would not relent, their debts would all be waiting for them on November's dockets, when merchants in Boston and Worcester, in Hartford and Springfield and Great Barrington would be anxious to take as much as they could get from them in payment.

So even as they brought in their crops, the prominent men in Massachusetts farm towns, from Rehoboth in the east to Great Barrington in the west, continued to call each other together at the end of their long days' labors, and when they read their newspapers from the tavern walls, they found one of the River God merchants, Caleb Strong, writing under the pen name "Aristedes," inflaming the people by accusing "the heads and fomenters of these troubles" of being "bankrupt, dishonest prodigals who have wasted their estates by vice and folly, by idleness and gaming."[56] Until their complaints were resolved and this inflammation died down, the farmers did not allow themselves to rest, but they spent long hours debating what they thought was likely to happen, laying the groundwork for further actions in case the government still refused to reform the taxes and policies that tortured them.

The farmers' optimism did not last a full week from the time the last court was closed in Great Barrington. On Tuesday, September 19, messengers raced through the commonwealth with news that the Massachusetts Supreme Judicial Court had convened in Worcester. The judges there had issued arrest warrants for Adam Wheeler—the veteran who had stepped forward to explain the people's grievances to Artemas Ward—and also for Henry and Abraham Gale and eight other men whom the court called "disorderly, riotous and seditious persons."[57]

In the taverns where they heard this news, the farmers were caught off guard. No one had suggested that they should close the criminal courts, since foreclosures were civil affairs. When the local militias had refused to muster, or when they took the protestors' side, they thought their local authorities had effectively endorsed their protests. Now the judges in Worcester betrayed the compromises the judges had made when they had agreed to adjourn the September courts.

Bringing this news into their homes—slamming doors or throwing down tools, gloves, or hats to announce this new fact with their violence—the men of Hampshire County saw dread in their wives and children's eyes as they feared for their farms' fate. They saw their own frustrations mirrored back at them in the raised faces, but now they also saw distrust. For how could their wives and children or anyone believe them when they claimed they would not be putting themselves in danger by staging protests? How could anyone trust that closing the courts would bring relief if the government was responding by issuing arrest warrants?

This news created a panic of new debates in Hampshire County in particular, for within a week—on Monday next, the twenty-fifth of September—the same judges who had handed down indictments in Worcester would arrive in Springfield to open the Hampshire County Supreme Judicial Court. Surely, they would authorize warrants for West Springfield's Luke Day and Pelham's John Thompson, Colonel Powers and Captains Conkey and Gray as well as Joel Billings of Amherst, and any other men Sheriff Porter identified as ringleaders.

At Conkey's Tavern and at the taverns where every Hampshire County town had organized its men in August, the small rooms were crammed with furious bodies once again. A few conservative landowners and merchants urged their neighbors not to stir up any more trouble. Now that their cellars and storerooms were full of their whole year's harvests, they said they should not compound their sufferings by giving the governor reason to send troops to ransack their homes.

A few men's reluctance did not restore their townsmen's confidence that flowery petitions would win the reforms they needed. In all the towns that had sent men to Northampton, their warnings were elbowed aside by men who said they would not back down when powerless government men waved meaningless papers and made empty threats. They said they had not fought a war, they had not suffered to free themselves from lords, in order to lower their heads and give up their land at the first sign of trouble.

When angry men called for volunteers to stop the Springfield court, men came forward by the hundreds. Men who had not bothered to ride to the first protest in Northampton now promised to bring their guns or pitchforks, or clubs from their woodpiles, to show Bowdoin they would not be intimidated by warrants.[58] Towns that had not sent men to Northampton to protest the economic conditions now promised to send men to Springfield to ward off what they saw as the danger of tyranny.

Some men said they should go to Springfield before the court opened and arm themselves from the federal arsenal on the hill above the river, where the Continental army maintained a stockpile of seven thousand muskets, a handful of cannon, two hundred tons of ammunition, and hundreds of barrels of gunpowder, in addition to uniforms and provisions.[59] They said that if they armed themselves with the arsenal's weapons, Bowdoin would not be able to assert his law in their towns. They would no longer just be citizens—they themselves would become the commonwealth's army, and their calls for reform would have to be respected.

Some even said they should declare themselves independent from Boston and form their own state, the same as they had done when it was the Crown that oppressed them. Some proposed merging Hampshire and Berkshire Counties into the independent republic of Vermont, but the stomping boots and applause were mixed with laughter when this proposal was presented, and men who called to arm themselves in Springfield were shouted down: it was still much too early to think about taking a step that would be seen as a declaration of war and might justify other states sending troops to defend Bowdoin's unjust policies with bloodshed.

By the time these discussions had ended, messengers were racing along the ridges toward Pelham, bringing Colonel Powers and William Conkey the news from the hill towns that hundreds of furious men were preparing to make a huge protest outside the Springfield courthouse—and many were threatening violence.

On hearing this news, the leading men of Pelham summoned each other to meet in Conkey's Tavern to plot a middle path by which they could close the court but also restrain the people's anger. Violence would threaten them all if they gave the governor an excuse to send soldiers west and force martial law on their region.

In tense meetings, they drafted letters to officers in the loyal towns' militias with instructions to organize and discipline the men and to start recruiting supplies to support their men for at least the five days it would take them to march to Springfield and back.

Even as their messengers fanned out across the hills from Pelham, reports from New Hampshire cast a cloud of deep dread and danger over their plans. On Thursday, September 21, only four days before the Springfield court, messengers burst into Conkey's Tavern to say that farmers much like themselves had been arrested in Exeter, outside of Portsmouth, not far northeast of Worcester.[60]

Following in the Massachusetts farmers' footsteps, two hundred New Hampshire farmers had marched six miles from a protest convention to Exeter, where they surrounded the building in which the legislature was meeting. The men, who believed that they still acted in the role of official convention, submitted a petition demanding an issue of paper money to reform the steep taxes and austerity measures New Hampshire Governor John Sullivan had imposed on his people.[61] Thousands of farmers had gathered to keep the judges from seizing their land and property for debts, but Sullivan had watched the disruptions in Massachusetts, and he refused to tolerate dissent in his state.

As a general in the Revolution, Sullivan had earned George Washington's praise for running a scorched-earth campaign against upstate New York's Iroquois Indians. He had burned out forty villages, and those Native food stores he did not destroy he used for his own army, leaving the Iroquois with nothing on the verge of winter.[62] Now he did not have any scruples about collecting two thousand militiamen to suppress his people's protests.

In the courtyard in Exeter, Sullivan and his men surrounded the New Hampshire farmers, cutting off their retreat. The farmers submitted without a fight. Sullivan's men identified the leaders, and Sullivan forced thirty-nine of his region's prominent landowners to march hatless and humiliated through a gauntlet of doubled lines of militia.[63]

In the end, Sullivan allowed almost all the men to return to their homes, but he kept five of their leaders in prison to make examples of the state's force and its leniency. In five households in the countryside around Exeter, families and communities lived with the threat that the governor might try his prisoners for treason and execute them when they were convicted.[64]

This news from New Hampshire set the Pelham men on edge. For now, if they were going to stop the Springfield court, they had to weigh the chance that Governor Bowdoin's deputies might feel encouraged by Sullivan's show of force and make a similar display. They would also have to make sure that their own men would not riot if Bowdoin did send men against them.

In Pelham, Colonel Powers and Captains Conkey and Gray devised a strategy that would stop the court and still minimize the dangers. In letters to leaders in other towns, they encouraged their countrymen to recruit as many of their neighbors as they could so the people could make a strong show of solidarity. But they also said that Luke Day should not lead the protest again or speak from the top of the courthouse steps. They said it would be too dangerous, since tensions were already running high in the wake of the warrants from Worcester.[65] They wanted to avoid any chance that Bowdoin's agents might try to seize Captain Day or any of the other leaders who had put themselves forward in August. If their townsmen tried to protect their leaders from arrest, it would only take one or two men's anguished cries to wash away any restraint and unleash the anger coiled in everyone's shoulders and forearms and start a full-blown riot as men lashed out. If the leaders could not prevent a riot, violence would turn their countrymen against them, and their own neighbors would call for the government to institute law and order by force if necessary.

On Friday, September 22, messengers carried their letters town to town through the dark night when the new moon did not appear in the sky.[66] It would return as a fingernail paring at sunset tomorrow, but now they conducted their deliberations by starlight or by their own lights. At the same time, the earth reached the equinox, and now if men raised their eyes to the sky for guidance, for more than half of each day for the next six months, the sky would answer with darkness and cold, remote stars.

In letters and visits that carried them all through their country, the leaders of seventeen Hampshire County towns nominated new leaders. In Pelham, the officers evaluated each town's veterans' and prominent men's characters and temperaments, testing them against the danger they thought they might face in Springfield.

In the absence of Captain Day of West Springfield, the men of New Braintree nominated their neighbor, Francis Stone, who had distinguished himself in battle at Crown Point on Lake Champlain in the French and Indian War, and then again in the Revolution. But Stone kept himself back. He volunteered to give advice but would not let the people take his name.[67]

From Chicopee, north of Springfield, men put Eli Parsons's name forward. Parsons was a respected artillery officer who spent the brutal winter of 1778 with General Washington at Valley Forge, but he too refused to lead more than his own town's men.[68]

From Pelham, where the opposition to Bowdoin's courts was being organized, any number of veterans and respected men could have stepped forward to lead. The Conkeys and Grays, the Johnsons and Powers had lived in Pelham since the town was chartered in 1743.[69] Officers from these clans had led hundreds of men in the wars. They commanded respect in their town, for they had brought large numbers men in their families to their protests. Now the Grays promised twelve men to the Springfield protest, the Johnsons eight.[70] All the first families of Pelham were sending their fathers and sons, their uncles and cousins, and even the men who were courting their women were drawn into their ranks.[71] But none of the patriarchs would assume responsibility for stepping forward to turn the towns' self-governing militias into a unified force that represented their whole region.

Once again, the leaders in Pelham turned to Daniel Shays as the best man to impose order on their proceedings. Shays had only lived in Pelham since he moved from Shutesbury in 1780, but he had commanded the town's militia since 1782. He had worked himself up from laborer to gentleman farmer and enjoyed the respect of men in every station.

In a new country that had just freed itself from a tyrannical king, the people were still afraid of investing any one man with too much power, but Shays had already proved his lack of ambition when he had refused to lead the people's first protest in August.

Shays had a lot to lose if he accepted responsibility for keeping a protest with thousands of men from devolving into a riot. Even if he did prevent the outraged farmers from committing acts of violence, the next time any courts did convene, he among all his countrymen would be singled out as the leader of an insurrection. He would be putting himself in the same danger men faced in Worcester, of living under threat of arrest for obstructing the courts. There would not be any safety for him till the crisis was resolved.

Shays could not answer his townsmen's request on his behalf alone. He had to consider his wife, Abigail, and their five children, the oldest of whom, Daniel Junior, was only thirteen and too young to run the farm. If Shays were arrested or injured, Abigail would not be able to go to her family in Brookfield for help, either, as her father, Captain Daniel Gilbert, had taken the government's side in this crisis. Even if Shays did come home unscathed, he would still have to explain why he had betrayed the man who had raised him into the class of gentlemen farmers with Abigail's dowry.

There was not much time for Shays to weigh his scruples, though. The news of the Worcester arrest warrants had arrived in Pelham on Tuesday night. On Thursday, the leading men of Pelham had heard from New Hampshire that Governor Sullivan had arrested the Exeter protesters. If the men of Hampshire County intended to stop the court in Springfield on Monday morning, it would take them a day and a half to cover the twenty-eight miles from Pelham. They were going to have to recruit and discipline men and gather provisions for days of marching. They would have to set out on the road no later than midday Saturday if they were going to have time to march to Springfield and establish their authority and organize the other towns' officers in advance of Monday's protest.

Pressed by the hard demands of the moment, Shays bowed to necessity and agreed to lead the men. He and his neighbors—now his officers—set up their center of operations at Conkey's Tavern, half a mile downhill from his house in its hollow on East Hill, a mile downhill from the meeting house on West Hill opposite.

The news from Exeter smoldered over the autumn-bright hills like low, choking smoke. The threat of a confrontation in Springfield loomed like a gathering storm. Shays and his officers sent instructions to leaders in other towns to make sure they were organized with officers and proper lines of command. They finished as much as they could of their farm work and or-ganized neighbors who volunteered to carry on the work in their absence.

If Shays's wife Abigail rode down the hill to interrupt her husband in his planning—if she or any of the wives came to ask their husbands why they had to be gone for this week, what answer could their husbands offer? The explanation was all around them; the question itself was just a protest against necessity.

The only explanation they could make was to promise to come home safe and return to their fields, to bring in their corn away from the threat of bailiffs coming to seize their harvests. All they could do now was keep protesting until there was no more danger.

Finally, the late-September dawn broke cool and crisp on Saturday morn-ing the twenty-third, and men rose from their beds on farms in Pelham and Amherst. They loaded food, blankets, and clothing in backpacks and sad-dlebags, straightened their uniforms or homespun coats, hung swords from their belts if they had them. A quarter of the men cleaned their muskets and polished bayonets, draped powder horns over their shoulders, slung pouches full of musket balls from their belts. Their military bearing would show the bystanders who were their audience that they had all made sacri-fices for their nation—it would demonstrate their willingness to make sac-rifices again, if necessary.

They said goodbye to their families and set out, stiff and encumbered in their gear, through the fields and orchards they had harvested in lighter clothing yesterday, climbing the hill to the meeting house to join Shays and the others.

All morning the men streamed in, their boots wet with September dew. They arrived at the clapboard meeting house on West Hill in Pelham in sixes and eights. They arrived in dozens, and their numbers grew throughout the morning. A month ago, Deacon Thompson had marched down the hill leading seventy men, but now Daniel Shays was preparing to ride out with seven hundred who were already weary with anticipation of the roads that stretched ahead of them. They would cover twenty miles today, to Ludlow, then the eight miles to Springfield tomorrow. At the end of two days' marching, they would have to see how far the Springfield militia's leader, Westfield General William Shepard, was willing to go to force the governor's laws on the region.

Electric with anticipation, the farmers and militiamen milled around in the perfect September morning. Finally, at a sign from their officers, they drew themselves apart from the wives and children and aunts and parents who had come to see them off. They hoisted their backpacks and shouldered their muskets and clubs. Each town's men raised the staffs with their handmade flags. The officers formed the men in lines eight abreast, as wide as the roads could accommodate. Drummers and fifers tuned their instruments, and Shays mounted the white horse that had been lent to him for the occasion.

He gave the orders any of the other veterans knew by heart and could have given themselves, to start the musicians and set the lines in motion. The column of seven hundred men marched off south from the West Hill meeting house, climbing the short rise south of the green before they descended the long road out of the sandy and rocky hills toward the courts in the bottom lands where rich men tended to contracts and loans that ripened into profits.

Shays and his men followed the Swift River south from Belchertown to Three Rivers, where the Swift River joined the Quaboag. In the crystalline, cool-warm September weather, the music of their passing brought farmers and their wives and children out of their houses in homespun coats to cheer them, and the towns' militias came out to join their column. They continued alongside the river to Ludlow, where sympathetic families welcomed them with food, beer, and brandy out of their harvests. Ludlow's leading families took Shays and his officers into their homes and showed the others to beds or barns, while hundreds of men pitched tents or rolled up in their blankets beneath the autumn night sky.

On Sunday morning, Shays and his men rose, packed their gear, formed their lines, and continued west through flatter and richer fields. Step by step, they approached the Connecticut River, where Springfield merchants and businessmen would treat their crude coats with contempt and report their presence as a threat to order and good government.

By the time Shays and his men crossed the bridge over the Connecticut River from Chicopee into West Springfield on Sunday afternoon, angry men had been pouring down into the valley from the hill towns of Hampshire County, from Colrain and Montague, from Chesterfield, Conway, and Charlemont.[72] In dozens and hundreds, they had marched through the flat floodplain farmland, each town's militia beneath their flag, each to their own music, in the shirts and coats woven in patterns distinctive to their people.

Town by town, the militias arrived in the West Springfield green and made their camps in bunches, filling the field with their voices over the sound of hammers staking out tents to shelter a force of two thousand men. Many of the farmers had served together in the war, so the meeting had the air of a reunion beneath the anxious anticipation of tomorrow. Men greeted each other and remarked at their numbers: if Governor Bowdoin threatened to take men to prison for protesting, the legislature would have to build new jails to house them all.

When enough of the men had arrived, Shays and his men from Pelham met with the leaders from other towns. Each town's officers pledged to restrain their men to ensure a peaceful demonstration, and they agreed on the steps they would take if the government men tried to arrest them. After they had spoken and the officers had conveyed these orders to their men, they drilled their men all together, wheeling and turning to Shays's and to their own officers' commands, rehearsing their obedience in advance of tomorrow's display.[73]

The late September sun went down Sunday night, and soon after sunset, the fattening sliver of first-quarter moon followed it into the black hills. The men fought the chill with their fires. Some had brought beer and rum, but the dangers they might face tomorrow kept them sober, and their officers did not have trouble keeping order.[74]

Close by, in the night, they could see the fires where government men had gathered and set up their tents, but guards kept the men on either side from instigating trouble. The two bodies of men camped close to each other recalled the war, when disciplined men waited for their officers to choose the time and place for their confrontations.[75]

Beneath the crisp stars, the people of Massachusetts slept poorly, uncertain what demands tomorrow might make on their solidarity and restraint, or on their courage in battle.

On the chilly morning of September 25, Shays and his men marched across the bridge from West Springfield toward the Springfield courthouse. When they arrived, they halted. Their restless horses shifted their weight from one foot to another, and each town's flags nosed the breeze as Shays and his men discovered that Westfield's state representative, Major General William Shepard, had already surrounded the courthouse with nine hundred men.[76] His men had even rolled out two small cannon, which the men called puppies, for their high bark.[77]

Studying the government men through the tension that stretched across the courtyard, Shays and his officers identified some of the most opulent and respectable landowners and merchants in the region.[78] They did not recognize Shepard's officers, though, for all but 14 of the 295 Revolutionary War veterans from Shepard's town of Westfield now served with the farmers against him. Most of the officers at Shepard's side now were not even old enough to have fought in the war.[79]

Shays and his men knew Shepard from the army. They had all served together from Bunker Hill to Saratoga to Newark, and some continued on as far south as Yorktown. In battles and in long marches and in long starving months in camps, they had all bent their backs together to execute their generals' commands against their common enemy. The solidarity that had bound them once had not simply dissolved for the insults and threats the newspapers had been printing these last four months. With the threat of arrest in the air, and the danger of being surrounded as in New Hampshire, neither side made a move. Shays's men outnumbered the merchants and clerks two to one, but they did not attack. Neither did Shepard and his officers try to follow in Sullivan's footsteps to surround the protesting farmers or try to arrest them. Both sides' officers kept their men's arms at their shoulders.

Finally, Shays ordered his officers to lead their men into positions surrounding the courthouse and Shepard's men, but after they had completed this maneuver, nothing happened.[80] The minutes accumulated, and three thousand men acknowledged together what everyone knew: that Governor Bowdoin and the men in the General Court would not solve this crisis by setting them against each other.

The General Court might have refused to acknowledge the people's concerns, but General Shepard did not force Bowdoin's will on the people he faced in person. Some merchants had urged him to fight to subdue the arrogant farmers, but the numbers were all against him. Even if Shepard had been inclined to enforce Bowdoin's laws, he refused to risk his men against experienced veterans who had faced down the redcoats' muskets.[81]

After Shays's men had surrounded Shepard's, the leaders called for a parley to settle the terms by which the court might be opened or closed, or either side might withdraw.[82] Neither side's leaders would agree to concede the day and send their men home. Shays asked for Shepard's permission to break up the tension by parading his men in the courtyard, as Day's men had paraded his men before Sheriff Porter in Northampton. Shepard agreed, provided Shays's men would not insult the government men.[83]

Under homemade flags, with muskets or clubs on their shoulders, to the surging music of fifes and drums, the men in their homespun uniforms whirled and turned in ordered lines again. Disciplined and dignified, they again showed the government men and the bystanders who had gathered that they were not a rabble but a proud people who could keep themselves obedient to officers' commands.

When the Regulators had finished, they cleared the courtyard, and Shepard's militia paraded beneath their flags in answer, as fathers and brothers on either side rebuked each other with their strictly regulated maneuvers. When Shepard's men resumed their positions, Shays and a delegation of men met with Chief Justice David Sewall to deliver the petition drafted by a "committee chosen by the people" for the "cause of moderating government."[84] The petition said the people found it "inconvenient" to hear the court's judgments before the General Court had addressed their grievances. They did not ask the judges to close the courts, only to defer hearing cases in which men stood to lose money or property. Their petition also asked the judges to pardon the men who had stopped the Northampton Court and to send the militiamen home without pay, since they themselves were not being paid to march to the courtyard to represent justice.[85]

When the negotiations were finished, the judges had not agreed to strike cases for debt from their docket. They insisted on opening the court, and in the end they did convene the court formally, but only among themselves. They could not hear cases because the farmers' blockade prevented them from impaneling a jury.[86]

Merchants pressed the judges to make a stand for law and enforcement of contracts, but Shepard refused to use force to disperse the protestors, so the judges adjourned till December. For the sixth time in six weeks, they put off any question of taxes and war debts, of tender laws and paper currency. They also tabled the question of whether men should be arrested for having closed the August court in Northampton. These questions would have to be answered in some other place, at some other time—not in the courtyard with fists and clubs—or bullets—in the crisp September weather.

When Shays and his officers came out to tell the men that the court had been closed, the farmers cheered, and they cheered again when they learned that the judges had also decided they would not bother traveling to Great Barrington to hold the Berkshire County Court's October session a week from now.[87]

The tension that clouded the courtyard dissolved as Shepard formed his nine hundred men into lines and marched them east up the hill, where they discharged their guns and occupied the arsenal grounds, the barracks and workshops, the powder magazine, and the storehouses filled with stockpiles of weapons and provisions. (Black powder muskets cannot be unloaded except by firing them.) All day, the grounds had sat undefended on the hill overlooking the town. None of Shays's movements had given Shepard reason to station men there to defend it, but Shepard marched off to secure it now, and Shays's men enjoyed the symbolic victory of occupying the courthouse.[88] Once again, they had demonstrated their power to represent law in the region. Again, their celebrations were light with relief, for even after the outrageous and inflammatory letter Samuel Adams had published two week ago—even after the warrants from Worcester, then the arrests in Exeter—no blood had been spilled.

Through their own act of organized protest, they had bought themselves and their neighbors in Berkshire County two more months of freedom from the threat of arrest. For two more months, they could try to win reforms through petitions, and the courts would not be able to reckon their debts by the cold light of Bowdoin's laws.

When Shepard's men had abandoned the courthouse, Shays formed his men into lines for the long march home. They marched up Continental Hill to the arsenal where Shepard's men occupied the buildings. They marched around the grounds twice, to fife and drum, before they too discharged their guns and continued out of town, back to their families.[89]

For the rest of the day, Shays followed the roads back to Ludlow, then the next day marched his men north again, to Three Rivers, then back up into their hills. As his men ascended from the rich country in the fertile flood plains, they watched the wealth fall off the bones of the earth. They marched past older farms up into rolling hills where farms that were only thirty or forty years old were scratching a bare subsistence from rocky, sandy soil.

Arriving in Pelham at the top of the long hill up from Belchertown, Shays disbanded his men, and they watched the militias from Shutesbury and New Salem continue north with their drums. Their return was more businesslike than triumphant. The action against the court had still not been followed by news from Boston that the governor was reforming his austerity measures. The unjust laws that oppressed them were all still on the books. Shays and the other leaders had just compounded their outstanding debts and taxes by adding this debt to the commonwealth, owing the state restitution for the crime of stopping the court. If the General Court would not pardon them for their peaceful obstruction of government business, the next time the courts did open, Shays and each of his officers would be subject to arrest. Government prosecutors would call them to answer for all of their debts at once. Judges and juries would decide how much of their property or how many years of their lives the state should claim in payment.

By closing the Springfield Supreme Judicial Court, the men had just committed themselves to closing every subsequent court until their concerns were heard. So they did not squander a day in celebrating their victory. They simply returned to their work, swinging their scythes through acres of corn stalks, husking the cobs, and threshing their oats and wheat and carting them to the mills for grinding. Courts or no, their flour corn would not feed anyone if it was not brought in from the fields. Debts or no, their farms must be ready for winter.

In the clear, bright, late-September weather, where trees blazed gold and scarlet along their fields' edges, they worked in teams, the same as their people had always done at this time of the year, finishing the growing season's exhausting labors, laying up stores that would seem like riches if they did not have to last through six cold, fallow months.

Chapter Five

The Government Swings into Action

I N THE DAYS AFTER THE SPRINGFIELD COURT CLOSING, the farmers found that the arguments in the newspapers continued as before. By the end of the month, Shays and his neighbors were reading a new paper on the walls of Conkey's Tavern: Northampton printer William Butler had launched the *Hampshire Gazette* to give merchants a platform to defend Governor Bowdoin's policies and to make the case for suppressing the farmers' protests.[1]

Chief Justice William Cushing of the Springfield court used these pages to declare that the leaders of the insurgents were "evil-minded persons" who were intent on waging war "against the Commonwealth, to bring the whole government, and all the good people of this state, if not continent, under absolute command and subjugation." Even within the week of the orderly closing Shays and his men had orchestrated with General Shepard, he wrote to tell the world that the farmers were led by "ignorant, unprincipled, bankrupt, desperate individuals," and he predicted that Shays would "erect a military government for the coercion of the state" and "declare himself dictator of the whole union."[2]

"An Old Republican" extended the justice's disdain by saying, "They are not people, but a class of disaffected individuals, spirited on by wicked men," and "men of desperate circumstances and morals" who "design to prevent the collection of private debts and the payment of public taxes." He accused them of being "excited, supported and encouraged by the emissaries of that nation to which we were formerly subject" and asked if "men of property and weight [will] put themselves under the conduct of those persons who so notoriously are governed by selfish, if not dishonest motives?"[3]

A few days later, a man who called himself simply "a Regulator" answered these distortions with exaggerations of his own, saying that the people would not stop their protests until they had completely subverted the government.

"We mean to make thorough work of it," this writer claimed. "We won't put our hands to the plow and look back. We have advanced too far—we know that there is no safety for us, except in completing the business, marching to Boston, and leaving not one stone on another."[4]

These insults continued to stoke indignation on both sides and polarized the region. Still Bowdoin's government did not send troops to arrest the protesters' leaders, and on their side, the farmers still refused to sneak out at night, to break into merchants' stores or judges' offices or homes, to make them pay for supporting the government's taxes. But the tension lay over the land like clouds that might break in heavy rain at any minute.

For days at the end of September, the cash-poor farmers of Worcester, Hampshire, and Berkshire Counties waited in vain for news of reforms. The courts were not scheduled to meet again until after the commonwealth's farmers had brought in the last of their harvests, so they did not have to decide whether to oppose another court until the Worcester court was scheduled to open in the third week of November.

For now, they only heard from Taunton that Major General John Brooks and two thousand men had opened the court there without opposition and without bloodshed. From Boston, though, the farmers heard that rumors had inflated their two thousand orderly men to a mob of thirty thousand or forty thousand rabble who had rioted in the streets.[5] From their friends in the market towns, the farmers heard that panicked merchants were telling Bowdoin that Shays was collecting an army to wage a new war and ultimately rule in the governor's place. In other rumors, the farmers were supposedly planning to confiscate rich men's lands and distribute all their wealth among themselves. They were said to be planning to set up a state where every man enforced his own rules, where laws were enforced by the whims of violent mobs.

In each new day's newspapers, men exercised their ingenuity in long letters, asserting their innocence, enumerating their sufferings to defend themselves against these ridiculous claims and bring their countrymen to their side.

In their taverns' long discussions, farmers who had traveled to Boston or served alongside Boston merchants in the war tried to explain to their townsmen what the merchants must be seeing. They explained that the men in Boston had seen firsthand how well-organized colonists had brought the British government's business to a standstill in the commonwealth. They looked at themselves through Bowdoin's eyes and recognized that he could see their court closings as a reprise of the protests of 1774, when the people effectively ended the Crown's control over the whole state west of Boston. Of course, they said, their constitutionally authorized town meetings and now their protests would look like a challenge to Bowdoin's central authority.[6]

Even though everyone knew that Bowdoin had put himself in this position by passing unjust taxes and laws and then ignoring the people's calls for justice, in their long discussions, the people looked at the puzzle of their situation from every point of view and wondered why Bowdoin and his advisers could not see through their eyes in return, to recognize that the taxes and currency policies might look like tyranny from their hills.

Bowdoin and the wealthy senators in Boston did not send envoys to Pelham or Worcester or Great Barrington to negotiate a compromise that would quell the protests and keep the commonwealth's business moving. But the farmers learned from Springfield that the general who had once written to praise their restraint had recently written to Bowdoin to recommend that the government make a display of authority. "It would appear," William Shepard said, "unreasonable and ill timed to either procrastinate or introduce lenient measures until the government have given proofs of their force and ability, otherwise clemency appears to proceed from inability or pusillanimity, and comes from ill grace."[7]

News had also come down from Canada that Lord Dorchester, Sir Guy Carleton, the royal governor, had arrived in Quebec from England, and the fertile fears of British power spawned rumors that he had brought troops. Now the government men said that Dorchester intended to exploit the divisions in Massachusetts and reinstitute "a monarchical government in the country," with one of "George's sons on the throne."[8]

With these wild claims filling the air, the people heard reports, in the first week of October, that Bowdoin had summoned lawmakers back to Boston for an emergency session of the legislature. He issued a proclamation that denounced the "destructive measures" of "artful and wicked men" in the farm towns, and he begged legislators to "vindicate the insulted dignity of government."[9]

Visitors from Boston reported that Bowdoin had asked Secretary of War Henry Knox, who lived in the city, to inventory the commonwealth's militia and measure the Springfield arsenal's defenses against any possible threats.[10] A few days later, they heard that Knox had sent a report to Congress in Philadelphia to support a formal request for $530,000, to garrison a force of seven hundred Continental soldiers in the arsenal.[11]

The farmers' peaceful opposition to unjust taxes and court fees had already been widely reported throughout the country, so Shays and the farmers of Pelham guffawed when they heard that Knox had justified his request for troops by claiming that the Connecticut River valley had to be defended from a possible Indian uprising.[12] As outraged as the people were to learn that their government had reduced them to the same status as the Natives whom the commonwealth's armies had always killed with impunity and long ago hounded off their lands,[13] they did not hear that Secretary Knox's request was being followed by any actual steps to suppress their protests.[14]

The lack of action did not give the people any peace. They still jumped up at the sound of horse's hooves in the road, for a messenger might yet bring news that Bowdoin was sending troops to apprehend their leaders. Day to day, Adam Wheeler and Henry and Abraham Gale and the eight other men who had been named by the court in Worcester went about their business under this fear. Every day, they also knew that their liberty could be seen from other states or from abroad as a demonstration of the government's impotence, and instead of a protest over taxes and currency policies, their protests could be seen as a bold assertion that the farmers who had thrown off the British were refusing to be governed at all.

With every day that the sun set on these troubles, the afternoons got a little bit shorter. In the brilliant autumn clarity, in the chilly houses and barns where they tended their livestock and wrapped up the last chores of the growing season, Shays and the other leaders had to explain to their wives and to their apprehensive neighbors how they would keep their movement from ending the way the North Carolinian Regulators' had ended. They calmed their wives' and parents' apprehensions by recalling that too many people in too many towns were suffering under the same unjust taxes and laws for them to stand down now. They assured their families that Bowdoin was only making hollow threats, that their countrymen would not turn against them to enforce rich men's taxes or press the governor's warrants. They said that in any case, it was already too late in the season to escape from these troubles by moving out of the state. Their harvests were in, the first snows were only six weeks away. There was nothing to do now but see it through.

Nevertheless, as the sun set earlier and earlier through the first fine days of October—as the tensions mounted, week to week—some of the wealthier landowners who had tried to stay neutral did start to leave. They claimed they were traveling for business, or they closed up their farms for the winter and set out to visit family in Boston or Connecticut. Wherever they went, they told the story that they did not trust their safety in a country where people were taking sides and preparing for armed confrontations.[15]

A few weeks later, when the cold had got deeper at night and the trees were shedding their leaves in every breeze, the people heard from Philadelphia that the federal government had approved Henry Knox's request for funds to garrison Continental soldiers in the Springfield arsenal. They had even increased from 700 to 1,340 the number of troops who would be raised from Massachusetts, Connecticut, Rhode Island, and New Hampshire.[16] But the people also cheered a victory, for every state but Virginia had refused to contribute funds to support these troops.[17] The other states' delegates said that Massachusetts's aristocratic elites had created this crisis, and Bowdoin should figure out how to clean up his own mess.

If the farmers of Massachusetts had hoped that this news might cause Bowdoin to ease their oppressive taxes, they were filled with despair on October 12, when riders sprinted town to town to say that Samuel Adams had been drafting a Riot Act.[18] The law became more oppressive as news of it traveled west, and rumors magnified both the insult and the danger it contained. The reality, when men learned it, was bad enough. The law would prohibit any gatherings of twelve or more armed persons. If such a crowd did gather, a sheriff should read the act aloud, and if the men did not disband within an hour, they could be arrested and "whipped thirty-nine stripes on the naked back, at the public whipping post, and suffer imprisonment for a term not exceeding twelve months, nor less than six."[19]

This was only the start. The law would also require convicted rioters to "forfeit all their lands, tenements, good, and chattels, to the commonwealth." If the men could still stand upright after they had heard this, they had to sit down when they learned that Adams's Riot Act would also indemnify the government's deputies against any liability if they injured or killed the men they were sent to disperse or arrest.[20] If the governor and his fellow elites could find enough eastern men to enforce their laws, their soldiers would be within their rights to simply shoot the farmers down before the courts pushed their families and their neighbors off their land.

From the western counties of Massachusetts, it looked very much like Bowdoin's government was going to use the same threats of violence the Crown had used to force them into submission. In a public address on October 18, members of the aristocratic Society of the Cincinnati assured the people of Massachusetts that they would "never tamely suffer those inestimable blessings to be rested from their hands by foreign force or domestick faction."[21]

In the evenings now, katydids were lifting their last exhausted groans into the cold trees' newly bare branches as men in Concord and Taunton, in Worcester and Rutland, in Pelham and Amherst, in Shutesbury and New Salem—as men in Montague, Conway, and Colrain, in Ashfield, Chesterfield, and Williamsburg—as men in Chicopee, Springfield, and Westfield—as men from Worthington out to Great Barrington sought each other and repeated this news. And when they had greeted the news with curses, they set out to tell their neighbors in turn, as if they could relieve their disgust by pressing the news into other men's ears.

When this news had spread throughout the state, the farmers once again summoned each other to meetings, but nothing the farmers said in those meetings could discharge the threat from Boston. Their constitutional emergency meetings did not give them any power to debate or vote against the law Adams was drafting. If Governor Bowdoin and his senators agreed, it would become law.

In Pelham, Shays and the officers were gathered at Conkey's Tavern almost all the time now, reading correspondence from officers in other towns, debating how to respond. They did not need to answer Adams's threat right away. Unless the governor put a force in the field immediately, they still had time, for there was still almost a month before this Riot Act might be tested in Worcester and Great Barrington on November 21.

Nevertheless, on October 23, messengers carried a letter to the selectmen of sympathetic Hampshire County towns.

"Gentlemen," the note said, "by information from the General Court, they are determined to call all those who appeared to stop the courts to condign punishment"—which is to say the punishment they deem fitting: imprisonment and whippings for a year, and forfeit of lands and property to the commonwealth—and all with the threat of injury or death in being arrested.

"Therefore," their letter continued, "you are requested to assemble your men together, to see that they are well armed and equipped, with sixty rounds each man, and be ready to turn out at a minute's warning; likewise to be properly organized with officers."[22]

All the people's letters and petitions had been signed by committees, but this letter circulated over Daniel Shays's name alone.[23] If anyone found this suspicious, the intent was clear and the cause was urgent: the time had come to start preparing for their defense.

While messengers were carrying the Pelham men's request through Hampshire County, they crossed paths with messengers carrying news that the legislature in Boston had finally passed measures designed to lighten the economic burden on Massachusetts farmers. New laws extended the tax deadline from January 1 to April 1, 1787, suspended suits for collection of debt in specie, and allowed the people to pay their taxes with produce from their farms, or, for artisans, with products from their workshops.[24] In a gesture meant to appease the rural populace, the legislature passed a new duty on imported hemp, to incentivize domestic hemp production, in addition to passing new taxes on luxury goods such as imported silver and jewelry.[25] They also issued reforms that removed the fees on cases affirming debts of under £4, and allowed the value of any property creditors wanted to seize to be determined by panels of local merchants—instead of at auction, where the prices would be much lower.[26] The General Court had also passed a law reducing the governor's yearly salary from £1,100 to £800—the town of Dracut proposed an even steeper cut, to £500, which "Represents as much Property at this time . . . as eleven hundred pounds did when the governor's salary was Established"—but no one was surprised to learn that Bowdoin vetoed this measure.[27]

Even if the farmers of western Massachusetts wanted to accept these reforms—even if they thought they could accept the galling news that the law would still allow their creditors to inventory their homes and choose which goods to seize—they found that the men in the General Court had still not finished threatening them. Instead of alleviating the people's troubles, they undermined their attempts at conciliation by passing a series of ominous measures designed to bolster the commonwealth's militias. Since the other states would not fund troops to help them, and the Articles of Confederation forbade each state's army from crossing state lines, the General Court had passed a Militia Act that threatened the commonwealth's soldiers with court-martial or execution if they refused to muster, or if they took the people's side of the road. They could even be punished for suggesting that others refuse to serve.[28]

The news of these measures reached Hampshire County at about the same time that the note arrived in Boston bearing Shays's name on the request for the towns to keep men ready with arms. A few days later, Shays and his officers heard that the delivery of his note gave birth to the very measures the people dreaded: the legislature made the Riot Act the law of the land.[29] If more than twelve armed men gathered and a sheriff read the act aloud to disperse them, then if they stayed to obstruct the court for more than another hour, their names would be taken, and they could be arrested any time the state saw fit to send deputies to their homes. Individual farmers would no longer be able to hide in the crowds. Their leaders would no longer bear the brunt of responsibility alone. Each man who followed his officers' orders would be risking his freedom as well as his property—and even his life, if the government men tried to disperse the crowds with bayonets or muskets.

Through the last week of October, the news of these repressive measures rippled through the farms of Massachusetts. Now when men worked in their fields or woods, they watched the roads in the valley, in the distance, squinting and straining their eyes to identify each rider, to see what further news might yet pour into their region. Every knock at the door froze the farmers' hearts, and the fear of further oppressions preceded every messenger. Every family was full of dread till the messenger had entered and delivered the actual news.

Still, the news of the Riot Act was not followed by news of arrests. No messengers whipped their horses along the post road from Boston to confirm that the government deputies had executed their warrants for Adam Wheeler or Henry and Abraham Gale. Nor did the farmers hear that the government was recruiting and drilling soldiers, preparing to make a show of force in Worcester on November 21.

After the General Court passed the Riot Act, Shays and the leading men of Pelham met regularly at Conkey's Tavern to forge chains of command and coordination with officers in the sixteen other Hampshire County towns that had sent their militias to the protests.[30]

They asked for reports of the people's preparations from Captain John Powers in Shutesbury to their north and from Captain Joel Billings down

Overleaf: A 1798 map of western Massachusetts, showing the Connecticut River valley, with the court towns of Northampton and Springfield in the floodplain along the river, ringed by Regulator towns Pelham, Montague, Colrain, and Chesterfield in the hills. Published and sold by O. Carleton and I. Norman, Boston [1798?]. (*John Carter Brown Library, Brown University*)

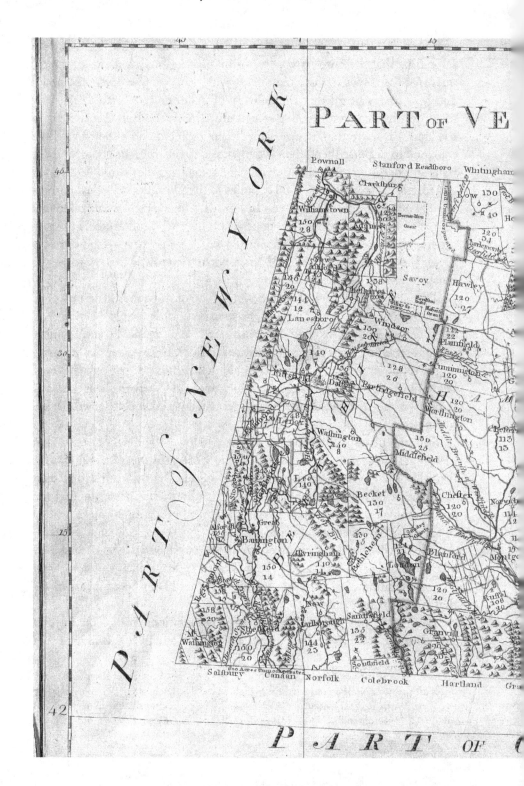

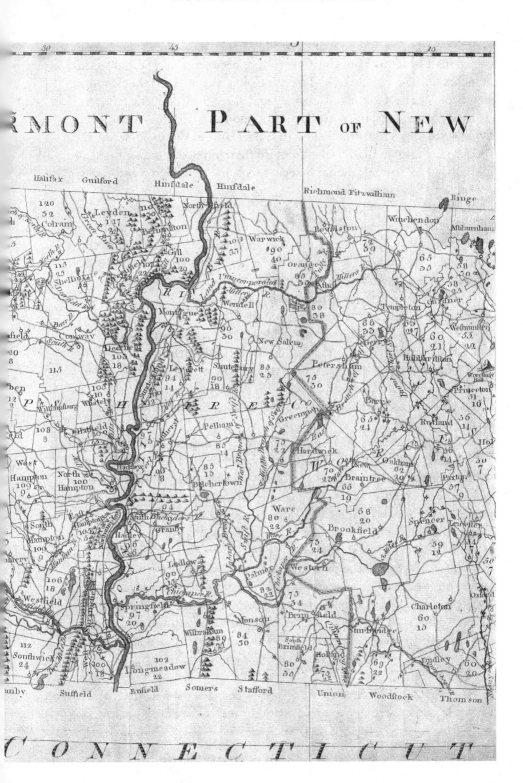

the hill in Amherst to their west. They dispatched messengers to deliver instructions to Joseph Hines in Greenwich, between the east and middle branches of the Swift River, and to Asa Fisk in Brimfield to their south, as well as to Alpheus Colton in Longmeadow, along the Connecticut border.[31]

In regular circuits, riders traveled back and forth between West Springfield, where they left instructions with Luke Day, and Westfield, where they sought out Captain Gad Sackett, before they traveled into the Berkshire foothills, where they sought out Samuel Morse in Worthington and Captain Aaron Jewett in Chesterfield.

In Whately, east of Chesterfield, Captain John Brown listened for riders who were bringing news toward Pelham, and he sent them off with his letters in turn. Messengers carried the news through Conway in the hills north of Whately, to pick up letters from Captain Abel Dinsmore, who had protested with Samuel Ely in 1782, then farther north to Charlemont, near the Vermont border, to hear from Samuel Hill.[32]

Bringing their letters back east toward the Connecticut River, they passed them to messengers in Colrain, who added Captain Matthew Clark's letters and carried them all to Captain Obed Foot in Greenfield.

Yet further riders crossed the river and sought out Captain Thomas Grover in Montague, where he added his reports to the pile of papers for Pelham, or poured them into the messengers' ears, that the riders could pour them out in turn.

In each of these towns, militia leaders had been drilling their men with guns in their town's green since the war. Now their hills were reverberating with the sound of their drums and flutes, and families were setting aside sacks of flour and oats in case the men needed to march on a moment's notice. They were economizing even more stringently than before, in case their leaders should ask them to sustain an extended campaign.

Eastward the messengers returned to the hills of Pelham and descended to Conkey's Tavern on the west branch of the Swift River, where they delivered news of the whole country's preparations to Shays and his officers.

When Shays was finished with long days of planning and rode up the hill to his home in its hollow, his view ran for miles and miles to the west and southwest, and he watched the cold sun set over the bowl of towns that were banding together to protect each other's harvests through the coming winter.

As November 21 inched closer on their calendars, the houses of western Massachusetts stewed in the government's threats. The first frosts had long ago burst the fibers that held September's grasses high, and now the winds and rains wove fallen reeds in mats across the meadows. Only tenacious seed pods and tangled briars stripped of their berries still stuck up from gray-brown, yellow-brown fields. The gray-green, green-brown woods were bare of leaves now, and the farmers and their families could see through the trees, all the way to the purple-blue hills in the distance, remote beneath the yellow-blue wintering sky, where geese flew over in long vees, solitary hawks soared over the ridges, and crows played over the valleys, grunting and croaking, assessing the naked landscape.

By the last week of October, the last corn was in, and there was nothing left in the orchards and fields. The cold rains drained the hills of their vibrant colors. The nights came earlier now, and the cold spoke of deeper cold and longer darkness to come.

As the farmers of Massachusetts moved their work inside, the threat of loss and the dread of imprisonment salted all their conversations. In their kitchens, wives kneaded dough in fear that armies would march from Boston. At their hearths, in their barns, they dreaded that their husbands might be forced to bare their backs to be whipped in the cold. They feared the danger of battle with government agents, but now they also feared for their safety if they dared to tell their neighbors they wanted to stay out of it and leave Shays and his committed men to bear the burden alone. Nor would they be safe if they simply submitted to the government's aggressive schedule of taxes.

The people performed all their work under fogs of apprehension, and their fears did not release them when they lay their heads down at night, but they seeped into the children's dreams, so they cried out with visions of persecution and nightmares of loss and grief, and their parents had to get out of their warm beds and cross through chilly rooms to soothe them.

A few days after the General Court had passed the Riot Act into law, the sun reached the midpoint between the autumn equinox and the winter solstice, but the people of Massachusetts did not turn this Halloween into a statewide Funeral for Liberty, as they had done in 1765, when the Crown had voided the colony's charter.[33]

When they lit their bonfires at dusk, the younger men in the farm towns warmed themselves with the same resentment their forefathers felt for the government's distant authority. With the light of their towering fires licking the hemlocks' and the oaks' bare branches at the edge of their clearings, younger men renewed their offer to fight, to finish the opposition their fathers had started, but the older men remembered too well their sufferings during their wars. To the hiss and snap of flaring brush piles they had been building for months—with light flickering on their foreheads and throats, and smoke choking their eyes—veterans told their sons and young neighbors that they would have to bundle themselves against colds much deeper than this October chill if they were going to fight a war for their liberties.

With warmth on their faces and winter cold on their backs, they looked at their tiny houses and little barns sprinkled across the vast landscape of darkened, exhausted fields, with the other towns' bonfires winking on hills across the way. They looked at the earth, still wild in so many woods. It had given them all they had planted, and now it lay fallow for its season. They looked at their harvest celebrations through winter's eyes and knew that there were aged parents and children who would not survive winter's trials to plant seeds with them in the spring. They looked down at their farms from the icy stars, they saw themselves through the eyes of their ancestors, who had been watching them work all this time. They prayed for their peace, and they hoped that they had been keeping faith with their customs well enough to let them sleep undisturbed through All Hallow's Eve and through winter.

Still, they could not help seeing their land through the eyes of the Boston nobles who thought they could claim their lands' wealth with their papers. For hours, the bonfires' bright flames ate through the wood the people had stacked, till the younger men ventured out into the forests to fetch wood to build up the flames, to drive the circle of warmth and light farther into the woods, higher toward the darkness between the stars.

When their fires died down and the spooky first-quarter Halloween moon set at midnight, the farmers of Massachusetts still did not disguise themselves with feathers in their hair and war paint on their faces and venture out to wealthy men's homes to make them pay their own tax for speaking in favor of government, taxes, and tyranny.

When they woke, the calendar had turned to November, and the court dates on the twenty-first loomed large only three weeks away.[34]

Day to day, the people of Massachusetts waited for news that the governor had ended the crisis by offering reforms, but each day passed, and the season of crisis persisted. When the farmers of Hampshire County did get news, a few days after Halloween, they learned that the late October courts in Taunton and Cambridge had been forced open by armed government forces.[35] They also learned that the legislature had made another gesture designed to give the appearance of conciliation. But the messengers' voices were sharp with contempt when they reported that the government had not offered actual reforms. It had passed an Indemnity Act, which offered to pardon men who had closed the courts but only on the condition that they would vow not to join further protests.[36] All the original causes of the crisis would remain in place. The pardons would not stop the courts from seizing land or taking men to prison for unjust debts, but individual men could assure their safety if they abandoned their cause and their townsmen.

The people had been saying since summer that they could not accept peace on these terms, but now that the Riot Act was law, husbands and wives in houses all through Massachusetts washed their cookware in the hard discussions, arguing back and forth about whether the men should sign their names to these pardons and leave their neighbors to keep up the protests without them.

It had been easy to march to the courts when crops were still in the fields. But now, as they looked out their autumn windows, where naked tree trunks turned black in the cold autumn rain and leaves skittered in the cold winds along the roads, some wives could already feel their late-winter hungers. Every time they went down into their cellars for squash or turnips, for beets or potatoes, they dreaded losing everything they had stored up. In terse discussions, they promised their husbands they would economize—they said they would make sacrifices, they said they would gladly withstand the foreclosures and loss of livestock so long as they did not have to suffer through any more years when their men were away and daily in danger of dying.

When wives entreated their husbands to accept the government's pardons and keep themselves alive till they could seek redress in elections, their husbands answered that clemency without reforms would only make them slaves. They would live at Governor Bowdoin's mercy. Their land would be taken, the men would be taken to prison again, and men who tried to protect their farms and communities would be jailed and whipped for the crime of exercising the liberties they had fought a war to establish.

In an address that was carried from Boston starting on October 30, the General Court doubled down on the importance of paying the state's debts, accusing any opposition of being misled by "false representation" propagated by "evil and designing men."[37] Ignoring the lack of money that plagued the state's farmers, the General Court stated that if a soldier had sold his notes for shillings on the pound, he should still be able to "purchase them again at a lower rate than he sold them" and share in the windfall when the notes were redeemed at full value. In a long and detailed accounting, the General Court justified its expenses and accused the people of having "greedily adopted the luxurious modes of foreign nations" in importing "the necessaries of life" from abroad and of having "indulged . . . in fantastical and expensive fashions and intemperate living."[38] It said that the people had effectively brought the crisis on themselves with their "habits of luxury," buying "gewgaws imported from Europe" and squandering their money on rum, "the pernicious produce of the West Indies."[39] It said that "whenever a people are dissatisfied with government, it may at least deserve reflection, whether the difficulty is not with themselves." It accused the people of "unreasonable jealousy and a complaining temper," so that even "if Angels . . . were to govern us, opposition would be made to their administration." The address accused "instigators" of wanting "to subvert all order and government, and reduce the commonwealth, to the most deplorable state of wretchedness and contempt."

"The man who attempts to subvert those laws and that constitution," the address concluded, "does in effect make an attempt upon the life, liberty and property of every member of the community."

In a proclamation, Governor Bowdoin extended the insult of the Indemnity Act by publishing an address in which he claimed the people did not have a "sufficient or justifiable reason" for protesting. He said they were not even really suffering, for if a law happened to get passed that produced any harmful effects, those effects would also be felt by the legislators themselves.[40] He declared for all the world to hear that the men in the legislature were not suffering from the crisis that panicked the farmers and he did not believe that his policies had given the farmers legitimate reasons to complain. Bowdoin continued that the people had been misled to "incautiously support artful and wicked men" who seduced them to adopt "destructive measures."[41] He then claimed that the people's constitutionally authorized meetings were "anti-constitutional, & of very dangerous tendency, even when attempted in a peaceable manner."[42] He said that the only legitimate avenue for winning reforms was through the very same legislature that had so far refused to respond to the people's concerns.[43]

Adam Wheeler responded in an open letter that ran in the Worcester paper.[44] He spoke for himself alone, and he spoke for all the men by refusing to presume to speak for anyone else, for the others were also free to speak their minds, but in their silence, they signified that his statement expressed their sentiments. He said that he had "no intention to destroy the public government," only to suspend the courts to prevent abuses. He said that he was "distressed to see valuable and industrious members of society dragged from their families to prison, to the great damage, not only of their families but the community at large."[45] He said that he did not intend to oppose the law in general, only to reform oppressive laws. He said he was waiting "to have redress of grievances in a constitutional way" and asserted that "liberty is the prize I still have in view." "In that glorious cause," he wrote, "I am determined to stand with firmness and resolution."[46]

Editorials in the *Hampshire Herald*, the *Worcester Centinel*, and now in the *Northampton Gazette* kept the country tense with apprehension, but the facts remained unchanged: the commonwealth's taxes and austerity measures were crushing the people. A petition from forty-one towns claimed that the lack of currency "subjects the inhabitants to the greatest inconveniences. The people in general are extremely embarrassed with public and private debts . . . no money can be obtained by the sale or mortgage of real estate. The produce of the present year, and the remainder of our cattle—even were we to sell the whole, are totally inadequate to the present demands for money."[47]

In the days after Bowdoin's offer of indemnity spread town to town, Daniel Shays and the men of Pelham did not hear reports that the communities of western Massachusetts were shattering into thousands of individual households—where each family calculated its own best interests—and sent their men to find their magistrates to swear the oaths and sign their names to the pardons on terms the government laid out.

In the Scots-Irish towns of Pelham and Colrain, the families had been knit together in solidarity that ran back generations, since long before they had founded their towns. They had volunteered in large numbers for both the French and Indian War and the Revolution. In the taverns and meeting houses, in their homes, each man pledged himself to the others and to their communities. They would bear the same things the other families bore, and they would bear it in the same silent solidarity that protects the mysterious bond of any marriage or community.

If they could not convince Governor Bowdoin that he and his legislature should share in the people's sacrifices—if no one could show him that he, as the leader who exemplified the state, should take the first portion of losses—they still would not agree to surrender their land and liberties and let him treat them as subjects whose experiences were not important.

But when men's parents and wives and children prayed that someone would show James Bowdoin the consequences of his actions and soften his heart to their plight, an elder would have to explain that the governor was not the source of their troubles. Even if Bowdoin had a change of heart, they explained, the other powerful merchants in the Senate would still refuse to take losses in their investments. They said that even if Bowdoin changed his mind and proposed reforms, the other men in his class would replace him with someone who would still press the people for money and seize their land.

In the cold, early morning forests where the farmers set out together to hunt for deer and moose to complement their harvests with fresh meat, they speculated how the crisis would end. In the swamps and lakes where they hunted ducks and geese at dawn, some men predicted that Bowdoin's fever of fear would feed on itself until blood had to be shed. In hushed tones behind their hunting blinds, they confessed their fear that nothing would change till the sound of gunshots and lamentations on either side showed the influential men in Boston that they and the farmers depended on each other and suffered one fate together.

As November 21 and the next courts in Worcester and Great Barrington drew closer, Shays and the men who refused to beg for the governor's pardons had to decide whether they would go to the courts to close them.

When Abigail Shays and the other wives warned their husbands that they were tying their own nooses by continuing to organize opposition to Bowdoin's laws, Shays and the men of Pelham, Adam Wheeler and the men of Worcester, Job Shattuck and the men of Concord, and William Whiting and the farmers of Great Barrington consoled their families by saying that they would only be outlaws as John Hancock and John and Samuel Adams had all been outlaws in their time. Their righteous opposition to unjust power would be redeemed in justice for their people, even if they themselves were shot down or arrested.

They reassured their families by telling them that they would continue to show up in the courtyards in such large numbers that they would overwhelm any forces Bowdoin's marshals could gather. They pledged to keep themselves pure in the countryside's eyes and not let their townsmen indulge in violence. They said that they trusted their countrymen to recognize right and wrong and to take their side. They repeated their assurances that the commonwealth's militias consisted of their own neighbors and fellow veterans and that without a loyal and disciplined army of his own, Bowdoin would still be powerless to act, no matter what violence he threatened. If he gathered a force to shoot them down, they would rally their countrymen and fight as they had fought the British. They promised to fight another war to free themselves if they had to before they would live as serfs on the land they had carved from wilderness with their own hands.

They said that when their rights had been secured, their people would thank them, even for taking to arms if it went that far. But they said their children would never thank them for submitting to unjust laws to keep the peace.

The first weeks of November passed, but even with grounds for warfare written into law, Governor Bowdoin still was not finished making threats and impugning his people's characters. On November 14, the General Court suspended the right of habeas corpus. Now the governor's agents could arrest "in any part of the Commonwealth any person whom [an official] shall suspect is unfriendly to government" and take that man to prison in Boston, far from his people, without due process of law.[48]

A few days later—with a clear recollection of the protests of 1774 and the antigovernment ferment that had led to the Revolution—the wealthy men in the General Court made the act of speaking against the government a crime. Even moderate merchants who urged the government to issue reforms—now even wealthy men like Great Barrington's Justice Whiting— would be subject to arrest if they argued for leniency, on the grounds that they would be feeding what the government was calling an insurrection.

Finally, on November 18—after having ignored dozens of petitions submitted from farmers' constitutional meetings—having protected the merchant elites' investments by placing their business income beyond the reach of taxes—having refused to depreciate war debts or allow the people the dignity of an issue of paper money—having pledged to pay speculators the full value of the promissory notes the veterans themselves had parted with for shillings—having slighted the people's authority to hold their town meetings—having tried to compel their militiamen's loyalty with threats— having suspended their citizens' rights—having threatened to arrest the people's leaders and seize their property—having promised sheriffs and militiamen immunity from punishment if they injured or killed insubordinate farmers—having stripped the people of any place within the law from which to even protest—having left the people's torments all in place—the wealthy merchants who constituted the General Court agreed they had done enough. They voted to adjourn till the tenth of January and returned to their homes to prepare their own estates for winter.

Chapter Six

Confronting
the Courts

B Y THE TIME WESTERN MASSACHUSETTS FARMERS received the news
that the General Court had once more adjourned without issuing reforms, the last of the leaves had been plucked from the trees by cold winds.
The distances over the valleys were cold through bare branches. Only the
beech leaves clung to branches, drying brown and crisp so that every November breeze sounded like court papers rustling in their woods.

Only the most hopeful men still waited to hear that Governor Bowdoin
had bowed to their pressure and issued reforms. Everyone else waited, tense
with anticipation of November 21 when two Courts of Sessions were scheduled to hear suits for debt and foreclosure, one in Worcester, one in Great
Barrington.

No one imagined Bowdoin might challenge the people of Berkshire
County by sending troops the length of the commonwealth to force that
court open, so Shays and the other Regulator leaders did not send Luke Day
or anyone else west with men to protect that court. Worcester, however, was
only a two-day, forty-five-mile march from Boston, and Adam Wheeler and
the other foremost men in that region were anxious about what might happen. In correspondence with Shays and the other leaders of Pelham, they
debated whether to carry on their protests under the threats contained in
the Riot Act.

In long discussions pacing in front of the hearth of Conkey's Tavern,
Shays and the men of Pelham decided that they could not afford to abandon

their demands for reforms and submit to unjust taxes and laws that would force them off their farms, to start again with nothing somewhere else. The Worcester court would have to be closed.

Reports coming in from the countryside said that once again hundreds of men were willing to demonstrate, but the leading Regulators in Pelham and Worcester felt that they had made their point by bringing large numbers to Springfield in September. With Bowdoin's threats in the air now, there was more danger than security in large numbers.

In deliberations that ran back and forth between towns, the leading men of Pelham resolved to send a force of just 350 picked, disciplined men to Worcester. These trusted men would keep angry Worcester farmers in line and also keep General Warner's militiamen from trying to force the court open with bayonets.

The Regulators' leaders also decided that Adam Wheeler should stay at home for the same reason Luke Day had yielded to Shays in Springfield: to prevent a riot or a massacre if the government tried to enforce its warrants and seize the men who had closed the September court.

Again, the leaders in Pelham turned to Daniel Shays, who had not yet been named in a warrant. Shays did not refuse to ride at the head of this force.

On Sunday, the nineteenth of November, with only two days before the Worcester court was scheduled to open, he collected his volunteers and prepared to march east to Worcester.

There was danger of warfare in the body he and his men made when they formed their lines in the cold. Bowdoin's threats had all been passed into law. The consequences of breaking those laws had been published. But so had the people published their objections to the commonwealth's policies. Those objections would have to be represented in the courtyard before the court could convene and hear the merchants' business.

There was also a new danger in the weather, for the air had turned much colder since the last time they had marched to a court in September. The season's first sleet had already threaded cold darts into their eyes and down their collars. The first snowflakes had already drifted down lazy and slow over their meadows, sifting through their hemlocks and pines. The men and their families had already stepped out of their houses in the mornings to see the distant hilltops frosted silver with snow.

Now as they set out from the Pelham meeting house, the wan November light slanted weak and low on their faces and heavy coats and breeches. Provisions were cumbersome in their packs, and the flags on their staffs and muskets and bayonets pinned the clouds of their cold breath to the sky. Over their heads, the croaking crows measured the distances between the long naked hills as the men's feet on the cold-hardened road chewed the distances step by step. More than a few of the men in Shays's lines had held equal or higher ranks in the war. Many had lived in Pelham much longer than he had, but they started and stopped on his command.

They did not expect to march all thirty-five miles to Worcester in one day. They headed to the town of Rutland, high on a rounded hilltop twelve miles northwest of Worcester. The Massachusetts army had constructed barracks there during the war, to house the five thousand redcoats they had taken prisoner when rebel General Horatio Gates captured General John Burgoyne's army at Saratoga.[1]

From Rutland, Shays and his men would be safely out of range of Worcester if Bowdoin had in fact sent soldiers, but the barracks were also close enough that they could reach the Worcester court in a few hours' march tomorrow.

Soon enough they were warm with the rhythm of walking through their country, and the cold air crisp in their faces was welcome. On the long plateaus between forests and clear-cut woodlots—on long hills between growing towns—they could see opportunity everywhere around them. They themselves were the citizen farmers who would turn these rough hills into towns and a nation. They were the ones who would create the value on which any government levied its taxes. It followed that they should be the ones who would institute law in this country.

Shays and his men marched past farms and fields where they had worked together. They passed hillsides where they had celebrated festivals, and churches where they had attended their neighbors' families' funerals and weddings.

Cresting each hill, they took in long views of their country, barren under the soaring vultures, the migrating geese and hawks, the low, wan autumn clouds. Leaving the Connecticut River valley behind them, they continued east, climbing and then descending each of the long north-south ridges that separated the three branches of the Swift River.

When they arrived in Rutland at the end of the day, they were not opposed. They opened the doors to the dusty barracks, put down their packs and muskets, and gathered wood to make fires in the cold hearths.

As the early dark fell, Shays posted guards in case Bowdoin might have sent a force to besiege them, but sentries who listened all night heard only the distant sounds of deer and turkey, foxes and owls, calling in the woods around Rutland's farms.

The next morning, Shays and his 350 men formed lines again under their flags and marched the remaining twelve miles to Worcester to get there the night before court would open on Tuesday.

The blood was jaunty in their veins as they entered the town, for their presence was an open instigation. They were practically daring their government to make a show of force, but there were no government men waiting for them. The people of Worcester came out to cheer as they rode into town.[2]

They occupied the courthouse, and at the end of the day, the people of Worcester fed them and made beds for them in their houses and barns, defying the governor's threats as they endorsed the people's resistance with hospitality and support.

Again that evening, Shays's officers posted sentries, but again, the night was quiet, and no one reported movements of government men from Boston.

When Tuesday's dawn broke the moonless dark, Shays and his men surrounded the building where judges expected to open the Court of Sessions.[3] Soon after the weak sun rose from its glow low in the southeast, their numbers started to swell as men from Worcester joined them in the cold.

Again, Chief Justice Artemas Ward arrived without a militia, as his men had once more refused to muster, this time in defiance of the laws that made it a crime not to come when summoned. Again, Ward's strident rhetoric and threats failed to move the protesting farmers. Nor did Sheriff Greenleaf break their resolve when he told them that if they were upset by the high cost of court fees, he would gladly hang them for free.[4] Without reinforcements to back him, though, this threat was just banter, ornamenting the central fact that the judges would not convene court on this day.

For hours, the farmers waited, repeating a routine that was becoming familiar. Their leaders met with Ward and the judges to no purpose, as Ward was not authorized to reform the laws that tormented them. They paraded in the courtyard, drilling for pride and for warmth. The slant sun that reached them never soaked November's chills out of their bones. All day they bore the cold, disdaining to break into taverns for rum, or to break up rich men's furniture or carriages for firewood.

Finally, Ward stopped waiting for reinforcements. On the very public stage Governor Bowdoin and the legislature had set with threats, Shays and his men and the farmers in Massachusetts prevailed. Poor farmers and governors watching from other states, the British and the French in Europe looked on as Ward and his judges wrote in their books that they had once more adjourned *sine die* without bloodshed.

Again, Shays and his men cheered as the judges and merchants departed without holding court. All Samuel Adams's threats and Governor Bowdoin's Riot Act were so much hot air. Their people had won another two months without suits for debt, without government men challenging their authority, although again, their relief was tempered by the danger that Bowdoin might still insist on extracting certain amounts of the people's land, or perhaps a measure of blood to show what his words were worth.

When the early dark settled, Shays and his men dispersed to the homes of the farmers and townsmen who had hosted them last night, and their hosts stoked fires and poured them drinks to chase the chill of the hours they had spent in the courtyard representing the people's laws.

On Wednesday morning, November 22, with frost sparkling in the fields, Shays led his picked men back to Rutland, a half-day's march through brown meadows and naked woods.[5] They did not continue the twenty-five miles back through the purple-gray hills to come home to Pelham. Another court was scheduled to open in Worcester in two weeks, on Tuesday, December 5. They would wait in Rutland like prisoners themselves, held captive by the danger threatening their homes.

When Shays installed his men in the barracks again, the winter months spread out before them, cold and daunting. No one could say how much longer this confrontation with Bowdoin's courts might last. The men were low on provisions and sore to lose their winter's labor, so they started to look for men of higher rank who would use their authority to broker a peace.

From Rutland, they wrote to Brigadier General Josiah Whitney of Harvard, just west of Boston.[6] Whitney had crossed the Delaware with Washington and led a brigade in the victory over Burgoyne at Saratoga. Since the troubles started last summer, he had written editorials that argued the people's side. Now Shays wrote to ask Whitney whether he would help them convince Bowdoin and the elites in Boston to solve the commonwealth's fiscal problems in ways that would not force them off their farms.

Shays also dispatched Captains Luke Day and Eli Parsons from Chicopee to ride the hundred miles northwest to Arlington, Vermont, to make the same invitation in person to Ethan Allen.[7] Shays and his officers hoped to harness Allen's celebrity to their cause and galvanize the people against Bowdoin's threats, as Allen had done in the spring when he helped the farmers of the Wyoming Valley resist the demands of the Pennsylvania courts.

Biding their time in the barracks in Rutland, Shays and his men had two weeks until they were going to close the next Worcester court. They had not brought enough food to see them through two idle weeks, but they still refused to break into merchants' warehouses to commandeer goods for themselves, so they knocked at the doors of local farms and asked for support. They were careful to say that they were not an army and had not come to press foreign demands on their countryside. They said that they were the people themselves, confronted by the same threats the farmers faced, of foreclosure, of debtor's prison. With three months of peaceful protests behind them, they assured the local farmers that they were not a mob but a dignified force who refused to let tyranny reign in their country again.[8]

The farms around Rutland were not very rich, but the farmers there gave them as much as they could afford, willingly paying a kind of tax to support the defense of their region.

While they waited for the next Worcester court to open December 5, the first blizzard of the winter blew in. Softly, at first, then thickening— melting at first, then blanketing the ground, the snow changed the landscape from autumn to winter all at once. Snowflakes rattled the beech leaves while they were icy, then hushed out all sound as the cold got deeper, as snowflakes softened and filled the sky, erasing the distant hills in a blurry hush.

Close in the stuffy barracks, with nothing to do while the snow piled up outside, Shays and his men fed wood into the great hearths and whetted each other's hungers recalling the stews and roasts their wives and mothers might even now be making, the feasts that might be waiting for them if the crisis ever ended and they could afford to keep all their harvests.

Sometimes the storm shook the building, or the snow fell against the windowpanes with a clatter, but inside the men told long stories to pass the time, living each of the lives of their country by turns. They reminisced about their days in camp and their battles during the war. They talked about the work they planned to do on their farms after Governor Bowdoin and Samuel Adams and the merchant elites finally backed away from their threats and reformed the unjust taxes. Some speculated what life would be like on the frontier in Ohio, with land to be worked if they would defend it from Natives who had not yet relinquished their claims.

When the snow stopped, Shays and his officers dug out from the storm and drilled in the cold, snowy fields in the fine first cold days of wintry weather. When the sun broke through the low, gray clouds, the fields were layered in silver and white, gleaming between the woodlots. Up close, the snow sparkled every color in the sunlight, and by afternoon the long stripes of trees' shadows showed the curve of each hill in long purple lines.

Another snowstorm blew through a few days later. The grasses that had poked through the first snow were buried again. The rolling fields were blanketed. The solstice was still three weeks off, but now the winter weather descended in earnest, and Shays and his men speculated whether the confrontation with their government would pause until spring, since the cold and the snow-filled roads would make it harder to send large numbers of men west into their hills.

Their optimism dissolved, though, and the shut-in air of the Rutland barracks turned sour with frustration when a messenger brought a letter from General Whitney in Harvard saying that he would not help them. Soon after, Luke Day's and Eli Parsons's messengers brought the same news from Vermont: Ethan Allen had not only turned them down, he had denied their request with abhorrence.[9] Allen was still so popular that many of the men in Rutland were willing to discount his statement of abhorrence as just a diplomatic concession to Bowdoin. Everyone knew that he and Vermont Governor Thomas Chittenden planned to bring Vermont into the union as the fourteenth state and could not afford to alienate Massachusetts's elites.

However Shays's men tried to justify General Whitney's or Ethan Allen's refusals, a sense of despair spread through the barracks when they understood that they would not be able to count on men who had influence in Bowdoin's circles. They were going to have to see themselves through the crisis. If the governor did end up fielding a force, they were the ones who would have to flee or defend their farms, and their own people's cellars would have to provision their protests for as long as their force was necessary.

Now instead of looking forward to going home to chip ice from the troughs outside their barns before they spent their days laying up firewood, or cutting shingles or tying brooms, or working beside their wives making cloth or lace for the merchants, Shays and the men in Rutland projected the costs of keeping their force together for another six weeks, at least till the General Court returned to Boston in the second week of January.

Some men argued that they would not have to do very much more once they had closed this next court in Worcester, on Monday the fifth. They said that the snows would only get deeper and deeper in the roads, and the governor would not be able to send a force to open the courts till the snow had melted and the mud in the roads firmed up in April. They said that they expected to return to their homes, and Shays could keep a small force together if that was what the leaders decided. Others, though, distrusted Bowdoin's government, and they estimated how much food and funding they would need to keep their force together for an additional ten weeks, from January through early April, when the people could finally go to the polls and vote Bowdoin out of office.

Through long days riding the roads around Rutland, recruiting support and provisions, through cold nights in the barracks, they speculated whether their force would ultimately be tested by battles. Would they ever return to the rhythms of their families, livestock, and land, or would they have to endure a long hungry winter, waiting for attacks that never came, in order to see their people through till elections when they would win reforms without fighting?

In the taverns where Shays and his officers visited Rutland's farmers, some men still clamored to march to Boston, to toss the governor and senators out of their mansions. They fantasized about cleaning out rich men's cellars and gorging themselves on wines and smoked meats before winter closed the roads. But Shays and his officers kept a tight lid on that talk, and no one took the first step to lead that march.

Still, no one could say how far they would have to go, and they waited through long idle days. Trapped by the looming confrontations, exiled from their families, the men put on their coats and scarves and went out in teams to shovel the trails between the barracks and stables and outbuildings. They piled the snow beside the narrow paths, in walls that hemmed them in and froze overnight and would not melt for months yet.

Chapter Seven

Blood in the Snow

O N THE NIGHT OF THE TWENTY-SEVENTH, six days after they had closed the Worcester Court of Sessions, riders tracked snow into the Rutland barracks bringing news that Bowdoin's forces had redeemed their failure to open the Worcester court. Militiamen from Boston had surprised everyone by marching twenty miles through the snow to open the court in Concord.

Shays and his officers had never planned to march from Rutland to Concord to close that court. They had expected Groton's Job Shattuck—the distinguished veteran and prominent landowner whose men closed that court in September—to do it. But now they learned that Shattuck had quarreled with Oliver Prescott of neighboring Shirley about who should lead.[1] In the end, no one had staked out the courthouse to keep the judges and merchants from entering the court to conduct their business.

This news set Shays and all his men on edge. They had not kept their presence in Rutland a secret, so they pressed their messengers for any sign that the governor's force might send men ahead to Worcester, to wait there and oppose them if they should come back on December 5 or even to march the twelve miles to Rutland to attack them here in the barracks.

Some men predicted the government's forces would not range farther than Concord.[2] Worcester was farther than the British had dared to venture in 1775, to confiscate the weapons and supplies the rebels had stockpiled there. No one could say for sure, but still the barracks were cold with anticipation, regardless of how many logs the men laid on the hearths.

After a long, anxious night fueled by breathless rumors and speculation, Shays and his officers spent Tuesday the twenty-eighth collecting intelligence, trying to learn where the governor's force had gone from Concord—trying to predict where they might go next.

With apprehension clammy in their cold fingers, the men cooked and shoveled and drilled through the day, as had become their routine. Finally, that evening, a rider whipped his horse into the barracks courtyard, to make the report everyone dreaded.

The soldiers had not returned to Boston after forcing the Concord court open. They had proceeded to Groton, where they had spilled blood in making the first arrests.

On hearing the early reports—that Bowdoin's men had "put out the eye of a woman, and stabbed and cut off the breast of another, and mangled an infant in the cradle"[3]— some men clamored to ride out for revenge before they lost the light of the first quarter moon.

But Daniel Shays and his officers had restrained their men for three months, and they were not going to let them answer blood with blood now, to risk starting a bidding war over who could drive the price of the people's blood highest. Shays kept them in the barracks until other messengers could confirm or refute the rumors of atrocities.

Soon enough, they learned the actual news: three hundred horsemen from Roxbury and Boston, led by Boston lawyer Benjamin Hichborn, merchant Stephen Higginson, and Harvard graduate John Warren, had ridden northwest from Concord to Groton with a warrant for Shattuck's arrest.[4] In Groton, Colonel Henry Wood joined them with another hundred men.[5]

Job Shattuck was not at his home when they sought him there, but they ransacked his house and menaced his wife and children. They found him at a cabin on the banks of the Nashua River, and when they tried to seize him, he resisted arrest.

In the struggle that followed, Boston militiaman John Rand subdued Shattuck by slashing his leg with his saber, severing the tendons behind Shattuck's knee.[6] The injury had likely crippled Shattuck for life, but he had been carted to Boston, swaddled in bloody bandages, to molder in prison with fellow Groton Regulators John Hapsgood, who had also been injured in the hand, and yeoman Benjamin Page.

With the sharp scent of blood in the snowy late-November air, Shays and his men kept waiting to hear that the hundreds of soldiers were even now coming to rout them out of Rutland. They heard that a separate party had set out in search of Adam Wheeler, and Henry and Abraham Gale. They had not found them, but they had menaced Worcester tavern keeper Thomas Farmer, threatening him with their pistols in his house.[7]

In the end, after some tense hours, messengers finally arrived to report that Hichborn and Warren had retreated to Boston with their three prisoners. They rode in haste, lest Shattuck's angry townsmen rally to avenge Shattuck's blood and recapture him and the others.

As the evening deepened to night in the Rutland barracks, some men argued that it was time to raise an army and march to Boston, to liberate Shattuck, Hapsgood, and Page, and to punish the aristocrats who thought they could steal their farms.[8]

Still Daniel Shays did not lead his men out into the cold November night to seek revenge. Nor did he let them use the excuse of Job Shattuck's arrest as a justification for beating down Worcester merchants' warehouse doors and pillaging their stores of salt beef and rum.

For long tense hours in the drafty barracks, Shays and his men stayed where they were, debating whether they should dare to ride into Worcester in six days to close the next court. Some men predicted that Bowdoin would send another army to Worcester, but other men countered that Bowdoin would simply hold Shattuck and the others as ringleaders of the insurrection. Now that he had his scapegoats, he would be able to say that he had made a show of force: finally, he would be able to issue reforms without showing weakness.

In their hours of speculation that night, some men predicted that other states' governments would probably step in, to offer loans and negotiate depreciation of debts, in order to keep the commonwealth from falling into civil war and threatening the union. They said that men like Alexander Hamilton and Stephen Higginson had been waiting for just such a crisis as this to expose the weaknesses in the Articles of Confederation. Everyone knew that Hamilton and the nationalists who wanted a stronger, centralized government would use this crisis to advocate for a central bank and a standing army.[9] Nonetheless the farmers hoped that now that Bowdoin had hostages, the crisis would become an issue in national politics and be resolved without further bloodshed.

Not everyone could believe that the other states' delegates would help them. The merchant elites in other states were much more likely to turn against them and back Bowdoin and Adams's calls for harsh treatment for the men they called rebels and traitors. They said that it was only a matter of time till they would be forced to murder their leaders, the same as the desperate men who had walked off their lines in New Jersey in the first months of 1781.

When they had argued every side of the situation, the men circled back to the horror of Job Shattuck's severed tendons, but Shays and his officers still could not see any justification for starting a war with Bowdoin by trying to rescue him from prison. They had committed themselves to their innocence from the beginning, and they would not abandon it now.

When the debates were over, the men settled down to a restless sleep. No one ventured out into the crisp late-November night to increase their countryside's sufferings by taking revenge on the deputies or the families who had helped them.

Nevertheless, the day after Shattuck's arrest, Montague's Thomas Grover and Shattuck's townsman Elisha Pownell wrote a letter from Rutland, addressed to the farmers of Massachusetts.

"The seeds of war are now sown," they said. "Two of our men are now bleeding that were wounded by light horse that came from Boston and Roxbury."

"Let this letter be read," they urged their readers, "and for you and every man to supply men and provisions and relieve us with a reinforcement. We are determined to carry our point. Our case is yours."[10]

Bluntly, Amherst's Sylvanus Billings wrote to tell his countrymen, "our lives and families will be taken from us if we don't defend them."[11]

Later that day, the men who had choked down their anger sent up a cheer when they learned that farmers far up the Connecticut River had avenged Shattuck's tendons by burning the courthouse in Grafton County, New Hampshire.[12] These flames melted the false tranquility Governor Sullivan had forced on his state in September when his soldiers had humiliated thirty-nine of the people's leaders in Essex.

Sometime later, the men learned that farmers in Groton had reprised the Grafton farmers' protest by torching their own courthouse. Groton men also burned Sheriff Aaron Brown's potash works to punish him for his role in Shattuck's arrest. Reports said they also laid incendiary materials beneath one Ebenezer Champney's law offices, but these had been discovered before they could be lit.[13]

From the barracks where they still waited, Shays and his men heard that every tavern and meeting house was crazed with rumors of fires and with speculation about whose house might burn or whose blood might be spilled next.

They never did hear news that anyone in Pelham or Montague, or in Colrain or Worcester, had rampaged through wealthy men's houses or orchards, tearing up fences or assaulting the men themselves. But through the angry hours of November 29, Shays and his officers listened with dread as they tried to gauge whether their force and authority would still be respected among the people, or whether the country would slide into open rebellion in spite of all their attempts at restraint.

Shays and his men never took the first step toward Boston, but they heard that Governor Bowdoin had posted a guard on each of the main roads into the city.[14] This defensive gesture created the very hysteria Bowdoin claimed he was protecting his people from.[15] For now reports from Boston said the city was crazed with rumors that rampaging farmers backed by British troops and even hostile Canadian Indians were coming to loot the houses and set the wharves and warehouses on fire.

The wealthy families in Boston remembered all too clearly August 1765, when mobs of Boston patriots destroyed British tax stamp administrator Andrew Oliver's and Royal Comptroller Benjamin Hallowell's houses, then ransacked Governor Hutchinson's house, to express their opposition to Parliament's Stamp Act. Now wealthy men feared what they called the leveling impulse would take hold of the people. They dreaded being dragged from their parlors and carriages and forced into the streets and tarred and feathered.

With their backs to the sea, the people of Boston clamored for their government to subdue this threat. From Westfield, General Shepard fanned Bowdoin's fears when he told the governor that "nothing will restore order and peace to these counties now but superior forces" and requested two thousand men "with two companies of artillery and a hundred light horse."[16]

Even as the commonwealth was convulsed with rumors and anticipation, Shays and his men bided their time in Rutland. They listened with dread to reports that twenty horsemen, men of large fortunes, had set out to break up a meeting of four hundred Regulators in Shrewsbury, east of Worcester. The Regulators were warned of their approach, and they moved their meeting to the neighboring town of Holden instead of staying to welcome the mismatched fight with wealthy government supporters. But the people's restraint nearly broke when a small faction split from the main body of Regulators and returned to Shrewsbury, looking for a fight. Fortunately, the horsemen had retreated by the time they returned, and the atmosphere of tense anticipation never rained down in blows or further bloodshed.[17]

Sour with dread in the cold, Shays and his men stayed in Rutland. November turned to December. Dawn broke later and colder every day. The thin light was no longer high enough or strong enough to dissolve the morning chill before the sun sunk down again, lighting the clouds in the west with cold scarlet and purple fires.

They should have been home on their farms, languidly starting their winter's work, relaxing after the back-breaking harvest. But when messengers confirmed reports that Bowdoin had not stationed troops in Worcester, they prepared to return there to close the next court.

On Sunday, the third of December, two days before the court was slated to open, Shays and his 350 men formed lines again in the snow.[18] On Shays's order, they raised their flags, and their fife and drum struck up the cascading rhythms to carry them back the twelve miles to Worcester, along the borders of snowy fields and woodlots.

Bowdoin had posted sentries at all the entrances to Boston, but no one kept Shays's men from entering Worcester at the end of a half-day's cold march, on Sunday night.[19] Without opposition, they lodged in houses and barns throughout the city.[20]

The next day they published a formal statement of their position, to "inform you of some of the principal causes of the late risings of the people."[21]

Their letter made it clear that their complaints were not coming from a few fractious or discontented men but that "almost every individual who derives his living from the labour of his hands or an income of a farm" shared their feelings.[22]

They explained that the crisis had started not when they had closed the courts but when they were burdened disproportionately with taxes they could not afford—all to pay windfall profits to rich financiers.[23]

They lamented the shortage of coin, which was filling the jails with "unhappy debtors" and rendering "a reputable body of the people incapable of being serviceable either to themselves or to their community."[24]

They complained about the "suspension of the writ of *habeas corpus*, by which those persons who have stepped forth to assert and maintain the rights of the people are liable to be taken and conveyed even to the most distant part of the commonwealth, and thereby subjected to unjust punishment." They noted the "unlimited power granted to justices of the peace, sheriffs, deputy sheriffs and constables, by the Riot Act," which allowed them to act "from a principle of revenge, hatred and envy." This suspension of law, they said, was "dangerous if not absolutely destructive to a republican government."[25]

"Be assured," their letter concluded, "that this body now in arms despise the idea of being instigated by British emissaries, which is so strenuously propagated by enemies of our liberties."

The letter went out over Pelham Captain Daniel Gray's name as chairman of the committee for stating the people's grievances.

In a similar letter to the *Republican Herald*, Montague's Thomas Grover, "a hearty well wisher to the real rights of the people," explained the people's concerns, hoping that their "brethren in the commonwealth who do not see with us as yet, shall find we shall be as peaceable as they are."[26]

Daniel Shays did not sign this letter, but that did not stop government men in their proclamations and merchants in their letters from continuing to call all the protestors Shaysites. It did not matter that the people's letters were signed by officers beside Shays, or that many men still signed their letters to the newspapers as Regulators. The long tradition of common people protecting their rights against unjust laws was reduced to the caricature of one charismatic man holding sway over deluded or drunken mobs of base men who believed they would place their man in the seat of power and claim rich men's wealth for themselves.

The swirling rumors and talk did not prevent Shays and his men from surrounding the Worcester County courthouse in the early morning cold on Monday, December 4, a day before court would open Tuesday morning.

Once again, a government force marched into the town to oppose them. Captain Joel Howe led a column of 170 Worcester militiamen into the courtyard beneath the commonwealth's flag.[27] But this time instead of simply taking up a position opposite Shays, Howe gave his men the order to fix bayonets and advance, and Shays and his men did not let Howe's men get too close before they withdrew.

The two bodies of men traded positions: Howe's militia occupied the courthouse, but Shays and his men kept the courtyard surrounded to turn away any judges, lawyers, or merchants who meant to take property from the people.[28]

The forces faced each other across the courtyard, and yet again Bowdoin's threats dissolved in the air as moment to moment the two sides held their positions and the cold wind blew the smoke from Worcester's chimneys over their heads. Howe never read the Riot Act aloud. His men never attempted to arrest Shays or the other leaders, or even to disperse them. The standoff dragged on through afternoon, and the protest drew farmers from Worcester and the neighboring towns. Soon there were more than a thousand men surrounding Howe's 170 men inside the courthouse.[29]

Still no one broke into homes or businesses, or warmed themselves by plundering houses for chairs and tables to set alight in the courtyard. Still no one warmed themselves by throwing stones or firing muskets.

The parties' positions had not changed by nightfall, when yet another snowstorm hushed the town and buried the streets in fresh blankets, reducing the tension between the two sides to a boring routine of waiting.[30]

The only disturbance came from unruly children, who called out warnings that horsemen were coming from Boston. Shays's sentries had taken shelter in the Hancock Arms Tavern, and they panicked to hear this alarm, then panicked anew when they discovered that their muskets were missing from the hall where they had stood them.[31] They rushed into the courtyard to form their lines without arms. They waited in agonized silence while their sentries studied the night, but they did not hear anyone coming.[32] Eventually the alarm subsided, and the men identified the mischievous children who had made off with their guns, then called out the false alarm.

The men on either side returned to their hours of uneasy expectation, but the night was troubled further when some of Shays's men began to vomit violently. They summoned a local doctor who increased their despair when he told them they had been poisoned. The men searched the tavern and found that someone had simply spilled snuff into the sugar they had mixed with their rum. It was only tobacco that turned their stomachs, but the men, far from home and in danger of battle, spent hours in nauseous dismay, afraid that their hosts might finally have turned against them.[33]

Still their ordeal was not over, but all night long, children continued to plague them will false alarms. The winter quiet was never ruptured by horsemen from Boston, but Shays's men slept on edge if they slept at all, praying through the long, cold winter night for an end to their nightmare.

Shays and his men rose from their pallets and floors stiff and irritable on the morning of Tuesday, December 5. But still the crimps in their spines and the exhaustion behind their eyes did not blur their consciences so much that they vented their anger in violence against Howe's men or the merchants who backed them.

Shays led his men back to the courthouse in orderly lines. The snow had stopped, but Captain Howe's men still occupied the building. Shays ordered his men to surround the court as before and to turn away any lawyers or merchants.

Again, farmers poured into Worcester to join Shays's lines, and soon there were more than a thousand farmers again, backing his 350 picked men.

From the courthouse, Howe's two hundred men did not dare to charge on their lines, and the merchants who could not collect their debts could not persuade Howe to start such a mismatched fight.

By mid-morning, Shays and Howe started negotiations. Shays petitioned for the release of prisoners and restoration of habeas corpus, and he asked for the judges to issue a blanket pardon for men who had protested at the courts.[34]

The commonwealth's leaders were still dead set against reconciliation, though, and neither the judges nor Howe had been authorized to settle the farmers' complaints, so none of their talks came to anything, and Shays and his men addressed their concerns in yet another petition they posted to Boston that afternoon.

They were not afraid of death or war, they said, or "the injuries of hunger, cold, nakedness and the infamous name of rebel, as under all these disadvantages they once before engaged and through the blessing of God came off victorious.

"To that God [your petitioners] now appeal,—conscious of the innocence of their intention—from a love of the people and horror of the thoughts of the cruelty and devastation of a civil war. For the prevention of so great an evil, your petitioners humbly pray for the love and candor of your excellency and honors in releasing our unfortunate and suffering friends."[35]

At the end of the day, with this fresh petition posted to Boston, the Worcester judges agreed to adjourn till the twenty-third of January. By that time, the General Court would have opened again in the second week of January, and everyone hoped they would have found a solution to the commonwealth's troubles by then.

Finally, the judges retreated from the tavern where they had negotiated this resolution, and Shays's men cheered again when he told them that yet another court had been adjourned without hearing suits against their property.

At dusk, Shays and his officers formed the men into lines again and marched away from the courtyard. They had taken another day from the government's calendars. They had not been tested by armed men from Boston. Captain Howe's militia had not challenged them in battle. Once again, no blood had been spilled. All of Governor Bowdoin's ominous rhetoric had blown over their protest like so much acrid wood smoke. Now the clear winter night and the regular sounds of their countryside, nestled in its snowy hills, were emblems of the people's patience and long-enduring strength. In orderly lines, they returned to the taverns and houses and barns where sympathetic residents of Worcester had lodged them these past few nights, and these homes too were emblems of the people's strong position and their deep support in their country.

Reforms were only six weeks away now. There was only one more court to close, in Springfield on December 26. Then, after months of impotent threats, Bowdoin and the General Court would convene the legislature in early January. Everyone prayed that they would finally acknowledge their errors and reform the taxes and currency policies that had driven the people into the courtyards.

Chapter Eight

Shoring Up Support

S HAYS AND HIS MEN STAYED IN WORCESTER on Wednesday night. On
Thursday morning, they marched the twelve miles back up into the
hills to their Rutland barracks.[1]

They could not stay in Rutland much longer though. The farmers there
had provisioned them out of their storerooms these past two weeks, but no
one's farms had produced such rich harvests that they could afford to feed
350 men indefinitely.

Shays refused to drain his countrymen's cellars any longer, so he sent
most of his men home.[2] He could not go back to Abigail and the children
though. He had allowed himself to take a position of trust among his people
and could not back down until he was certain that Bowdoin's horsemen
would not come for him as they had come for Shattuck. He kept a small
force together, thirty men who would protect him and help him organize
his region until the laws and the taxes that tortured them were stricken from
the books.[3]

In the nearly empty barracks, Shays and his men laid plans to ride
through the region, shoring up support for their cause by recruiting men
and supplies in case the governor did try to enforce his threats in the spring.[4]

The snow lay thick on the fields as Shays and his men rode south out of
Rutland at the end of the first week of December. With hemlock in their
hatbands, they churned the snow toward New Braintree and the Quaboag
River beyond that. In the winter light on the snowy fields, they recognized
the purple of every different time of day. Tears ran down their cheeks from

December's cold winds, and icicles grew in their beards as they rode past farms much like their own, where families were doing the same work they themselves hoped to return to. Every time they crested a hill and looked out over a patchwork of farms, they knew that they were condemned to the roads until their government heard their demands.[5]

As they made their way south through their region down long country lanes, Shays and his men were always dispatching messengers to sound the men in nearby towns for invitations. They measured the country's loyalties with their horses' reins, steering by their sense of where they might find families friendly enough to their cause and wealthy enough to offer them men and supplies, but not so wealthy that they would have taken the government's side, to send for their sheriffs, and try to have them captured in the road and sent to Boston.

They did not take the road to Brookfield, where Shays's father-in-law was one of the town's most prominent men, for Captain Daniel Gilbert had joined the Brookfield militia against the local Regulators.

Cold in their coats and heavy breeches and boots, Shays and his officers arrived at the taverns, meeting houses, and private homes where men they had known in the war welcomed them in. Men who had never met Captain Shays recognized him as one of the people. They could see signs of their work in his shoulders, in the brogue of his Scots-Irish customs, in his clothing of homespun linen and wool—even though an editorial in the *Worcester Centinel* reported that Shays had been seen "with a green leaf in his hair, lolling on two soft cushions. In his right hand, he held the life of the pious St. Augustin, and with his left hand he pointed to the passage: 'While the timid guide we have nought to fear.'"[6]

In the evenings, neighbors came to meetings at these houses, to see for themselves the men who were being called rebels and traitors for standing for justice. When the people had gathered and the roar of conversation peaked, someone tapped a glass with a spoon, and introduced Shays and his men, who dispelled the myths that there had been rioting mobs, violence, or murders. Beneath their countrymen's critical eyes, they personally disavowed any desire to rule in Bowdoin's place.

Patiently, they painted the picture of how things would go in their country if the people could not protect themselves should Bowdoin make a show of force in the spring. Everyone knew they would all lose their farms. It was not just the people's leaders who would be arrested and possibly hung as traitors, not just the men who protested. All the men who could not afford to pay the governor's taxes and court fees—in hard coin or in inflated prices for produce—would have to surrender their property to the courts. The country would be emptied out, and rich men would buy up their towns. They would all become refugees, packing their houses in carts and riding west into the wilderness—or else they would come under lordships again, as their parents had lived under the English.[7]

In meetings grim with consequence, Shays and his men answered each of the charges the newspapers had printed, and they answered their countrymen's objections that lawless protests were not the way to oppose a constitutional, republican government. They reminded the people of their long tradition, running back to England, of common people protecting their society as a whole by taking action when their leaders misused the law and ignored the people's welfare.[8] When they felt that the men had heard enough of their story and seen enough of the future that waited for them, they asked the farmers for help. They asked the men to keep themselves organized with officers and lines of communication. They begged them to keep their reckless men in check.

Lastly, they begged for material support. They said that they needed food for the men who had given up their winter's work to protect their countrymen's liberties. They asked for guns and ammunition so they could balance the government's forces musket for musket and never have to negotiate from weakness. Again, they promised not to use force and pointed to almost four months of peaceful protests. But they told their countrymen that bodies in the courtyards would not be enough. To keep the peace, they would need to show the government that the entire countryside was with them and that they were ready to counter force with force if need be. At the very least, they begged their hosts to keep their neighbors at home when the government called out their militias, to show solidarity with the people's peaceful protests.

When they finished making their requests, the farmers calculated what they could afford to give. In the government's eyes, it was treason to give Shays anything, but the men broke the silence and pledged what they could, because giving was what made them one people.

After these meetings, prominent men competed among themselves for the honor of hosting Shays and his officers, nurturing their opposition to government by taking them into their homes. In every house they entered, their arrival was a holiday, as they interrupted the farms' slow winter routines with their urgent campaign. In long discussions through late winter nights, they tallied the chances of winning reforms in January, and the danger of war in spring.

In one house after another, Shays and his officers witnessed their people's sufferings. They took stock of their debts and their thin resources for winter, and they estimated the quality of their indignation and their willingness to fight to protect themselves if the conflict came to blows.

But every morning, Shays and his men stifled any desire to stay and enter into the simple routines of honest work on the farms. They packed their things and got back on the road to make their requests for support in another town.

For hours on the roads along fields and snowed-over streams, Shays and his officers measured their preparations against each test they might face. With their breath dissolving in clouds of vapor, they guessed where Bowdoin might try to find men to send against them. They estimated the quality of any force he might raise, and they rated the quality of the men in each of the towns they had visited to estimate their chances if the crisis continued to escalate.

For three weeks of short days and long nights, they estimated what it would cost them if they had to fight in the end. They counted and recounted the numbers of men, the numbers of muskets, the numbers of barrels of flour and salt beef their neighbors had pledged, and estimated how much they would still need, if they were going to wage a ten-week campaign, for hundreds or thousands of men. They estimated how much more they would need for each additional month they might have to spend, drilling and demonstrating at the courts while they neglected their farms. They speculated what would happen if they could not get reforms through elections, but elites refused to alter the commonwealth's laws, or worse, suspended elections. Sometimes they grew disgusted with calculating how much their resistance had already cost them, and they tallied the costs of fleeing their country, and starting anew in Vermont or Ohio. They tried to muster dismissive laughter when an editorial in the *Massachusetts Centinel* punned on Shays's and Shattuck's names and listed an ad for a used "fallback shaise" with the "maker's name Sedition," which had last been seen "on the road to Pelham, the body then almost broken in pieces, and the head in a very shatter'd condition."[9]

Night after night, they met with their people and saw to their preparations. They could not do anything more than they were doing. They ranged as far south as Windham, Connecticut, south of Brookfield, where sympathetic farmers were suffering under Governor Samuel Huntington's austerity measures as well.[10] All through that country, regardless of what borders they crossed, the threat of government action hung over the people's winter labors like a sudden spring thaw that might rush through their farms and sweep away all their work if they failed to shore up their towns' defenses.

In the mid-December evenings, spring and the campaigning season were still months away. The cold was still building at night, the stars getting sharper and sharper in crystalline darkness. The country they rode through still waited for the real deep of winter to phrase its questions, to see how their harvests and months of preparations would answer.

Finally the earth swung through the solstice. Now the evenings would lengthen again, even by just a minute every day. There would start to be more and more light in the sky. The cold would keep getting deeper, and snowstorms would bury their fields from view, but in just a few weeks, the sun would start to fall on their shoulders with stronger warmth, and they would have to be ready when more snow melted each day than fell in each new storm.

With the solstice behind them, Shays and his officers circled back toward Springfield to collect the men who had returned to their homes while they had been recruiting. On Tuesday, December 26, they marched into Springfield with three hundred men to close the Court of Common Pleas there.[11] General Shepard did not defend the court. All of Bowdoin's threats and oppressive laws drifted over the courtyard like distant clouds. Nor did the Springfield sheriff read the Riot Act or threaten to enforce the government's laws. Shays's men simply surrounded the courthouse and turned away any lawyers and businessmen who had come to ask for the court's help collecting their debts.

In the note they submitted to the judges, Shays and Luke Day and Montague's Thomas Grover asked the "honorable judges of this court not to open said court at this time, nor do any kind of business whatsoever, but all kind of business to remain as though no such court had been appointed."[12]

The Springfield judges conceded the day, as they had done in September. They could not say that they agreed with the people's position, so they issued a statement of abhorrence, like Ethan Allen had done.

In his official report to Governor Bowdoin in Boston, the Springfield sheriff claimed he was surprised when three hundred Regulators poured down from the snowy hills to keep the court from opening.[13] He could not admit that he had known they were coming, since he himself was charged with enforcing the Riot Act and apprehending the leaders. Nor could he say that he sympathized with their cause, since Bowdoin had made it a crime to speak against government, so he attributed his surprise to the people's stealth and cunning.[14] This report of the people's armed, disciplined, and now stealthy resistance would not reassure Bowdoin when it reached Boston.

After they had closed the court, Daniel Shays, Luke Day, and Thomas Grover gathered their officers together to decide what they should do next. Some of them argued that they should return to their homes and wait two weeks until the General Court reconvened. They said that they had effectively won, that the conflict was over, for the roads would not be passable till after the election. The men who wanted to resume their winter's work promised to keep themselves ready to muster at a moment's notice.

Others refused to believe that a man like James Bowdoin would let himself be humiliated by their humble force. He and his advisers still stood to lose huge sums of their own money if they abandoned their program of taxes and austerity policies. They said that Bowdoin would fear for his commonwealth's stability if foreign creditors saw the lowly farmers' protests as a sign of his government's powerlessness.

They argued that they should keep their force together until the governor's agents had traveled the length of the state distributing printed proclamations that pardoned the protestors and freed the people from their economic ordeal.

In the conference of officers, some men argued that if they were already subject to arrest, they might as well stay in Springfield. Again they suggested occupying the Continental army's arsenal grounds, which still sat undefended at the top of the hill, overlooking the town. They should arm themselves with the government's muskets and draw down the government's stockpiles of flour and salt beef instead of returning to Pelham or Rutland to chew through their neighbors' supplies. They felt they were entitled to the federal stores since they had already sacrificed their own to represent law.

Full of their power, they puffed themselves up on their triumph, but Shays and the other leaders would not allow their men to seize the federal arsenal. They had ignored the stockpiled weapons for months, but so had General Shepard refused to use those guns against them.[15] Now they flatly declined to fulfill the governor's fear that they were arming themselves and preparing to wage a war against the commonwealth, so they turned their backs on the strategic advantage they might have gained by controlling the stockpiles of gunpowder and weapons.

Still, Shays agreed that they should not back down yet either, so he said that he would take his three hundred picked men back to Rutland to keep their force together for the two weeks before the General Court would finally meet and issue reforms.

When this meeting ended, Day and Grover said that they would accept the judges' invitation to dine, but Shays said that he would set out toward Rutland that evening.[16]

Before he left, he told his men that he did not expect he would need to call them out again for another such occasion.[17] Soon, he promised, they would be able to go back to their homes and work their land in teams together and salvage what they could of their winter's work.

Shays returned to Rutland with his men before the new year. Without any further courts to close or provocations from Boston, the peace of the season finally lay thick on the fields. Smoke drifted up from chimneys in the hollows and lay across snowy meadows. The winter days drifted over them at the slow pace of cows ambling out to the snowy pasture, to scratch through the snow to the frozen grasses, then wallowing through the snow, back to the barns and their hay at dusk.

In the deepening cold of early January, Shays and his men could almost adjust themselves to the slow pace of their country again. With the General Court only two weeks away from reconvening, they could almost sleep through the nights.

They had kept the peace. In months of threats and fiery rhetoric in the face of bald injustice, they had only suffered three men to be arrested in the whole region from Concord west to the Berkshires. The Regulators had given their people the time they needed to bring in their crops and now to keep them through the first months of winter. They had made their case to the people in the courtyards, and even the commonwealth's militias and elected officials had allowed them to protect their liberties without a fight.

This was the freedom they had fought for in the war. For four months, they had shown the merchants in Boston and all the world that America's hardscrabble farmers were capable of representing justice in their own region without interference from a corrupt government in Boston.

Back in Rutland, Shays and his officers still drilled their men in the snow-covered green by the barracks. When they were not meeting with local farmers to gather supplies, they were busy keeping up correspondence with men in the towns that had marched with them and also with men in the towns where they had gone recruiting.

From time to time, messengers brought copies of the petitions the towns had still been posting to Boston all this time, begging for pardons and for reforms. By dozens and scores, the towns continued to tell the government that the Regulators were not lowly rabble but "a large number of the calm, steady and sensible yeomanry, men of good principals and large property," who feared that they might be brought to a state of slavery by the common-wealth's laws.[18]

Other towns warned that it would not be fitting to settle these matters "by fire and sword," and suggested that it would be better to suffer a little by making reforms than that a civil war should take place.[19]

In this first week of January, in one of his trips to visit with local farmers, Shays met his former general, Rufus Putnam, in the road.[20] Putnam had grown up in Rutland and now lived in a fine house that had been confiscated from a Loyalist family.[21]

Putnam had commanded Shays's regiment at the battles of Saratoga and Stony Point, and he was not unfamiliar with the soldiers' frustrations, for the government had failed to pay him along with the others. At the end of the French and Indian War, he had gone so far as to renounce soldiering when the army withheld his pay and extended his enlistment against his will.[22] He had joined up again to fight the British, but near the end of the war, he joined a group of fellow officers who had nearly mutinied over their lack of pay. They petitioned the state to pay them in grants of western land if the state could not give them money.[23]

The years since the war had nevertheless been good to Putnam, for he had come through with funds to invest. While the people of Massachusetts had been organizing conventions and begging for reforms, Putnam had been meeting with other retired officers to establish the Ohio Company of Associates, who had arranged for Congress to sell them a million acres of land in the western territories.[24] They were preparing to build towns at their own expense, letting settlers join them at bargain prices, so they could profit when each successive wave of settlers paid higher prices for land that became more valuable with each family's improvements.

Putnam and his associates had friends in the federal Congress in Philadelphia who were even now preparing to pass the Northwest Ordinance in the spring. They were going to define a path to statehood for new territories so farmers in the towns they settled would not be troubled by conflicts between the states where new towns were chartered and the distant territories where those new towns put down their roots.[25]

When Daniel Shays met Rufus Putnam in the road in the first week of January, Putnam was preparing to take settlers west to land he had surveyed before the war, at the junction of the Ohio and Muskingum Rivers.[26] The crisis of debts and taxes had actually been an opportunity for Putnam. He had recruited men like Shays with military training who might be glad to escape from the crushing taxes and economic turmoil in Massachusetts.[27] They would represent law in a country of their own creation, far from the nobles who had already made their fortunes developing towns and expanding their businesses along the coast.[28]

Shays and Putnam met in the road in the low-slanted, cold light of early January. Shays asked Putnam if he knew whether his petition had been forwarded to the governor. When Putnam told him that it had not, but that it did not have any chance of success, Shays said that in the absence of a pardon, he "must fight it out."[29]

Putnam told his former subordinate that if he continued to stand against Bowdoin, he would have to flee the country or else be hung. Shays said he would not run.

Putnam asked why and recalled that Shays had once admitted that the people had been wrong to take arms.

Shays did not disavow his role, but he said that his only motive for taking command at Springfield in September had been to prevent the shedding of blood.

He said that it certainly would have been shed had he not stepped in.

He said that he could hardly consider his actions a crime. He said that it seemed to him that the government was indebted to him for his service.

Putnam pressed to know why Shays had persisted in arms, after he knew that the Riot Act had forbidden men gathering, but Shays said simply that he did not want to be taken.

Putnam asked how Shays came to write the letter requesting certain towns to choose officers and arm their men with guns and ammunition, and Shays said that he never did.

"It was a cursed falsehood," he said. "Somebody else, who I don't know, put my name to the copy and sent it to the Governor and the Court."

He said he had never had half as much to do with the movement as Putnam might think. He explained that he and his men had not heard the governor's offer of pardons which was only five days old when they had closed the Worcester court on the twenty-first.

He did concede that it might have been better for him if he had quit, but still he could not see why stopping the Worcester court was such a crime that if he might have been excused before, now he should not be pardoned.

Putnam could not answer. He only circled back to his one grudging question: what would Shays do if he could not obtain a pardon?

Shays replied he would collect all the force he could and fight it out.

"And I swear so would you, or anybody else," he said, "instead of being hanged."[30]

Putnam told Shays he could not see how he would escape since he was the head of the people's force, but Shays did not agree he was the head. He flatly denied he was.

Putnam suggested that Shays set off for Boston immediately to beg for Bowdoin's pardon, but Shays said that the risk was too great.

Putnam offered to hang beside him if Bowdoin betrayed him and denied him a pardon, but Shays answered that he would not have his general hung.

The two men regarded each other in the silence of irreconcilable differences before Shays returned to his men in the Rutland barracks and Putnam to his plans for Ohio.[31]

Chapter Nine

"Murder, Murder"

FOUR DAYS AFTER DANIEL SHAYS and Rufus Putnam spoke in the road, legislators gaveled the General Court back into session in Boston.

Shays and his people had been waiting to hear that the governor had found a way to pardon them, but the proclamation Bowdoin printed and sent to the towns only condemned them again. The governor boldly stated that the "object of the insurgents is to annihilate our present happy constitution." He said that if they succeeded, it would be "the result of force undirected by any moral principle; it must finally terminate in despotism." He accused the farmers of profaning the sacred Revolution with their demonstrations, and he asked his countrymen whether "the goodly fabric of freedom which cost us so much blood and treasure [was] so soon to be thrown into ruin," or whether it was to "stand but just long enough to flatter the tyrants of the earth in their daring maxim that mankind is not born to be free."[1] In *Worcester Magazine*, John Billings of Amherst replied that "we are a republic. Government rests upon the shoulders of the people. The staff of the government is in the hands of the people."[2]

Two weeks before, Shays had been optimistic enough to have told his men that they should not have to close any further courts, but if the men had told their wives that they would be home soon, they choked on their words now. For Bowdoin's condemnations only prefaced more indictments, the first since September's warrants for Adam Wheeler and Henry and Abraham Gale and the eight other men in Worcester.

In his proclamation, Bowdoin vowed to arrest the ringleaders of what he called an insurgency. He singled out each of the officers. From Charlemont, in the foothills of the Berkshires northwest of Springfield, he named Samuel Hill an enemy of the commonwealth. From Colrain, a Scots-Irish town on Vermont's southern border, he named Captain Matthew Clark. From the hill town of Worthington, far from the river, he named Samuel Morse for arrest, and from neighboring Chesterfield, Captain Aaron Jewett.

From Conway, in the high fields above the steep streams running down to the Connecticut River, he named Captain Abel Dinsmore. From farther south, close to the floodplain in Whately, he named Captain John Brown. From Greenfield just north of the Deerfield River's junction with the Connecticut, where men and women in their eighties remembered the Indians burning the town and marching its inhabitants to Montréal through the snow, he called Captain Obed Foot a rebel for leading his people.[3]

From south of there, across the river in Montague, he named for arrest Captain Thomas Grover, who had dined with the judges in Springfield just two weeks ago. From Shutesbury in the hills northeast of Amherst, he named Captain John Powers. From Pelham, he named Daniel Shays, and from Greenwich on the Swift River's eastern branch, he called Joseph Hines to answer to the state for the sin of rebellion.

From Amherst on its plateau he called for Captain Joel Billings to answer for treason, and from Brimfield, Asa Fisk. From farther south of there, on the Connecticut border, he named Longmeadow's Alpheus Colton, and from farther west, toward the mountains again, from West Springfield, Luke Day. Finally, completing the ring of the people's leaders, he named Captain Gad Sackett of Westfield a rebel against law and order.[4]

All of these men were prominent in their towns. Eleven of them were respected veterans, if not officers from the war. But now the people of Massachusetts read their leaders' names in the proclamation and had to decide how far they would be willing to go to protect them if hundreds of deputies came for them as they had come for Shattuck and Page.

At any time in the last four months—all through summer and fall into winter, the farmers of Massachusetts might still have laughed at Bowdoin's indictments, since he still had not managed to demonstrate his authority anywhere farther than twenty miles west of Boston. But now messengers whipped their horses through January snow from Boston to Framingham, to Worcester, then up the hills to find Shays and his men in the Rutland barracks to tell them that Bowdoin was not waiting for spring to send an army.

Fresh riders threw on their coats and launched into the snow, spurring their foaming horses over snow-sloppy roads, letting the whole country know that the government was preparing to force the courts open and arrest the people's leaders.

Ringing their towns' bells, blowing the conches that normally summoned men to house fires or alarms, they gathered their neighbors and told them that 129 Boston elites—who could not find funds to relieve the people's embarrassments when English credit contracted—had pledged £6,000 to recruit and outfit an army of forty-four hundred Boston merchants and clerks, servants and laborers, sailors and longshoremen.[5] Rich men were donating hundreds of pounds to finance the force that would lead to full payment of notes worth thousands of pounds.[6]

The General Court was not even in session. The legislature had not approved these loans or passed resolutions requesting supplies for a state-sanctioned expedition.[7] Even the people's town meetings were more legitimate and constitutional than this army. But Bowdoin himself was the commonwealth, and whatever he did, he could call it the law. After months of humiliating and impotent waffling, he had taken rich investors' money in private and he had given them receipts, promising to pay them back with money from taxes, plus interest at the customary rate.[8]

With the funds he collected, Bowdoin contracted with wealthy friends to supply his expedition with tents and supplies, with muskets and gunpowder, rum, and other provisions. He sent notices to each loyal town, asking for a contribution of soldiers, and he paid recruiters to scour Boston neighborhoods for able men who would take £2 pay and a daily half pint of rum for a month of cold campaigning to put down what he was calling a rebellion. (He would not, however, take Blacks, even though Prince Hall, the head of Boston's African Masons, offered to bring seven hundred African-American soldiers.)[9] To the poor laborers who agreed to march the length of Massachusetts in January, Bowdoin's recruiters would provide food, guns, and immunity from prosecution if they should injure or kill the farmers they would be marching west to subdue.

In their Rutland barracks, Shays and his men learned that Bowdoin's army would be commanded by General Benjamin Lincoln, who had defended the city of Charleston, South Carolina, from the very same redcoats Shays and the men of the 5th Massachusetts Regiment had humiliated at Stony Point in October 1779.[10] General Henry Clinton had loaded those soldiers onto ships and sailed them south for the winter, and in March 1780, they had laid siege to the port of Charleston. When Lincoln surrendered in May, the five thousand men he commanded were taken captive, to starve and die on British prison ships. Lincoln was paroled and exchanged for a captured major general.[11]

Lincoln's defeat was redeemed a year later, at Yorktown, when General Washington gave him the honor of taking Cornwallis's sword when Cornwallis sent his second in command to offer it in surrender.[12] Now, though, in the first weeks of January, Lincoln was one of the leaders of the elite officers' group, the Society of the Cincinnati, and he was recruiting officers, collecting provisions, and drilling his men in order to impose Governor Bowdoin's idea of law and order, not to redeem the people's losses.[13]

In the Rutland barracks where Shays convened a meeting of his officers to consider what they should do, the blazing hearths could not chase the sickening chill of their vulnerability. The men who had refused to indulge in violence at every step now shook their heads and cursed for having been backed into this corner. If they fought now, they could die. If they refused to fight, or fought and lost, Lincoln's army of servants and clerks would flood into their region. The courts would be protected by lines of men armed with muskets and cannon. The courts' bailiffs would ride to their people's farms with armed escorts to seize their livestock, if they did not force them off their land entirely. Then the hunt for the people's leaders would begin. Lincoln's army would come to their towns and ransack their houses, and who could say what violence the eastern men might do to their wives and children.

If they fled, they would be abandoning their farms, losing all their improvements in addition to all the wealth they had in their neighbors' teamwork. They would be forced to start over as landless laborers, refugees new to any country they tried to settle in.

In the same barracks where the men had insisted on rushing into the night to avenge Job Shattuck's blood six weeks ago, Shays and his officers finally acknowledged that they could not afford the luxury of innocence any longer. The only way to protect themselves and their land was to occupy the arsenal in Springfield, where the federal government stockpiled weapons and stores. If they were well armed—even if they did nothing more than keep General Lincoln from using those weapons against them—they might be able to negotiate for peace with Bowdoin's army on equal terms.

If Lincoln thought his only hope for dispersing the protesting farmers was to face them in battle with untested men, he might prefer to end the standoff peacefully, regardless of what he had been ordered to do in Boston. If Shays and his men held the arsenal grounds, Lincoln would have to camp his city men in the cold or else quarter them in unwilling Springfield houses, which would help turn the people against them.

If they needed to fight—perhaps they could prevail in a fight against untrained men, and so summon federal intervention. Perhaps they would flee before they were backed into that final corner, where freedom would have to be purchased in their blood and their countrymen's.

The bluff of seizing the arsenal was their last chance, short of forming an actual army, and preparing to march into battle.

Shays and his officers were not in any hurry, though, to reinforce Bowdoin's panic by taking the arsenal. With their grim options laid out before them, they still refused to take the aggressive stance of setting out for Springfield before they learned that Lincoln's army had departed from Boston, to start his men on the ninety mile march from Boston to Springfield on snowy roads.

Shays and his officers devised a plan that was so simple it could be drawn in the snow with a stick, and they dispatched riders into the cold with letters to each of their officers in the towns. When the time came, they would make a three-pronged approach to the arsenal, with forces approaching from east, west, and north, to overwhelm any defenses General Shepard might gather.[14]

West through Hampshire County, east as far as Worcester, their riders summoned all the sympathetic men from the hill towns, asking them to gather in Pelham on January 19, well armed and equipped, with ten days' provisions. From there they would be poised to march south to Ludlow, and approach the Springfield arsenal from the east.

To the towns in Connecticut and in the western hill towns, their riders directed men to gather in West Springfield, where Captain Luke Day would mass men on the arsenal's western flank. In the towns along the river, their riders instructed men to collect in Chicopee, where Eli Parsons would cut off the arsenal's northern approach, and from there to "hold themselves in readiness to march at a moment's warning."[15]

In their dispatches, Shays and his officers made it clear that they were still only getting into position around the arsenal. They would gather on January 19, but they would not move on the grounds till the government's army was close enough to pose an immediate danger. They needed to show their countrymen that they were not seizing arms to start a war against their government. They were only defending themselves against Bowdoin's private army.

These instructions did not go out above Shays's name alone. His signature was accompanied by those of Amherst's Sylvanus Billings and Shutesbury's John Powers, as well as Williamsburg's Perez Bardwell, who put their names forward to share responsibility with Shays.[16]

The Regulators' instructions set the whole countryside on edge. In the brutal cold of Massachusetts winter—under thin clouds that sucked the warmth from the slant light that striped their floorboards—men in the towns of Hampshire County had to say what they would do: would they risk their lives and liberties to defend their land, or would they accommodate themselves to Bowdoin's authority and to his taxes?[17]

In the week that followed Bowdoin's proclamation, hundreds of men pledged to join Shays, Day, and Parsons at the meeting places. They gathered provisions and made arrangements for the work that would need to be done in their absence and for the contingencies that might occur if they were captured or had to stay away from home for long weeks of campaigning.

When all their plans were in place, men shouldered their muskets and clubs and set out to meet their townsmen. With their wives and mothers' cornbread in their packs—with fish they themselves had caught and salted in summer, with strips of beef and venison they had butchered and smoked, with beans they had planted and picked with their own hands—the men who marched to Pelham were not even an army. They were the land itself, armed against the invasion of debts written down in foreign ledgers.

They were gathering to resist an actual army, though, hired by private men who had loaned the commonwealth money and now expected to be paid back—if not in hard coin then in land they could get at cheap prices, then rent or sell to farmers, or to speculators for coin, once the crisis had passed.

On January 17 and 18, men from every corner of Hampshire County arrived at their towns' taverns and meeting houses. They filled the rooms with their packs and their weapons, their bulky coats and gloves.

Eventually their militias' leaders stopped waiting to see who else was coming and which towns had failed to send the men they had promised. They pulled their men away from their fires and called them out into the cold where they took their men under command. They formed them into lines and gave them orders to raise their flags, then to start their fifes and drums, then to set out to Pelham, Chicopee, or West Springfield.

In dozens and scores, from towns all through the commonwealth, men wallowed over the same miles they had covered easily in September, when summer had baked the roads to stony ruts. If they became impatient with the snow that sapped their momentum at every step, the danger of an army marching into their region kept their knees grinding forward. Onward they stumbled, and in between their marching songs they cursed the governor and the merchant elites and the influential men who had refused to help them.

Down from their hills, in from their forests, they rode and walked alongside the blanketed hayfields and cornfields and wheat fields they had worked in teams all summer. For long hours of marching they kept stride with their drums, and at the end of the day, they slept in bunches in sympathetic farmers' houses and barns. In the mornings they ate together and packed their things before they stepped out into the same yellow-gray morning light that had always shone on their mid-January fields, though now their bayonets and guns glinted bright with the threat of war.

From Rutland, Daniel Shays and his men marched to Pelham as well, retracing their steps from November, down and up and down again over the miles. When they finally descended from Hines's Tavern in Prescott toward Conkey's at the river, they passed the road to Shays's hollow, where Abigail and the children could hear their drums. They crossed the frozen river and climbed the long hill to the meeting house, where they warmed themselves at the hearth as they set up their headquarters.

Down the long ridges from farther hill towns—from Montague through Shutesbury, and up from towns as far east as Worcester, or west up the hill from Amherst—their countrymen arrived in platoons, their faces red with cold, their mustaches snotted, stamping feet impatient for fire, throats burning for rum to spread the glow of warmth through their bellies back to their fingers.

From the meeting house on West Hill, Shays and his men greeted each town's contingent and still watched the road like anxious wedding guests, searching the farthest turns to see who else would ride up to join them.

When the meeting house was full, Shays and his officers dispatched the men to the taverns on both sides of the Swift River valley, to the houses and barns that would quarter them out of the cold. When the houses and sheds and barns of Pelham were full, men set up tents in the snow along the edge of the meeting house green, where Shays and the other militia leaders had drilled them in September. They dug their shallow fire pits and huddled over their fires, blowing on coals to make them flare up and catch so they could rub the warmth into their hands.

From their headquarters at the meeting house, Shays and his officers were occupied day and night with billeting and provisioning men and coordinating with leaders in West Springfield and Chicopee. Messengers were constantly arriving up the hill, with reports from Luke Day or Eli Parsons or officers in the other hill towns, so the roads to Pelham resembled a harbor, with messengers' coattails flapping like canvas as they wheeled in, delivered their cargo of news, then rode off again with their leather bags' bellies bulging with further instructions.

By the end of the day on Thursday the eighteenth of January, the towns of Pelham, Chicopee, and West Springfield were full of men, horses, and carts. Local farmers who could not afford their taxes brought sleds full of provisions, as if the families of Hampshire County were hosting a huge, dreadful banquet, pouring out all the wealth of their harvests as offerings to the fate that threatened their independence. The people's numbers grew and grew, but Shays and his officers still refused to take the offensive by marching to Springfield to occupy the arsenal's barracks and seize the stores of weapons and provisions. Until the government's army was so close by that everyone in the country would see that they were marching in self-defense, they would stay where they were.

By the end of the day on Friday the nineteenth, Pelham was bursting with twelve hundred men. Luke Day and his neighbors were hosting six hundred men in West Springfield, and Eli Parsons's townsmen were finding food and beds for four hundred in Chicopee.

If Shays and his officers hoped to convene larger numbers, their combined force of twenty-two hundred men was all the army their towns could afford to field to defend their rights against the forty-four hundred men Lincoln was said to be leading.[18]

The government men must have learned of their plans, for now Shays's officers heard from Springfield that General Shepard had gathered nine hundred men and occupied the arsenal grounds to keep the farmers from seizing it for themselves. Shepard was not authorized to take control of the federal stores—any more than Bowdoin had been authorized to raise and equip an army—but like the governor, Shepard could argue that his action had been necessary for the commonwealth's safety, and the action could be made legal retroactively.[19]

In the Pelham meeting house, this news forced Shays and his officers to reevaluate their plans. For weeks, the arsenal buildings had stood undefended on the hill overlooking Springfield and the frozen Connecticut River.

Now they could no longer simply march up and enter the grounds unopposed, as they had done in Rutland. Now they were going to have to drive one army out of the arsenal before they could think about confronting the other army Lincoln was bringing.

No one could say whether Shepard was likely to fight them. When Shays had closed the Springfield court in September, Shepard had kept his men in line and allowed the farmers to make their dignified protest. At the end of the day, he had withdrawn his men to the arsenal while Shays's farmers enjoyed the symbolic victory of occupying the courthouse.

With an army on its way west now, no one could say whether Shepard would dare order his men to fire on them if they marched up and told him to leave. They hoped that the three-pronged approach of seasoned veterans—Shays's from the east, Day's from the west, and Parsons's from the north—would compel Shepard to march his outnumbered and inexperienced force south away from the grounds.

Shays and his officers kept their men in Pelham, drilling them to keep them busy and disciplined and restrained, but the *Massachusetts Centinel* inflamed tensions throughout the region by printing an inflammatory letter from someone who claimed to have visited Shays's house in Pelham, describing it as a "stye" that looked more like "a den for brutes than a habitation of men."[20] This report quoted Regulators who claimed they were raising an army of ten thousand men who would "march directly to Boston . . . and destroy the nest of devils who by their influence make the courts enact what they please."[21]

Another letter claimed that the people were planning to overthrow the merchants' unjust constitution—that they were going to "plunder the city, burn it and lay the town of Boston in ashes."[22] This letter was not signed with the name of the man who wrote it. It was signed with Daniel Shays's name, the name Shays himself had handed to his people when he accepted his townsmen's invitation to lead. This had always been one of the dangers— that men would make all kinds of claims over his name—but it was too late to take his name back now.

Shays himself only told his fellow Regulators that he was sorry he had ever engaged in the scrape.[23] His friends recorded him saying that he had taken charge "against his inclinations" but that "importunity was used which he could not withstand."[24] He said he "knew no more what government to set up, than . . . the dimensions of eternity." He said that "he had put his hand to the plough and could not now look back."[25] They could not fight it out. The men with muskets had only three or four rounds of ammunition, and only one in ten had a bayonet, but they were going to show their colors and see if a show of force would command enough respect to compel negotiations for reforms.[26]

So Shays let the newspapers say what they would and returned to the business of organizing the movements of more than two thousand men in three camps within thirty-five miles of Springfield, making sure they were ready to meet Lincoln's army when it arrived.

Finally, at the end of the day on Friday, January 19, Shays and his officers learned that Lincoln's army had set out from Boston in a snowstorm.[27]

Men who kept track of the sun's and moon's movements told their neighbors that the moon had compounded the storm by eclipsing the sun on that day.[28] The eclipse had ended before the people of Massachusetts could see the spooky, unnatural shadow sliding over their hills, but their almanacs told them that the disorder in their commonwealth's affairs was echoed in the heavens.

Even with Lincoln's army on its way west, Shays and his men did not move from Pelham. They waited, tense and tired, cold with apprehension, impatient to act and anxious about the battles they might have to fight with Shepard or with Lincoln.

They still did not move on Saturday, when they heard that Lincoln's army of two thousand men from Boston had marched into Worcester. They stayed where they were through Sunday the twenty-first, waiting on edge to hear whether Lincoln was really intent on marching the sixty remaining miles through the cold to confront them in Springfield.

They waited as well for any indication that Shepard's nine hundred men were preparing to venture out from the arsenal barracks to rout Eli Parsons's men out of Chicopee or Day's men out of West Springfield. But each day the sun set, and Shepard's and Parsons's and Day's men stayed where they were.

Shays and his officers did not order their men to prepare to march until Tuesday the twenty-third, when they heard from Worcester that Lincoln's two thousand men, with an additional six hundred men from Worcester, had forced the Worcester court open.[29]

With snow on the roads, Lincoln's army was four days from Springfield, but now his columns were approaching by the hour. Shays and his men were two days away themselves. It was time. They would have to defend themselves. They could not care any longer whether their countrymen might accuse them of treason or insurrection. Let them say they were starting a civil war. They had to defend their farms or else submit to martial law and watch the army arrest their leaders, let the courts seize their farms.

That afternoon, Shays and his officers sent word through their camps, to the leaders of each town's militia, to pack their supplies and gather at the meeting house ready to march in the morning. They were finally going to Springfield, to see whether they would be forced to fight or whether Generals Shepard and Lincoln would let them settle their differences without bloodshed.

On the icy morning of January 24, Shays and his officers met their men at the Pelham meeting house. From all the houses and barns around Pelham, the Hampshire County militias marched in, each band beneath their flag. They displayed their discipline even here, obeying their officers' terse commands with uniform obedience until the moment their officers released them and they would mill about with the others in the cold.

Many of the region's families had come to see the men off. A huge crowd filled the meeting house benches, upstairs and down. The stone fireplace was constantly losing its heat as men and women tramped in and out of the doors, tracking in snow and bringing the cold in their coats.

Apprehension was thick in the air, for no one could say what they would find in Springfield. Some found reasons for optimism in the close-knit circles of western Massachusetts society. Plenty of men knew General Shepard personally. Many of their farmers had fathers, sons, and brothers inside the arsenal with him, including Shays's own father-in-law, Captain Daniel Gilbert, as well as Shays's brother and also Francis Stone's brother Jonathan.[30] No one expected kinsmen to fire on kinsmen.

Still, an army was coming to enforce the governor's warrants, and it was hard to know whether the eastern men would feel any solidarity with their suffering countrymen when their officers ordered them to fix bayonets or load muskets.

From the meeting house where their twelve hundred men had gathered, Shays and his officers sent word to Day in West Springfield and to Parsons in Chicopee to have their men ready to act together, and they appointed the time and day for their approach.

The threat of battle loomed over their preparations for departure. In the crowd that had gathered, men promised their wives and children that they would come home safe and return to their work, but as the moment of departure came closer, their words wavered in the air. No one could be certain what would be true at the end of the day the day after tomorrow, when they would have arrived in Springfield, or what would be true in another two or three days, after Lincoln arrived. General Shepard was waiting to greet them in Springfield in buildings stocked with muskets and cannon, ammunition, and gunpowder. Lincoln's men were sledding cannon in their direction even now.

In the nervous groups, men and their wives looked to the veterans of the wars for their predictions, but the Revolution itself had shattered all precedents, so the men turned their histories over in conversation, testing their memories back to the English civil war, recalling each of the disturbances that had happened in living memory to see if they could find a pattern, but their guesses faltered as men awaited the events that would confirm their fate one way or another.

On the other side of two days' cold marching, some kind of confrontation waited like a wilderness no one had seen yet. Until they had actually set up their beds in the arsenal barracks, no one would be able to say for sure whether the last five months' peaceful victories really confirmed the liberties they had won in the war. Bowdoin's army might still banish their independence and establish tyranny and force as the laws of the land again, and all their meetings and protests could have come to nothing.

Finally, Shays and his officers put an end to the men's debates and predictions. It was time to go. Officers routed the men out of the meeting house pews, upstairs and down.

With apprehension thick and sickening in the air, men mustered outside in the snowy green. Shays and his officers formed them into one long column of twelve hundred men, almost twice as many men as had gathered in Pelham in September.

In lines eight abreast, they waited, their breath steaming into the cold. Town by town, beneath their flags, they shivered and stamped, awaiting the order to march.

On the white horse that distinguished him among the other officers, Daniel Shays inspected his men in their army uniforms and in their homemade coats of every color and cut. These men would be an army soon enough, armed with regular guns, housed in regular barracks, sobered by the danger of a hostile army approaching.

When the last of his officers signaled that they were ready, Shays told them what he and his officers had said in a letter they published in the *Northampton Gazette*.

He said that the governor and his adherents were resolved to support the courts by the point of the sword, to "crush the people's power at one bold stroke and render them incapable of opposing the cruel power, Tyranny." He said they would not allow themselves to be ruined by "unconditional submission" or subjected to the governor's "infamous punishment." Shays said that they had even offered to let the government open its court in Springfield, provided that Bowdoin "withhold his troops from marching"— but since Lincoln's army was on its way, they would have to go meet it.[31]

They stood there together, cold in their coats, and stared off down the road, at the long miles to Ludlow, trying to see the danger that waited for them in Springfield.

This moment of their departure might be the last daring step they would have to take in defense of their righteous cause. It might be the start of years of arrests and seizures of land. The people might have to rally support from farmers in other states, to fight a new war and free themselves again, this time from their own nobles.

They would not know anything till they had heard Lincoln's drums, confronted his guns in the snow, and witnessed whatever outcome fate had in store.

Shays gave the order to start. The fifes and drums snapped to life, and the column of twelve hundred men began to move. For a few moments as they marched away down the hill, some of the men could still see their wives and children over their shoulders, waving from the snowy green till they disappeared behind the bare trees. It was not long till the families were darting out of the biting cold back to the meeting house hearth, and soon enough, the men were alone with the rhythm of their fifes and drums, with long rolling hills and the vast sky with its hawks and crows, accompanying them through the long miles south to Ludlow.

Some of the men had marched out of Pelham with Deacon John Thompson in August. More had marched this same route with Shays in September. Now the whole country was pouring its men into the Connecticut River valley. Whatever the men expected to happen, whatever they feared, they stayed in the ranks and put one foot in front of the other, in time with the marching songs, to the sound of the other men's boots. For men at the front and sides of the column, the landscape revealed itself, one turn, one crest at a time. The fields and woodlots, the houses and barns spread out before them, the fields white and purple with shadows, the woods brown-gray and green, the hills in the distance fading to leaden blue translucency under low, yellow-white clouds on the cold horizon.

To men in the middle of the column, the march was a tedious jostling, hemmed in by other men's coats and the smell of their damp wool and the mutter of their curses against the slippery snow and the biting cold and the governor and the elites. For men in the rear, every crest revealed a living column snaking past houses and snowy fields ahead of them, with muskets and bayonets glinting in the sun, and families at the windows of the houses, watching them pass with quiet concern or loud cheers.

Step by step, Shays and his men passed through the farmland between Pelham and Belchertown and Three Rivers. The men knew all too well that up close, the farms themselves consisted of dirty barnyards and bawling cattle, of endless work and constant debts and shortages. They knew by heart their mothers', aunts', and wives' complaints about this life, and they shared their impatience to leave for the comforts in a town or longed for the freedom and independence of life on a farther frontier. But still, from the road, the farmhouses dotting the hills, the fields and woodlots, the snaking streams, the smoke rising from the hollows showed them the life of their people—a life in common that justified all kinds of sacrifices.

Late in the afternoon, the four-day-old crescent moon emerged in the blue sky, then edged toward the horizon, and finally, as the sun began to set, their front lines emerged from the open fields and entered the town of Ludlow. Families came out to the road to steer them toward the houses and barns, the churches and taverns, where they could come in from the cold. They had stoked the fires to warm their icy fingers and dry their boots, and they had laid out as much food and drink as they could afford.

That evening, Shays and his officers posted sentries against the chance that Lincoln might send an advance guard to arrest them here while they slept, but the night passed without any sign of Lincoln's soldiers. Still Shays's sentries kept their own men inside their camps, and no one ventured out into the night to pillage wealthy farmers' houses or break into merchants' shops or even just to protest injustice by throwing stones through their windows.

When they woke on Thursday, the twenty-fifth, though, they heard from West Springfield that Luke Day's men had not shown the same restraint. They had broken into warehouses and commandeered four thousand bushels of grain in addition to barrels of beef and pork.[32] They had also taken merchants hostage in case the government captured their men and they would have to redeem them by trading captives.

The act was sure to turn their countrymen against them, but the morning's messengers also brought news that a troop of Berkshire men had isolated General Shepard by seizing the bridge north of Springfield.[33] They reported that Shepard's men were low on provisions and desperate for reinforcements. The word from inside the arsenal was that the general had been paying the men's salaries himself, in the absence of government funding.

Bolstered by this news, Shays and his twelve hundred men packed their bedding expecting to sleep in the arsenal barracks the next time they laid their heads down.

The sun climbed the sky on Thursday morning, and Shays and his men did not set out immediately. They only had eight miles to cover to Springfield, but they had agreed with Luke Day and Eli Parsons to arrive together at four in the afternoon, when dusk would blur their approaching outlines in the road.

If things went well, they would watch Shepard march his men south to Connecticut in the day's last light or else he would simply disband his force, and they would celebrate their victory with food from the arsenal's stockpiles of provisions. Then they could post their sentries and set up defenses and sleep in the barracks, warm while they waited for Lincoln.

If Shepard somehow managed to turn them away, dusk would hide any disorder in their withdrawal, and dark and January cold would discourage Shepard from sending men to harass them as they retreated.

By the time the sun had sunk into the hills, their fate would be settled, one way or another.

If Shays and his officers hoped to take Shepard by surprise, their plans were ruined when Deputy Sheriff Abel King rode to Springfield from Wilbraham, south of Ludlow.[34] He had pushed through fields of crusted snow that bloodied his horse's legs to notify Shepard that Shays was marching—using Shays's name alone to refer to all twelve hundred of his men.

Regal by all accounts on his borrowed white horse, Shays had only led his men three miles from Ludlow when two of Shepard's officers, Captains Samuel Buffington and Joshua Woodbridge, met him in the road. They came to see whether they might resolve this crisis by trading words at a distance instead of exchanging gunfire at closer range.

When Buffington asked what Shays wanted, Shays answered barracks and stores.[35]

Buffington said that Shays threatened to destroy the country that Buffington and others had come to defend.

Shays answered that if he had come to defend the country, they should take the same side.

Buffington said he suspected that they would take very different parts, but Shays said he would take the part on the hill, where the arsenal and public buildings stood.

Shays asked whether Shepard would fire. When Buffington answered he would, Shays answered, "It's all we want."[36]

He urged his men forward, and Buffington rode back to let Shepard know that Shays would not be put off.

Shays and his men continued on alongside the snowy fields. Soon the houses came closer together, as the front of the column entered into Springfield. The closer they came, though, the less they saw women and children running to the road to cheer their approach; now they saw farmers running into their houses, afraid to be caught in a battle.

By the time the arsenal buildings appeared on the hill above the river, the red bricks of the buildings glowed warm in the slant light of the setting sun, and the lapping hills on the other side of the river were dark blue silhouettes under the sunset.

When Shays and his men were 250 yards from the arsenal grounds, Buffington rode out again, this time with Major William Lyman, a Springfield retailer, to parley with the farmers.[37]

Shays halted his lines to hear whether Buffington had come to negotiate Shepard's retreat. He had not. Again he warned that Shepard would fire if they approached any closer, but now it was Adam Wheeler who repeated Shays's response: It's all we want.[38]

Seeing he could not slow Shays's approach, Buffington returned to his post.[39] Shays's officers ordered their men with muskets to come forward and load their guns. He ordered them to shoulder their arms and advance.[40] As Shays's lines came closer and closer to Shepard's men in front of the arsenal, they did not see any sign of Parsons's or Day's men in the roads on the other sides of the grounds. But Shays did not halt to confer with his officers and figure out what they would do without half their force.

Even without Day and Parsons, their force of farmers and veterans outnumbered Shepard's merchants and clerks, though now it was four to three instead of better than two to one. They knew they had had the country on their side for five months. In twelve court closings the length of the state, the government's men had not yet fired a shot or made any attempts to arrest them.

Shays pressed his advance, daring Shepard to fire. He did not stop to scout Shepard's defenses and search for strategic advantages in the landscape, as he had seen his generals do any number of times in battle. He did not order his men to fan out and surround the arsenal grounds, or calculate which approach would cost him the fewest casualties.[41] Trusting his innocence, he simply ordered his men onward, and they advanced as if their righteous presence in the road in their homespun coats should be sufficient to show that they were the ones who had a right to the Confederation's reserves.[42]

When Shays and his men were a hundred yards from the entrance to the grounds where they would take arms and become an army at last, General Shepard ordered Major William Stevens, Colrain's justice of the peace and colonel in the town's militia, to fire warning shots over their column.[43]

At the howitzers and at the three four-pound cannon they had sledded out to face the road, militiamen answered his orders with ready hands. They had served alongside the men who now faced them, but they fired one volley, then another.[44]

If Shepard thought the flash and roar of shots would scare the farmers off, he found they had the opposite effect: Shays's men quickened their steps and drew closer together as men will hunch their shoulders and put their heads down to push through the curtain of cold drops raining down from their eaves to make the last step into the warmth of their houses.

When Shays and his men did not stop, Shepard gave the order to fire grapeshot at waistband height at the men in the road. Artillery men reloaded the cannon and lowered their aim. Again they touched the wicks to the cannon, and too fast for any eye to follow, the spreading shot fired out.

The shots could only be seen in their effects: the men in the road broke and ran. Smoke rose from the hot mouths of the cannon, and the air in the road a hundred yards from the arsenal filled with cries of "murder, murder."[45]

Cries were going up close to the cannon as well, for one artilleryman, John Chaloner of Springfield, had stepped in front of a cannon as it had gone off, and his arms had been hurled against the approaching men in a spray of blood and bone.[46]

In the moment of Shepard's second volley, Shays's men ceased to respond to his commands.[47] He urged them to continue forward, but his authority had been shredded in the instant when the men in his first three lines collapsed. The men behind turned and ran, and then the men behind them turned as well, heedless of anything Shays or his officers said.

All through their autumn exercises, Shays and the leaders of seventeen towns had steadied their neighbors, toughening them against this very panic.

All through fall into winter, Bowdoin had dreaded the people's disciplined army, but nothing Shays said now could keep his men from acting just like a flock of birds, each afraid to be either the rear or the center of the crazed crowd that only a minute ago had executed his orders as one body.

In the chaos, the men still refused to abandon their innocence, though. They did not wheel on the men in the road by the arsenal and fire their muskets for rage or revenge: they dropped them as they fled.

When Shepard's men ventured out later, they collected three loaded muskets and discharged them into the snow so they could safely add them to the arsenal's stores.[48]

Shays fled with his men from the arsenal gates. Over their shoulders, the men in the rear—the men who had only a minute ago formed the front of the column—did not see Shepard's men charging after them to rout them and cut them to pieces, so the men who still had their muskets were never tempted to turn and fire and draw down the guilt on their columns for shedding blood. They maintained their innocence to the end, following their countrymen in a blind rush.

By the time the men slowed in the road, they were already more than a mile from the spot where their advance had been repulsed. They gathered their wits and shook their fingers, testing their senses, testing their bodies' evidence that they had survived. When they counted, they were missing twenty-four men, most of their first three lines.

The gaps in their lines galvanized the men into action again. Some said they should return to the arsenal. The men who still had their muskets begged to fire them into the clusters of men at the cannon, to fight through the curtain of grapeshot, to punish Shepard's men and claim the arsenal grounds in one cruel push.[49]

The strong scent of blood on men's coats sapped the strength from their lines, though. The horror of blood in the snow behind them numbed and confused them, and they could not focus themselves in one force again.

Some stunned men looked down at their cold boots, or studied the snowy fields glowing silver in the dusk. Some watched dully as winter sunset glowed in the southwest, watching for any sign that Shepard's force might be pursuing. Some looked up at the cold stars that were already blinking icy and sharp in the east, and they tested the air for the sound of Lincoln's army arriving to reinforce Shepard's merchants and lawyers.

When Shays and his officers caught up with their defeated men, they started to take charge again. Against the men who clamored to fight, they said that the blood of kin had not stopped Shepard's men firing on them once, and it would not keep him from firing at them again. They were merely a mob of strangers in Shepard's eyes, enemies to be killed.

They said they refused to lead the men back to be massacred. Nor would they sleep in the barracks if they had to pay for their lodging in blood.

They said they had to go. They said they had done enough, by forcing the government's hand. With blood in the snow now, it was only a matter of time till their countrymen throughout the state and poor farmers in other states heard their lamentations, saw this scene through their eyes, and were horrified by their government's actions.

In grief and defeat, they withdrew to spread the word through the commonwealth that the government's unjust policies and threats had finally cost men their lives.

Cartoon of Daniel Shays and fellow Regulator Job Shattuck. This is the only surviving contemporary image of Daniel Shays. It seems hard to imagine that a Boston illustrator would have met Daniel Shays in person, to make this a likeness. Shays and Shattuck are depicted here as a military threat to the commonwealth, holding swords with cannon in the background. From *Bickerstaff's Genuine Boston Almanack for 1787*. (*National Portrait Gallery*)

Wealthy merchant John Hancock, Massachusetts's first governor, who betrayed his class by cultivating popularity with the people. He withdrew from government in 1785, when legislative gridlock was compounding the post-war financial crisis. His reelection in 1786 ended James Bowdoin's crisis of taxation and protests. Engraving after the 1765 portrait by John Singleton Copley. (*New York Public Library*)

James Bowdoin II, wealthy merchant with huge holdings in real estate throughout Massachusetts and Maine, and founding member of the American Academy of Arts and Sciences. When he was elected Massachusetts's second governor in 1785, his unforgiving policies and his failure to negotiate reforms drove the people to open resistance. For months, he treated opposition as an existential threat to the state, but waffled and refused to exacerbate the problem by sending troops. He ultimately raised money from private donors to fund an army of 3,000 troops in January 1787. By April, the people of Massachusetts had had enough, and Bowdoin lost his bid for re-election by a two to one margin to former governor John Hancock. Portrait by Christian Gullager, 1791. (*Bowdoin College Museum of Art*)

Samuel Adams, close advisor to Governor James Bowdoin, and co-author of the aristocratic 1780 Massachusetts Constitution, which raised property requirements for holding office and established Congregationalism (Puritanism) as the state's official religion. Adams had made a tour to western Massachusetts during the troubles of 1782, and concluded that the people did not have any legitimate complaints, so he supported a hard line response in 1786. When Bowdoin lost his election in 1787, Adams became the president of the Massachusetts Senate, and he and other wealthy hardliners prevented Governor Hancock from pardoning Shays and the final protestors. Portrait by John Singleton Copley, c. 1772, detail. (*Museum of Fine Arts Boston*)

Top: Conkey's Tavern, one of the centers where Pelham farmers organized the protests, on the west branch of the Swift River, half a mile downhill from Daniel Shays's house. This photograph is from 1883 when the building was in disrepair, nearly a hundred years after the protests. The site of is now underwater as part of the Quabbin reservoir. (*John Lovell Photograph Collection, Jones Library Special Collections, Amherst, Massachusetts*) Bottom: An interpretive reconstruction of the interior of Conkey's Tavern with the original hearthstone at the American Museum and Gardens in Bath, England. (*American Museum and Gardens*)

Pelham (Massachusetts) Meeting House, where Daniel Shays drilled his militia, and which served as another headquarters where the Regulators planned their opposition to the courts. Completed in 1743, it is the oldest continuously operating town hall in the United States. (*Author*)

Left: Westfield Major General William Shepard, who occupied the Springfield arsenal in advance of the Regulators' arrival in January 1787. Shepard ordered his men to fire the arsenal's cannon as Shays's men advanced, killing four and wounding twenty. The people revenged themselves afterward by destroying two of Shepard's purebred horses, burning his woodlot, and tearing up his fences. Reprinted from John Lockwood, *Westfield and its Historic Influences, 1669-1919*, 1922. Right: Portrait of General Benjamin Lincoln from life by Charles Willson Peale, c. 1781–1783. Lincoln led Governor Bowdoin's army against the protestors. Lincoln wisely applied only enough pressure to dissolve the people's force, without sparking a larger insurgency against government authority. (*Independence National Historical Park*)

"General Lincoln in Massachusetts," map by Ezra Stiles. This map shows General Lincoln's movements in Massachusetts, from January 23 when he left Worcester, through the rout in Petersham on February 4, 1787, which put Shays and his men to flight. (*Beinecke Rare Books Collection, Yale University*)

Monument at the site of the shootout between Perez Hamlin's lawless band and Colonel John Ashley's militia, in Sheffield, Massachusetts. At the same time, Daniel Shays and his officers were hundreds of miles away seeking asylum in Quebec. The stone came from nearby Goodale Quarry and was erected and inscribed incorrectly by James Tully in 1904, "The last battle of Shays Rebellion was here Feb. 27 1787." (*Author*)

Chapter Ten

Retreat into the Cold

I N THE REAR OF THE COLUMN he had led just a minute ago, Shays only stopped to write a letter to General Shepard in Springfield to ask for his wounded, the bodies of his dead. He begged for a general truce till the people could get legislative relief from "the insupportable burdens their region had been laboring under since spring." He said that he wanted to restore "peace and harmony to this convulsed Commonwealth" and refused to be "an accessory, in any way, to the shedding of further blood."[1]

Shays gave this letter to one of his lieutenants and sent him back under a white flag of truce before he joined what was by this point an organized retreat.[2]

With defeat heavy in their packs, Shays and his column set off in retreat. Defeat slid their feet sideways and crossways in the sloppy snow. They struggled under the heavy knowledge that Luke Day and Eli Parsons had not shown up as planned. They cursed them for having betrayed them. The burden of this hard knowledge twisted their packs sideways on their backs and threatened to topple them over whenever they thought that their relatives in Shepard's ranks had betrayed them as well. None of their fathers or brothers had kept the shots from being fired.

Hot in their panic, they shivered with icy shame when they thought that in one terrible moment they had just shown everyone in the country the real value of their rhetoric and their constitutional meetings. Their polite petitions, their democratic votes, their martial pride, and their virtuous restraint in the courtyards were not worth any more than this ignominious flight.

Swimming through the snowy road, men who thought they had been poisoned in Worcester felt their gorges rise in their throats again, as the putrid smell of suspicion was compounded with the stink of blood and gunpowder, the sting of January cold, and the throbbing absence of twenty-four men from their ranks.

The men who marched in what were now the front lines had not seen the fire from Shepard's cannon, but every time they crested a hill or rounded a turn in the road, they dreaded that they might stumble into Lincoln's army, and the shots that had just been fired in Springfield might prove to be just the start of the violence they had avoided all this time.

The nauseous tang of blood on their clothing stuck to them as they sweated into their coats, but they would not be able to return to their houses to cleanse themselves. They would not be able to protect their houses unless they were willing to answer the government's guns with their own fire. Unless they returned to the arsenal at dawn and damned themselves by battling with Shepard's men, they would not be able to keep Lincoln's men out of the country. They would have to either flee or submit to martial law.

The stars flickered cold and inconsistent through the gloaming ahead of them. The purple fields reflected the deep glowing blue of the sky, as the men were accustomed to seeing it do, at this hour in this season. But the beauty of the landscape could not console them. They were not at home, and they still had miles to cover before they could bury this day in sleep.

Eventually messengers caught up with them from Springfield to tell them that four of their men had been killed by the volleys of grapeshot: Ezekiel Root and Ariel Webster, from Gill upriver from Turners Falls, and Jabez Spicer, from Leyden, north of Colrain, had been killed immediately. John Hunter, from Shelburne, had died afterward of his wounds. Twenty others' wounds were being tended.[3]

General Shepard responded that he would not hand over the bodies nor allow the wounded to be tended by their own people, for fear that the wounded men's cries and their bloody clothes would testify again to the government's violence and spark a wider insurrection.

He refused to agree to a truce. He only invited Shays to come and get the men himself, to surrender and end their troubles.

Shays and his men cursed at Shepard's offer and continued their retreat toward Ludlow. As darkness deepened ahead of them, some men made bitter jokes or muttered threats, or else piercing cries were ripped from them, prayers for justice pulled from their throats up toward God. Nothing anyone said could purge the rhythms of defeat from their ears, though, or lift the heavy stone of defeat off of their hearts.

Still, sometimes the farmers were overtaken by moments of unaccountable joy, something like grace, for the simple sensation of being alive. They could, after all, be singing the one long, silent note four men sang into the road now. Cold as their fingers and noses were, they could not complain when their comrades' blood had probably already frozen into the snow in the road and would not thaw till horses tramped it to mud in a warm day's traffic. The uncomfortable joy of having survived swelled in their chests, and the colors of the night overwhelmed them, the color of their neighbors' faces and coats with the last of the slender moon's light on their backs overwhelmed them, and the emotion that rose in their throats leapt out in sobs, and they caught themselves before they cried out, or else they simply wept with wrong joy as they walked.

Onward they marched, enduring the black despair of the men who had seen the horrifying shots at close range, who watched their neighbors' bodies explode into red mist.

They started to calculate what it would mean to return and fight at last. They tallied the gratification of venting their rage against what it would cost them to submit to the governor's taxes. They started to estimate whether they could afford to sit back and watch while he executed his threats against their leaders. And even if they could not see how they would ever bear this new experience, they prayed that justice might greet them and relieve them of it at the end of their cold retreat.

In hope and despair, they continued. Whatever they loved in the world now carried them through the dark miles. Their wives in their dresses, their children's faces, the sound of their parents' voices—the other men in whom they were a people—the houses and taverns where they were known and at home—their dogs' or cats' soft ears—the barns and sheds where their tools knew their hands—the stalls and enclosures where their horses and oxen nuzzled their chests—the mist in the trees at the edge of their meadows—their hills curving off in their distances, stars in their treetops—whatever they loved now carried them, or else they were just bodies walking, animals being herded by bayonets.

They retreated into the cold, and their bodies themselves answered their prayers. By walking to Ludlow, they would live. In injustice, it's true, but they would live. As refugees, even in prison, if it went so far, but they would live, and life would be its own blessing.

They were not, in the end, void of consolations. The country they marched into was wrong, but they knew where they were, at every turn, even in near total darkness. Their state might not have justice, but they had loyal friends who would give them beds and food, and even if their accommodations were rough, they would lie down all clustered together for warmth, and sleep would carry them through the long, dark season when power protects injustice. If they woke each other with nightmares, the sound of the others' regular breathing would comfort them back to sleep.

Tomorrow they would wake at dawn, and when they saw each other in the morning light, they could decide together what they were going to do. They might have to give up their homes in Massachusetts at last. They might have to start again with nothing on a new frontier in winter. Whatever they did, they would stay together, and they would survive as their people had always survived. They would pay the price in labor or taxes or blood, as their times demanded, and they would fight for their freedom when it was within their power to fight.

They did not need to stay and die for their rights, here. This was not an ancestral homeland, with soil full of their predecessors' bones. They had arrived here as settlers a generation ago, in flight from the east. They could simply walk away from this conflict. They could start new lives on raw land in the west or in the north, where American freedoms had not yet been stifled by unjust laws.[4] There were still wild acres where they could plant crops in springtime. The nation they had fought a war for could still be established in any number of farther frontiers.

For eight cold miles, Shays and his men marched into deeper and deeper darkness. The first-quarter moon followed the sun into dark hills behind them. Orion climbed the sky before them as the last warmth of the day was carried off by the night winds.

Finally, they arrived in Ludlow, in the full dark of January night. The men lay down to sleep, exhausted from marching to Springfield and back in the snow, shocked by the appearance of death in their ranks. But Shays and his officers could not sleep until they had decided, once and for all, whether to issue orders for another attack at dawn. It would be their last chance to arm themselves, and to face Lincoln's army on equal terms.

Shays had dispatched riders to sound out Day's and Parsons's intentions, but none of his riders returned by starlight from Chicopee or West Springfield with news that Parsons or Day were willing to make a second attack. None of the leaders from the towns that had promised them men or supplies were willing to help them now that blood had been shed. None of the officers indicated that their men were willing to risk their own lives in order to compensate their dead neighbors' families with the blood of government men.

Quietly, under the soft midnight lamps of a Ludlow tavern, Shays and his officers let the hour pass when they would have had to issue orders for a dawn march. They gave up the chance to revenge themselves on General Shepard's men or to defend their country from Lincoln. They simply posted their watch and let their men sleep.

When dawn broke late over snow-covered fields on Friday, January 26, Shays and his men rose and put on yesterday's retreat like a cold coat that would not warm up or sit right on their shoulders.

He and his officers gave the orders to form the men in lines again.[5] They were going to march west to Chicopee, to join Eli Parsons's men, to merge their force and put some distance between themselves and Lincoln in the east.

Again the men stowed their gear and formed lines. Again they set out when their officers gave the order. For men who still refused to fight, this march was taking them farther from home. Every step they took through the January cold would have to be retraced before they could rest. For men who still felt a fight throbbing in their fists and shoulders, though, the order to march to Chicopee banked their anger and kept it alive like smoldering coals that might still leap into flame. From Chicopee, they might still be given the chance to feel the percussion of shots. They might still swing their clubs and feel the impact of justice in blows. When they added Eli Parsons's four hundred men to their twelve hundred, they would only be six miles north of Springfield. With Luke Day's six hundred men directly across the frozen Connecticut River, they would still have the power to strike at the men who had killed them yesterday, and they warmed themselves with the hope that a swift march would take them to Springfield, where they could still fight it out with Shepard.

As the cold morning sun rose into the southeast sky, Shays and his men advanced into their shadows, west toward Chicopee. Messengers from farther west found them in the road to tell them that Major General John Paterson was on his way east from the Berkshires to reinforce Shepard, but Paterson's army was still a few days away and would not affect their immediate plans.[6]

After forcing their toes through the snow for another nine miles, Shays's men arrived in Chicopee without incident, and Parsons's men found them lodging and food.

The rest of the afternoon passed, and Shays and his officers never gave orders to start their lines toward Springfield. They heard that Shepard's men were expecting another attack and fortifying their position at the top of the hill, but they were not venturing out to confront them where they waited.[7]

When darkness fell, they posted sentries to keep a strict watch against advances from either Shepard or Lincoln, but again, the night passed without incident.

The countryside was tranquil as the sun rose from the hills on Saturday, the twenty-seventh, to find Shays's and Parsons's men camped near the river.

From Chicopee, Shays wrote to Shepard again, reminding him of his connections to the dead and wounded men's families, naming their brothers and in-laws and friends, whom Shepard also knew. Shays hoped that Shepard would soften his stance and at least let the people recover their dead and wounded.[8]

After they dispatched their messengers, Shays and Parsons and their sixteen hundred men waited. The January sun climbed the sky, glaring bright on the snow with feeble warmth. Icicles dripped from shingled roofs, and still there was no news of Lincoln. Saturday morning slid toward noon, and Shays and Parsons kept their men where they were.

Across the river, Luke Day's men also waited. Moment to moment the chance to return in arms to the arsenal slipped away, but the men did not break up their force and return to their homes.

Afternoon chills had stripped the warmth from the sun's rays by the time a messenger thundered in on horseback to tell Shays and Parsons that Lincoln's front lines had finally entered Springfield and assumed command of the arsenal.

When Lincoln arrived, General Shepard had set out with four regiments, four field guns, and a troop of light horse, marching west to isolate Day's six hundred men in West Springfield and keep them from crossing the river to merge with Parsons and Shays.[9]

By the time Shays learned this news, it was three thirty in the afternoon.[10] The sun was already low in the sky. They would only have light for another hour, but Shays and his officers formed their sixteen hundred men into lines and set out northeast toward South Hadley, intent on Amherst, eighteen miles away.

Cold in the weak light, they marched into their shadows again. When the January sun broke through the afternoon clouds, the clapboards of white houses glowed warm and yellow ahead of them. Soon enough, though, the sun sank into the hills behind them, and once again they warmed themselves in the cold by marching through it.

Leaving Chicopee, they entered farmland again. Shays and his men were retreating back toward their own homes at last, though now Eli Parsons's men were leaving their homes behind them in their flight from Lincoln.

Altogether, they gave up any hope of warming themselves at the hearths in the arsenal barracks or of striking a peace on terms that protected their land.

Why should they stay to fight, after all? What longstanding traditions should they stay and martyr themselves to? Their forebears had abandoned their own ancestral lands long before they had come to Massachusetts, and they themselves had raised their children on promises that their towns would become an ancestral homeland in two more generations. Now they prepared to follow in their people's best-established tradition, of leaving one land for another. They set their mind's eyes on western New York or Vermont, on Ohio or Pennsylvania.

Shays and his people had built their houses and barns with their own hands before. Those same hands could make barns and houses wherever they could find land and timber to build with. Their horses and cows, their chickens and pigs, their dogs would reproduce themselves in Vermont as well as they could in Massachusetts. With sacks of seeds, with muskets and axes, they could start again almost anywhere—even in January, if necessary. They had friends throughout the country and family members who would lend them their labor and tools to help them make a new start. They did not need to submit to unjust law or corrupt themselves by waging war.

For an hour after the sun went down, they marched into the gloaming, dreading the sound of messengers galloping up with news that Lincoln was close on their trail.

Their force largely stayed together. Only about a hundred men slipped away back to their homes. The rest marched into the darkness along familiar roads. The sky would be light with tomorrow's sunrise before they were finished marching, but they would be back in their own country, in steep hills protected by narrow approaches where Lincoln would not be wise to risk his men.

The first-quarter moon had only been down for a couple of hours when Shays and Parsons's column arrived in South Hadley. When some of them stopped to warm themselves and eat at Butt's Tavern, South Hadley's friends of government, inspired by Shepard's attack, loaded their muskets and fired on them from the horse shed behind Smith's Tavern nearby.[11]

Everyone took cover and loaded their guns, but Amos Call of Montague and Joseph Bellows of Palmer had been killed before Shays ended the stand-off by threatening to burn down the buildings from which the snipers had fired their guns.[12]

Now that Shays's men felt the town's gunsights trained on their backs, they finally lost their restraint and broke into South Hadley houses, where they plundered food and two barrels of rum. Like Day's men, they also took hostages—Sunderland shopkeepers Cotton Graves, Noahdiah Leonard, and Martin Cooley, and Ebenezer Barnard from Deerfield—collecting them as coins to exchange for captives or as savings to lower the cost of the government's punishments.[13]

With captives in their midst now, and rum in clouds in their eyes, with defeat over their heads and the unforgiving winter's night wind in their faces, Shays and his men kept walking north as one body.

In the middle of the night, messengers found them and told them that Lincoln's army had crossed the frozen Connecticut River in pursuit of Day's men. The pickets Day posted in West Springfield had fled north through Easthampton toward Northampton.[14]

A group of Day's men under a Captain Luddington of Southampton had fled west, then turned on their pursuers in Southampton and captured fifty-nine of Shepard's men under one Captain Bannister.[15] But Colonel Ebenezer Crafts of Worcester, with one hundred horsemen, and Colonel Baldwin and one hundred Brookfield volunteers in sleighs, overtook Luddington and his men and their captives. In Middlefield, they found the Regulators on their way into the hills. They surrounded the house where they had taken shelter and captured them without firing a shot.

The rest of Day's men fled north through Northampton, with Lincoln's and Shepard's men close behind them, collecting the muskets and supplies they abandoned in the road.

Now the messengers reported that Day was on his way east to join Shays and Parsons in Amherst.

All through the night, the Regulators of Hampshire County converged on the East Amherst green. The first-quarter moon had long ago sunk into the hills, but they covered the last cold miles by icy starlight.

Ten miles north Shays marched with his men, from South Hadley up through the woods on the Seven Sisters mountains and through the Notch and downhill through farmland again. Support for their cause was strong in this country, so when the men needed to warm themselves, the farmers along the way took them into their homes and fed them and warmed them before they got back on the road.[16]

Of the sixteen hundred men who had departed from Chicopee yesterday afternoon, more than twelve hundred arrived at the green by Clapp's Tavern in East Amherst, at the foot of the road up to Pelham.

Back in their own country at last, in the late hours of the night, they slipped their heavy packs off their shoulders and fed and watered their horses.

Landlord Clapp offered what provisions he had and told the men that fresh supplies were waiting for them in Pelham. The same Berkshire County farmers who had pleaded poverty when the state pressed them for taxes had forwarded food and provisions that filled ten sleighs, to help the towns of Hampshire County pay the price of supporting their men.[17] Clapp said he might have kept the teamsters in Amherst but had hurried them up the hill the last six miles to keep the supplies from falling into Lincoln's scouts' hands.

Having fled through the night, Shays and his men now threw themselves down on every available surface in every church and barn. In every home that would open its doors, they slept the troubled, exhausted sleep of men who had been walking all night and might still need to leap up and race through the snowy roads if Lincoln's army pursued them.

On Sunday morning, the twenty-eighth of January, Luke Day and his routed men straggled in out of the cold after crossing the frozen Connecticut River and marching through the night.[18]

Finally, Shays could demand to know why Day and his men had failed them.

Day said he had sent Shays a note asking for one day's delay, but Shays had not received a note.

Shays said he must have sent a note to Parsons as well, because Parsons had not arrived either. He and his men had never heard anything about a day's delay. He said Shepard must have known they were coming alone because he had concentrated all of his thousand men in defense of the arsenal's eastern approach.

Day said he had wanted to give Shepard a chance to leave the arsenal without a fight. He had sent the general an ultimatum, instructing the government's volunteers to lay down their arms, to leave the stores in the arsenal and go home on parole.[19]

When Shays asked why he had not moved at the time they had agreed to in advance, Day said his pastor, Joseph Lathrop, had warned him that he would be putting his own soul at risk of the sin of murder if men under his command were killed.[20]

By this time, Shays had already lost six men killed—four at the arsenal and two who had been shot in South Hadley—and twenty had been wounded by grapeshot. Day said that he had lost a man on the march, when his rear guard shot a straggler after mistaking him for the advance ranks of Lincoln's army.[21] Nevertheless, their men had stayed with them through long marches on short rations for three icy days, but whatever the state of their souls, Shays ordered his officers to take Day and his men into their ranks and find them provisions and shelter with the others.

Shays, Day, and Parsons could not let their men rest in Amherst for long. That morning, messengers from the Berkshires arrived to say that General Paterson's force of 300 men had encountered 250 Regulators who agreed to disband on condition that Paterson would represent their cause in negotiations with the government.[22]

Messengers from Chicopee and Northampton also came to warn them that Lincoln was driving his hired army close on their heels.

His men had pursued Day as far as Northampton, then camped in Northampton last night. Now his troops had been seen crossing the frozen river to Hadley, putting them only seven miles away.[23]

Luke Day's force had shrunk in retreat, but his numbers replaced men who had departed from Shays's and Parsons's. Together they still commanded more than twelve hundred men. They would be badly outnumbered by Lincoln's army of three thousand, who were armed with muskets and cannon, while only a quarter of Shays's men had been armed with muskets, and not a few of his men had lost their guns in their several retreats.

Outnumbered and still unwilling to fight, Shays, Day, and Parsons roused their exhausted men and formed them into lines again to march up the hill through the narrow approach to Pelham.

From Clapp's in East Amherst they crossed the frozen Fort River and marched up the hill, leaving the Connecticut River behind them as they crested over back into the Swift River valley. From the last hill that commanded a view of the roads from Amherst, Shays posted a watch to give them some warning if Lincoln's army should follow.

He could have posted armed men along the roadside to aggravate Lincoln's army with withering fire from behind stone walls and buildings, but he still refused to condemn his people by letting individuals shoot at government men.

After a long morning's march, Shays and his men arrived at the Pelham meeting house at the top of West Hill.

When the wives and children of Pelham heard their drums, they came to welcome them back. For seven days they had listened to rumors from Springfield, Ludlow, and Chicopee, and now they came together to hear their men's firsthand accounts.

The men arrived and put down their gear and opened the parcels their Berkshire friends sent them. They told what they had seen, and no one interrupted them with warnings that they were in danger from Lincoln's men. His army might have caught them in the green at East Amherst with a quick march from Hadley, but now that they had fled to Pelham, they had put another eleven miles, a half-day's march, between them.

All day, the Regulators waited for news of Lincoln's approach, but their scouts only reported that Lincoln had camped his three thousand men near the river, in Hadley, lodging his soldiers in almost every house in the village. He had parked his cannon on the north side of the meeting house to let the Hampshire County farmers feel the ominous presence of foreign men poised in the heart of their country, with the state's authority in their guns.[24]

Shays, Day, and Parsons set up their headquarters at the Pelham meeting house. The leading families of Pelham sheltered the men in the taverns and houses and barns, extending their hospitality to their countrymen, the same as their own men had been hosted in Rutland and Worcester, in Ludlow and in Chicopee.

Amid the thousand details of housing and feeding their men, Shays and his officers sent messengers back to Springfield with letters for General Shepard, continuing to negotiate for their dead and wounded.[25] But they could not make any headway now that Shepard and Lincoln considered them enemies of government.

Shays and his officers also wrote to leaders in neighboring towns, begging for supplies and reinforcements, and pleading with them to keep their angry men from firing on Lincoln's force. All day they were gratified not to hear news of attacks against rich men's property or businesses or against families who supported the government. Their authority in the region was still respected, even after their retreat had announced their powerlessness to the world.

Soon the cold dusk fell, and again the men slept in dread and apprehension. Again, the night's peace was never ruptured by cries of alarm that Lincoln's force had followed them.

Monday's dawn broke, and the sun rose over the people's barren fields and cold, clustered tents. The men in both forces stayed where they were. By mid-afternoon of Monday, January 29, the swelling moon appeared in the east and climbed the sky in pursuit of the sun. The farmers in Pelham heard that Lincoln had ordered provisions and firewood from Hadley merchants to supply his camp ringed with cannon. By the time the moon had followed the sun into the hills that evening, there was still no indication that Lincoln was getting ready to march his men east from Hadley.

For a second night, Lincoln kept his men in their camp and let Samuel Adams's calls for blood, and Governor Bowdoin's accusations of treason and threats of arrest, resound through the countryside like the haunting cry of owls while Shays and his people nestled into their hills.

Nervous beneath this danger, the men of Hampshire County maintained a watch on the road to Pelham, but their men slept in the same beds and haylofts and tents they had slept in last night.

When they woke and ate their breakfasts on Tuesday morning, the thirtieth of January, they could already start to see an end to the supplies from the Berkshires, so Pelham families opened their pantries and raided their stores of salted fish and meat, their grain and gourds, apples and barrels of cider, spreading their wealth on boards in camps.

Their men had already lost their winter's labor in the weeks they had spent marching from town to town to close the courts—now they began to eat through supplies that should have seen them through till spring. From other towns, wives and families came to Pelham afoot, on horseback, and in sleighs. They brought flour and corn, bread, jam and beans, and bundles of dried fruit—as many provisions as they could carry, to share in the burden of feeding their men.

They should have been traveling town to town in preparation for the holiday of February 2, when the sun reached the halfway point between the solstice and new warmth and life at the equinox. There should have been a festival instead of this ragged and hungry encampment, the stifling fear from Hadley, the lamentations for their wounded men plus the six who had been killed.

When wives and children begged their men to come home with them, Shays and his officers did not keep them from going, but the men did not depart from their camps in large numbers. They stayed together, to protect their leaders, to make sure that they were not alone when Lincoln brought the government's force to bear on the insubordinate towns.

During the day Tuesday, January thirtieth, the cold deepened danger-
ously.[26] Rhododendron leaves hung withered and black on their branches,
and the cold brought tears to men's eyes the moment they stepped out of
warm buildings. Soon it was dangerous to spend any time outside.

It was too cold for the government's army to set out after them into the
hills, so Shays's men abandoned their tents and huddled cold in barns or
stables, passing another day on thin rations.

That afternoon, a messenger braved the cold to bring Shays a letter from
Lincoln:

> Whether or not you're convinced of your error in flying to arms, I am
> fully persuaded that before this hour, you must have the fullest con-
> viction upon your own minds, that you are not able to execute your
> original purposes.
>
> Your resources are few, your forces inconsiderable, and hourly de-
> creasing from disaffection of your men. You are in a post where you
> have neither cover nor supplies, and in a situation in which you can
> neither give aid to your friends, nor discomfort to the supporters of
> good order and government.
>
> Under these circumstances, you cannot hesitate a moment to dis-
> band your deluded followers. If you should not, I must approach and
> apprehend the most influential characters among you. Should you at-
> tempt to fire on troops of government, the consequences must be fatal
> to many of your men, the least guilty.
>
> To prevent bloodshed, you will communicate to your privates, that
> if they will instantly lay down their arms, surrender themselves to gov-
> ernment, and take and subscribe an oath of allegiance, they shall be
> recommended to the General Court for mercy. If you should either
> withhold this information from them, or suffer your people to fire
> upon our approach, you yourself must be answerable for all the ills
> which may exist in consequence thereof.[27]

Lincoln had also published this open letter in the *Hampshire Gazette* so
all the taverns in Hampshire County should bear this warning on their walls.

By the time Shays and his men received Lincoln's letter, they had just
dispatched a rider of their own into the cold, carrying yet another petition
to Boston, begging for peace and reforms:

> We, the Officers of the Counties of Worcester, Hampshire, Middlesex
> and Berkshire Now at Arms humbly petition to say that we are sen-

sible that we have been in error, in having recourse to arms, and not seeking redress in a Constitutional way.

We therefore heartily pray your honors, to overlook our failing, in respect to our rising in arms, as your honours must be sensible we had great cause of uneasiness. It is our hearts' desire that good government may be kept in a constitutional way.

It appears to us, that the time is near approaching when much human blood will be spilt unless a reconcilliation can immediately take place—which scene strikes us with horror, let the foundation cause be what it may.

We therefore solemnly promise that we will lay down our arms, and repair to our respective homes, in a peaceable and quiet manner, and so remain, provided your honors will grant to our petitioners— and all those our brethren who have recourse to arms, or otherwise aided or assisted our cause—a general pardon for their past offenses.

All of which we humbly submit to the wisdom, candour and benevolence of your honours, as we in duty bound shall ever pray.[28]

This petition was signed not by Daniel Shays but by Francis Stone, with the title of "Chairman of the Committee for the above counties." It included a postscript to say that the petition had been read and accepted by the officers in constitutional fashion.

With this abject letter already on its way to Boston, Shays and his officers ordered their men to carry General Lincoln's warning around to the houses and barns of Pelham, to read it aloud so everyone would know where they stood in the government's eyes.

They composed their answer and sent a messenger back to Lincoln in Hadley that evening:[29]

Sir,

The people assembled in arms from the counties of Middlesex, Worcester, Hampshire and Berkshire, taking into serious considera-tion the purport of the flag just received, return for answer, that how-ever unjustifiable the measures may be which the people have adopted, in having recourse to arms, various circumstances have induced them thereto.

We are sensible of the embarrassments the people are under, but that virtue which truly characterizes the citizens of a republican gov-ernment, have hitherto marked our paths with a degree of innocence; and we wish and trust it will still be the case.

At the same time, the people are willing to lay down their arms, on condition of general pardon, and return to their respective homes, as they are unwilling to stay in the land, which we in the late war purchased at so dear a rate, with the blood of our brethren and neighbors.

Therefore, we pray that hostilities may cease, on your part, until our united prayers may be presented to the General Court, and we receive an answer, as a person is gone for that purpose. If this request may be complied with, government shall meet with no interruption from the people, but let each army occupy the post where they now are.[30]

Shays alone signed this letter, and even though his men had addressed him as general while they were marching to close the courts, he signed with the title the commonwealth itself had given him during the war: Captain Daniel Shays.

The sun set after this exchange of letters on Tuesday, and it rose through the brutal cold on Wednesday the thirty-first, and still neither side moved from their camps. All day the cold remained sharp in men's lungs and numbed their fingertips as soon as they stepped outside. Snowflakes got small and light and slipped across the crusted fields like sand as all moisture froze out of the air.

Huddled in Hadley, Lincoln did not try to move his troops, but he sent a messenger into the hills to answer yesterday's plea for a truce with a terse ultimatum:

"Gentlemen, your request is completely inadmissible, as no powers were delegated to me which would justify the delay of my operation. Hostilities I have not commenced. I have again to warn men in arms against government, immediately to disband, if they would avoid the ill consequences which may ensue, should they be inattentive to this caution."[31]

Still Lincoln's men did not move through the cold. Neither did Shays's men disband. The sun set again, and the blinking stars circled over the fields in icy darkness, and on Thursday morning the first of February, there still was not any change in the weather. The sun rose, and more than a thousand farmers refused to abandon their officers, even under the pressure of three thousand men camped so close by.

General Lincoln was not in any rush. From Hadley on the river, loyal local merchants could provision his men indefinitely. The expense would simply be added to the commonwealth's accounts. The debts would be paid with money raised by levying taxes.

In Pelham, Shays and his people were not in any rush to move either. They were at home in their hills. They were eating through their winter supplies, but provisions were pouring in from neighboring towns. The whole region was draining its stores in order to keep their men together—if not to fight, then at least to protect their leaders and to let them negotiate a peace that would include all the people together.

In the houses and barns and taverns and tents in Pelham, Shays and his people waited for word from Boston, hoping that the stain of blood in the snow and their humble petition might turn the legislators' hearts, that they would finally issue reforms and pardon the people.

They watched the roads in the east, but when the rider finally arrived from Boston, and Shays and his officers broke the seal and read the letter aloud, they only cursed and spat into their fires. The wealthy men in the legislature said that the farmers' abject petition could not be sustained because they "openly avow themselves in arms, and in a state of hostility against the government."

"For this reason alone," they wrote, "the paper would be unsustainable."[32]

They then complained that "the applicants appear to view themselves on equal, if not better standing than the legislature, by proposing a 'reconcilliation,'" and they complained that the farmers "appear to threaten the authority and Government Commonwealth with a great effusion of blood, unless this 'reconcilliation' can immediately take place."[33]

Even with four of the people's bodies lying in the road with twenty wounded, seventeen men named for arrest, and thousands at risk of losing their homes, legislators in Boston had read the people's groveling petition and still refused to admit that the people had any legitimate grievances. Still they refused to answer any of the people's concerns, and only mocked them by drawing attention to the extra "l" their scribes had added to the single most important word in their petition.

At the same time that the men in Pelham heard that their last appeal had failed, they learned from Hadley that Lincoln had punished seven of his men for looting Hadley homes.[34] When a military tribunal found them guilty, Lincoln forced them to march between lines of militia, with signs hung from their necks that read "for plundering."[35]

When news of this light punishment reached Pelham, though, the seven humiliated men filled the people with fear for the crimes Lincoln's lawless men might commit if they marched up the hill to ransack the houses and barns in search of Shays and his officers, for they still recalled that the Riot

Act indemnified government agents from punishment for injuring or murdering protesting farmers.

In the end, the punishment for looting only reassured the wealthy men who had business with the courts, while they terrorized the people.[36]

In the Pelham meeting house, Shays and his officers debated how much longer they would be able to keep their force together if Lincoln was bent on arresting them. Some said that as soon as the cold broke, Lincoln would set his army on the road, but others predicted that Lincoln would never risk his army of dandies and doctors, lawyers, servants, and store clerks so far from their suppliers by the river.

They said that they were safe in Pelham, for the road from Amherst was too steep and narrow for Lincoln to dare approach. They said that they would have plenty of time to withdraw if Lincoln took his men to Belchertown, to approach up the ridge from the south, or up to Shutesbury, to come down the ridge from the north.

They said they should plan to stay in Pelham till early April, when they would win reforms through elections.

But men who had already seen more blood than they could bear recommended withdrawing. In the long shadows of the Hadley cannon, they argued that they should suspend their resistance and concede the last nine weeks until April elections. They said that their total defeat was inevitable now. If Lincoln did march his men through the narrow hills up to Pelham, they did not have any intention of opposing them, so why keep their force together any longer?

They said their officers should flee from the country and wait till the people could win reforms at the polls, but Shays and the majority of his officers refused to flee. Again they told their men that they could leave if they wanted to see to their own safety. They themselves had stood for justice for months, and they were not about to discredit the sacrifices their people had made to support them, so even after the officers gave them leave to return to their homes, they stayed close to their leaders.

At the end of their long discussions, Shays and his officers only agreed that they should take the thousand men they still commanded farther beyond Lincoln's reach, away from the river and the merchants who were supplying him.

In long hours of debate inside windows frosted with ice, Shays and his officers considered where they might retreat to. They could not stay within the commonwealth's borders, where Lincoln's army was authorized to apprehend them. They could not flee to Connecticut, Rhode Island, or New Hampshire, for the governors of these neighboring states had pledged to arrest any fugitives and return them to Massachusetts.[37]

Shays and his officers dispatched messengers into the cold with letters to leaders in other hill towns to see who might be able to support them. They also wrote to friends in Vermont and New York to beg for asylum if they could not negotiate a peace.

For two more days, the deep cold persisted, and Lincoln waited frigid in Hadley while Shays's men stayed put in Pelham.

On Friday night, the sun went down icy and clear. The moon rose almost full from the pitch-black hills, and still both sides stayed where they were.

It was not till Saturday, February 3, that warmer air moved into the region, and people could step outside without feeling stabbed by the cold. Now that the forces could move again, Shays's men spotted Lincoln's spies reconnoitering their camp.[38] The Regulators could not stay in Pelham any longer. If Lincoln pushed his men hard, they could be here in under three hours.

Shays sent riders to rouse men out of the houses and barns where they had passed these last five days. When they had collected in the meeting house lawn, he told them that he and his officers had arranged to flee to friends farther from the river. The people of Petersham, high in the hills toward the New Hampshire border, had offered to feed and house them for as long as they could.

The town was remote from the market towns, just northwest of Rutland and the country that had sheltered Shays's 350 picked men from November into December. It was a region where Lincoln would have a hard time provisioning three thousand men.

Once again, Shays and his officers told their men they were free to return to their homes. They told them they should ask for the government's pardons if they felt that was what they needed to do, but the solidarity was still strong among them, and more than a thousand men formed lines in the cold to escort their officers up through the snowbound forests to safety farther from Lincoln.

Before they set out, Shays treated his officers to drinks at Nehemiah Hines's Tavern in east Pelham, then dispatched an envoy to Hadley to stall Lincoln with proposals for terms by which men might be pardoned or prisoners exchanged.[39]

By the time the sun reached its peak at noon, Shays and his men had already covered miles on the road east into the hills. Past snowy fields and forests, up and down hills and across frozen lakes, they trudged the twenty miles. Now the families who were drawn to the roadside by fife and drums beheld a column of ragged men who looked more like refugees than soldiers, and they brought them food to carry them through their retreat.

Through two weeks of marching, Shays and his men had maintained their innocence at every step, but now in the middle of the afternoon, they were joined in the road by a band of armed New Braintree men who had finally abandoned the dignified restraint that had characterized their conduct these last six months.

They came with two captives they had taken yesterday, John Stanton and Samuel Flagg, and they came with the stink of gunpowder on their cold coats.[40] They reported that after they had taken the prisoners, 130 soldiers had come to the tavern where they were being kept. The Regulators said that they had ambushed this party, shooting from behind fences and trees, and the government men had formed lines and traded fire. By the time the farmers fled, two government men had been hit, one in the hand, the other in the knee.

If the exiles from Pelham had longed to fire their own guns into the lines of government men, they heard this story with satisfaction, but Shays and his officers listened with dread. In General Lincoln's blind justice, any of them could now be made to pay for the government men's injuries. It would not matter whether the right men were made to pay. They were all stained with guilt by this act, the officers more than the others.

With more blood in the snow now, some of Shays's men wanted to march back to Pelham to protect their families and farms against Lincoln's soldiers' reprisals, but Shays and his officers still refused to be baited into battle. They entrusted their wives and children to their innocence, and they formed their men into lines again, threatening to arrest and whip any men who lingered behind to station themselves by the road with loaded muskets.

All day, Shays and his men marched the twenty cold miles from Pelham to Petersham, leaving Lincoln's men more than thirty miles in their rear.

By the time the full moon rose from the hills at sunset, Petersham's Captain Joseph Gallants and the town's other leading men had settled Shays and his officers in their houses and barns and showed the rest of Shays's men where to set up their tents in the sloping green ringed with houses.

The full moon lost its yellow glow as it rose, and it whitened and shrunk in the sky overhead. The air was thick and sweet with the scent of approaching snow as a thousand men tended their fires and cooked what evening meals they had.

The January sun had set into the valley behind them, but the full moon lit their labors through the trees, replacing the sun's light with its silver glow. Bit by bit, the outlines of the houses retreated, till the houses themselves were only yellow windows in moon-lit shadows, sprinkled across the moon-blue, snow-covered hills, and the men settled down to sleep in the heart of the region where their friends and relatives sheltered them from injustice.

Shays, Day, and Parsons did not know that Lincoln had set his column of men in motion by early afternoon that same day. Lincoln had not followed the thousand Regulators' week-old footprints up the steep notch in the hills into Pelham, nor the hours-old prints east from Pelham.[41] His scouts in the country had told him that Shays's force was heading to Petersham, so he had charted a course north through Amherst to Shutesbury, then east through the hills of New Salem, where Shays would not have left pickets to slow his advance.[42]

When Shays and his men were settling in Petersham at dusk, they did not know that Lincoln had refused to allow his men to stop to set up a camp when the full moon rose huge and swollen out of the hills. In Petersham, Shays's men did not have any idea that Lincoln was driving his men underneath the full moon's light.

As the moon shrunk in the distance above the treetops, Lincoln pressed his men on with torches and lamps. The cold deepened as the night wore on, but they forged ahead through deeply shadowed forests. After midnight, the moon disappeared behind clouds. Lincoln's force had covered the sixteen miles from Hadley to New Salem by two in the morning when the wind picked up, and soon the gusts were prickling soldiers' faces with icy snow. The temperature started to drop, and the snowflakes fell thick on the paths, filling Lincoln's soldiers' collars and ears, erasing their footprints, but their guides led them on through the hostile towns toward Petersham.[43]

Soon the road drifted deep with blowing snow, and Lincoln's supply train fell five miles behind the field guns in advance.[44] Still he pressed his men past the region's thinly spread farms to cover the last fifteen miles to Petersham in blowing snow and miserable darkness.

When dawn suffused the low clouds with a faint glow and Lincoln's men could see where they were putting their feet again, the landscape of hemlocks and mountain lakes was buried under eighteen inches of fresh-fallen snow.[45]

By the time the sun rose and lit the backs of the ebbing storm clouds, they still had two hours to march before they reached Petersham, and Lincoln and his officers drove their wallowing men with a mixture of encouragements and threats.

Shays and his officers woke in the houses of Petersham and looked out the windows at quiet woods where the last gusts were raising eddies and swirls from the fields that glowed white in the eerie, yellow-wan, post-storm light.

Lincoln did not pause to reconnoiter Shays's camp or surround it as General William Tryon surrounded the Regulators at Alamance Creek in North Carolina, as General Robert Howe had surrounded the Pennsylvania soldiers who had walked off their line in New Jersey, as Governor John Sullivan's men had surrounded the protestors at Exeter in September. Nor did Lincoln send envoys to give Shays time to consider his hopeless position and negotiate his surrender.

In their houses and tents on the Petersham green, Shays and his men had not set sentries to warn them, so the first sign that Shays had that Lincoln's force was so close by was when Lincoln's men charged up the hill into the town center with loaded guns.[46]

When Lincoln's advance guard burst into their camp, the men had been lazily cooking their Sunday breakfasts. In an instant, their camp was thrown into chaos. Some of the men leapt up, formed lines, and started to load their guns.

As soon as Lincoln's officers saw them, they ordered their soldiers to raise their loaded muskets. They ordered them to fire, and even though they only fired into the snow, the flash of their muzzles, the smell of exploding gunpowder turned Shays's men's lines inside-out once again.[47]

Neither Shays nor any of his officers rallied their men or tried to repel Lincoln's soldiers. Their organized opposition to government dissolved at last as all thousand men abandoned their muskets and dropped their gear, the same as they had abandoned their guns in Springfield eleven days earlier. They melted into the snowy roads around Petersham, and Lincoln's men did not charge on their flanks to pursue and destroy them.[48] They showed the same restraint Shepard's men had shown when they did not charge out from the Springfield barracks to cut Shays's men to pieces when they might have.

Famished and freezing after marching all night through a blizzard, Lincoln's men only arrested the men who fell into their hands. In the end, they caught about 150 farmers, but not Daniel Shays or any of his officers.[49]

After the tumult of flight and chase ended, Lincoln's men collected their captives in the Petersham green. Lincoln administered oaths of allegiance to Bowdoin's government, and Shays's men swore and signed their names.[50]

Lincoln sent them back to their homes on parole, and his soldiers from Boston warmed themselves at the rebels' fires, breakfasting from their pots of bubbling beans.[51]

Chapter Eleven

The Force Dissolves

B URNING WITH PANIC, Shays and the last remnants of his force, about three hundred men, barreled through the fresh-fallen snow in the roads. Once again Shays gave up command, as each man looked only to his own safety.

When the impulse to flee passed, no one tried to stop the mad rush, to organize the men, to return to the center of Petersham to wrest control of the town from Lincoln's troops.

Men who had not given any orders in this army simply cut through the farms and the woods to find the roads that would take them back to their families. They would have to ask for pardons now, or make their peace with the government however they might. But Shays and the men who had been singled out for arrest in Bowdoin's proclamations did not dare return to their homes.

A few minutes out of Petersham, when their first rush of panic subsided and they realized they were not being pursued, they settled into a steady pace that would carry them through twenty miles of fresh snow north toward Athol and into New Hampshire, where Lincoln's army was not authorized to follow.[1]

Cold in whatever clothing they were wearing when Lincoln arrived, they forged fresh trails on the roads out of Petersham, passing houses where farmers were only starting to shovel their paths. They proceeded through the thick, high forests where the snow had only been tracked by the squirrels and mice, by rabbits and deer. Hour to hour, they spelled each other at breaking the trail, to keep the forward-most men from exhausting themselves.

They had not made it all the way to New Hampshire before they were overtaken by riders who told them that Adam Wheeler had been captured, though the messengers also reported that Wheeler's men had rallied and captured him back.[2] No one had been killed or injured in the skirmish, but now Shays's men's eyes were always anxious, their necks spinning on pivots, searching out the source of each distant sound.

In the wake of this news, every farmer who looked at them sideways and every rider they passed in the road filled them with dread of arrest. Heartbroken leaving their country, they wondered aloud how many friends Governor Sullivan might have in this region.

Even if they could not say exactly how they would survive their cold despair, though, they knew in their hearts that they would. Every heartbeat affirmed it. They had already seen more than this, in the war. They had come home, and their communities had taken them in, and they had set to work, and the nightmares of battle had been softened by the recognizable rhythms of the seasons and the work their people had been doing since time immemorial.

They would still have to march a hundred miles through the snow, though, before they would be safe. They could not stay in New Hampshire, where Governor Sullivan had promised to send refugees back to Bowdoin for trial. They would head for western Vermont. Shays and others had family and friends there, and no one expected Governor Thomas Chittenden to arrest them and return them to Massachusetts for hanging.

They would only have to keep themselves moving, to press ahead though their hearts broke for their defeat. The hills patched with fields blanketed with snow, the icy streams chuckling down from the hills did not offer any respite.

They fled past farms where wealthy men had taken the government's side, but even after everything, Shays's men still refused to indulge the anger they carried in their fists. They did not bash in wealthy men's doors or ransack their houses or take captives from the houses or pillage their cellars to feed themselves in flight.[3] The wealthy men let them pass without attempting to capture them.

In the clear fine weather that followed the storm, Shays and his men fled north unimpeded, with only the thin provisions they had managed to grab when they fled. They steered by jurisdiction, by friendships or by family

connections, stopping only at houses and taverns where they knew that kinsmen would offer their hospitality.

By late afternoon, Shays and his three hundred men crossed out of Massachusetts into southwestern New Hampshire, a hilly rural region where
Sullivan's authority was not very strong.

Cold in their saddles, cold in their wet boots, they made their way west
down the valley beside the brook that bubbled beneath the snow, toward
the Connecticut River and Vermont.

They were overtaken by messengers who told them that Bowdoin had
declared martial law in Massachusetts. In a proclamation his messengers
were taking town to town, he portrayed the people's constitutional meetings,
their nonviolent protests, their defensive maneuvers, and their servile petitions as an "open, unnatural, unprovoked and wicked rebellion" against the
dignity and authority of the commonwealth.[4]

Shays and his men were well beyond the state's borders, but now that
they had been branded rebels, there would not be any going back for things
they had left behind. If they were captured, the penalty would almost surely
be death for Shays and the other leaders, and imprisonment if not execution
for many of the others.

When the sun started to slide behind the steep hills, they arrived in the
town of Winchester.[5] They knocked at friendly doors where they were offered food and lodging. They posted their watches and slept however they
could through their panic and grief and dreams of flashing muskets and icy
cold.

When they woke on Monday, February 5, they had to tell themselves
the whole improbable story about how they came to wake in these strange
beds.

Shays and his three hundred men continued west toward Vermont. They
did not take the road that led toward Brattleboro, where merchants loyal to
Governor Bowdoin might try to catch them and turn them in. Instead, they
made their way northwest through New Hampshire's steep hills and crossed
the frozen Connecticut River north of Brattleboro, near Putney.

Their travels were hardly finished when they entered the independent
republic of Vermont. They were aiming for farms in Arlington, in Vermont's
southwestern corner, which bordered both Massachusetts and New York,
where both Ethan Allen and Vermont Governor Thomas Chittenden had
farms, and also near Shays's wife's brother in Bennington.[6] They would not
be able to hang their horses' saddles in barns and sleep in safe beds till they

had crossed another fifty miles through the snowy mountains that separated the state's eastern and western valleys.

Many of the men who rode with Shays knew the way through these mountains. Some men had made this same trip before. Shays himself had considered moving to the region around Bennington after the war. Abigail's brother and many of Shays's comrades were founding new towns that would not be burdened by Massachusetts's taxes, but Shays and his wife had chosen Pelham, closer to her father and family in Brookfield, a day's ride away.

Shays and his men might have arrived in Bennington from the south after days of easier marching if they had skirted the Green Mountains' southernmost ridges by aiming for Fort Massachusett, on the border north of Williamstown. But that would have taken them back into the state where they were wanted for arrest. Instead, they joined the road that followed the West River northwest from Brattleboro, which would take them up to the Windham Road through the mountains. They would climb through the hills and cross the state's central ridge between Grout Pond and Stratton Mountain and then ride down into Arlington, in the state's western valley.

They rode through Newfane and Townsend, which had only been chartered twenty years ago. The farther they rode, the younger the farms were, till soon they were riding past clearings that were not even ten years old. The towering trees and wooded hills still waited to be civilized, and the individual families in straggling houses were still only making crude assaults on the wilds.[7]

In the primitive barns and enclosures built on the edges of ancient forests, the refugees witnessed a country much like their own being born out of the elements themselves. But they were not riding through this rough country to establish a civilization—they were refugees from the very civilization they and their parents had come to this country to settle.

The farms they passed through were much like the farms they had left behind, but this landscape was not the landscape they knew in Massachusetts. The laurel and straggling oak trees they recognized only dotted the bases of these hills, but maple and ash, enormous hemlock and pines rose up the flanks of snowy mountains that were shaggy at their tips with stunted spruces and firs. In the layered ridges and mountaintops they could see when they crested each hill, they beheld a remote and frozen wasteland where they could easily die if they did not pass quickly.

By the time dusk's shadows were starting to darken the snowy forests, they had reached the wild foothills of the state's central ridge of mountains.

At the end of their second long day on the road, they stopped at houses and begged for food and shelter. Like primitive pilgrims, they threw themselves on the mercy of poor farmers. They slept in whatever barns and sheds they could find to get out of the cold, although once the farmers recognized Shays as the leader of the people's resistance to Bowdoin, they tried to find him the best lodgings they could, to honor him for the sacrifices he had made for his people.

When dawn broke, Shays and his men packed their gear and set out in the snowy roads, warming themselves with the exertion of climbing the rolling hills toward the plateau of Wardsboro. Soon the only houses were hesitant cabins, or cold shacks where men had abandoned their work for winter. Foundation stones poked out of the snow, waiting for sills and joists in the spring.

Through towering mountains purple and gray with deep cold, they forged ahead, enduring their hunger, enduring their exhaustion and despair. Higher and higher they continued into the mountains, following streams where the water rumbled spookily beneath the ice.

They tried to let themselves be lifted by the beauty of the rugged land they passed through, with mountains laid out around them in lapping rows. Sometimes they would still find themselves admiring a curl of the landscape—a river, a plain, a stand of trees—and the force of habit was so strong that they would imagine how they and their neighbors might put that land to use.

They could not stop here to start new settlements, though. The cold and the threat of arrest spurred them onward and up through the hills. If the landscape's beauty consoled them for moments, they were haunted by the families and homes they were leaving farther behind with each step. They speculated whether they would be able to go home by spring, or whether they would have to start new lives in this republic and force themselves to forget the farms and communities they had abandoned.

Finally, they reached the high frozen marshes of Grout Pond and crested the gap that separates Vermont's eastern and western valleys. From the pass through the mountains, they descended toward civilization again, with the rippled hills of southern Vermont and eastern New York sliding translucent, silver and blue-gray behind the trees ahead of them as they descended.

Eventually they could start to see the towns in the valley below, then after another night in the mountains, they pushed through the last notch in the hills and rode into country where they encountered first the high farms, then, as they descended, settlements again. Now Shays and the others who had visited this country started to recognize the hills along the road, the curves around certain fields. They knew where they were and could tell the others what they should expect to see next, and how much farther they would have to march before they could rest at last.

On February 7, the fourth day of their exile, Shays and three hundred men reached the bottom of the broad Walloomsac River valley and the marshes alongside the river.[8] At the frozen river itself, the east-west road ended. On their right-hand side, the road ran north, to Manchester and Rutland, with Lake Champlain and Montreal beyond. To their left, it led south toward Bennington and back toward Massachusetts.

Some of the refugees parted from Shays and set off north to family or friends in Pittsford, just north of Rutland. Some continued north for a short way before they would turn west again and climb through another gap that would take them through the north-south Taconic Mountains and into New York, to friends in Salem, where Shays's sister lived, or else to friends in Cambridge, New Canaan, or New Lebanon.[9]

Shays and the final remnants of his force continued into Arlington, where the leading landowners, the Masons from Arlington's Newton Lodge and humble Scots-Irish families, were waiting to take them in.

In Arlington, Shays made arrangements for the hundreds of men who still accompanied him to camp on land next to the governor's farm.[10] He himself continued south through Shaftsbury to Bennington, where he was welcomed at last by his brother-in-law Jonathan Gilbert and his wife Hannah Converse and their five children, a hundred miles from Petersham, where he and his men had been ambushed four days ago.[11]

Shays and his men created a stir of excitement when they disrupted the slow routines of the towns strung through this valley remote from Albany and Boston, equally distant from the commercial centers of New Haven on the coast and Montreal on the St. Lawrence River.

The farmers here were used to watching the lights shift slowly across the face of the purple-green, purple-brown bowl of mountains that hemmed in their towns east and west, but now their fields were filled with bustling tents, and the air was full of hot debates about whether the Massachusetts farmers were justified in turning against their government, and whether the flinty Vermonters were obligated to offer them asylum.

Soon after Shays arrived, Eli Parsons, Joel Billings, and Reuben Dickinson descended out of the purple and silver mountains with even more men,

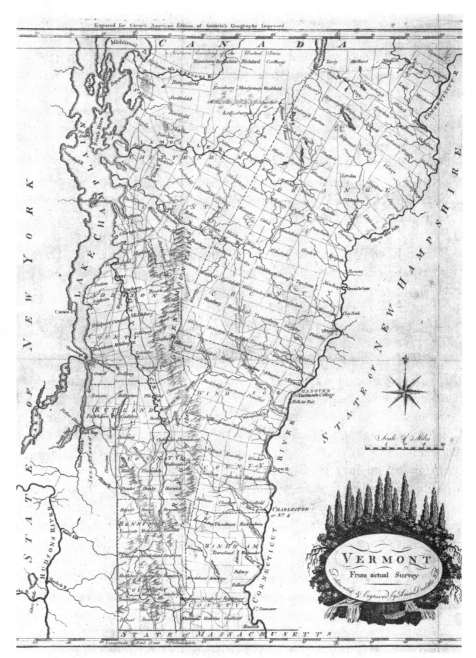

"Vermont, from Actual Survey" by Amos Doolittle. This 1795 map shows the central ridge-line of the Green Mountains as well as the northern end of the Taconic mountain range, on the western border, where Shays and his followers ultimately settled. (*Library of Congress*)

and it was not long before Luke Day and his brother Elijah joined them. The Days were preceded by reports that they had brandished pistols and stirred up talk of revenge at their brother Giles Day's house in Marlborough, west of Brattleboro along the Massachusetts border, before they came west to join the others.[12]

In the Walloomsac River valley, the Massachusetts farmers buzzed with talk of insurrection and arrests at home, as they heard reports that after the skirmish at Petersham, "soldiers of Government took the advantage to . . . vent all the spite, malice, and spleen, their jealousies and ill will, . . . taking some under pretense of warrant and Civil authority, taking others by the force of the Bayonet and Military power, some out of spite and malace in them that complaind, others upon bare suspicion, many of them Innocent, others more or less Guilty."[13]

This talk brought the fear of surprise attacks to the valley, for the Day brothers came with news that Governor Bowdoin had issued a proclamation offering £150—ten years' pay at laborer's rates—to any man who would capture Daniel Shays and bring him back to face justice in Massachusetts. Eli Parsons, Luke Day, and Adam Wheeler were each worth £100 in the governor's eyes.[14]

The danger that their hosts or their townsmen could report them and claim the reward spoiled any relief Shays and his men might have felt. This sense of dread was compounded by news that Lincoln had not kept his men in Springfield or Northampton, to institute martial law in Hampshire County, as the people had feared. After Petersham, he dismissed his artillery, sending them back to Boston, and shadowed Shays's journey west with three companies of infantry. He had arrived in Pittsfield, Massachusetts, a few days after Shays got to Arlington and set up his headquarters thirty-five miles south of Bennington, a day's march from Shays.[15]

One of Lincoln's agents, Royall Tyler, a lawyer hungry for the drama of hunting refugees, started to be seen around Arlington, offering money for information that might lead him to Shays, but the men of Arlington, Shaftsbury, and Bennington knew each other well enough to distrust the wealthy Boston lawyer and the men he recruited to help him.[16] The Regulators and Vermonters alike closed ranks and distrusted anyone they did not already know.

With Lincoln in Pittsfield, Shays and his officers could never feel secure in their safety, and they debated whether Governor Chittenden might authorize General Lincoln to cross the border north into Arlington, forcing them to continue west and cross another border into New York.

With danger of government agents in every shadow and in the whistle of every cold breeze, the families who hosted the Regulators took the precaution of moving them every night or every other night.[17] Shays and his men were always shaking new hands and mustering apologetic smiles for wives and children whose winter work they were interrupting, as they turned their houses upside-down with suspicion and guards at their doors. Every night or every other night, Shays put himself in debt to a different family. The families promised that they were giving their hospitality for free—they told him that they were all the same people and were only paying him for his service—but every morning or every other morning, he left in their debt nonetheless.

Even as the refugees' family members and their friends in Vermont provided for Shays and his men in exile, they heard from Massachusetts that the commonwealth had borrowed another £40,000 from the state's richest financiers, adding the sum to the commonwealth's other debts, as a "Loan to Suppress the Rebellion."[18]

The General Court had also passed a law that made it a crime to spread information prejudicial to government, but the refugees were beyond Bowdoin's authority. They paid their hosts with their stories, dispelling the rumors, telling the hungry Vermont farmers what it had cost them to organize opposition to government. They described the tense encounters at each of the court closings, the loathing they saw in the wealthy merchants' faces, and the respect they were shown by people in the towns, and even by some of the government's militias.

The families who had opened their homes to them knew these stories. Most of them had already taken sides simply by being cash-poor farmers. They knew well enough how merchants in cities wrote laws to squeeze profits out of the people. The farmers had fled to Vermont from the coasts of Connecticut and Massachusetts. They had accepted the trials of setting up farms in rocky hills, far from commercial centers, to get away from precisely these injustices.

Night to night, Shays and his men paid for their lodgings with their stories, but they moved too frequently to repay their hosts by entering into the rhythms of their farms and working beside them, making themselves at home in the routine of work in the snowy valley.[19]

In spite of the sleepless fear and suspicion, Shays and his men were never seriously menaced by Royall Tyler or Lincoln's men. Samuel Buffington, who had met Shays in the road as he approached the Springfield arsenal, had tried to come north with twenty horsemen, following in Shays's footsteps through the mountains, but the people of Brattleboro banded together and formed a crowd too thick for him to penetrate, and Buffington's horsemen retreated to Massachusetts.[20]

Still, hard news followed the refugees into the hills. The governor's militias were still pursuing the men who had not made it out of the state, and news came north that the governor's men had arrested Longmeadow's Alpheus Colton, Colrain's Matthew Clark, and Captain John Brown from Whately.[21]

In the houses where Shays and his officers were harbored, they heard reports of Royall Tyler's movements throughout the valley as he tried to seduce poor farmers with offers of money for information. Vigilant apprehension was thick in the valley, but a report from New Lebanon, New York, told them that Lincoln was subject to the same danger: Regulators had narrowly missed capturing the general at the hot springs there.[22]

Through the long bowl of southern Vermont's Walloomsac valley, tension and fear made the cold nights longer, even as they grew shorter with every dawn, and the growing season inched closer.

After a week of alarms and rumors in black hills under frigid stars, on February 16, Shays and his men heard that the General Court had made another half-hearted attempt to settle the crisis on the governor's terms.

The law they passed was not a compromise. It did not make any concessions on the economic issues that had been torturing the people these last two years. Really, it only spelled out the rules by which the Regulators would capitulate. The commonwealth itself named the law the Disqualification Act, because it offered men pardons on the condition that they surrender their muskets, pay a fine of nine pence, and agree to be disqualified from voting or serving on juries for three years. Nor would they be able to teach or sell liquor or run a tavern.[23] Men who signed this oath could ask their towns to reinstate their rights, but the magistrates who would hear their appeals had all been appointed by Bowdoin himself.

From Bennington, Eli Parsons responded to news of this act by publishing a letter that reminded his people that they had fought a war to establish the very rights the Disqualification Act now took from them. "Friends and fellow sufferers," he wrote, "Will you now tamely suffer your arms to be taken from you, your estates to be confiscated and even swear to support a Constitution and form of Government, and likewise a code of laws, which common sense and your consciences declare to be iniquitous and cruel? Can you bear to see and hear of the yeomanry of this commonwealth being patched and cut to pieces by the cruel and merciless tools of tyrannical power, and not resent it even unto relentless bloodshed?

"Would to God I had the tongue of a ready writer that I might impress on your minds the idea of the obligation you, as citizens of a republican government, are under, to support those rights and privileges that the God of nature hath entitled you to.

"Let me now persuade you, by all the sacred ties of friendship which natural affection inspires the human heart with, immediately to turn out and assert your rights."[24]

This letter ran in the Massachusetts newspapers beside letters brimming with inflammatory claims that promised to renew the people's resistance as soon as "the woods are covered with leaves."[25] And in the same newspapers, government supporters suggested that "a plenty of hemp" would solve the commonwealth's problems.[26]

In the cold, bright, mid-February days, Shays and his fellow exiles in southern Vermont did not take any steps to back those threats with action, though. Neither Shays nor his officers called meetings to organize further actions against Massachusetts courts, which were opening without interruption again. They did not make plans to rally the men of the country and march to Pittsfield to challenge Lincoln and his army.

Nor did the people who had stayed in Massachusetts call new meetings themselves, to nominate leaders to take Shays's place and carry on his work of organizing resistance. Almost as soon as Shays's force had been routed from Petersham, the towns of Massachusetts had started to post new petitions to Boston, confessing that they had been in error for having stopped the courts. In one petition after another, they apologized for having turned against government "under the mistaken notion of its being the only way to obtain redress of certain grievances." Gently they pointed out that the underlying causes that had led to the problems had not been dealt with satisfactorily, but now they openly pleaded that "allowance ought to be made on account of the ignorance and great distress of the people in general." They protested that many of their neighbors had "brothers and near relations among the insurgents," and they begged the state to issue pardons, to let them return to the fold.[27]

At the same time, though, men choked down the words they had spoken back in November, when they refused to seek out their magistrates. In the weeks that followed the Disqualification Act, almost eight hundred men sought their magistrates and surrendered their guns, signed their names, and swore the government's oath of loyalty, abandoning their rights in exchange for peace.[28]

While other men either swore to challenge the law or signed the oaths and submitted to it, Daniel Shays made plans to withdraw his family from Massachusetts. From Bennington, he dispatched his brother-in-law, Jonathan Gilbert, back through the snowy hills, past General Lincoln's patrols, to find Abigail in Pelham. Gilbert took instructions from Shays that she and the children should load their things in a sleigh, close up their house, and come join him in exile.

The General Court had passed a law prohibiting citizens from buying livestock and property from fleeing Regulators, but General Lincoln had not stayed in Hampshire County to force this law on the people.[29] When Jonathan Gilbert pulled up to the house and gave Abigail Shays this message from her husband, she made the rounds to her neighbors to raise money selling her things, and her neighbors offered her what they could as a way of redeeming her sacrifices.

One man had offered her money in exchange for information about Shays's whereabouts, but she knew that he must be a government man, for who among their people would have needed that information, and who but a government man would offer money?[30]

When her brother touched the draft horses into motion a the head of their sleigh full of trunks and tools, Abigail and the children turned their backs on all the improvements they and their neighbors had made on their land since the war. Daniel Junior and Hannah and Lucy compared this move to their previous moves, from Shutesbury to Brookfield during the war, and then to Pelham when Shays came home. But Gilbert and Polly departed from the only house they had ever known.

Abigail Shays and the children were hardly the only ones leaving Pelham. When the *Worcester Magazine* reported that they passed through Northampton en route to Bennington on February 21, they were joining columns of seven hundred refugee families pouring over the northern border into Vermont, with "livestock, household furniture and all moveable property" in their sleighs. In some towns, so many people departed that there were not enough inhabitants left to fill the town offices.[31]

Like their ancestors before them, they were leaving an unjust country, setting out into harsh, cold winter hills in the hope they might still be able to live by their own laws in another land.

Daniel Shays was not in Bennington to greet his wife when she arrived with her brother and the children at the end of February. At the same time Jonathan Gilbert was leading their jostling sleigh through the long valleys of the Berkshires and over the hills, Shays had taken to the road again, to visit Vermont Governor Thomas Chittenden in Williston east of Burlington, one hundred miles north.

He and his men had learned that a party in Vermont's legislature had been insisting that the state should keep itself independent of Massachusetts's troubles. They had drafted a proclamation that would deny Shays and the Regulators refuge, and now that petition sat on Chittenden's desk, awaiting his signature.[32]

Chittenden had held off signing the bill in hopes the matter would settle itself, but the crisis had dragged on, and his legislators were pressuring him to sign, so Shays, Adam Wheeler, Sylvanus Billings, and Pelham men William Conkey, Nehemiah Hines, Cornell, and Daniel Gray left their hundreds of men camped near Ethan Allen's farm in Arlington.[33] They bundled themselves against the winter weather and headed north to make their case for asylum to Chittenden in person.

If they had traveled in summer, they could have stabled their horses northwest of Rutland and rowed or sailed the length of Lake Champlain in a couple of days, but now their horses would have to wallow step by step through the snow for the whole hundred miles.

They rode from fire to fire. They passed through rough towns where the oldest buildings were not even thirty years old, and through primitive country where the new farms had still barely spread their roots into the forests. From tavern to tavern, no one tried to capture them, to claim the reward Bowdoin offered.

Cold in their saddles, they pressed their horses along the edges of snow-covered fields and frozen rivers. North of Rutland, the valley opened wide, and they rode north along the plains toward Lake Champlain. On their right, the jagged Green Mountain ridgeline followed their eyes as far as the northern horizon, and across the frozen lake, the Adirondack foothills and the mountains themselves behind them turned pink at dawn, then silver in glistening sunlight, a deep green and slate in the shadows, then a bruised purple as the sun swung behind them at dusk.

Row upon row, the mountains in the distance ground their teeth on each other as the refugees passed the length of the state. In every forested peak and in every plateau in the mountains, the men saw virgin land that promised freedom and independence, but they could not stop in their tracks to build those farms.

The late-February cold was still profound. Even when it was not snowing, crystal flakes sifted down on their hats and coats, and they wrapped themselves tight in their scarves, hastening over the miles, spurred by the urgent question of asylum. When the sun did break through the clouds, it warmed their backs, as if to assure them that spring was coming and that winter and their exile would not last forever. Nevertheless, hour after hour through four long days of riding and nights of short rest, they pushed north to settle the question of their future.

After days of passing along the frozen Lake Champlain, Shays and his officers rode into the port town of Burlington. They followed eastward and uphill along the Onion River in search of Governor Chittenden's grand brick house on its rise looking east out over that river.[34]

When they arrived, Chittenden entertained their plea for refuge but said he could not help them. He said that he recognized the desperate farmers' righteous cause and their pride, and he even admired them for refusing to bow to Bowdoin's tyranny, but he was not free to let them stay, not as the state's official policy, anyway.[35] He explained that Bowdoin had written to demand their arrest. Alexander Hamilton had introduced a bill in the federal Congress supporting Vermont's bid for statehood on the condition that Chittenden turn them over.[36] Chittenden explained that he and Ethan Allen and the others had formed the state as an independent republic during the turmoil of the Revolution, but they had always expected to bring Vermont into the union. He could not afford to jeopardize years of negotiations by openly insulting Bowdoin and Hamilton now.

Still, Chittenden said that he did not respect Bowdoin's wishes enough to arrest Shays or Wheeler or any of the others, to return them to Massachusetts for trial. He told them that even if his legislature forced him to sign the proclamation denying them refuge, he would not take steps to enforce it.[37] He lamented that he was not in a position to disregard Bowdoin's demands entirely, but he offered Shays and his men hospitality after their long trip north.

Shays and his road-weary officers stayed with Chittenden in Williston for a few days, but when they left, they did not ride south back to Arlington. They pressed farther north, following along the lake from Burlington, riding the hundred miles across the windy floodplains toward Quebec.

They were going to repeat the same request for refuge before the Canadian Royal Governor Sir Guy Carleton, Lord Dorchester. He had earned a reputation as a decent and principled man when he oversaw the evacuation of New York Loyalists to Prince Edward Island and Newfoundland after the war. He would not agree that the Loyalists' slaves were rightful property, and he forced New York slave owners to leave their oppressed men and women behind with their children, terminating any claims of ownership.[38] Now Shays and his officers hoped he would be able to see how things stood and give them protection from Bowdoin's army.

When Shays and his men crossed the frozen St. Lawrence River and entered the city, Lord Dorchester heard their pleas, but he told them, as Chittenden had told them, that he had been getting letters from Bowdoin insisting that Shays be arrested and sent back to Boston for trial. Dorchester also told them that his ministers in London had counseled him not to get entangled in Americans' affairs. He was told to let conditions devolve until the American ministers sent a formal request to London to beg for Britain's protection again.[39]

Like Chittenden, Lord Dorchester refused to commit the injustice of arresting Shays and his officers, but since he could not give them sanctuary, he simply denied having met with them.[40] The commanding officer at the Canadian fort on Ile aux Noix in the St. Lawrence, south of Montreal, refused to either assist or arrest Shays's party and refused to turn them over to Lincoln's agents, who arrived two hours after Shays had departed.[41]

Rebuffed in Quebec, Shays, Wheeler, and Billings and Conkey, Hines, Cornell, and Gray set out south to retrace their steps, two hundred miles through the snow, back at last toward their families and their men in Arlington.

Tavern to tavern, fireplace to fireplace, they rode back through the cold. Stopping again in Williston, they heard that Chittenden had yielded to his legislature and signed the proclamation denying them refuge. In person, though, he assured them that he still intended to flout his lawmakers and Bowdoin alike: he would not enforce the edict and either drive Shays out or arrest him.

Shays and his envoys continued south from Williston undisturbed. All the way back to Arlington, though, all the length of Vermont, they begrudged Chittenden and Dorchester their neutral stances and resented the power by which Bowdoin forced unjust authority on his neighbors. Without any channels through which to appeal the governors' decisions, they could only return to their hosts, whose private hospitality was all the state they had now.

When Shays and his envoys returned to Arlington in the first week of March, their reunion with their wives and children was spoiled by news that more than one hundred New York and Berkshire men had shattered the peace in their absence.

On February 21, aggrieved men had seen a window to act when Lincoln's army's enlistments expired, and most of his three thousand men marched back to Boston. Lincoln's men had taken the post road, passing south of most of the towns that had sent men to interrupt the courts. The hired army did not encounter resistance on their way home, but they left Lincoln in Pittsfield with only thirty men, waiting for Bowdoin to send reinforcements.[42]

Shays and his men were still unpacking their saddlebags when their friends welcomed them home with the news that a few days after Lincoln's men left, a New York captain, Perez Hamlin, had marched into Massachusetts near Stockbridge, twenty miles south of Pittsfield.[43] He rode at the head of 130 exiled Regulators and sympathetic New Yorkers who promised death to merchants, lawyers, and judges and to any men who had taken the government's side. Their force liberated rebels and debtors from prison and looted seventeen houses, including Silas Pepoon's general store.[44] They had also plundered the warehouse of a wealthy merchant, Captain Walter Pynchon, after they had forced his daughter Mary to unlock the doors at bayonet point.[45] From Stockbridge, they marched to Great Barrington, where they sought out their chief tormenter, Judge Theodore Sedgwick.[46] They did not find him at home, so they ransacked the house he had furnished with the thousands of pounds he had stolen from the people in court fees.

Warming themselves at last in front of their hosts' fires in Arlington, Shays and his officers read the newspapers that celebrated Sedgwick's Black housekeeper, Mum Bett, who had protected the judge's silver by hiding it in her own trunk.[47] The farmers had not had any reason to pillage the servants' quarters, but the merchants' editorials celebrated the servant's loyalty to the man who had challenged Massachusetts's slavery laws to free her.[48]

From Sedgwick's house, the mob had gone to search for him in his office. When they still failed to find him, they took his two clerks captive and proceeded southeast along the snowy roads toward Sheffield to punish whatever wealthy men they could find.[49]

Shays and his men listened with heavy hearts to the predictable conclusion of Hamlin's raid. In the absence of General Lincoln's army, eighty Berkshire County militiamen rallied under Sheffield's Colonel John Ashley, the lawyer who had listed Mum Bett among his possessions before Sedgwick sued on her behalf.

Ashley's force found Hamlin's men in the snowy road between Great Barrington and Sheffield, eighty rods south of the marble sawmill at the Goodale marble quarry.[50] Like Tryon and Howe—like Lincoln before him—Ashley did not surround the insurgents or dispatch envoys to start negotiations. He simply rushed his men into the trees on either side of the road and shot into Hamlin's ranks when they approached on the road.[51]

The parties exchanged fire for only a couple of minutes, but when the sharp stink of gunpowder and the sounds of wounded men's cries drained the fight out of Hamlin's men, two had been killed in each party, and thirty writhed in their injuries. Ashley's men surged forward to capture Hamlin and eighty-four others, while the rest fled through the fields.[52]

If Shays and his officers still hoped they might be pardoned, they gave up their hope with this news. They had not played any part in planning this raid, but now Hamlin's daring affront would condemn them all. Bowdoin would not be able to end the crisis until the state had shown men of property that lawlessness would be punished. The fact that Shays was not involved would hardly protect him if Bowdoin's agents ever laid hands on him.

In the days after Hamlin's raid, the news of his defeat and arrest had still not sparked a wider lawlessness, but more of the families who had taken the government's side found reasons to lock up their houses and leave the region, to visit their friends and family in Boston, New York, or Connecticut.[53] As they left their homes, they spread the rumor that Shays was collecting an army of fifteen thousand disaffected men and was even now stockpiling supplies and preparing to march an army into Massachusetts. They said Ethan Allen was planning to annex Hampshire and Berkshire Counties into the independent republic of Vermont. They even spread the alarming story that the British fleet was waiting offshore, hungry for a chance to retake the colonies.[54]

In reality, though, Shays and his men still refused to organize a force to invade their country or to take revenge on Colonel Ashley and his men or Lincoln and his. But facts did not matter now that newspapers were inflaming the country with wild speculations, and day to day, the tensions were thick throughout southern Vermont and northern Berkshire County. The people's fears were bolstered by anonymous letters—or by letters that ran above Shays's name—in which exiled men swore that they would rather die "by the bayonet than by the halter."[55]

Day to day, the newspapers still did not print reports that anyone was actually setting these plans in motion, but in Boston, these rumors triggered a frenzy of suppression. Shays and his people in exile heard that Bowdoin's allies were arresting anyone who dared to criticize the government. New Hampshire Governor Sullivan's brother wrote that it was even dangerous to be silent. He said that a man could be "accused of rebellion if he does not loudly approve every measure as prudent, necessary, wise and constitutional."[56]

To quell the panic gripping the commonwealth, Bowdoin deployed militias in the towns along Massachusetts's northern border to intercept Shays's army if he came south. The militias patrolled the roads for attacks that never came. They only captured individual men who were returning to their homes for tools or provisions.

Hungry for evidence of insurrection, the newspapers pounced on the story of Jason Parmenter, whom Bowdoin's patrols had tried to arrest at the end of February. Parmenter, a farmer in his fifties, had fought with Shays at Fort Ticonderoga, when the rebels had surrendered the fort to General Burgoyne. He had been with Shays again when they defeated Burgoyne a month later at Saratoga. Like so many other farmers in the region, Parmenter had suffered under Bowdoin's austerity measures, so he had joined the people's protests in Northampton and Springfield, and he had fled with them to Vermont after their force was surprised in Petersham.

When Parmenter slipped back across the border to retrieve some supplies from his house in Bernardston south of Brattleboro, he and the men in his party had collided with one of Bowdoin's patrols in the perfect dark of a new-moon night. In the entanglement of horses and reins, Parmenter's loaded musket had gone off.[57] He had made his escape, but when he returned in the morning and found blood in the snow, he learned that his blind shot had killed a government sergeant, Jacob Walker of Whately. Stung with guilt, Parmenter turned himself in. He was taken to prison and charged with murder, and now in the court of editorials, his accidental musket ball compounded the charges against Shays and his officers, staining them all with the bloodshed they had always tried to prevent.

As the crisis of fear and panic spiraled deeper in western Massachusetts and southern Vermont, Shays and his men were trapped in a stateless limbo. But now that February was yielding to March, the growing season was starting to come into view. Every day, the sun was rising a little bit higher in the east, and winter was losing its grip on the hills as the earth inched toward the equinox.

When it snowed now, the snowflakes were flecked with ice and sometimes they were even softened with rain. On every sunny day, the snow that had fallen in January and February blizzards was starting to melt off the farmhouses' and taverns' roofs in long icicles like bars of light that closed them inside, and the streams rushing down from the mountains were noisy and ragged with foam.

Shays and his officers were still moving house to house in Arlington, Shaftsbury, and Bennington, but now the families who hosted them were watching the first patches of bare earth appear in their fields where the snow melted. They were starting to tend their equipment in advance of plowing their fields for the seeds they would plant in May, and now Shays and his family, his men and their wives, were going to have to settle the question of where they would plant their own seeds, to grow the crops that would see them through the coming winter.

In the letters their messengers carried back and forth between Jonathan Gilbert's house in Bennington and the houses where Arlington families kept Shays out of sight, Shays and his wife estimated the likelihood that he might be pardoned in Massachusetts, that they could return to Pelham to plant their seeds there. They weighed the chance that Chittenden would allow them to stay in Vermont officially against the possibility that the legislators who had forced him to sign their proclamation would ultimately drive them out.

Determined not to run farther than they had already run, Shays and his people started to ask their hosts where they could find land they could rent or buy, and Shays wrote to his sister, to see whether she could find him a place on her side of the border.

Shays and his wife's plans were complicated in early March when they heard from Massachusetts that ten of their creditors had filed papers with the Hampshire County Court of Common Pleas asking for the right to seize their land and property as payment for debts they had left behind when they fled.

Some of these suits had been filed by their neighbors. Three had been brought by men who had obeyed Shays's orders and called him general when they marched from Springfield to Worcester and Rutland and back. Even Nehemiah Hines, one of the men who had asked Shays to lead, had submitted a claim against his land, trying to get what he could before Shays's assets were consumed by other men's claims.[58]

Shays had already pulled his wife and children out of the state. Abigail had already sold what she could to raise funds to start again in Vermont. They were going to lose their farm if Shays could not answer the charges in court or borrow money from family or from fellow refugees to pay the debts.

All the improvements they had made in six years were going to be taken from them for his crime of having restrained his townsmen and government men alike from the violence that was coiled in everyone's fists.

Daniel Shays made one last attempt to win a pardon. On the tenth of March, he and Eli Parsons posted a humble apology to Governor Bowdoin, expressing regret for their errors and begging to be pardoned for their role in stopping the courts.[59] They told the government officials that their petitioners would "never cease to remember with regret their not having trusted for relief to the wisdom and integrity of the ruling power." They said that their errors "proceeded from a misapprehension of the facts, from a failure of judgment, and a too precipitate resentment, but by no means from an abandoned principle." They denied having fomented an insurrection from out of the state. "However criminal they may have been in other respects," they said, "they could not be justly reproached with this enormity."

Shays and Parsons closed by saying there was "scarcely an inconvenience or misfortune to which they have not already been exposed," and they wished "to have an opportunity of proving to the world the sincerity of their reformation, and of adding another happy instance to those which have been already so conspicuous from the clemency of this Honorable Court."[60]

Unfortunately, their letter was delivered to Boston only a few days after men in South Hadley had burned down a glass factory to punish its owner, Josiah Woodbridge, for having loaned the commonwealth money and supplies. If the legislators in Boston had even looked at Shays and Parsons's request, their discussions were halted two days later when the state was alarmed by news that two Berkshire County retailers had watched their warehouses in Nobletown, New York, go up in flames.[61]

Shays and Parsons had not stirred from Arlington to play any part in setting those fires. They had restrained their men at every step. They had not moved to arm themselves against the government men at the Springfield arsenal until the last moment, and even then, they had not spilled any blood on the government's side before they had been chased from the state and ultimately lost their ability to rein in their people's outrage.

Nevertheless, the government men called all the arsonists Shaysites, and the papers kept the country inflamed with further threats of violence, so the legislators in Boston never responded to Shays and Parsons's petition.

Notwithstanding the violence and the fires that eclipsed their petition, Shays and his wife and Eli Parsons waited for an answer from Boston. Through the middle of March, they continued to hope that Governor Bowdoin would respond with a list of terms they could negotiate, to win pardons in the end.

They never did hear those terms, but week to week, the news that did come from Massachusetts was all against them. The dignity and discipline Shays and his officers had instilled in their townsmen had melted in Hamlin's raid, and now the fires in Nobletown and South Hadley sparked other fires.

Within a week after Shays and Parsons had posted their petition, yet another wealthy man, a Pittsfield lawyer and merchant and former Tory, Woodbridge Little, lost his barn to a fire.[62] The merchants and wealthy men were crying out for their government to give them relief from the tax of violence the people were imposing.

Beneath the dark clouds of these fires, Shays gave up his hope of returning home. He spoke to the men who had followed him into exile, men who had refused to surrender their guns and sign the governor's oath of disqualification. Shays asked them to join him in starting a new settlement in Vermont. More than a hundred men said that they would stay with him, working at his side to make a place where they could farm in peace and live by their own strict Presbyterian laws.

Chapter Twelve

Refugees and Settlers

O NCE AGAIN, DANIEL SHAYS SPOKE for his people when he asked his hosts in Arlington for permission to start a settlement within the town's borders. The people of Arlington called a town meeting to take up the question. It was not a simple matter. The legislature in Vermont had passed its resolution denying them refuge, and even though Governor Chittenden had refused to enforce this order, Arlington's leaders were afraid of the consequences if Chittenden changed his mind. Or perhaps the next election would bring in another governor who would punish them for letting Shays's men plant their roots there. Prominent men pleaded Shays's case, but when they put the question to a vote, their town decided not to let them stay.[1]

Shays and his officers submitted the same request to the leaders of Shaftsbury, south of Arlington, but they got the same answer there. The people could not risk letting them charter a settlement within their borders. Like Chittenden and Dorchester, they did not have the authority to grant them official asylum, although they did not vote to expel them either, or to turn them over to Bowdoin.

Shays and his men were not willing to pack their possessions in carts and ride farther west, or farther north, to start new lives as strangers far from their region. They asked their hosts to recommend land, in a private capacity, where they could build homes and plant crops safe from Lincoln's agents and also far enough from the towns that no one would be putting themselves in danger by letting them build.

One of their hosts, David Cowden, who had fought with Shays in the war, owned land in the uncut hills of Sandgate, Vermont, adjacent to the New York border.[2] He told Shays about a high plateau where he and his men could start again, out of the way but still within a short ride of their friends and relatives.

Shays and his officers put down their correspondence, their drafts of petitions begging for asylum or pardons. They dressed themselves for an outing into the woods and followed Cowden along the snowy roads beside the Battenkill River west from Arlington and crossed into New York State before they turned northeast and crossed back into Vermont. They followed roads through farmland, then forested roads that zigzagged up into bare hills, then entered woods that had never been logged and followed foot paths into the uninhabited hills, ascending a long ridge into the heart of the mountains.

The site Cowden offered sat on a south-facing shoulder of Egg Mountain, surrounded by a bowl of five other mountains.[3] A wide plateau would be broad enough for crops. A stream nearby flowed down from the heights, and the valley below opened southwest across the border into New York, close to Salem, where Shays's sister Polly lived with her husband and children.

From a narrow promontory south of the plateau, Shays and his men could see through the bare trees out over a long view of ridges and mountains that stretched off into the distance, much like Shays's vista in Pelham. Whatever settlement Shays and his men could foresee as they surveyed this south-facing hillside, they would need to slave for years before they had made homes like the farms they had abandoned in Massachusetts.

These forests had been neglected for a generation. For thousands of years, Mohican and Abenaki people had maintained the hills, burning out underbrush to clear the forests for hunting and to encourage the nut-bearing hickories, chestnuts, and oaks.[4] But ever since the natives had been driven out of these hills at the end of the French and Indian War, the forests had been sliding back toward wild nature. The parklike forests had been ruined by neglect, and the ground that had been grassy and open beneath the huge trunks' cathedral-like columns was snarled and tangled with thickets and blown-down limbs. Vines and saplings, striving against each other, had narrowed the paths and choked out the light.

All of this riotous growth would have to be cleared before the refugees from Massachusetts could plant the seeds that would carry them through the coming winter's cold, hungry months. Their guides pointed out that the hills did have the advantage of bountiful wild game. If they brought their muskets, they could feed themselves like frontiersmen on squirrels and rabbits, geese and robins, before they domesticated the hillside by planting crops in their clearings.

Slipping and sliding in snowy mud as they descended back to the valley, Shays and his men alternated between laying their plans and lamenting the rough conditions in which they would have to begin. There was nothing else to do, though. They had asked for help in every direction, and no one had offered them civilized land to settle. They could not return to their homes in Pelham now, any more than the exiled Scots could have returned to Ulster where their people had established plantations for English landlords almost two hundred years ago, nor to their people's ancestral homes in the Scottish Lowlands, nor to the homelands of any of the people like the Gilberts, with whom they had crossed their blood in their years in America. They could only follow their new world tradition of starting from scratch on wild land.

When Shays and his scouting party returned to their hosts' homes in the valley, more than a hundred men started to gather supplies and provisions and plan their attack on the hillside. Through the middle of March, as the days swung forward toward summer and the nights swung back toward winter chills, they spent their days loading sleighs with the tools their wives and children had brought from home, plus supplies for a camp, and provisions their hosts had donated. They spent the money they had saved from home and bought supplies on credit from Bennington merchants.

When they had filled the carts as full as they could and still steer them over the rough tracks up into the hills, they said goodbye to their wives and children, entrusting them to their family members and friends for a little longer.

With oxen and draft horses hauling their cargo, they followed a longer road that took them into New York so they could approach the site from the west where the climb was not so steep. The snow still had not all melted, but they drove up the rough paths, filling in ditches with stones and saplings, to keep the loads from bogging down in mud. For miles uphill through the forests, more than a hundred men followed the oxen until they arrived at the site Shays and Cowden had marked.

As some men unloaded supplies in the open forest, others started to set up their tents in the cold, late-March snow, hammering tent stakes the best they could into the frozen ground and digging shallow pits for cook fires and for latrines. As this work commenced, drovers sawed the oxen around and returned to the valley to bring up another load. When the creaking carts disappeared beyond hearing, Shays and his men stopped running at last and started to make their home in land they would call their own.

When he served in the army, Shays had overseen the construction of breastworks around his camp on the Hudson River. Now he worked alongside men who were skilled in the art of building. They would start their settlement the same as every settlement had started before them, with a central blockhouse where they would sleep and cook together until they could frame other buildings. They chose a site for their first foundation and marked off a square perimeter where they would build walls a hundred feet long on each side to protect themselves—not from Natives' arrows, but from their own government's bullets.[5]

High on their hillside, a hundred men made themselves at home in endless toil and became, for this time, the first settlers themselves. For months, the exiled men had restrained their anger in disciplined shoulders, but now they could finally pour out all the force they had held back. In teams, they hacked at the ancient trees, clearing the view from the promontory, so they could keep a watch on the roads below. Teams of men trimmed the fallen trees, wrestling branches and roots into long piles along the edge of a clearing that expanded as one tree after another came crashing down. Teams of men drove the horses and oxen that sledded the cut logs to the site where further teams had been digging up what stones they could wrest from the south-facing soil, to start on the foundation.

At the site itself, men squared the logs with broadaxes and sawed them with pit saws, and soon men were leaning into drills and chisels, carving dovetails, and mortise and tenon joints, and holes for pegs, while other men whittled trunnels to peg the timbers in place.[6]

On sunny days, when the late-March weather was mild and the growing season seemed rich and close by, their labors were paid by their pride in the quick work a hundred men's hands were making in the woods, and they could already start to see houses in the stacks of lumber and crops in neat rows in the muddy clearings. On cold days when the weather slid back toward winter, though—when sleet accumulated in muddy puddles, and their fires could never chase the damp chill from their bones, the stacks of lumber looked nothing like a shelter. The men hunkered cold in their tents and tortured themselves dreaming dreams in which they were still on the road with an army behind them, or, equally painful, dreaming of home fires they had left behind.

Cold in their hills, they braced each other up. They recalled the heroic feats their parents' generation had accomplished when they had carved towns out of wilderness. They reminded each other that they were not the first people pushed off their land for organizing opposition to powerful men. They reminded each other how much worse their conditions had been in camp during the war, without provisions or blankets, when they were fighting a disciplined army, and all their liberties hung in the balance.

They consoled each other with the same hymns and ballads and fighting songs they had sung through the war.[7] They quoted the same Bible verses that had soothed their parents' and grandparents' resentments when they were starting with nothing in wilderness in their turn.

All through the Revolution, they had told themselves that they would be the ones who lived in freedom, but now they returned to the long tradition of settlers who sunk themselves in hard work, slaving in faith that their children's children might one day realize those dreams.

For Daniel Shays, the numbing, impersonal work was a respite from the cares he had carried for months. He was no longer responsible for thousands of men. He was not still caught between factions who wanted to fight and others who hoped to negotiate peace.

Everyone knew what they needed to do here, and Shays was merely one man among the others. He could even allow himself to take orders again, from men who had more experience laying joists or floorboards, or lifting logs into place for the blockhouse beams. High on the hillside, Shays was subject to the same cold fingers, the same nicks and cuts, the same hungers and exhaustions, the same heartsickness and loss, the same longings that afflicted every man. Through long days of crushing labor, Shays and his men found purpose and consolation in work. They sweated out their anger and only observed rough Sabbaths by pausing briefly in work that was in itself a kind of prayer for safety and independence.

Through the end of March, Shays and his men were visited on their hillside by men who brought word from their wives and children and families in the valleys. They brought reports that crocuses and snowdrops and daffodils had started to send up their buds, and messengers were glad to give an accounting of the songbirds that were returning to the thickets.

As they entered into the rhythm of their settlement, the reports that continued to come from Massachusetts registered strangely. It was news from a foreign country now, but they listened almost in spite of themselves. In the last week of March, visitors brought reports that judges had opened the Berkshire County Supreme Judicial Court without disturbance. In their robes and wigs, they heard the government's lawyers make their cases against two hundred men who had been charged with riot and treason, sedition and insurrection.

The state's attorney general, Robert Treat Paine, had been riding throughout the commonwealth gathering evidence for these trials. For weeks, the settlers high on their hillside heard the visitors relate men's complaints, that it did not take very much testimony to convict men of having joined the insurrection. Even wealthy landowners had been complaining that they were just being framed by their townsmen, who were using the courts' investigations and trials to vent private resentments.[8]

When the government's lawyers had finished presenting their evidence in Great Barrington, the judges rode to Northampton, where government prosecutors laid out their evidence against another two hundred men from Hampshire County, including the capital case against Jason Parmenter.[9] No one brought news that the men on trial denounced Daniel Shays, or accused him of having seduced them to insurrection. Reports said that the dominant tone in the trials was contrition, as communities repented their men's actions and timidly begged for the state's forgiveness.[10]

In the last weeks of March, they had also heard that John Hancock had been campaigning to take the governor's seat back from Bowdoin in April elections. Hancock was still one of the richest men in the commonwealth, but the papers said that he had been riding through Massachusetts in a plain, two-wheeled trap, to draw the contrast with Bowdoin's extravagant personal carriage.[11]

The people were not blind to the irony of this gesture, since one of the things that had always infuriated Hancock's critics was the ornate carriage he had driven before the war, emblazoned with a showy coat of arms with three crowing cocks and an open hand.[12] Now, in rallies and speeches and campaign proclamations, Hancock was making himself popular again by promising to pass the very reforms the farmers had been asking for all this time.

Shays and his fellow settlers listened with curious interest, but elections would not change anything for them now. It was too late. They had already lost their farms. They were already building new lives. The problems Hancock promised to solve belonged to another people, to men who had been defeated, to officials in towns that had never sent men to the protests, to commercial men and lawyers who had accused them of being lazy and wanting something for nothing.

On the second of April, in Pelham and Amherst, in Rutland and Worcester, in Concord, Taunton, and Hopkinton, in Sheffield and Great Barrington, the free men of Massachusetts whose wealth exceeded £60 went to the polls to cast their votes for governor, lieutenant governor, and senators in the commonwealth's referendum on Bowdoin's crisis. In the beginning of May, they would repeat the process to vote for representatives.[13]

Their votes would not be tallied till early summer, though, so the elections themselves did not put an end to acts of arson in the commonwealth. Everyone knew that the governor's Disqualification Act was an illegal strategy to suppress the vote against him, so the people were not optimistic about having won reforms.

Even as the votes were being counted, men who had surrendered the right to vote when they swore the disqualification's loyalty oath continued to take the law into their own hands, and they imposed their version of justice on merchants who had oppressed them. News ran through the state, and up to Vermont, that Westfield merchant Enoch Loomis's store had burned on April 4. A few days later, Greenfield merchant William Moore lost half his potash works to fire.[14]

Some of the men proposed marching back to help the government institute order, to keep their state from being consumed by lawless revenge and descending into civil war, but the men who had started their work in the hills did not put down their tools to march home with muskets.

The government had not yet announced the election results when the judges returned their verdicts in the middle of April. Muddy in their work site high in the forest, Shays and his men heard that the Berkshire County judges had sentenced six men to the gallows, including Nathaniel Austin from Sheffield and Peter Wilcox Jr. from Lee, for firing on government men, and Joseph Williams, from New Marlboro, for being taken in flight with a loaded gun. For high treason, they convicted Enoch Taylor from Egremont and Samuel Rust from Pittsfield.[15]

Four more men were sentenced to lesser penalties, among these Justice Whiting, who had stopped General Paterson's men in September, then published the pamphlet that accused the government of plundering the people.[16]

From Northampton a few weeks later, they heard that the Hampshire County court had condemned Jason Parmenter—whose musket ball had killed Jacob Walker—and also thirty-six-year-old Henry McCullough of West Hill in Pelham. McCullough had not held any leadership position in Shays's ranks. He had only distinguished himself by having ridden a good horse to Springfield in January, but everyone knew that Bowdoin's judges needed to make a show of force, and it did not matter to them who was killed in order to prove the commonwealth's authority.[17]

From Hampshire County, the judges selected nine other men for fines and imprisonment. Some of the protestors were condemned to demonstrate their submission by standing on the gallows for an hour with a noose about their necks.

By the time the judges handed down the last of their sentences, one more man from Worcester Country, Henry Gale, and one from Middlesex County, Job Shattuck, had also been named for hanging. The executions were scheduled to begin at the end of May, starting with McCullough and Parmenter in Northampton on the twenty-fourth.[18]

The men on Egg Mountain scoffed at this news. They knew that their people would never allow their townsmen to be killed. If they did not capture them back from prison, their neighbors would mob and prevent the executions themselves.[19] Shays and his men had always refused to return to Massachusetts, but now they promised their visitors that they would prevent the hangings if it came to that.

When their visitors descended back to their homes in Sandgate and Arlington, or to Shaftsbury and Bennington in the valley, Shays and his fellow settlers returned to their blockhouse and the long ordeal of preparing unbroken soil to take their seeds.

Every day, the sounds of their work were answered from the valleys by the sounds of men splitting wood or hammering on houses and barns. At dusk, they cooked their suppers and slept in the timeless quiet of the forest.

As April turned toward May, visitors brought reports from Massachusetts that the looming threat of executions had also started to thaw the hostilities in their old towns. The wealthy merchants who had taken the government's side had been dreading the danger of losing their barns and homes in fires for long enough. They finally started to use their influence on the convicted men's behalf in order to regain their townsmen's trust.

Amherst's retired general, Ebenezer Mattoon, had led the 4th Massachusetts Regiment during the Revolution, but he had kept himself out of sight while his neighbors in Amherst and Pelham were marching to stop the courts.[20] His business had been suffering, though, as the people had been avoiding his store, so now he wrote letters to the governor and the courts, attesting to Parmenter's character and begging the governor not to inflame the populace by putting him to death.

From the Berkshires, Shays and his men heard that the other Regulators were not waiting for help from prominent men. Two Regulators' wives, Abigail Austin and Molly Wilcox, had freed their husbands by smuggling saw blades to them in loaves of bread, though some reports said in their underclothes.[21] Their townsmen conspired to keep the fugitives hidden when government men came to capture them back, but all through the countryside, people's hearts were sore with concern for the men in prison.

Chapter Thirteen

Starting Anew

B Y THE END OF APRIL, vote totals started to trickle out from town offices, and the news came up the hill to the settlement that John Hancock had been elected in a landslide. A thousand men had given up their right to vote in exchange for being pardoned for stopping the courts, but thirty-two thousand men—almost twice as many as had ever voted in Massachusetts elections—turned out, and they overwhelmingly blamed Governor Bowdoin for creating and then exacerbating the crisis. In every county in the commonwealth—even Bowdoin's stronghold in Suffolk—by an overall ratio of three-to-one, they repudiated his policies and refused to renew his authority.[1]

Hancock would not take office till the first of June, but now that Bowdoin's days were numbered, he feared that Hancock would take the credit for ending the crisis. On April 25, he stole Hancock's thunder by issuing a blanket pardon for men who had closed courts in the fall. He also rescinded eight of the sixteen death sentences the Supreme Judicial Court had handed down.[2]

Daniel Shays was not one of the men who could feel that justice had finally been served. He, Day, Parsons, Hamlin, and four other men were exempted from pardons. Bowdoin had left their cases as well as the eight capital sentences for Hancock to resolve: either to vindicate Bowdoin's policies by exercising the state's authority and going ahead with executions or else show his weakness by issuing pardons.

For Shays and his men, this news of the blanket pardon did not change anything. By this point, the men who had wanted to return to their homes in Massachusetts had found their way back. The rest had made themselves at home in the settlement they were building in their clearing. In six weeks, more than a hundred men had framed the blockhouse. They had built a hearth and a chimney, and they had piled stones in walls a hundred feet square to protect against any attack.[3] At the end of April, they were starting to put a roof on the structure, so they finally had a place to sleep and cook out of the weather—and just in time, as mosquitoes were starting to swarm their heads while they worked, and buzz in their ears while they slept.

As they finished the blockhouse, the settlers started another common building, to serve as a barracks and also a tavern and meeting house. They also started to plan what crops they would plant when their hillside was finally free of the last threat of frost in another few weeks.

In everything they envisioned and debated as they laid these plans, they wove themselves into the coming months on Egg Mountain. The news from Massachusetts no longer applied to them. When it stung them to remember how their government and even some of their townsmen had betrayed them, they soothed that sting by blistering their fingers cutting trees, or bruising their shoulders lifting beams into place.

However they had come to feel at home in their new routines on Egg Mountain, the people of western Massachusetts and southern Vermont could not ignore the black mark on their calendars as April turned to May: in three and a half weeks, the Commonwealth of Massachusetts was going to execute Henry McCullough and Jason Parmenter in Northampton.

On the second of May, the moon rose full in the east behind the Green Mountain ridge, and every night as it rose later and thinner, Shays and his people waited in vain to hear that the men had been pardoned or rescued from prison.

Some of Shays's men started to talk about going back to Massachusetts to stop the hangings by force. Men who had fled their country to keep themselves innocent of violence considered the cost to their consciences if they did not prevent the hangings. They weighed this against the cost to their souls if they should either spill blood to prevent them—or if they themselves were injured or killed.

Debate though they might, the men refused to budge from Vermont, although they heard from Massachusetts that their people were taking action without them. Regulators in Colrain had captured Colonel Hugh McClellan and Major William Stevens, the artillery officers whose men had fired grapeshot into the people's ranks at Springfield. They promised to hang them both if the government followed through with its threatened executions. In Warwick east of Northfield, Regulators abducted Dr. Medad Pomeroy and Esquire Metcalf and let the state know that they too would be put to death if McCullough and Parmenter were hanged.[4]

From Westfield, Shays's men heard the terrible news that Regulators had enforced a law more ancient than any state authority. In retribution for the shots General Shepard had ordered his men to fire and for the deaths of the four men at Springfield, Regulators had torn up Shepard's fences and burned his woodlot beyond "recovery for many years."[5] They had also killed two of his purebred horses: they gouged out their eyes and cut off their ears, to make sure that Shepard tasted his share of the grief and disgust four men's families felt.

None of the men who had ridden horses through the snowy mountains from Petersham to Bennington could savor that act of revenge, but men who had heard their comrades' cries in the road in Springfield, and men who had come home to hear those men's mothers and wives and children and relatives keening, could not say that the mutilated horses were worth half as much as the men who had been shot down.

These bloody acts cast all of Shays's men as savage criminals. But they also showed Bowdoin and other hardliners in the government that the people themselves still held a certain power in reserve. If the commonwealth was prepared to be cruel in its justice, the people could be cruel and dispassionate in implementing their own.

Day to day, the outrage of the commonwealth's sanctioned murders lay like a fog on the hills of western Massachusetts and southern Vermont. But every day, the springtime sunshine shone warm on the fields and forests, bringing the soil to life. The fields in the valleys below them were already starting to green. The trees burst into flower, and the hills were tinged purple and orange with flowering maples and oaks, then brilliant yellow-green as the first gleaming leaves came in.

High on Egg Mountain, Shays and his men debated their obligations, but they could not agree that they should risk their lives to either free their men or restrain the people who had let them be driven into exile.

They waited to hear that Bowdoin had followed his pardons of April 25 by pardoning Parmenter and McCullough, but no visitors came to Egg Mountain with news of reprieves.

In the letters they submitted to the newspapers, the farmers of Massachusetts declared that they were going to prevent the executions, and merchants answered with furious denunciations of the men who were preparing to war against their state.[6] The *Massachusetts Centinel* dismissed the Regulators' concerns and printed an editorial declaring that "those who are not decidedly in favor of [the government's] present exertions [against the farmers] are against the Constitution."[7]

On the seventh of May, some of the refugees from Egg Mountain and other exiles from Massachusetts joined Vermont farmers at a meeting in Shaftsbury south of Arlington to debate what they should do. More than a hundred men gathered, but Daniel Shays did not attend. He only sent a letter in which he promised that the people would have relief if they could wait a few more weeks, till Hancock took over as governor.[8]

The men convened their constitutional meeting the same as ever and argued back and forth, urgent for justice. They had not come to any conclusions by the time Shaftsbury Sheriff Jonas Galusha arrived and called their meeting a threat to public safety and dispersed them.[9] The meeting withdrew across the border to White Creek, New York, where the men continued their council unmolested. In the end, they did not decide to take action, but this fact did not prevent Shaftsbury's Reverend Jeremy Belknap from inflaming tensions in Boston by reporting that "the insurgents are mustering again—either to rescue those culprits ordered for execution or commit predatory mischief."[10]

Night to night, the moon that had been waning since the full moon on May second measured the commonwealth's inescapable progress toward the horrifying spectacle. On the seventeenth, the moon swung past the sun again in the dark, and now all of New England waited on edge for news of pardons, watching with dread as the moon grew again, from a fragile sliver at sunset toward the ripe first-quarter moon that would mean death for two men.

The cloud of suspicion and danger grew darker when news came north to the hills of Sandgate that sheriffs in Connecticut had arrested four Berkshire men on charges of recruiting farmers to form an army, with plans to march to Northampton to interrupt the hangings.[11] Some reports went so far as to claim that the men were planning to start a war.

When the hangings were only a few days away, riders brought news that Bowdoin had halted the executions.[12] The news did not give the people the sense of relief they had hoped for, though, since Bowdoin had only set the date back. Parmenter and McCullough would march to the gallows four weeks from now, on June 21. By that time, Bowdoin would have stepped down, and the hangings would be Hancock's problem to solve.

Released from the urgent threat of the hangings, the people returned to their work, and now the leaves on their wooded hillsides unfolded in earnest, all the way to the mountaintops. In the mornings, fog hung cool and damp over fields that had held their heat through the night, and the valleys resounded with lowing cows, and now the bleat of their calves.

All throughout western Massachusetts and southern Vermont, farmers took up the back-breaking task of plowing and planting, working in teams from the valleys up into the hills. The people still did not stop writing letters and composing petitions to Boston, pleading with Bowdoin and his legislature to use the last days of their terms to pardon Parmenter and McCullough.

In letter after letter, they testified that neither man had had anything to do with leading the people's protests. Henry McCullough's townsmen swore that he had never given orders. He had only brandished a sword at Springfield because someone thought that he looked like an officer on his fine horse. They had only found a sword for him to complete the costume.[13]

Amherst's General Ebenezer Mattoon posted additional letters begging for clemency for Jason Parmenter, citing his generous support of his dependent mother.[14] But nothing he or any of Parmenter's townsmen said succeeded in striking the hangings off the calendar. The state continued to hold the men as hostages against further protests or arson, and now the people of Massachusetts turned their calendars to June with the same dread they had felt when the hangings had appeared on their calendars in May.

By the end of May, when the blockhouse was finished and the men had plowed as much land as they could, they called their wives and children to join them, to mark an end to their hapless campaign as protestors and a return to their lives as farmers. Abigail Shays and the children and as many other wives and children as dared to live rough in the hills rode their carts up the track from Salem, loaded with pots and plates and kitchen utensils and clothing, as well as sacks of seeds, and potatoes and sweet potatoes with vines starting out of their eyes.

Abigail had grown up in relative comfort as the great-granddaughter of Brookfield's first settlers, but the blockhouse before which her cart came to rest was rougher than anything she and the children had left behind. Her ancestors must have dwelt in such rough houses, where the log walls were not papered, where the doorways and windows lacked moldings, where the hand-sawn floorboards were raw without paint or rugs, and the mud of men's boots had worn the fresh cut wood dark with their traffic. Now her cart was one of the seeds out of which her family would start to grow back the community whose roots Governor Bowdoin had cut.

Abigail and the children and the other families unpacked the things they had salvaged from Pelham and joined their men in the work of founding a town. Daniel Junior was fourteen and could work alongside the men. Lucy and Hannah were old enough to work in the fields, in addition to helping Abigail and the other women with cooking and washing, with spinning and weaving, and tending Gilbert and Polly and the other young children.

They might have to live on thin rations for this first year, they might have to run into debt to meet all their needs, but they would only be suffering the same trials their own parents or grandparents endured when they had founded towns. They were not starting with nothing. They could still call on friends in the valleys for help if they needed, or Abigail's brother and sister-in-law in Bennington, or Shays's sister Polly, not far across the border in Salem.

If the blockhouse and mountainside fields were still raw and unfinished, the crisp air on this hillside and the long vistas into the mountains were just like the air and the views from their farm in Pelham. Long valleys spread out below them, and farms across the way mirrored their own farms' progress.

The seeds and tools Shays and the other families brought from Pelham and planted on Egg Mountain were all their wealth now. In the fields they had cleared, they planted flax and corn, wheat and oats, in addition to potatoes, pumpkin, and squash, and orchards of apples, peaches, and pears. In soil they enclosed with tight fencing, they planted a kitchen garden with carrots and beets, turnips and lettuce, radishes, garlic, onions.

They put their seeds in the soil, and now the muddy earth was no longer a wilderness. Now it was an investment they would tend through the summer. In the fall, when they harvested, they would have wealth in their cellars again. They might still be in debt by the end of their first year here, but every year they would coax the earth to satisfy more of their needs.

All summer, they would keep cutting timber for buildings to enlarge their settlement. They would leach the ashes from cooking fires and burned brush piles for potash they could use in their soil or trade for supplies while their fields kept expanding.

Once their crops had taken root, they could start on a mill so they could grind their corn and cut lumber themselves. In ten years, when suitors came to ask Daniel and Abigail Shays for their three daughters' hands, they would be bowing their heads to the town's leading family.

Now that the seeds were planted, the men continued to build. The leaves fleshed out on the trees, hiding the hillsides' rock ribs in forests again. The bright green leaves lost their dewy yellow-green innocence and started to wave in a deep oceanic green when the gusts ran up the ridges. They brought down the trees they had girdled when they first arrived, and their buildings expanded into the clearings.

In large pots over their open hearths, the women and children who had come to the settlement stirred their stews. In ovens that blackened with use immediately, they baked the same breads their ancestors baked. They dreamed the dreams their ancestors dreamed when they had come into this country, of drawing enough wealth from the land that they would be free from foreign financiers' squabbles over currencies and trade.

In the first week of June, messengers came to Egg Mountain with news the Shayses and the families there had waited a year to hear: Hancock had taken power from Bowdoin, and his government had passed all the reforms the people had been begging for since last summer.

The news came too late for Shays and the hundreds of men who had followed him into exile. It came too late for Job Shattuck's tendons, or for Ezekiel Root or Ariel Webster, Jabez Spicer or John Hunter. It came too late for the merchants' warehouses, or William Shepard's horses, but finally Governor Hancock vindicated the people's protests. Their campaign of peaceful and dignified protests had finally released them from Governor Bowdoin's oppressions.

Striking at the source of the crisis, Hancock declared a moratorium on debts and reduced Massachusetts taxes from three pounds, on average, to less than two shillings.[15] He specified that revenues from taxes would only be used to pay the commonwealth's operating expenses. He could not push through an issue of paper money, but he cut injustice out of the government's economic policy by saying he would not use tax receipts to reimburse the investors who held bonds from the war. Overnight, these reforms drove the value of government bonds and soldiers' notes down by more than 30 percent from the amounts for which Boston financiers had been driving the people out of their homes six months ago.[16]

Hancock also set caps on the fees judges and lawyers could impose on the parties who came to the courts with their suits. He outlawed imprisonment for debt and restored habeas corpus. [17] He repealed the Disqualification Act and the repressive measures Massachusetts' legislators had passed in their futile attempt to force the people into submission.

To show the people of Massachusetts that he was willing to share in their sacrifices, Hancock made the concession Bowdoin had vetoed in his time: he allowed his £1,100 salary to be reduced to £800, although Bowdoin's allies in the Senate made it clear that this was a one-time arrangement that would not establish a precedent that would affect future governors' pay.[18] He would still have to solve the problem of taxes, though, for he found that in the period between October 1786 and March 1787, the commonwealth's treasurer, Thomas Ivers, had collected only £103 in gold and silver for taxes.[19]

In the rough buildings and primitive fields where Shays and his men heard this news, the satisfaction of justice for their people was sour with loss. The commonwealth's official heavy demands had been lifted, its fever of distrust had finally been cured by elections, but they did not have justice in their own accounts. Bowdoin and the wealthy senators in the General Court and the merchants they represented would continue to collect rents from their real estate and profit from their trade as before. Merchants and financiers and land speculators would adjust their books to reflect their losses, and search for new opportunities to buy land at bargain prices, in order to turn it around when the settlements expanded into the frontiers. Bondholders would go to exchanges and sell their government bonds or their soldiers' notes, but other men would buy up the notes, continuing to bet their money that merchant elites would prevail in pressuring the government to pay them one day.

Shays and the men who had risked their lives to stand for justice could not feel satisfied with this peace. The lives they had lived till last summer were utterly sundered. Whatever status Daniel Shays had won through his work and his marriage and through his bravery during the war had been trampled. His name had become a word for treason, for laziness, greed, for drunkenness, for manipulative cunning, for ambition—all the distasteful traits wealthy men heaped on the poor to keep them from feeling dignified when they stood up for justice.[20]

Daniel Shays could not return to anything he had before. He and his family had been hounded out of the state under threat of arrest or death. They had been driven away from their farms and their communities. They had had to abandon all the improvements they made with their own hands, on their own land and on their neighbors'. It would still be years before the crude houses they erected high on this hillside could carry them comfortably through long winters or give them any leisure above the constant strains of farming.

There was nothing they could do, though. No one was going to pay them for their losses. Hancock had not even pardoned them, and hardliners in the Massachusetts Senate demanded that the commonwealth continue to keep Parmenter and McCullough beneath the shadow of the gallows in case the people were not finished pillaging rich men's homes or setting their stores on fire.

Shays and his people heard this news and returned to their rough fields, to work their crops and livestock as the looming winter demanded. The sun and the rain on their fields, the satisfaction of doing good work and keeping their traditions and recognizing each other's dignity were all the blessing they would get.

They knew how to live on this land. Their ancestors had made their lives in hills like these for generations. Weather much like this had always washed over their troubles. The political and financial cycles of borrowing and austerity and resistance had not moved them from their rounds. The refugees' flax and hay fields filled in with grasses that waved in the breezes as towering clouds lumbered through the deep sky overhead. As their crops began to grow, they followed their shoots' progress with nervous fear of late frosts, and they tramped the country to work in each other's fields, weeding and haying, and harvesting the first berries from the woods, the first early greens from their gardens.

They returned to the rhythms that had always given their people's lives meaning. On Sundays, their ministers offered them words to help drive the anger and outrage and grief out of their hearts, or at least to help them carry their hard feelings through their work by giving them stories from the Bible and other examples they could follow.

Visitors continued to bring news up from Massachusetts that summer, as the last details of the crisis were still unfolding. Governor Hancock finally canceled the bounties on Shays, Wheeler, Parsons, and Day, but only as a budgetary matter.[21] He still had not pardoned them, so they could still be arrested if they missed their homes so much that they thought it would be worthwhile to abandon their work in Vermont and return to start from scratch two months behind the season.

Hancock's measures had still not settled the country. The people still waited for news that McCullough and Parmenter had been pardoned, but every day's sun set without that relief. Everyone in the country waited with dread for June 21. The people of Massachusetts continued to fill the regional papers with letters that threatened violence if the state insisted on hanging them. Farmers in southern Vermont and western Massachusetts still held their constitutional meetings and posted petitions to Boston, pleading for clemency.

They prayed that Hancock's new legislature would issue pardons. The elections that brought him into power had also increased the size of the legislature by almost a third. The western towns that had never bothered to send representatives found ways to raise the money to send them now. As a consequence, Hancock's legislature had 76 more representatives than the 190 who had answered the roll calls to authorize Bowdoin's laws.[22]

The quality of the legislature had changed as well. Out of forty-two men who ran for reelection in the senate, only twelve were returned by their constituents. The legislature filled up with new representatives who were sympathetic to the people's cause, or at least hesitant to repeat James Bowdoin's mistakes. Even Harvard's Brigadier General Josiah Whitney took a seat in the legislature, flouting Bowdoin's attempts to bar men from holding office for having spoken against his government.[23]

Whitney and others rode to Boston to press for reforms and pardons, but they still failed to win reprieves for McCullough and Parmenter. Hancock's party did not command enough votes in the senate, where Samuel Adams had been elected senate president and Bowdoin's wealthy peers still held power. Adams did not prevent Hancock from repealing Bowdoin's austerity measures, but he still refused to allow the state to show weakness by delaying the hangings that had already been pushed back from May.

It was no longer clear that the hangings would have the sobering effect Adams thought they would have, for the rash of fires and violence had effectively stopped with Hancock's election. With reforms in the air, Hancock had taken away the anger that fueled those fires, although the newspapers were as full of inflammatory rhetoric as ever.

Still, Hancock could not convince Adams to drop the execution; Adams and his fellow elites insisted that the commonwealth's dignity demanded that Parmenter and McCullough be sacrificed for the state's peace. As in May, the people of western Massachusetts, Connecticut, and Vermont watched apprehensively as the June moon waned through the early weeks of the month. As in May, they watched it shrink to an early morning sliver and disappear in the sky for a night. Once again, its return as a slender shaving in the evening of the sixteenth filled them with dread. They waited for news as it fattened toward the twenty-first, and they held the long meetings in which they debated what to do.

Governor Hancock both soothed and inflamed the country's anxieties by sending a troop of soldiers west from Boston to Northampton to enforce peace during the hanging.[24] Apprehension filled the bowls of the valleys and washed up into the hills of southern Vermont, but still Daniel Shays and his men stayed in their settlement. This trouble was not a trouble they could take on their own shoulders. Shays had still not been pardoned. He was not in any position to ride back to Massachusetts and risk his life obstructing the executions, unjust as they were.

When the sun came up on June 21, Shays and his people high on Egg Mountain observed the solstice with prayers of thanksgiving for this year's crops. They went about their work under the cloud of the executions. Late in the day, church bells rang the news west from Northampton, and farther towns' churches forwarded the peal town to town through the Berkshires and up to Vermont. Messengers followed the tolling bells to say that justice had prevailed: McCullough and Parmenter had not been hung.

It was not till the next few days that Shays and his men heard detailed reports from men who had been in Northampton. Visitors told them that the hanging day had dawned on huge crowds that had gathered from neighboring towns to witness the commonwealth's demonstration of force. Anger and danger buzzed thick through the crowds, but Reverend Moses Baldwin of Palmer was not disturbed when he preached the execution sermon.[25]

Nor was Sheriff Elisha Porter disturbed when he escorted the prisoners to the gallows with grim accompaniment from muffled drums. Tension and dread weighed heavier and heavier moment to moment. To the hundreds of people who had gathered, the presence of the militia was so imposing that no one tried to interrupt the procession or turn against Porter's men, and the soldiers mastered their nerves and kept their formations without inciting a riot.[26]

Step by step, the convicts were led past the coffins that were waiting to cart them away.[27] They ascended the platform, and now the visitors who told the news on Egg Mountain described the crowd's prayers and bitter anticipation as Porter placed the nooses around the condemned men's necks.

Shays and his men had already heard the outcome from the church bells that carried it west, but now their visitors described in detail how Porter had paused. He did not spring the traps that would drop the condemned men's souls into empty space and take their lifeless bodies as payments for the people's disturbances. Under the dreadful scrutiny of thousands of eyes, he took a paper from his pocket and read a stay of execution.[28]

The crowd erupted with groans and protests as they understood that Porter had been carrying that note in his pocket all this time. The condescending sermon, the muffled drums, the pleas for mercy had only been an exercise in submission and abasement, and the people shouted indignant objections against the state's power.[29]

Nor were the people satisfied that the injustice of the death sentences had been righted, for the men had still not been freed from the danger of hanging. Hancock had not been able to pardon the men, only to put the executions off for another six weeks. Samuel Adams and the merchant elites in the senate still demanded that the commonwealth keep McCullough and Parmenter as hostages, holding their lives on credit against any unauthorized gatherings or violence. Through the rest of the summer, the people of Massachusetts would have to repeat the ritual of writing petitions and pleading for mercy in hopes that the threat of executions might finally be lifted.

On the hillside in Sandgate where Shays and his people heard this news, the state's charade only showed Shays and others how vulnerable their lives had always been. They were farmers and soldiers. They would always have to accept the fact that God would demand that they suffer in one way or another. In their crude settlement, the cruel whims of nature were always close at hand. Rain might still drench their seeds or drought or blight kill their crops, destroying all the labor they had invested in their first-year harvests. They might still have to retreat to the towns, to burden their friends and relatives with supporting them. They might still have to break up their homes and work in other men's fields as common laborers. The state and its injustices, the whims of men in power, were only additional trials they would be tasked to endure in their season.

So Daniel Shays and his people heard these reports from Northampton in stony indifference. They returned to their fields and they prayed and they prepared to face whatever fate required of them, working at the tasks that were close at hand and leaving people in distant countries to see to their own business.

Chapter Fourteen

New Life, Old Life

N OW THAT HANCOCK'S REFORMS had legitimized the people's pro-
tracted protests, he settled the crisis that had roiled the commonwealth since last spring, and the Shayses and the families on Egg Mountain
relinquished more of their friends back to Massachusetts. Hancock's reforms
were starting to take effect, and some of the settlers calculated that their efforts would be better spent recovering from the past year's losses than in
turning a raw hillside into a settlement.

Some families disdained to return to Massachusetts and moved to land
farther north in Vermont. Some traveled west, to central New York or Ohio.
Some went west to join Rufus Putnam's settlement in Marietta, Ohio, on
the Muskingum River, or else they joined other settlements where land was
cheap for the working.[1] Of the families who stayed in Vermont, some sent
their young men west to scout land for next year's plantings, the same as
they would have done if they had stayed in Massachusetts. Some went to
see for themselves, packing their things in carts, leaving their crops to battle
the weeds while they looked for a place where they could start from scratch
yet again.

Daniel and Abigail Shays and their children stayed in the settlement
high on Egg Mountain, along with the remnants of their community. The
breezes turned warmer and heavier as June gave way to July, and men came
in from the fields bright red where the sun had touched them. The clouds
drifted over the fields on Egg Mountain the same as they had flown over

Pelham and Colrain. The scents in the air, the humid earth, the growing grasses and crops, and the lives of the birds and insects told them where they were at every moment of the season.

As the summer progressed, the teams of men worked together the same as ever. New buildings grew beneath their hammers. The same crops they had always grown spread their leaves in the fields. The same fogs lay over the valleys. The same clouds mottled the green hillsides purple, the same sunshine striped the floors of their kitchens and bedrooms. The same June winds that had always warmed their fields in Massachusetts brought the same July thunderstorms rolling through from the Midwest. The same hurricanes barreled up from the south, or in from the Atlantic, and they cleaned up the blown-down limbs and tended the crops that had not been flooded by rain or shredded by hail.

From time to time, Shays and his people traveled down to the houses and fields of the farmers who had hosted them through the winter, to repay their hospitality and trust with long days of camaraderie and teamwork. They left their fields to ride down to the rivers and fill their baskets with fish they would salt for the coming winter, the same as their parents had done in their early days in their hills.

From time to time, the scents on the wind brought back the panic and outrage of this time last year, and the settlers choked on their memories of the humid days when their troubles were just beginning. They still spoke of their lost homes with bitterness in their throats, but they consoled themselves with the knowledge that they lived in an independent country now, where all adult men were allowed to vote.[2] The Vermont legislature did not have an upper house in which a cabal of merchant elites could overpower a house of small merchants and farmers, to pass laws that would enrich them at the common people's expense. The mountainous state had not even settled its capital in one commercial center. Over the past five years, the legislature had met in Manchester, then in Windsor on the Connecticut River, then Rutland in the center of the state, and then in Norwich, so the towns were all burdened in their turn by the expense of having to travel to join its sessions.[3]

Week to week, Daniel Shays and his wife and children adjusted themselves to the scent of the air on their hillside, the shape of the sky as it slid across their clearings, as it stretched across the hillsides across the way. When they went to the promontory on the shoulder south of their settlement and surveyed the landscape of farms spread out below them, they no longer watched the roads below for soldiers. Soon it was just to hope for news or excitement from towns or cities farther away, to break up the long routines of endless work.

The days turned heavy and humid through August. Soon the same katy-dids they were used to hearing every August in Massachusetts were filling the muggy evenings with the same incessant call and response. The people turned their eyes to the skies, wondering whether they would get the rain they needed, to keep their crops from drying out under the sun. They calculated whether their crops would carry them through the winter or whether the wives and children would need to go live with friends or relatives in the valleys. They tallied the sums they might need to borrow from local merchants to supplement their harvests with provisions, and they balanced their debts against the money they could raise out of their land.

Finally, in the middle of August, the families in their mountain settlement heard that Hancock had settled the last of the peace in Massachusetts: he called off the hangings postponed in May and again in June. In the absence of further violence, Samuel Adams and other hardliners in the Senate had finally relented and allowed the governor to pardon McCullough and Parmenter. In the end, none of the men Shays had marched with had been hung. The commonwealth had only executed two of Perez Hamlin's men who had been convicted of robbery during their ill-fated raid.[4]

With these pardons, Hancock had released the last breath of steam from the people's resistance. The commonwealth resumed its business. Hancock's administration still refused to repay war debts with taxes, and the merchants who had backed Bowdoin's strict austerity measures last summer resigned themselves to Hancock's policies and bided their time to redeem their losses. The value of soldiers' notes continued to decline, but for every man who sold his notes at a loss, another was willing to risk his money and hope that they would be paid. For rumors had started to run around Boston that the federal government might pay them if Hancock's government would not. Speculators invested whatever money they could afford to part with. They waited, much like the farmers, who had invested their seeds in the soil.[5]

Now that the people were free from excessive debts and taxes, money and goods were circulating again. Merchants were letting farmers run credit for supplies, and shopkeepers were taking produce in exchange for goods. The coastal merchants turned their eyes westward and started to compensate for their lost Indies trade with new trade on the frontiers.

Summer 1787 yielded to autumn the same as every other year had yielded, with the same blazing trees and the same blasts of cold winds and rains blowing down from Canada. When their thin crops came ripe in September, the settlers on Egg Mountain went to their fields with carts and sacks and gathered their produce, taking wheat, corn, and vegetables, taking pumpkins and squash to the cellars of the homes they had constructed all summer. They filled their storerooms the same as their ancestors had harvested crops in their first autumn in Worcester—the same as they had harvested thin crops in their first autumn in Pelham, after the Worcester Puritans had driven them west in 1743.

As thin as their first harvests were, the settlers reminded themselves that the towns they grew up in had started from just such beginnings. Parents promised their children that subsequent harvests would come in thicker and easier as their clearings expanded, and they worked the stones out of their fields and fed the sandy soil with compost and manure.

After Shays and the families of Egg Mountain had finished harvesting their crops, the men took their muskets into the forests the same as ever. They took their fowling pieces and nets to the marshes and lakes as they had always done to supplement their crops with meat, while their wives and daughters cleaned flax stalks, in preparation for spinning and weaving thread for new clothing through winter.

It might still be years before their farms were as prosperous as the farms they had abandoned. They might not be able to make enough linen to trade for fine clothing or lamps or fashionable wallpaper or rugs, but the wives and daughters stole moments from their work to make exquisite lace and fine embroidered pieces they could trade for good money.

Their people had lived with less than this, and in their Sunday sermons and at their meals, they thanked the Lord for seeing them through the trials they had endured and for providing for them in His grace.

Epilogue

Reverberations and Echoes

B Y THE TIME THEY HAD BROUGHT IN THEIR CROPS at the end of that first summer in Vermont, Daniel Shays and his family, his men and their families, largely disappeared into the history of their region. They ran the same farms and harvested the same crops under the same weather as everyone else. No urgent troubles threatened their crops or their title to their land. No one man needed to put himself forward to advocate for his people and to let them hide by signing his name to their letters in the papers.

While Shays and his men slid back into the lives and seasons they had been raised in, though, their protests against their government were still not finished rippling through the country. In August, they heard that Hancock was making a military tour of western Massachusetts, and they suggested Shays and Parsons go to meet him in person to plead for pardons, or else they joked about the depopulated towns that must have greeted him.[1] In September, visitors came to Egg Mountain with news that in May—while Massachusetts had still been convulsed with dread of the hangings—wealthy merchants and businessmen in other states had taken steps to make sure that their states' governments were never again as impotent in the face of their people's protests. They had summoned each state's delegations to Philadelphia to form a Constitutional Convention, and in long meetings shrouded in secrecy, they drafted a constitution to replace the Articles of Confederation.[2]

Everyone in the country knew that ever since the articles were ratified in 1781, Alexander Hamilton and James Madison and reformers had been proposing to strengthen the confederation and increase the government's authority to issue taxes and regulate commerce.[3] Delegates had held conventions to address these issues in 1784 and also in September 1786. While the people of western Massachusetts were waiting in vain for reforms from Boston, nine states had sent representatives to a Meeting of Commissioners to Remedy Defects of the Federal Government in Annapolis, Maryland, where delegates discussed the need for reforms and laid the foundation for another meeting in Philadelphia in May 1787.

That meeting had taken place in the wake of the tumultuous news from Massachusetts, where the government had infuriated the people by levying taxes "beyond what prudence would authorize," as Congressman Rufus King said in a December open letter. The subsequent turmoil was not seen as another chapter in the country's proud history of popular movements checking irresponsible elites but rather as an insurrection against the state's authority. The draft Constitution that emerged from the convention in September proposed reforms that would strengthen the states' governments against internal disturbances and stabilize their economies.[4]

As the people of the independent republic of Vermont brought in their harvests, the delegates of the Constitutional Convention had submitted their draft to the states for ratification, and visitors to the tavern high on Egg Mountain brought copies of this proposed Constitution and read it aloud while Shays and his men drank beer and brandy they had brewed out of their own crops. Too late for them and their farms, the draft Constitution proposed reforms that would have prevented the problems that brought Massachusetts's business to a standstill. It gave the federal government the right to tax the people and to borrow money to pay its debts, which promised to lift the burden of war debts off individual states.[5]

Too late to help Governor Bowdoin, the Constitution proposed a standing army that would be authorized to cross state borders. The provision was mainly included to assure wealthy southern planters that other states could not refuse to help them if their slaves ever tried to free themselves, as they themselves had refused to help Bowdoin's government suppress the resistance his laws created. But the right of rebellion and the natural rights Thomas Jefferson had offered the country in the Declaration of Independence were now replaced with a government that authorized itself to write and enforce its laws and subdue insurrections with soldiers who felt no kinship to the people they forced the law on.

Vermont was still an independent republic, so Shays and the families on Egg Mountain were not directly threatened by the tyranny many men saw in this Constitution. But the Massachusetts papers filled up again with furious letters as men despaired that the document was creating the same strong central government their people had just fought a war and then staged five months of nonviolent resistance to free themselves from.

Shays did not contribute any editorials to stake out a public position on either side. No one from Massachusetts rode up to Egg Mountain to solicit his opinion. He and the other refugees simply went about their business through the autumn. Massachusetts's vote on ratification would not affect how they harvested the last of their crops or cured their beef or made the tools or furniture, the cloth or lace they would trade for provisions in spring. It would not matter to them how New England merchants regulated their commerce. They in their hills could not change the fact that northern merchants were willing to purchase the nation's unity by looking away when southern planters bought and sold African men and women as property or instituted a national army to keep them in submission. Their own timber and salted fish and rough linen tow cloth were exported by local merchants to Indies traders where they housed, fed, and clothed enslaved people, so they themselves were not entirely free from the trade.

All through the fall into winter, Shays's old neighbors in Massachusetts debated ratification in their newspapers and town meetings. When they finally cast their votes in February 1788, only seven out of the ninety-seven towns that had sent men to stop the courts with Shays had instructed their delegates to vote for ratification. They feared that the Constitution would only subject them to wealthy nobles in other states, in addition to the nobles who had already oppressed them from Boston. They did not want to pay taxes to suppress slave rebellions and to patrol the Appalachian frontier, nor to have to redeem the war bonds the wealthy speculators still held. But the Constitution had strong support among eastern towns, who closely balanced the western towns' opposition. Ultimately, the commonwealth's decision rested in John Hancock's hands. He voted to ratify the document along with a Bill of Rights to protect individuals' property and liberties.[6]

In February 1788, Massachusetts was the sixth state to vote for ratification. Its vote was influential. By June that year, when Shays and his people were cutting the first hay of their second spring in Vermont, enough other states had also voted for ratification that the Constitution had become the law of the land.

Two years after the other states had denied Governor Bowdoin's request for troops, the states authorized the central government to maintain a federal army. The men in that army would not know the people they policed, so nothing would stop them from using force against protestors. They would not need to assess the legitimacy or righteousness of the protestors' claims for themselves or be bound by personal ties when officers gave them the order to fire their guns.

Fortunately, at least for now, the people no longer needed to interrupt the courts. Trade had resumed, and the promise of wealth in westward expansion let the delegates skirt the question of how those debts would be paid.

On June 25, 1788, Governor Hancock finally pardoned Daniel Shays for his role in the protests he had organized two years ago. Shays had submitted his final petition in February, begging for the state's absolution. When his request was granted, the pardon did not compensate him in any way for his ordeal. It simply closed his business with the Commonwealth of Massachusetts and made him his own man again. He and his family returned to the work they could do with their own hands on soil they had domesticated themselves, close to the seasons and God's strict laws.

For the rest of his life, Daniel Shays never put himself forward to speak for anyone but himself and his wife and their five children. He never gave the republic of Vermont or the federal government any reason to name him in any subsequent complaints.[7]

Through autumn 1788, he and his family stayed on Egg Mountain to harvest the second year's crops from their south-facing plateau. But now that Shays had been pardoned, he no longer needed to hide in the hills, and the following year, he moved his family down to the valley, to a farm south of Arlington along the road to Bennington.[8] The house faced the long Green Mountain ridgeline, whose west-facing slopes were silhouetted by sunrise each morning, whose tips glowed pink in the last of each day's light.

Now that their eldest son was sixteen, their elder daughters fourteen and eleven, Daniel and Abigail Shays had more help than ever, and even their youngest daughter and son, at nine and six, could contribute their work to rebuilding the family's fortunes in the independent republic of Vermont.

Shays was still farming in Arlington in autumn 1789 when newspapers up from the coast announced that peasants in France had rioted in the streets and then suspended nobles' privileges. In the chaotic scenes the papers described, the farmers recognized the distorted images Governor Bowdoin must have seen in their crowds. Here were the rich men's nightmares come to life, in the mobs that would ultimately haul their monarch and aristocrats to the guillotine.

As the troubles spread through France and infected Europe, the Massachusetts newspapers were filled with editorials in which Boston and Worcester merchants and Springfield and Northampton businessmen warned that any statements of sympathy for the French in their revolution were dangerous preludes to further insurrection on their own soil, an affront to their own government's legitimate and necessary authority.

Daniel Shays and his fellow veterans in Vermont did not call meetings to plan to further the French peasants' cause by waging war against their own nobles. Nor did they set sail to repay their comrade the Marquis de Lafayette for his assistance during the Revolution. Lafayette was installed as commander in chief of the French National Guard, but any loyalty Shays might have felt on account of the gold-handled sword the marquis had given him had long ago been tarnished by circumstance. The marquis's *Declaration of the Rights of Man and the Citizen* did not inspire the Regulators to return to the savageries of battle nor to trade their homes for the pestilence, starvation, and boredom of army camps.[9]

Shays and his people had already seen how their revolution replaced one set of aristocrats with new elites who made the same unjust demands—regardless of what Samuel Adams said to distinguish the new republican government from the previous monarchy. Their people had not been any better represented in the government they had established to replace the British monarchy, so they let the Europeans struggle for power among themselves and stayed close to their own crops.

The troubles that had roiled the Commonwealth of Massachusetts in 1786 echoed back from closer to home in 1791. From western Pennsylvania, the papers brought news of a crisis that followed the same exact pattern James Bowdoin's crisis had followed five years earlier.

Now it was Alexander Hamilton who was pressing the people with unjust taxes. After the Constitution had been approved, Hamilton's federal bank had assumed the state's war debts. With the new nation's debts on a single ledger, the federal government finally promised to pay the soldiers' notes that still had not been paid. Once again, the government now proposed to pay those notes in full.[10]

Everyone knew that the soldiers had long ago parted with their notes and that only a handful of wealthy speculators would benefit by this plan.

But Hamilton claimed that the concentration of wealth was one of the plan's chief advantages. He claimed that in many hands, money was merely money, but large amounts of money in only a few hands turned money into capital, which could be invested and used for nation building—even if that money had to be taken from poor farmers, artisans, and small merchants.[11]

In the newspapers, the northern farmers and southern planters and slave owners all opposed this plan for assumption of debts. They dreaded the rise of a powerful mercantile class in the north. But southern statesmen ultimately approved the plan in exchange for the symbolic victory of moving the new nation's capital to a new site on the Potomac, closer to Virginia's tobacco plantations than northern banks.[12]

The veterans who had received the government's notes as payment for their service could not affect the vote. Many of the men who now owned those promissory notes either held seats in the legislature or had powerful friends in Congress who would see to their interests. Once again, wealthy speculators essentially voted to pay themselves windfall profits.

From their houses in the broad valley south of Arlington, Daniel Shays and his townsmen watched George Washington's government follow James Bowdoin's blunders step for step. They repeated the injustice of voting to pay the notes to speculators instead of to the soldiers who had earned that pay. Then, just like Bowdoin, they voted to raise the funds to pay the notes by levying steep new taxes, this time on whiskey.[13]

The whiskey distillers of western Pennsylvania felt the tax was an insult. Like Shays and other subsistence farmers, they did not do business in cash, so they could not afford to pay the taxes Hamilton demanded, but they felt they were being singled out to suffer for living in frontier conditions: they only traded in whiskey because it was too expensive to ship their grain across the mountains to ports on the coast.[14]

The leading men in western Pennsylvania towns organized opposition to these taxes.[15] They did not call themselves Regulators, though. They did not send envoys to Shays, in Vermont, to ask for his help or guidance as men in the Wyoming Valley of Pennsylvania had asked for Ethan Allen's. Nor did Shays leave his farm in his son's or his neighbors' hands while he traveled west to Pennsylvania to help the distillers rein in their angry men and stage peaceful demonstrations. Shays did not stir from Arlington.[16] He simply followed the crisis in the newspapers with his neighbors, reading accounts of the people's attacks on the government's tax assessors, who were beaten then tarred and feathered in defiance of Hamilton's taxes.[17]

The protests dragged on for three years until they finally came to a head in 1794. The government issued inflammatory writs that could only be answered in person in Philadelphia, requiring the distillers to make the long and expensive trip there. Five hundred farmers answered this insult by mobbing tax inspector John Neville's house southwest of Pittsburgh. Neville shot and killed a man, and the armed standoff that followed only ended when Neville's mansion and slave quarters were burned to the ground.[18]

That August, President George Washington led an army of thirteen thousand eastern men as far as Carlisle, Pennsylvania. Like General Lincoln, he avoided an open battle with the angry distillers, refusing to galvanize opposition by martyring individual men.[19] He arrested a few dozen ringleaders and suppressed the people's protests by threatening to execute them. Like Governor Hancock, Washington never did hang anyone. He kept the men in prison for a year before he pardoned them. By that time, many of the distillers who refused to submit to the government's authority had packed their possessions in carts and moved farther west, to territories where tax assessors were not in a position to press them with unjust demands yet.[20]

Daniel Shays and his family heard of these troubles but never stirred to join them. They stayed in Arlington till 1795. When they moved, it was not because a crisis drove them west. They simply saw better prospects on flatter land in Rensselaerville, New York, southwest of Albany. A man named John Bay, from Claverack, near Albany—a wealthy lawyer who had fought against Hamilton and the Federalists in the ratification debate—offered Shays and his family support in the form of a generous price for the land he had bought and settled on Egg Mountain.[21] Shays did not move west as a gentleman farmer. He had long ago lost the title he held in Pelham and returned to the constant, pressing needs of subsistence farming.

By the time he took his family to New York, the community of families who remembered closing the Hampshire and Worcester County courts had scattered around New England and west into the frontiers. By now, the crisis seemed like a shameful, distant memory in a country that was trying to see evidence of its unification. Newcomers to the region did not have reason to bring that story of protest back to life out of their own troubles. The events of 1786 and 1787 passed into local legend, and the country turned its attention to contentious debates about whether America ought to take sides in the new war the French and English were fighting in Europe.

By the time Daniel Shays died almost thirty years later, at seventy-eight, in 1825, he had moved even farther west, to Sparta, New York, between the two westernmost Finger Lakes. Only his last son, Gilbert, was still with him to inherit his meager belongings: some books, household goods, and farm implements. Shays's other children had scattered farther west, first to Michigan and Wisconsin, then in every direction.[22] None of them had returned to Massachusetts, and none of Shays's descendants distinguished themselves by taking their people's troubles on their shoulders, risking their lives or property to advocate for justice for their communities.

Daniel Shays's name was largely forgotten, owing partly to time and also to the shame attached to his modest means later in life. Instead of the soldier and father who lost his farm for protecting his people, history remembered the caricature of a tipsy and genial tavern keeper, as if poverty or drinking confirmed the delinquency of the movement he had led.[23]

The name of the Regulators was not heard again for almost a hundred years after Shays fled to Vermont. In 1878—a year after Reconstruction was over and the federal government stepped back from the role of upholding the rule of law, conceding power to hooded mobs and vigilantes in the Jim Crow South[24]—East Coast newspapers printed breathless reports from the wild frontier of New Mexico, where Billy the Kid joined a group of cattlemen and ranch hands who called themselves the Lincoln County Regulators.[25] For weeks that spring into summer, city readers were riveted by accounts of their gunfights with corrupt deputies, which devolved soon enough into assassinations and ambushes, but stories about the Regulators fed the American myth that individual men with guns could hold the law in their own hands and represent justice, defying the men who used state-sanctioned power for their corrupt ends.[26]

The name of the Regulators fell out of use after that, but the protests that were remembered not as "the people's Regulation" but as "Shays's Rebellion" were hardly the last time Americans were forced to band together in opposition to unjust power.

When railroad companies and land speculators and local bosses and pineapple or banana growers or mine and factory owners corrupted the law or used blunt force to steal land or wages from their workers or forced them to work such long hours in such horrid conditions that they felt their liberties were being taken from them, the people called themselves leagues and unions, syndicates, and committees. They did not have to search through books to find that there were precedents for organizing resistance to unjust law nor for maintaining solidarity when men in power made threats against their resistance.

Whether or not they thought that they were following in the footsteps Daniel Shays and the men of Pelham and Colrain and West Springfield and Chicopee had set down, they were Americans. They recognized right and wrong. They spoke for themselves and their people and did not back down when men in power threatened them. They carried the stories inside themselves, and each generation knew what to do when it was time to go to the courtyard.

Notes

INTRODUCTION

1. Rock Brynner, *"Fire Beneath Our Feet": Shays' Rebellion and Its Constitutional Impact* (Ann Arbor, MI: University Microfilms International Dissertation Services, 1983), 319-320.

2. Brynner shows evidence that the portrait of "Shays' Rebellion" was deliberately created by elites who misrepresented the nonviolent protests to turn them into a threat to the nation, essentially using the protests as a propaganda tool to justify a nationalist project that was in no way assured of success, at the time. *"Fire Beneath Our Feet,"* 1-9.

3. George Washington to Henry Lee in Congress, October 1, 1786, *The Writings of George Washington: pt. III, Private letters from the time Washington resigned his commission as commander-in-chief of the Army to that of his inauguration as president of the United States: December, 1783–April, 1789,* ed. Jared Sparks (Boston: Russell, Odiorne and Metcalf, 1835), 204.

4. Thomas Jefferson to William Smith, November 13, 1787, Thomas Jefferson, *Political Writings,* ed. Joyce Appleby (Cambridge: Cambridge University Press, 1999), 109.

5. Marion Starkey, *A Little Rebellion* (New York: Knopf, 1955), 224.

6. As Robert Feer puts it, "enough material has survived to allow us to say with considerable conviction that the radical schemes of which the conservatives accused the dissidents and insurgents never existed in any serious form, and that such accusations were nothing but the work of over-wrought imaginations." *Shays's Rebellion* (New York: Garland, 1988), 103.

PRELUDE: JANUARY 25, 1787

1. This central episode of the 1786–1787 protests has been narrated in all of the histories. There were only a handful of contemporary accounts of this confrontation in Springfield. Westfield Major General William Shepard described it in a letter to Governor James Bowdoin, quoted in full in Ellery Crane's "Shays' Rebellion," in *Collections of the Worcester Society of Antiquity,* vol. 1, *Proceedings for the Year 1881* (Worcester, MA: Published by the Society, 1892), 93-95. We have firsthand accounts from one of Shepard's officers, Epaphras Hoyt ("They immediately broke into the greatest confusion," autographed letter from Springfield, MA, signed as "Epaphras Hoit," to brother Seth in Deerfield, MA, dated January 26, 1787, Sale 2380, Lot 161, Swann Galleries, New York, accessed July 2, 2021, https://catalogue.swanngalleries.com/Lots/LotDetails?salename=%28MASSACHUSETTS.%29-Hoyt%2C-Epaphras.-An-officers-long—2380%2B%2B%2B%2B%2B161%2B-%2B%2B698889&saleno=2380&lotNo=161&refNo=698889), as well as from a foot soldier, Daniel Stebbins, quoted extensively in Brynner, *"Fire Beneath Our Feet,"* 93-95, and from a Springfield Congregationalist minister, the Reverend Bezaleel Howard, reprinted in "Shays's Rebellion and Its Aftermath: A View from Springfield, Massachusetts, 1787," by Richard D. Brown, *William and Mary Quarterly* 40, no. 4 (Oct. 1983): 606ff.

Another Hoyt, David Jr., wrote a "Letter to his Father" that has been preserved at the Pocumtuck Valley Memorial Association, Deerfield, MA, and made available through the Springfield Technical Community College's Daniel Shays website, accessed June 28, 2021, http://shaysrebellion.stcc.edu/shaysapp/artifact.do?shortName=letter_dh26jan87.

Lastly, one of General Shepard's officers, Samuel Buffington, provided a deposition (Forbes Library Special Collections, Northampton, MA, via Springfield Technical Community College Daniel Shays website, accessed June 28, 2021, http://shaysrebellion.stcc.edu/shaysapp/artifactPage.do?shortName=deposition_sb1feb87&page=p002) relating his two interviews with Shays and his officers as they approached Springfield. This has been printed in James Russell Trumbull's and Seth Pomeroy's *History of Northampton, Massachusetts, from its settlement in 1654* (Northampton, MA: Press of Gazette Printing, 1898), 505-506.

This legendary moment was related in print again twenty-five years after the event, when George Minot wrote his official account of the "Rebellion," *History of the Insurrections in Massachusetts in 1786 and of the Rebellion Consequent Thereon* (New York: Da Capo, 1971), which was designed to salt the episode away in the history books as a minor disruption. Marion Starkey vivified the narrative of the Regulation in *A Little Rebellion*, and Robert Taylor described the economic and cultural pressures that led to Samuel Ely's and Shays's protests in *Western Massachusetts in the Revolution* (Providence, RI: Brown University Press, 1954).

As the 1986 bicentennial approached, interest in Shays flared up in a number of publications, starting with an academic analysis by David Szatmary, *Shays' Rebellion: The Making of an Agrarian Insurrection* (Amherst: University of Massachusetts Press, 1980), and *Shays' Rebellion: Selected Essays,* ed. Martin Kaufman (Westfield: Institute for Massachusetts Studies, 1987). These studies were accompanied by exceptionally thorough analyses of the underlying cultural and economic causes of the 1786 troubles, in excellent dissertations by Rock Brynner, *"Fire Beneath Our Feet"* (1983) and Robert Feer, *Shays's Rebellion.*

More recently, Leonard Richards dug into the archives and presented a history based on extensive tax, land, and military records, with *Shays's Rebellion: The American Revolution's Final Battle* (Philadelphia: University of Pennsylvania Press, 2002), and Sean Condon adds details in his slender account, *Shays's Rebellion: Authority and Distress in Post-Revolutionary America* (Baltimore: Johns Hopkins University Press, 2015).

In addition to the academic studies, many of the local towns in this area have added facts and local color from not-always-recent memory, domesticating the story but also sometimes giving birth to further legends. The best of these include Charles Parmenter's *History of Pelham, from 1738 to 1898 including the Early History of Prescott* (Amherst, MA: Carpenter & Morehouse, 1898), Mabel Cook Coolidge's *History of Petersham, Massachusetts, incorporated April 20, 1754: Volunteerstown or Voluntown, 1730-1733, Nichewaug, 1733-1754* (Petersham, MA: Petersham Historical Society, 1948), J. H. Temple's *History of North Brookfield, Massachusetts, Preceded by an account of old Quabaug, Indian and English occupation, 1647-1676* (published by the town, 1887) as well as Trumbull's *History of Northampton*, cited above. Regional histories have also included this scene in the snow at the arsenal, including John Lockwood's *Western Massachusetts: A History: 1636-1925*, vol. 1 (New York: Lewis Historical Publishing, 1926) and Josiah Gilbert Holland's *History of Western Massachusetts: The Counties of Hampden, Hampshire, Franklin and Berkshire* (Springfield, MA: Samuel Bowles, 1855).

These are the primary resources, but there are many others that narrate the approach to the arsenal, and the cannon fire.

I have supplemented these accounts with an idiosyncratic variety of information from the period, ranging from Eric Sloane's illustrated histories to Alice Morse Earle's *Home Life in Colonial Days* (Stockbridge, MA: Berkshire House, 1993) to George C. Neuman and Frank J. Kravic's *Collectors' Illustrated Encyclopedia of the American Revolution* (Texarkana, TX: Rebel Publishing, 1975), as well as natural histories and my own observations of the progress of the seasons through this region's hills and fields, rivers and skies. As you would imagine, each historian has selected the facts that showed what they considered the true narrative. I have made my own guesses about the facts that express the essence of the lived experience. The reader, of course, must weigh the available facts and form their own judgment about where this story sits in our region's and in our country's history, and in our own lived experience of the opposition between entrenched wealth and power and a proud American people.

2. Fife and drum music, and the military pageantry of flags and disciplined lines, is noted in some histories but assumed or omitted in others. A sampling of references would include Trumbull, *History of Northampton*, 488, and Brynner, *Shays's Rebellion*, 84.

3. These are the forces who would ultimately drive the last of Shays's force out of Petersham, as described in Stearns, *Shays' Rebellion: 1786–7: Americans Take Up Arms against Unjust Laws* (New York: Franklin Watts, 1968), 52.

4. Lincoln's army is often described as 4,400 strong, but this number seems to be aspirational. By Parmenter's count, it includes "700 from Suffolk, 500 Essex, [and] 1,200 from Middlesex" counties. It was meant to include 1,200 from Hampshire and 1,200 from Worcester, but these contingents had trouble meeting their recruiting goals. Lincoln seems to have left Boston with about 2,000 men, then picked up about 600 men in Worcester, then 400 out of the 900 or so with Shepard at the arsenal, making the total force pursuing Shays, Day, and Parsons about 3,000 men. *History of Pelham*, 375-376. See also, Richards, *Shays's Rebellion*, 25.

5. Leonard Richards, following Daniel Stebbins's diary (*Daniel Stebbins Notebook and Diary*, vol. 1, Forbes Library Special Collections, Northampton, MA), puts the snow at four feet deep. Richards, *Shays's Rebellion*, 29. Szatmary puts it at six inches. *Shays' Rebellion*, 17.

6. Historian Ellery Crane writes that "it seems more than probable that Shays and his men had no idea that the militia would fire upon them, and they were completely surprised. Had they not met before at this very place, when a compromise was effected, that recognized the presence and the authority of the Regulators? If Shays marched his men to the front would they not again be received as equals and another compromise be made? Civil war they certainly did not want or they could have returned fire." Crane, "Shays' Rebellion," 94-95.

7. As during the Worcester court closing in early September. When Artemas Ward demanded to know who was in charge, Adam Wheeler answered that no one was. This is a refrain in the people's actions if not their correspondence. Stearns, *Shays' Rebellion*, 25. John Lockwood cites a letter to the people saying that "as many as 'can conveniently march' should proceed to Springfield and, having informed themselves, 'join that party as they shall judge to be in the right of the cause, they acting entirely for themselves in the matter.'" *Western Massachusetts*, 132.

8. Richards, 63.

9. David Szatmary, "Shays' Rebellion in Springfield," in *Shays' Rebellion: Selected Essays*, ed. Martin Kaufman (Westfield: Institute for Massachusetts Studies, 1987), 17; Starkey, *Little Rebellion*, 131.

10. Hoyt, "They immediately broke."

11. Neuman and Kravic, *Collectors' Illustrated Encyclopedia*, 51.

12. Crane, "Shays' Rebellion," 92. Numbers of protestors vary, for this court closing and each of the subsequent demonstrations. In this case, estimates range between 900 and 1,200, but rumors put the crowds up to 10,000.

13. This is David Hoyt's account of the cannon: facing the farmers head-on. "Letter to his Father." Other accounts have cannon hidden alongside the road. None of the accounts indicate any pause in the Regulators' approach.

14. Richard Colton, "Conflict and Ambivalence in Shays's Rebellion," Springfield Armory National Historic Site, unpublished paper, 2007, 18.

15. Trumbull, *History of Northampton*, 506.

16. Starkey, *Little Rebellion*, 132.

17. Leonard Richards, *Shays's Rebellion*, 29; Crane, "Shays' Rebellion," 94.

18. Richards, *Shays's Rebellion*, 29.

19. The third and subsequent shots "gave them great uneasiness," Shepard said, and "put the whole column into the utmost confusion." Crane, "Shays' Rebellion," 94.
20. Parmenter, *History of Pelham*, 377.
21. Starkey, *Little Rebellion*, 71.
22. Crane, "Shays' Rebellion," 94; Starkey, *Little Rebellion*, 133.
23. Bezaleel Howard said that they "retreated with the utmost Disorder and precipitation." Brown, "Shays's Rebellion and Its Aftermath," 607.
24. Richards, *Shays's Rebellion*, 33, 38.
25. Stearns, *Shays' Rebellion*, 48. See also Bezaleel Howard's account in Brown, "Shays's Rebellion and Its Aftermath," 607.
26. Brynner makes it clear that the five months of protests, and even this fateful encounter, were not a rebellion but a "ritual demonstration" of resistance to unjust laws. He points out that "Regulators did not seek out tax collectors or judges to harass them, nor did they burn them in effigy, as they had done during the Stamp Act crisis. There was none of the 'rough music'[noisemaking] associated with Revolutionary crowd actions, no tar-and-feather treatment, or skimmington [satirical parading, with mockery], or other indignities. No property was stolen, defaced or damaged." Brynner, *"Fire Beneath Our Feet,"* 60.

CHAPTER ONE: THE CRISIS BEGINS

1. Elmer S. Smail, *The Family of Daniel Shays: From Descendants of Daniel Shays*, ed. Mary Ann Nicholson (November 1934; Boston: New England Historic Genealogical Society, 1987), 19.
2. For a detailed discussion of the economic situation in Massachusetts, see Robert F. Taylor, *Western Massachusetts in the Revolution*, ch. 4.
3. Szatmary, *Shays' Rebellion*, 23.
4. Ibid., 64.
5. Ibid., 23.
6. Ibid., 20, 21.
7. Ibid., 24.
8. Ibid., 26.
9. Ibid., 20.
10. Richards, *Shays's Rebellion*, 58. Taylor notes that "the year 1784 brought more imports than any two years before the war." Ibid., 123.
11. Szatmary, *Shays' Rebellion*, 21.
12. To provide a simple example: If I borrow $100 from you when $100 buys a cow, and then the value of currency decreases (or, put another way, prices increase), and $100 only buys an ax, you as the creditor would not be satisfied if I give you $100 to settle the debt. Nor, of course, could a farmer who had only borrowed money for an ax be satisfied if he had to sell his cow to settle the inflated value of his debt. Such was the crisis of currency and values in the Revolutionary era, with numerous contradictory systems for reckoning values of currency and produce. Sean Condon, *Shays's Rebellion*, 43.
13. Szatmary, *Shays' Rebellion*, 27, 28.
14. Ibid., 26, 28.
15. Richards, *Shays' Rebellion*, 82.
16. Szatmary, *Shays' Rebellion*, 67; Szatmary "Shays' Rebellion in Springfield," 6.
17. For more on the River Gods and their role in the political and commercial business in Hampshire and Berkshire Counties see Taylor, 11ff; Richards, 91; and Tom Goldscheider, "Shays' Rebellion: Reclaiming the Revolution," *Historical Journal of Massachusetts* 43, no. 1 (Winter 2015): 62-93. See also John L. Brooke, "To the Quiet of the People: Revolutionary Settlements and Civil Unrest in Western Massachusetts, 1774–1789," *William and Mary Quarterly* 46, no. 3 (July 1989): 435ff.

18. Szatmary, *Shays' Rebellion*, 31.

19. Woody Holton, "'From the Labours of Others': The War Bonds Controversy and the Origins of the Constitution in Massachusetts," *William & Mary Quarterly* 61, no. 2 (April 2004): 281.

20. The relative self-reliance of the western Massachusetts farmers and the cultural differences between western and eastern towns is addressed more fully in Richard W. Hale Jr., "The American Revolution in Western Massachusetts," *New England Historical & Genealogical Register* 129 (October 1975): 325-334.

21. For more on the people's resentment of the courts, the institutional-historical reasons that led to the courts being resented, and the differences between people's relationships with the courts in Worcester, Hampshire, and Berkshire Counties, see Brooke, "To the Quiet of the People," 425-462.

22. Brynner, *"Fire Beneath Our Feet,"* 63.

23. Taylor, *Western Massachusetts*, 115; Feer, *Shays's Rebellion*, 125ff.

24. Richards, *Shays' Rebellion*, 50.

25. James Russell Trumbull. *History of Northampton, Massachusetts*, 337. See also Szatmary, *Shays' Rebellion*, 34ff; Richards, *Shays's Rebellion*, 52-53; Stearns, *Shays' Rebellion*, 10. Robert Feer notes that the actual numbers of men imprisoned for debt were not significantly elevated at the time, but that it was the indignity in the fear of imprisonment, more than imprisonment for debt itself, that raised the people's ire. *Shays's Rebellion*, 63-68.

26. Starkey, *Little Rebellion*, 93.

27. Lockwood, *Western Massachusetts*, 131.

28. Richards, *Shays's Rebellion*, 25.

29. Ibid., 16.

30. Taylor, *Western Massachusetts*, 104.

31. Condon, *Shays' Rebellion*, 39; Brynner adds that this amount was "twenty times greater than the total value of [the state's] real and personal property." *"Fire Beneath Our Feet,"* 59.

32. Holton, "From the Labours," 282. See also Paul Marsella's "Propaganda Trends in the Essex Journal and the New Hampshire Packet, 1787–1788," *Essex Institute Historical Collections* 114, no. 3 (1978): 161-178. Marsella shows that "eighteenth-century American newspapers were a propaganda medium," and his analysis demonstrates that three primary topics—Shays, paper money and credit, and "Indians"—were all systematically presented in a light that was slanted to reinforce the federalist priorities of wealthy merchants.

33. Feer, *Shays's Rebellion*, 72.

34. William M. Fowler Jr., *The Baron of Beacon Hill: A Biography of John Hancock* (Boston: Houghton Mifflin, 1980), 103.

35. Richards, *Shays's Rebellion*, 75.

36. For a detailed treatment of the war bonds and their effect on the Shays protests, see Holton, "From the Labours," 271-316.

37. Richards, *Shays's Rebellion*, 75. Szatmary points out that in a commonwealth where most adults were literate, this information would have been public knowledge. *Shays' Rebellion*, 63.

38. Taylor, *Western Massachusetts*, 130.

39. For detailed discussions of the economics surrounding these notes, see Szatmary, *Shays' Rebellion*, 45-46; Richards, *Shays's Rebellion*, 75-83; Condon, *Shays's Rebellion*, 36-45; Taylor, *Western Massachusetts*, 128-136; and Brynner, *"Fire Beneath Our Feet,"* 53-62.

40. Condon, *Shays's Rebellion*, 41.

41. Holton, "From the Labours," 278.

42. Taylor, *Western Massachusetts*, 125.

43. Condon, *Shays's Rebellion*, 42, 48.

44. Szatmary, *Shays' Rebellion*, 124.

45. Condon, *Shays's Rebellion*, 47.

46. Taylor, *Western Massachusetts*, 125. For a detailed discussion of the British tradition of extralegal actions and of specific actions in the colonies in the decades leading up to these

protests, see Pauline Maier, "Popular Uprisings and Civil Authority in Eighteenth-Century America," *William & Mary Quarterly* 27, no. 1 (January 1970): 3-35.

47. Gordon E. Kershaw, *James Bowdoin II: Patriot and Man of the Enlightenment* (Lanham, MD: University Press of America, 1991), 11. James Sr. divided his estate between his sons, but James Jr. bought out his brother's interest in the business and consolidated its holdings.

48. Kershaw, *James Bowdoin II* , 64.

49. For an inventory of the holdings Bowdoin inherited, see ibid., 63.

50. Ibid., 20.

51. Frank E. Manuel and Fritzie P. Manuel, *James Bowdoin and the Patriot Philosophers*, Memoirs of the American Philosophical Society, vol. 247 (Philadelphia: American Philosophical Society, 2004), 54.

52. Kershaw, *James Bowdoin II*, 230, 114.

53. I use the term "improve" here as Bowdoin and his colleagues would have used it. It remains to be seen whether the enlightenment "improvements" included any improvements in justice for the societies that were displaced as this "progress" advanced through the country. New scholarship such as Charles Mann's *1491* and *1493* (New York: Vintage, 2005 and 2011, respectively) throw this question into a new and compelling light. Likewise, Lisa Brooks's history of the conflicts known inaccurately as King Phillip's War, *Our Beloved Kin* (New Haven, CT: Yale University Press, 2018), shows profound injustices at the root of the colonists' expansion through Massachusetts, and it is hard to frame the terms in which "progress" "repairs" that injustice. A full account of the debts America has paid for its growth, or the rituals that might reconcile those debts, is beyond the scope of this narrative.

54. Fowler. *Baron of Beacon Hill*, 258.

55. Richards, *Shays's Rebellion*, 77; Condon, *Shays's Rebellion*, 36.

56. Feer notes that the Revolutionary era had made regular people more involved in political discussions about the role and size of government and the proper strategy for setting up a government, and he suggests that this popular participation made the people more alert to and more willing to respond to injustices in their government's structure and policies. *Shays's Rebellion*, 69ff.

57. Stearns, *Shays' Rebellion*, 16.

58. Van Beck Hall, *Politics Without Parties: Massachusetts 1780–1791* (Pittsburgh: University of Pittsburgh Press, 1972), 136.

59. Brynner points out that Bowdoin was appointed according to rules he himself had written as one of the three authors of the 1780 Massachusetts Constitution, about which more below. Brynner, *"Fire Beneath Our Feet,"* 150.

60. Condon, *Shays's Rebellion*, 36. Brynner shows that the merchant elites also hoped that Bowdoin's election (appointment) would lead to a constitutional convention that would establish national power of taxation and create a standing army. *"Fire Beneath Our Feet,"* 151.

61. Feer points out that between 1780 and 1786, almost every town in Massachusetts asked for special dispensation to be excused from paying taxes, and he says the common theme in all the towns' pleas was the lack of specie money. *Shays's Rebellion*, 25ff.

CHAPTER TWO: THE COMMONWEALTH COMPOUNDS THE PROBLEM

1. Parmenter, *History of Pelham*, 370-371; Richards, *Shays's Rebellion*, 82.

2. Richards, *Shays's Rebellion*, 83.

3. Holton, "From the Labour of Others," 275.

4. Condon, *Shays's Rebellion*, 37, 71-72; Kershaw, *James Bowdoin II*, 91.

5. Feer points out that veterans were a large class of creditors to the government, having fronted their time and labors, but that the state had defaulted on their promised pay almost from the beginning. He adds that in 1780, some veterans in Northampton had petitioned against issuing paper money, on the grounds that it would depreciate their pay and make it almost worthless. *Shays's Rebellion*, 74.

6. Feer points out that during Samuel Ely's protests of 1782, Northampton Justice of the Peace Joseph Hawley feared that the unpaid veterans would turn against the state. *Shays's Rebellion*, 76. Apparently, the fear of the "democratic mobs" was founded in guilt for the state having failed to pay its soldiers.

7. Richards, *Shays's Rebellion*, 75.

8. Holton, "From the Labours," 277.

9. See Holton, "From the Labours," 279ff., for the story of Nicholas Brown, the Rhode Island merchant who held £80,000 in notes, and the efforts he took, to influence government policy on bond payment.

10. Richards, *Shays's Rebellion*, 75, 76, 85.

11. Smail, *Family of Daniel Shays*, 6.

12. Richards, *Shays's Rebellion*, 78.

13. Holton, "From the Labours," 291.

14. Holton, "From the Labours," 284. See also Robert A. Gross, "A Yankee Rebellion?: The Regulators, New England, and the New Nation," *New England Quarterly* 82, no. 1 (March 2009): 112-135. Gross points out that about 70 percent of Massachusetts's principal place-holders in government had been banished by the Revolutionary War and that the government's ranks had swelled with ambitious men from the coastal towns whose inexperience in government fed their insecurity about their status and anxiety about their investments.

15. Condon, *Shays's Rebellion*, 42.

16. Richards, *Shays's Rebellion*, 85.

17. See Starkey, *Little Rebellion*, 46; Pauline Maier, "Coming to Terms with Samuel Adams," *American Historical Review* 81, no. 1 (Feb. 1976): 14; William Pencak, "Samuel Adams and Shays' Rebellion," *New England Quarterly* 62, no. 1 (March 1989): 66ff. Maier's article has redeemed Samuel Adams from the caricature of the master manipulator and propagandist who pulled the strings that led the colonies to revolution—she describes him rather as a strict Calvinist who held rigidly to the notion that a legitimate, republican state should not be opposed—but this does not entirely justify the strong stance Adams took against the people's opposition to the 1785 austerity measures. He did not leave writings that explain his change of thinking, but his defenses of the new American government do not seem to account for the possibility that even a republican government could ignore its constituents and pass unjust laws that would not wait to be remedied through elections. His silence on the questions of economic injustice or class war undermines his outspoken defense of political stability and republican government, a view put forward by Pencak in "Samuel Adams and Shays's Rebellion."

18. John K. Alexander, *Samuel Adams: America's Revolutionary Politician* (Lanham, MD: Rowman & Littlefield, 2002), 27.

19. Condon, *Shays' Rebellion*, 43. Feer notes that debt collectors were not imprisoned frequently. *Shays's Rebellion*, 59.

20. Fred Anderson, *Crucible of War: The Seven Years' War and the Fate of Empire in British North America, 1754–1766* (New York: Vintage, 2000), 312.

21. See Timothy H. Breen, *American Insurgents, American Patriots: The Revolution of the People* (New York: Hill and Wang, 2011), for an extended discussion of the degree to which the Revolution proceeded from ordinary people's actions and activism, which led the way the "leaders" and "Founding Fathers" eventually followed.

22. Maier, "Popular Uprisings," 25.

23. Taylor, *Western Massachusetts*, 141-142.

24. Maier, "Popular Uprisings," 25, 28.

25. Holton, "From the Labours," 294.

26. Szatmary, *Shays' Rebellion*, 32.

27. Ibid., 32-33.

28. Richards, *Shays's Rebellion*, 67. Leading men in Vermont declared the state an independent republic in 1777, as a way of settling conflicting claims from New York and New Hampshire. In the tumult of the Revolution, there was not a clear avenue to join the colonists' union, so Vermont remained independent until 1791.

29. While I am telling this story from the farmers' point of view, I cannot ignore the reality that the "virginity" of the "wilderness" had been bought with the blood of the Native Americans who were killed off or driven out by more-lawless men than the merchants whose policies tormented Shays and his people. Poor farmers moving west served as the leading edge of empire, but they were also an aftereffect of the workings of capital and speculation in the cities, where powerful men used legal and illegal methods to manufacture opportunity out of the land itself. Again, a full accounting of this dynamic waits to be made, especially the influence of capital and real estate speculation.

30. Szatmary, *Shays' Rebellion*, 62-63.

31. Smail, *Family of Daniel Shays*, 12.

32. The "plantation" in Ulster seems to have been an early version of the colonization that would soon take place in North America, as internally displaced Britons were sent to settle in Ireland by investors and wealthy planters, where they were tasked with "reducing the Irish to servitude, and, if they resisted, killing and dispossessing them." Nicholas P. Canny, "The Ideology of English Colonization: From Ireland to America," *William and Mary Quarterly* 30, no. 4 (Oct. 1973), 590. See also David B. Quinn, *Ireland and America: Their Early Associations, 1500-1640.* (Liverpool: Liverpool University Press, 1991).

33. Richards, *Shays's Rebellion*, 100.

34. See Robert Lord Keyes, "Who Were the Pelham Shaysites?," *Historical Journal of Massachusetts* 28, no. 1 (Winter 2000), for a detailed demographic analysis of the Scots-Irish town's history and the known ninety-one Pelhamites' roles in the protest campaign.

35. Smail, *Family of Daniel Shays*, 6ff.

36. For a history of the conflict known inaccurately as King Philip's War, see Brooks' excellent history, *Our Beloved Kin*, which describes the troubles from the Natives' point of view.

37. Temple, *History of North Brookfield*, 164.

38. Smail, *Family of Daniel Shays*, 4; Trumbull. *History of Northampton, Massachusetts*, 492.

39. Smail, *Family of Daniel Shays*, 4, 5.

40. Brynner, *"Fire Beneath Our Feet,"* 80.

41. Stearns, *Shays' Rebellion*, 5.

42. Smail, *Family of Daniel Shays*, 6.

43. Nathaniel Philbrick, *Valiant Ambition: George Washington, Benedict Arnold, and the Fate of the American Revolution* (New York: Penguin, 2016), 247.

44. Richards, *Shays's Rebellion*, 48.

45. Ibid., 27, 48.

46. Stearns, *Shays' Rebellion*, 6.

47. Smail, *Family of Daniel Shays*, 6.

48. Leonard Richards (*Shays's Rebellion*, 58-62) and John Brooke ("To the Quiet of the People," 443ff) make clear that the economic situation in western Massachusetts was only one factor in the people's resistance to Boston. Szatmary notes that indebtedness rates were higher in Worcester than in Hampshire County (*Shays' Rebellion*, 29), but the Regulation was predominantly an affair of Hampshire County. Rather the fear of foreclosures and imprisonments for debt played on longstanding resentments among the people about the way they were treated by officials in Boston.

49. Again, see Maier, "Popular Uprisings," for a detailed discussion of the history of extralegal action in Massachusetts.

50. Ray Raphael and Marie Raphael, *The Spirit of '74* (New York: New Press, 2015), 76-92.

51. Rafael and Raphael, *Spirit of '74*, 29.

52. Crane, "Shays' Rebellion," 68; Taylor, *Western Massachusetts*, 120ff; Brooke, "To the Quiet of the People," 427ff. Most histories present Ely as merely an itinerant preacher and rabble-rouser who was upset about taxes. See Brynner for a detailed discussion of the importance of constitutional issues of representation in Ely's protests and the class-based bias in the taxes designed to fund an aristocratic class of retired officers. Brynner also discusses the role of the courts and their aggressive fee schedules as contributing to the disruptions that go under Ely's name. *"Fire Beneath Our Feet,"* 55-62.

53. For a detailed discussion of Ely and his political activities, see Feer, *Shays's Rebellion*, 142-174.

54. Condon, *Shays' Rebellion*, 22ff; Szatmary, *Shays' Rebellion*, 34; Trumbull, *History of Northampton*, 454ff; Crane, "Shays' Rebellion," 68.

55. Richards, *Shays's Rebellion*, 60.

56. Taylor, *Western Massachusetts*, 121.

57. Condon, *Shays' Rebellion*, 40.

58. Richards, *Shays's Rebellion*, 71-74; Condon, *Shays' Rebellion*, 45. In his essay "Shays' Rebellion and the Problem of Opposition Politics," J. R. Pole points out that Hampshire, Worcester, and Berkshire Counties sent only 67 of the 130 representatives they were entitled to send to the General Court, a shortfall he attributes to poverty and to the sense that the representatives would not have sufficient influence to counteract the wealthier towns' representatives. In *Major Problems in the Era of the American Revolution, 1760–1791: Documents and Essays,* ed. Richard Brown, 3rd ed. (Boston: Houghton Mifflin, Cengage Learning, 2000), 451.

59. Szatmary, *Shays' Rebellion*, 48-49; Condon, *Shays' Rebellion*, 45.

60. Maier's "Popular Uprisings" makes clear how the extralegal crowds operated, acting only when official avenues of seeking redress had been exhausted and staying within the bounds of their complaints without turning to broader violence or property damage. Nevertheless, Maier points out, to call a group of righteous men a mob was an effective strategy for dismissing their concerns in a new democracy where fear of "the levelling impulses" was strong. 22-24. As Brynner puts it, "generalizations about crowds of demonstrators are notoriously fallible, and always subject to deliberate as well as unintentional distortion." *"Fire Beneath Our Feet,"* 740.

61. Brooke points out that justices of the peace were relatively uncommon in Hampshire and Berkshire Counties, but the law was administered in the river towns, forced on a people who could not execute their own legal affairs. "To the Quiet of the People," 436.

62. Kershaw, *James Bowdoin II*, 74.

63. For a history of the role of slavery in Massachusetts, see Jared Hardesty, *Black Lives, Native Lands, White Worlds: A History of Slavery in New England* (Amherst, MA: Bright Leaf, 2019).

64. Carl Van Doren, *Mutiny in January* (New York: Viking Press, 1943), 107.

65. Michael Schellhammer, "Mutiny of the New Jersey Line," *Journal of the American Revolution* (March 19, 2014), accessed July 4, 2021, https://allthingsliberty.com/2014/03/mutiny-of-the-new-jersey-line/.

66. Richards, *Shays's Rebellion*, 101ff.

67. Ibid., 114; Keith Krawczynski, *Daily Life in the Colonial City* (Santa Barbara, CA: Greenwood, 2013), 133ff. Also, the 1780 Massachusetts Constitution established Congregationalism (Puritanism) as the state religion of Massachusetts and obligated the towns to maintain a Congregationalist church. Unsurprisingly, this provision created resentment in the Presbyterian towns of western Massachusetts. Brynner, *Shays's Rebellion*, 148.

68. Richards, *Shays's Rebellion*, 114.

69. Szatmary, *Shays' Rebellion*, 13.

70. For a detailed account of religious life in the Commonwealth and the differences between the sects central to the different communities, see Krawczynski, *Daily Life,* 117ff.

71. Richards, *Shays's Rebellion*, 101-102. Pelham farmers had recently been swindled by con man Stephen Burroughs, who had passed himself off as a minister and filled the pulpit for twenty weeks, then absconded one week shy of fulfilling his contract. His "Hay Mow Sermon," which Parmenter says was published after the 1786 crisis, mocked the country people for their crude speech and Irish brogues, which pronounced "faith" as "fath," as well as for their dishonesty, superstitions, and their factiousness. Parmenter, *History of Pelham*, 337-340. See also Richards, *Shays's Rebellion*, 102.

72. Richards, *Shays's Rebellion*, 98-100.

73. Alice Morse Earle. *Home Life in Colonial Days* (Mineola, NY: Dover, 2006), 39, 111.

74. Brown, "Shays's Rebellion and Its Aftermath," 83-84.

75. Terry Bouton's *Taming Democracy: "The People," the Founders, and the Troubled Ending of the American Revolution* (Oxford: Oxford University Press, 2009) shows a parallel case in Pennsylvania during and after the Revolution, where the postwar economic troubles and the founding elites' concentration of political and economic power through the US Constitution undermined the people's confidence that the Revolution had increased their economic opportunities and liberties. Bouton notes that it also redoubled their sense that "ordinary people . . . had the right to interpret law and decide what was legal under the 1776 Constitution, and what was unconstitutional." 166.

76. Szatmary, *Shays' Rebellion*, 124.

77. Ibid., 41.

78. Holton, "From the Labours," 292. Also, Massachusetts held yearly elections for governor, but in all the Shays literature, I have found reference to a March 1786 election only in Feer, *Shays's Rebellion*, 195.

79. Holton, "From the Labours," 294.

80. Richards, *Shays's Rebellion*, 83; Szatmary, *Shays' Rebellion*, 50.

81. Holton, "From the Labours," 290; Szatmary, *Shays' Rebellion*, 52.

82. Richards, *Shays's Rebellion*, 84.

83. Starkey, *Shays' Rebellion*, 161.

84. Szatmary, *Shays' Rebellion*, 58.

85. Richards, *Shays's Rebellion*, 52.

86. Szatmary, *Shays' Rebellion*, 67.

87. Szatmary, "Shays' Rebellion in Springfield," 5.

88. Condon, *Shays' Rebellion*, 34.

89. Starkey, *Little Rebellion*, 15.

90. Condon, *Shays's Rebellion*, 34.

91. Szatmary, *Shays' Rebellion*, 67.

92. Condon, *Shays's Rebellion*, 42.

93. Szatmary, "Shays' Rebellion in Springfield," 6.

94. Condon, *Shays' Rebellion*, 42.

95. Ibid., 46; Starkey, *Little Rebellion*, 15.

96. Richards, *Shays's Rebellion*, 80. For more on Benjamin Austin Jr., who wrote a series of letters under the pen name "Honestus," opposing lawyers and court fees, see Feer, *Shays's Rebellion*, 125-132.

97. Brynner notes that the invocation of the Roman populist brothers Tiberius and Gaius Gracchus cut in two directions: on one hand, it resonated as a call for regular people to band together to limit wealthy landowners' power and holdings; on the other hand, it haunted the 1786 protests with the specter of civil war, for the Gracchi were suppressed by violence, and their supporters were arrested and executed. *"Fire Beneath Our Feet,"* 126.

98. Szatmary, *Shays' Rebellion*, 57; Condon, *Shays' Rebellion*, 48.

99. Szatmary, *Shays' Rebellion*, 45, 73.

100. Ibid., *Shays' Rebellion*, 71.

101. See Brynner for a detailed discussion of the effect of these fears, and the elites' arguments, which fed the counter-revolutionary panic. There is also, of course, a counter-revolutionary aspect of this fearmongering, as the government that came into power through revolution sought to establish its legitimacy by casting its opposition as rebels against order and suppressing them.

102. Starkey, *Little Rebellion*, 31.

103. Szatmary, *Shays' Rebellion*, 73.

104. Condon, *Shays' Rebellion*, 43. For more examples of satire sharpened on the Regulators' cause, see William Pencak, "The Humorous Side of Shays' Rebellion," *Historical Journal of Massachusetts* 17, no. 2 (Oct. 1989): 164.

105. Howard Zinn. *A People's History of the United States*. (New York: Harper & Row, 1980) 93.

106. Kershaw, *James Bowdoin II*, 212; Manuel and Manuel, *James Bowdoin*, 93.

107. Starkey, *Little Rebellion*, 85; Kershaw, *James Bowdoin II*, 246.

108. Kershaw, *James Bowdoin II*, 94-99, 153.

109. Condon, *Shays' Rebellion*, 43ff.

110. See Richards for a detailed discussion of the leading Regulator families in Pelham and other towns. *Shays's Rebellion*, 56-57.

111. See Brooke for a discussion of the convention movement and the self-reliance of Hampshire County farmers, relative to farmers in Worcester or other eastern counties. "To the Quiet of the People," 452.

112. Raphael and Raphael, *Spirit of '74*, 46-48.

113. These town meetings and the conventions that came out of them had been seen as a threat to the Crown in the wake of the Boston Tea Party, and they were a source of contention to the Bowdoin administration as well, for they served the purpose of local government in an area where, as Brooke points out, not many towns had justices of the peace, to administer government business. For this reason, Brooke argues that the Massachusetts protests of 1786–87 were caused by Massachusetts's failure to establish a complete "revolutionary settlement of civil institutions" after the Revolution and the Massachusetts Constitution of 1780. "To the Quiet of the People," 436-441.

114. Richards, *Shays's Rebellion*, 5, 69.

115. Raphael and Raphael, *Spirit of '74*, 46-48.

116. Ibid., 46.

117. Richards, *Shays's Rebellion*, 68-69, 72

118. Brynner adds that the 1780 constitution calculated representation in the Senate not by population but by taxes paid, tilting influence toward eastern merchants and land speculators, and effectively disenfranchising towns with fewer than six hundred residents. *Shays's Rebellion*, 30-31.

119. The process by which the 1780 constitution was ratified was itself deeply undemocratic. The first draft of the constitution had been submitted to the towns for review, but it was returned to Boston with so many confusing or contradictory requests for changes from the various towns that when James Bowdoin and John and Samuel Adams finished a second draft, leaders in Boston sent it to the towns with simple instructions to the towns: vote to accept or reject the document as a whole. When the ratification convention took place, a heavy snowstorm closed roads the length of the state making travel impossible, meaning that hardly any of the western towns' delegates were in Boston to voice their concerns. For more on the 1779 and 1780 constitutions, see Richards, *Shays's Rebellion*, 71-72, and Robert Feer, *Shays's Rebellion*, 8-24. See also Brynner for a discussion of irregularities in the ratification process, "*Fire Beneath Our Feet*," 30n57. Brynner adds that the most inflammatory provision in the 1780 constitution established Congregationalism as the official religion, which is slightly to the side of this narrative, but the requirement that Presbyterian towns should pay to support Congregationalist churches surely fed the bilateral resentments between Boston and western Massachusetts. 148.

120. Richards, *Shays's Rebellion*, 74.
121. Condon, *Shays' Rebellion*, 48.
122. Stearns, *Shays's Rebellion*, 12.
123. Szatmary, *Shays' Rebellion*, 23.
124. Starkey, *Little Rebellion*, 41.
125. Condon, *Shays' Rebellion*, 50.
126. Szatmary, *Shays' Rebellion*, 40.
127. Parmenter, *History of Pelham*, 368.
128. Szatmary states that "between 1784 and 1787, yeomen in seventy-three rural Massachusetts towns—more than 30 percent of all communities in the state—sent petitions to the General Court in Boston." Szatmary, *Shays' Rebellion*, 38.
129. Holton, "From the Labours," 294.
130. Taylor, *Western Massachusetts*, 136-137.
131. Eric Sloane, *A Museum of Early Tools* (New York: Funk & Wagnalls, 1964).
132. Smail, *Family of Daniel Shays*, 19.

CHAPTER THREE: THE FARMERS ORGANIZE THEIR FIRST PROTEST

1. Richards, *Shays's Rebellion*, 4.
2. Feer notes that by September, half a dozen towns in northern Worcester County had entered into such pacts. Feer, *Shays's Rebellion*, 247.
3. Richards, *Shays's Rebellion*, 8.
4. Parmenter, *History of Pelham*, 367.
5. Taylor, *Western Massachusetts*, 137.
6. Parmenter, *History of Pelham*, 367-370.
7. Ibid., 368-369.
8. Ibid., 368.
9. For more about the divisions between towns and the decentralized nature of the protest campaign, see Richards, *Shays's Rebellion*, 56ff. See also Gregory Nobles' essay "The Promise of the Revolution, 'Satan, Smith, Shattuck, and Shays': The People's Leaders in the Massachusetts Regulation of 1786," in *Revolutionary Founders: Rebels, Radicals, and Reformers in the Making of the Nation*, ed. Alfred F. Young (New York: Knopf, 2011), 215-232.
10. Richards, *Shays's Rebellion*, 55.
11. Ibid., 101, 98ff.
12. For a discussion of the difference between Regulator towns and government towns or towns that remained neutral, see Richards, *Shays's Rebellion*, 53-62 and 110-116.
13. Ibid., 9.
14. Ibid., 57.
15. Szatmary, *Shays' Rebellion*, 66.
16. According to Bezaleel Howard, a Springfield Congregationalist pastor, when the Regulators discussed the question of bringing arms to the protests "They . . . signified that they should not be more obnoxious to Government to go with arms than they should with Bludgeons and Clubs, and it would show their Determinate Resolution to have those matters and things Redress'd of which they so much and ardently complain. . . . They Concluded to appear at Northampton, and those who lived Remote, to leave their arms at Home, them more Near, to appear with them." Brown, "Shays's Rebellion and Its Aftermath," 598-615
17. Stearns, *Shays' Rebellion*, 27.
18. Richards, *Shays' Rebellion*, 46.
19. Ibid., 44.
20. Ibid., 46, 48, 52.
21. Stearns, *Shays's Rebellion*, 13.
22. Ibid., 35; Taylor, *Western Massachusetts*, 146.
23. Richards, *Shays's Rebellion*, 9.

24. Stearns, *Shays's Rebellion*, 21.
25. Richards, *Shays's Rebellion*, 34.
26. Stearns, *Shays's Rebellion*, 21.
27. Trumbull, *History of Northampton*, 493ff.
28. Stearns, *Shays's Rebellion*, 21.
29. Starkey, *Little Rebellion*, 30; Stearns, *Shays's Rebellion*, 21, 22.

CHAPTER FOUR: A MIDDLE PATH

1. Holton, "From the Labours," 296.
2. Condon, *Shays' Rebellion*, 50; Taylor, *Western Massachusetts*, 143-144.
3. Feer points out that this statement was a rare instance of executive leadership from a governor whose response was characterized by vacillation. *Shays's Rebellion*, 250. For more on Bowdoin's wavering response to the protests, see ibid., 333ff.
4. Starkey, *Little Rebellion*, 35. Feer notes that eighteenth-century communication was famously slow and inconsistent. *Shays's Rebellion*, 266-267, 334. For the sake of narrative continuity, I have condensed the lag times and largely skirted the complex issues that arose from the inconsistent distribution of official communications. Feer adds that one of the outcomes of the 1786–1787 tumults was that the government resolved to publish its proclamations in Worcester and Springfield newspapers, not just in Boston. Ibid., 469.
5. Feer notes that Bowdoin did not act alone in responding to the first protests, but he met with a council consisting of "Benjamin Austin; . . . three senators, including Samuel Adams and the Phillipses, cousins Samuel and William; Chief Justice William Cushing of the Supreme Judicial Court and three of his colleagues; Attorney-General Robert Treat Paine; and four of Boston's representatives," most of whom were "merchants, or lived on wealth inherited from parents or in-laws who were merchants." *Shays's Rebellion*, 196. For more about their deliberations—in which council members were more concerned about avoiding bloodshed than about making reforms or even conferring with the affected farmers—see ibid., 196-200.
6. Szatmary, *Shays' Rebellion*, 108.
7. Starkey, *Little Rebellion*, 110.
8. Kershaw, *James Bowdoin II*, 72.
9. Brynner adds that the people of Massachusetts would have also remembered the "only precedent of non-monarchical government in British history: the elimination of Charles I," which set up the expectation that a monarchy might reestablish itself after a period of civil war. *Shays's Rebellion*, 15. Since Cromwell's interregnum lasted ten years, an expectation was set that America's confederation might be due for a transition back to monarchy. Ibid., 25.
10. Parmenter, *History of Pelham*, 7ff.
11. Richards, *Shays's Rebellion*, 100.
12. Cf. Richards, *Shays's Rebellion*, 65; Irving Mark, "Agrarian Revolt in Colonial New York, 1766," *American Journal of Economics and Sociology* 1, no. 2 (Jan. 1942): 111-124; Cynthia A. Kierner, *Revolutionary America, 1750–1815: Sources and Interpretation* (Upper Saddle River, NJ: Prentice Hall, 2003), 116ff; William Edward Fitch, MD, *Some Neglected History of North Carolina* (New York: self-published, 1914), 198.
13. Irving Mark, "Agrarian Revolt in Colonial New York, 1766," *American Journal of Economics and Sociology* 1, no. 2 (January 1942): 112.
14. Richards, *Shays's Rebellion*, 66.
15. Ibid., 67.
16. Anderson, *Crucible of War*, 479-481.
17. Raphael and Raphael, *Spirit of '74*, 24.
18. For a detailed account of Massachusetts's resistance to the Crown and its functional independence, see ibid., 39ff.
19. Willard Sterne Randall, *Ethan Allen: His Life and Times* (New York: W.W. Norton, 2011), 516.

20. For a detailed history of this conflict, see Bouton, *Taming Democracy*, 164-66.

21. Holland, *History of Western Massachusetts*, 241.

22. Trumbull, *History of Northampton*, 492.

23. Raphael, *Spirit of '74*, 153; Richards, *Shays's Rebellion*, 10; Brynner, *"Fire Beneath Our Feet,"* 76.

24. Richards, *Shays's Rebellion*, 11; Szatmary, *Shays' Rebellion*, 80.

25. Stearns, *Shays's Rebellion*, 26; Starkey, *Little Rebellion*, 37-38. Feer casts doubt on this narrative, as a "gross exaggeration" for which no verification can be found. *Shays's Rebellion*, 192. Feer quotes Artemas Ward's biographer as saying that Ward was "no orator" but was "inclined to stumble in public utterance." Ibid., 193.

26. Stearns, *Shays's Rebellion*, 24.

27. Richards, *Shays's Rebellion*, 111.

28. Stearns, *Shays's Rebellion*, 25.

29. Alden T. Vaughan, "The 'Horrid and Unnatural Rebellion' of Daniel Shays," *American Heritage* 17, no. 4 (June 1966): 63.

30. Stearns, *Shays's Rebellion*, 25-26.

31. Lewis Glazier. *History of Gardner, Massachusetts: From Its Earliest Settlement to 1860* (Worcester, MA: Charles Hamilton, 1860), 67.

32. Stearns, *Shays's Rebellion*, 26.

33. Ibid., 22.

34. Richards, *Shays's Rebellion*, 11.

35. Condon, *Shays' Rebellion*, 55.

36. For a detailed account of the Concord closing, see Feer, *Shays's Rebellion*, 205ff.

37. Zinn, *People's History*, 92.

38. Richard Mros, "Shays' Rebellion in Taunton," in Kaufman, ed., *Shays' Rebellion*, 27.

39. For a detailed account of the Taunton closing, see Feer, *Shays's Rebellion*, 207ff.

40. See Brooke, "To the Quiet of the People," 439ff, for a discussion of the politics surrounding the Berkshire County courts and the opposition that sprang up in fall 1786.

41. Condon, *Shays' Rebellion*, 44; Taylor, *Western Massachusetts*, 144.

42. Ibid., 145.

43. Condon, *Shays' Rebellion*, 57.

44. Stephen T. Riley, "Dr. William Whiting and Shays Rebellion," *American Antiquarian Society* (October 1956): 125-127.

45. John Spencer Bassett, *The Regulators of North Carolina (1765–1771)*, electronic edition (Chapel Hill: Academic Affairs Library, University of North Carolina, 2002). The parallels with the situation in western Massachusetts run deep: the western North Carolina farmers were largely excluded from the political process, and they were burdened by the lack of hard currency for paying taxes. This lack created a power disparity that allowed the judges, sheriffs, and courts to profit at their expense, swindling them out of their property with impunity.

46. Ibid., 150ff. Abby Chandler adds that the fee schedules and commissions associated with taxes, assessments, and other legal actions compounded the farmers' resentment and deepened their poverty. "'Unawed by the Laws of their Country': Local and Imperial Legitimacy in North Carolina's Regulator Rebellion," *North Carolina Historical Review* 93, no. 2 (April 2016): 119-146.

47. Bassett, *Regulators of North Carolina*, 167, 177ff.

48. Ibid., 164; Richards, *Shays's Rebellion*, 64.

49. Fitch, *Some Neglected History*, 198.

50. Cf. Riley, "Dr. William Whiting," 131ff. for the complete text.

51. Richards, *Shays's Rebellion*, 15; Riley, "Dr. William Whiting," 132.

52. Richards, *Shays's Rebellion*, 15.

53. Riley, "Dr. William Whiting," 127. For more on Sedgwick, who had begun construction of a prominent, new, brick home in spring 1786, see Feer, *Shays's Rebellion*, 237ff.

54. Richards, *Shays's Rebellion*, 16; Condon, *Shays's Rebellion*, 69. Maier points out that in the government's view, any nongovernmental organization was illegitimate and "seditious, undistinguishable from common 'mobs,'" making any resistance to duly authorized policies a form of treason. In this view, the state was the only authority, and county conventions were, in Adams's words, "not only useless, but dangerous." "Coming to Terms with Samuel Adams," 27.

55. Maier, "Coming to Terms with Samuel Adams," 27-28.

56. Goldscheider, *Shays' Rebellion*, 82.

57. Szatmary, *Shays' Rebellion*, 75.

58. Richards, *Shays's Rebellion*, 60.

59. Ibid., 27.

60. Ibid., 13.

61. See Holton, "From the Labours," 298ff., for a discussion of New Hampshire taxes and currency policy, including the "Exeter Riot," which was also known as the "Paper Money Riot." See also Charles Henry Bell, *History of the Town of Exeter, New Hampshire* (Boston: J. E. Farwell), 1888.

62. Glenn Williams, *Year of the Hangman: George Washington's Campaign against the Iroquois* (Yardley, PA: Westholme, 2005), 293.

63. Richards, *Shays's Rebellion*, 13.

64. Szatmary, *Shays' Rebellion*, 78-79.

65. Stearns, *Shays's Rebellion*, 32.

66. For this and other references to the phase of the moon throughout the months of protests, see Moongiant.com, accessed June 26, 2021, https://www.moongiant.com/calendar/september/1786/.

67. Temple, *History of North Brookfield*, 245.

68. Richards, *Shays's Rebellion*, 29.

69. See Keyes, "Who Were the Pelham Shaysites?," for demographic and personal information about the protestors from Pelham.

70. Szatmary, *Shays' Rebellion*, 61.

71. Richards, *Shays's Rebellion*, 91, 96.

72. Again, see Richards, *Shays's Rebellion*, 57ff, for a discussion of the differences between the towns that sent men and the towns that refrained.

73. Stearns, *Shays's Rebellion*, 35.

74. Crane, "Shays' Rebellion," 74.

75. Condon, *Shays' Rebellion*, 61.

76. Feer notes that Shepard "broke into the arsenal" to arm his men "over the protests of the superintendent." *Shays's Rebellion*, 230. Feer adds that Shepard had called for a "Total suspension of all political disquisition" among his troops, for fear that a clear discussion of the issues might dampen their enthusiasm for taking up arms against their countrymen. Ibid., 231.

77. William Dodge Herrick, *History of the town of Gardner, Worcester County, Mass., from the incorporation, June 27, 1785, to the present time* (Gardner, MA: Printed by A. G. Bushnell, 1878), 87.

78. Szatmary, *Shays' Rebellion*, 81.

79. Richards, *Shays's Rebellion*, 112.

80. Szatmary, *Shays' Rebellion*, 81.

81. Shays and the Regulators were not necessarily fighting for a military objective so much as they were fighting for the hearts of their people. As Brynner puts it: the protests were a ritual demonstration "designed to accomplish a single extra-constitutional goal: to postpone property seizures by the courts until the next elecction.Daniel Stebbins, eyewitness to the Springfield protest, wrote that while the outcome of the protest was uncertain, the loyalties of the bystanders were not clearly inclined toward either side: "Between the Court House and old Meeting House was a large open space, now filled with a dense crowd of spectators ready to join the strongest party." Brynner, *"Fire Beneath Our Feet,"* 85.

82. In reality, the court closing lasted up to three days, but I have consolidated the closings because reports frequently provided deeply contradictory or partial accounts, and there was not enough reliable material to portray a detailed or consistent scene. For the highly partial accounts of the Springfield closing in September 1786, see Trumbull, *History of Northampton*, 492ff., Holland, *History of Western Massachusetts* 230ff, and Feer, *Shays's Rebellion*, 232ff.

83. Holland, *History of Western Massachusetts*, 247.

84. Stearns, *Shays' Rebellion*, 35; Szatmary, "Shays' Rebellion in Springfield," 11.

85. Stearns, *Shays's Rebellion*, 35, 21; Starkey, *Little Rebellion*, 81.

86. Monroe Stearns describes a multiday negotiation in which the judges responded on September 27 that they would not do "anything inconsistent with the offices of this body," which inspired the protestors to threaten to attack and possibly kidnap the judges. Stearns, *Shays' Rebellion*, 35, 36.

87. Starkey, *Little Rebellion*, 83. See also Feer for an account of the preparations Berkshire men had made to obstruct that court. *Shays's Rebellion*, 237-283.

88. Brown, "Shays's Rebellion," 605; Starkey, *Little Rebellion*, 83.

89. Brown, "Shays's Rebellion," 605.

CHAPTER FIVE: THE GOVERNMENT SWINGS INTO ACTION

1. Butler's new newspaper was filling a gap for Hampshire County society. Brooke attributes some of the restiveness of Hampshire County to the lack of government infrastructure, lack of justices of the peace, and the absence of a regional newspaper as a mechanism for airing out local concerns. "To the Quiet of the People," 438.

2. Szatmary, *Shays' Rebellion*, 74

3. Goldscheider, "Shays's Rebellion," 72. Feer adds that accusations of British influence were widespread, not only in the 1786 protests but in numerous earlier troubles as well. For a detailed account of this provocative slander, see Brown, *Shays's Rebellion*, 289-301. Feer debunks this charge in detail and describes the measures British agents were actually taking to damage the new nation, including negotiating trade agreements with the Bahamas, smuggling out American textile machinery, and encouraging migration to Canada. Ibid., 295. Feer adds that Bowdoin's daughter's husband, John Temple, served as the British consul general to the United States, and he would hardly have fomented a rebellion against his father-in-law's authority. Ibid., 296. Feer also debunks the accusation that the protests were exacerbated by domestic agents provocateurs, who were supposedly backed by nationalists like Knox or Higginson, who thought that chaos in Massachusetts would lead to a constitutional convention and a stronger federal government. Ibid., 301-314.

4. Lockwood, *Western Massachusetts*, 140.

5. Crane, "Shays' Rebellion," 81; Starkey, *Little Rebellion*, 134.

6. Feer points out that county conventions existed in a legal gray area, not explicitly constitutionally authorized but not forbidden either. They functioned as a relief valve for local political concerns but also as a threat to state authority, depending on whether a speaker was advocating for or trying to suppress popular concerns. *Shays's Rebellion*, 89ff.

7. James Bowdoin, *The Bowdoin and Temple Papers*, vol. 2 (Boston: Massachusetts Historical Society, 1907), 119.

8. Szatmary, *Shays' Rebellion*, 74.

9. Starkey, *Little Rebellion*, 85; Condon, *Shays' Rebellion*, 65.

10. According to Feer, the federal arsenal in Springfield became a real source of discomfort to the government after the first round of statewide protests. Feer says that when Henry Knox visited the arsenal and met with Major General William Shepard, he wrote to Bowdoin for guidance about protecting the stockpiled weapons and ammunition, but Bowdoin delegated authority to Knox, who delegated it to Shepard, before leaving Springfield to return to New York. In the end, no guard was set, for fear that an armed force would antagonize the protestors and also for fear of incurring costs that would have to be borne by Congress. *Shays's Rebellion*, 214-215.

11. Richards, *Shays's Rebellion*, 15; Szatmary, *Shays' Rebellion*, 82. Brynner credits Henry Knox with creating the movement called "Shays' Rebellion" when he reported to Congress that the insurrection was led by Shays. Brynner shows that this report used the idea of Shays and his military leadership as a threat to frighten the elites into the drastic steps of bolstering the strength of the federal government by reforming the Articles of Confederation. *"Fire Beneath Our Feet,"* 128, 162-163.

12. Brynner shows that this ruse was part of a wider effort to garner support for a standing federal army and redeem the officer corps after the collapse of the Newburgh Conspiracy of 1783. Ibid., 125-131. In this case, James Swan, one of Henry Knox's conspirators, said "'Indians' is meant [to include] all who oppose the Dignity, Honour, and happiness of the United States." Ibid., 130. Feer finds that in congressional records withheld from the public for thirty years, Congress knew very well that it was authorizing funds for troops to oppose the farmers. *Shays's Rebellion*, 281.

13. This history has been thoroughly documented, but I recommend Brooks' *Our Beloved Kin* as a penetrating historical narrative from the Native American perspective. It is clear that the farmers and the Native Americans, opposed as they were in many cases, also had common enemies in land speculators and financiers.

14. For more on Knox's role in using "Shays' Rebellion" as a tool to spur Washington and the federal government into action, see Brynner, *"Fire Beneath Our Feet,"* 105ff.

15. Richards, *Shays's Rebellion*, 97.

16. Richards, *Shays's Rebellion*, 15; Szatmary, *Shays' Rebellion*, 82; Feer, *Shays's Rebellion*, 269. For a detailed account of this force, which was led by Henry Knox's friend Henry Jackson, see Feer, 271-289.

17. Szatmary, *Shays' Rebellion*, 84.

18. Ibid., 83.

19. Richards, *Shays's Rebellion*, 17, Szatmary, *Shays' Rebellion*, 83. The British Riot Act of 1714 formed the basis for this law, but Adams's version was much harsher than the original, which simply authorized the use of force against rioters and indemnified authorities against liability. The original did not contain provisions for whipping or surrendering land and property to the Commonwealth. Maier, "Popular Uprising," 28-30.

20. Szatmary, *Shays' Rebellion*, 83; Richards, *Shays's Rebellion*, 17.

21. Brynner, *"Fire Beneath Our Feet,"* 161.

22. Parmenter, *History of Pelham*, 374. It is worth mentioning that this note was sent at around the same time that Henry Knox had made his tour of the Springfield arsenal to survey its defenses and assess the danger from the protestors.

23. In his interview with Rufus Putnam in January 1787, Shays complained that his name was signed to letters he did not write. Parmenter, *History of Pelham*, 395-398. Others have commented on the decentralized nature of the people's protests, so I find it more than plausible that this letter could have been a forgery, manufactured by nervous merchants to give the government clear evidence that the people were mustering. Shays's leadership is not described consistently. Taylor fails to see Shays as the "generalissimo" the government saw and casts doubt on his participation in the court closings beyond the September 25, 1786, protest. *Western Massachusetts*, 151. Certain histories say Shays was not in Springfield for the December closing, though others place him there. For the sake of narrative continuity, I have placed him there. The facts to confirm his movements in detail, one way or the other, have not been preserved.

24. Feer, *Shays's Rebellion*, 257; Richards, *Shays's Rebellion*, 16; Condon, *Shays' Rebellion*, 68.

25. Feer, *Shays's Rebellion*, 254; Condon, *Shays' Rebellion*, 68.

26. Condon, *Shays' Rebellion*, 69.

27. Szatmary, *Shays' Rebellion*, 83; Crane, "Shays' Rebellion," 80; Holton, "From the Labours," 276.

28. Szatmary, "Shays' Rebellion in Springfield," 12.

29. Szatmary, *Shays' Rebellion*, 83.

30. We do not have this correspondence, we only have evidence that it existed. In his interview with Rufus Putnam in January, Shays states that he "wrote to a few towns in the counties of Worcester and Hampshire." Parmenter, *History of Pelham*, 396. Clearly some correspondence took place. (It seems plausible that these letters would have been destroyed, as the state had criminalized the protests, and any correspondence could have been used as evidence. Also, after the people won reforms in the 1787 elections, the controversial period of unrest came to seem shameful in the eyes of a country that was seeking unification through other crises, so the letters that showed coordination would not have been valued.) Still, the degree to which Shays commanded an organized force has been disputed, and there is evidence that the coordination was much looser than suspected, as the towns were largely self-governing, and many acted on their own. Nevertheless, the movements of large numbers of men do indicate some degree of coordination. Regarding the individuals named here, as based on Governor Bowdoin's arrest warrants, it is not likely that all of these men were actually leaders, either. The government's arrests smacked of political score settling, and many of these names appear nowhere else in the record of the protests. Richards's *Shays's Rebellion* is the best resource for detailing which towns sent the largest numbers of men and leaders.

31. All these officers were named for arrest in Bowdoin's January warrants.

32. Taylor, *Western Massachusetts*, 116.

33. Ray Raphael, *A People's History of the American Revolution: How Common People Shaped the Fight for Independence* (New York: New Press, 2016), 15.

34. At the same time that the people were praying for a peaceful resolution to their crisis, Brynner shows, Henry Knox's October 28 letter to George Washington was instrumental in convincing Washington that the Massachusetts protests posed a grave danger to the union. Only two weeks after Knox's letter, Washington wrote to Madison to suggest that he might be willing to return from retirement, a step nationalists like Knox, Higginson, and Bowdoin had seen as essential to any hope of advancing reforming the Articles of Confederation. *"Fire Beneath Our Feet,"* 133ff, appendix B.

35. For more on these courts, see Feer, *Shays's Rebellion*, 240-246.

36. Starkey, *Little Rebellion*, 92.

37. The quotations in the following paragraphs are from *An Address from the General Court, to the People of the Commonwealth Of Massachusetts* (Boston: Adams and Nourse, Printers to the Honourable General Court, Ordered to be distributed on October 30, 1786).

38. Feer notes that this detailed account of the state's taxes and expenses had been requested for years and that "bad public relations" had led to confusion about the state's demands for money. *Shays's Rebellion*, 84, 85.

39. Condon, *Shays' Rebellion*, 71-72. Feer notes that in 1786 and in earlier crises, "merchants were eagerly talking about the evils of luxury and of imported goods not in order to avoid or confuse the issues of [the 1786 protests], but rather, in order to hurt their foreign competitors and get more of the trade into their own hands." *Shays's Rebellion*, 485. For a detailed discussion about this rhetoric and the realities of tariffs and international commerce, see ibid., 477ff.

40. Condon, *Shays' Rebellion*, 65.

41. Ibid.; *Acts and Resolves of Massachusetts, 1786–87* (Boston: Secretary of the Commonwealth, 1893), accessed June 28, 2021, https://archive.org/details/actsresolvespass178687 mass, 930.

42. Condon, *Shays' Rebellion*, 65; Acts and Resolutions, 929.

43. It is not clear whether Governor Bowdoin was truly ignorant of the conditions the people were complaining about or whether he knew what they were experiencing and was only dismissing their concerns in a strategy designed to inflame their passions so he could then accuse them of irrational rage. Considering the distance between the coast and the interior of the

Commonwealth—and also the insulated distance between rich and poor—it may well have been the case that he simply did not understand that the people were suffering because of his policies.

44. Crane, "Shays' Rebellion," 82; Szatmary, *Shays' Rebellion*, 69.

45. Crane, "Shays' Rebellion," 82.

46. Ibid.; Szatmary, *Shays' Rebellion*, 69.

47. Brynner, *"Fire Beneath Our Feet,"* 58.

48. Richards, *Shays's Rebellion*, 17; Szatmary, *Shays' Rebellion*, 83.

CHAPTER SIX: CONFRONTING THE COURTS

1. Starkey, *Little Rebellion*, 103ff.

2. Parmenter, in *History of Pelham*, 375, places Shays in Worcester for this closing, but Stearns, *Shays' Rebellion*, 38, and Starkey, *Little Rebellion*, 98, have Wheeler and Abraham Gale leading this closing. Starkey (102) has Shays recruiting arms and soldiers nearby, returning to Rutland on the second of December. For the sake of narrative convenience, and in the absence of consistent documentation to settle this question, I have placed him there.

3. Feer credits Abraham Gale with leading the men in Worcester. He places Shays in Rutland at the time of this protest. *Shays's Rebellion*, 317, 326-327.

4. Stearns, *Shays's Rebellion*, 38.

5. Parmenter, *History of Pelham*, 375.

6. Starkey, *Little Rebellion*, 115.

7. Ibid.

8. Much has been made, in the histories of "Shays's Rebellion," of the "leveling impulses" and violent impulses expressed in the editorials, but the farmers' consistently nonviolent protests support the view that nonviolence was their plan all along—not some kind of failure of nerve, or incompetence, as some histories suggest (in disappointment, surely, that Shays did not live up to the rebel leader they wanted).

9. Starkey, *Little Rebellion*, 115.

CHAPTER SEVEN: BLOOD IN THE SNOW

1. Gary Shattuck. *Artful and Designing Men: The Trials of Job Shattuck and the Regulation of 1786–1787* (Mustang, OK: Tate Publishing, 2013), 282. For more about the hostility between Shattuck and Prescott, see Feer, *Shays's Rebellion*, 319.

2. Raphael, *Spirit of '74*, 147.

3. Richards, *Shays's Rebellion*, 21.

4. Ibid., 20; Szatmary, *Shays' Rebellion*, 92ff; Brynner, *Shays's Rebellion*, 165.

5. Crane, "Shays' Rebellion," 84.

6. Szatmary, *Shays' Rebellion*, 93.

7. Condon, *Shays' Rebellion*, 75; Szatmary, *Shays' Rebellion*, 93.

8. Lockwood, *Western Massachusetts*, 157.

9. See Brynner, *"Fire Beneath Our Feet,"* 136ff, for a detailed discussion of the elites' hopes that plundering and atrocities committed by "ignorant, restless desperadoes," in the words of Abigail Adams, would "prove salutary to the state at large" (157) by accomplishing what Knox and Hamilton and Stephen Higginson and Bowdoin would see as a "restoration to political health" (155), which is to stay the ascent of an aristocratic government of merchant elites and wealthy landowners.

10. See Crane, "Shays' Rebellion," 85, for the letter in full.

11. Szatmary, *Shays' Rebellion*, 94.

12. Ibid., 79.

13. Richards, *Shays's Rebellion*, 21.

14. Starkey, *Little Rebellion*, 106; Myron F. Wehtje, "Boston's Response to Disorder in the Commonwealth, 1783–1787," in Kaufman, ed., *Shays' Rebellion*, 59-61.

15. Lockwood, *Western Massachusetts*, 148.

16. Ibid., 145.

17. Holland, *History of Western Massachusetts*, 252.

18. Stearns, *Little Rebellion*, 39.

19. Wehtje, "Boston's Response," 60.

20. Crane, "Shays' Rebellion," 87.

21. Ibid., 88.

22. Condon, *Shays' Rebellion*, 78.

23. See Crane, "Shays' Rebellion," 88, for the letter in full.

24. Ibid.

25. Ibid.; Szatmary, *Shays' Rebellion*, 92.

26. Crane, "Shays' Rebellion," 88, 89.

27. Worcester Bank and Trust Company, *Historic Events of Worcester: A Brief Account of Some of the Most Interesting Events Which Have Occurred in Worcester During the Past Two Hundred Years* (Worcester, MA, 1922), 20; Condon, *Shays' Rebellion*, 77; Minot, *History of the Insurrections*, 81.

28. Worcester Bank, *Historic Events*, 20.

29. As noted earlier, numbers of protestors were famously unreliable. Feer says that Shays commanded one thousand men at this closing. Brynner says that "one anxious report in Boston put the number as high as 13,000." Feers, *Shays's Rebellion*, 91.

30. Ibid.

31. Ibid.; Glazier, *History of Gardner*, 76.

32. Crane, "Shays' Rebellion," 86.

33. Worcester Society of Antiquity, "Old-Time Taverns of Worcester," *Proceedings of the Worcester Society of Antiquity* 19, no. 2 (1903): 80.

34. Starkey, *Little Rebellion*, 108.

35. Ibid.; Glazier, *History of Gardner*, 80.

CHAPTER EIGHT: SHORING UP SUPPORT

1. Parmenter, *History of Pelham*, 375.

2. Ibid.

3. Lockwood, *Western Massachusetts*, 148.

4. Parmenter has the "insurgents," whom he says were estimated to constitute at least a third of the Massachusetts populace, holding a convention on November 23. *History of Pelham*, 375.

5. Parmenter has Shays in Rutland from the ninth of December until the December 26 closing in Springfield. Ibid.

6. Pencak, "Humorous Side," 164.

7. Richards, *Shays's Rebellion*, 25.

8. See Maier, "Popular Uprisings," 5ff.

9. Pencak, "Humorous Side," 165.

10. Starkey, *Little Rebellion*, 203.

11. Trumbull, *History of Northampton*, 501.

12. Szatmary, "Shays' Rebellion in Springfield," 13.

13. Richards, *Shays's Rebellion*, 21, 22.

14. Wehtje, "Boston's Response," 63.

15. Feer notes that Knox had been cagey about the federal arms, suggesting that Shepard might supply his troops from the arsenal but also warning that use of the weapons might fan the flames of opposition by giving the Regulators evidence to support their claims of tyranny. *Shays's Rebellion*, 338–339.

16. Stearns, *Shays's Rebellion*, 43.

17. Starkey, *Little Rebellion*, 117.

18. Condon, *Shays' Rebellion*, 83; Szatmary, *Shays' Rebellion*, 96.
19. Condon, *Shays' Rebellion*, 84; Starkey, *Little Rebellion*, 124.
20. See Smail, *Family of Daniel Shays*, 5; see Parmenter, *History of Pelham*, 395, for the full text.
21. Temple, *History of North Brookfield*, 715.
22. Anderson, *Crucible of War*, 371.
23. Rufus Putnam, *The Memoirs of Rufus Putnam and Certain Official Papers and Correspondence* (Boston and New York: Houghton, Mifflin, 1903), 93.
24. Szatmary, *Shays' Rebellion*, 86; Starkey, *Little Rebellion*, 119; Brynner, *"Fire Beneath Our Feet,"* 25.
25. Jack Rakove. *Revolutionaries: A New History of the Invention of America* (Boston: Houghton Mifflin, 2010), 311-312.
26. This settlement is now the town of Marietta, Ohio. Starkey, 241.
27. Brynner writes that "Reverend Manasseh Cutler, one of the co-founders of the Ohio Company, wrote that 'these commotions will tend to promote our plan and incline well disposed persons to become adventurers, for who would wish to live under a Government subject to such tumults and confusions." *"Fire Beneath Our Feet,"* 52.
28. This narrative really only gave farmers the chance to be perpetrators, in turn, instead of victims, since the Natives who lived in Ohio would not surrender their claims without violence, and the land could not be occupied without spoiling in advance any claim to innocence for the settlers. The opportunity to profit by speculation in real estate was a constant pressure behind the cycles of settlement, conflict, and displacement, which was inevitably followed by further waves of settlement, then further conflicts, then further displacements as the value of land increased.
29. See Parmenter, *History of Pelham*, 395ff, for the full text of Putnam's letter to Bowdoin. This is our only account of this conversation, but we cannot ignore the fact that this conversation was recounted in a letter to Bowdoin and that Putnam was therefore deeply circumscribed in what he could say.
30. Ibid., 397.
31. By stressing Shays's willingness to fight—and also Shays's distrust of Bowdoin's pardon—Putnam was sending his own message to Bowdoin, quite apart from anything Shays told him in the road. Regrettably, we do not have any other records of this conversation for comparison or verification.

CHAPTER NINE: "MURDER, MURDER"

1. Starkey, *Little Rebellion*, 126.
2. Szatmary, *Shays' Rebellion*, 97.
3. See John Putnam Demos's history *The Unredeemed Captive* (New York: Vintage, 2011) for a narrative of this raid and its consequences.
4. Parmenter, *History of Pelham*, 375.
5. Richards, *Shays's Rebellion*, 23; Szatmary, *Shays' Rebellion*, 87; Szatmary, "Shays' Rebellion in Springfield," 15.
6. Holton, "From the Labours," 296.
7. Richards, *Shays's Rebellion*, 32.
8. Trumbull, *History of Northampton*, 502. Bezaleel Howard also makes clear that the money raised was a loan from merchants. Brown, "Shays's Rebellion," 606.
9. Richards, *Shays's Rebellion*, 25.
10. Ibid., 23. For a more detailed description of Lincoln's background, see Feer, *Shays's Rebellion*, 349-355.
11. Charles Bracelen Flood, *Rise, and Fight Again: Perilous Times along the Road to Independence* (New York: Dodd Mead, 1976), 408.
12. Henry Phelps Johnston, *The Yorktown Campaign and the Surrender of Cornwallis, 1781* (New York: Harper & Brothers, 1881), 156.

13. Brynner notes that the Society of the Cincinnati was intent on redeeming the reputation of America's officer corps, which was tarnished by the Newburgh Conspiracy of 1783, in which soldiers' complaints about lack of pay had led to rumors that they were planning a coup. Created and led by Knox, the Cincinnati persuaded Congress to pass half-pay pensions for life for retired officers who had served three years. Congress commuted this pension to a one-time payment of five years of full pay, and this item in Massachusetts's budget caused a good deal of outrage among the retired enlisted men. For more on the Newburgh Conspiracy, the Cincinnati, and Knox's role, see Brynner, *"Fire Beneath Our Feet,"* 119ff.

14. Szatmary, *Shays' Rebellion*, 100.

15. Szatmary, *Shays' Rebellion*, 98.

16. Ibid., 97.

17. Szatmary notes that in private correspondence, Shepard expressed surprise "that they have not seized the arsenal long before this time and erected their standard at Springfield." Ibid., 99.

18. The numbers of men vary from account to account. For the numbers of men around Springfield in January, see Starkey, *Little Rebellion*, 128; Parmenter, *History of Pelham*, 376; and Crane, "Shays' Rebellion," 92.

19. Richards, *Shays's Rebellion*, 28.

20. Condon, *Shays' Rebellion*, 86.

21. Richards, *Shays's Rebellion*, 29-30.

22. Ibid.; Condon, *Shays' Rebellion*, 86.

23. Szatmary, "Shays' Rebellion in Springfield," 15.

24. Szatmary, *Shays' Rebellion*, 97; Smail, *Family of Daniel Shays*, 10.

25. Szatmary, *Shays' Rebellion*, 97.

26. Hoyt, "They immediately broke."

27. Richards, *Shays's Rebellion*, 25.

28. Szatmary, *Shays' Rebellion*, 56.

29. Richards, *Shays's Rebellion*, 25.

30. Temple, *History of North Brookfield*, 245.

31. Szatmary, "Shays' Rebellion in Springfield," 13; Condon, *Shays's Rebellion*, 84, 87.

32. Szatmary, *Shays' Rebellion*, 101.

33. Ibid., 100.

34. Starkey, *Little Rebellion*, 130.

35. This conversation, and the next one, at 250 yards from the arsenal, were recorded in Buffington's official report, printed in Trumbull, *History of Northampton*, 505-506. Like Putnam's letter to Bowdoin, Buffington's account was meant to serve an official purpose that was not impartial.

36. Buffington deposition. See also Trumbull, *History of Northampton*, 505-506. Again, this is Buffington's report and needs to be taken with a grain of salt. We do not have other corroborating accounts of this or the subsequent conversation in the road.

37. See Crane, "Shays' Rebellion," 93-94, for Shepard's whole account to Bowdoin.

38. Condon, *Shays' Rebellion*, 91.

39. Buffington deposition.

40. Crane, "Shays' Rebellion," 94. That the men advanced with their muskets at shoulders, see Szatmary, "Shays' Rebellion in Springfield," 17.

41. The question of Shays's intentions in marching his men into Shepard's grapeshot is the center in any theory about these protests. In the popular imagination, fed by inaccurate histories, Shays attacked the arsenal in order to try to overthrow the state. These histories do not consider his refusal to mount an aggressive attack. The suggestion that he ought to have mounted an aggressive attack is a curious one. It does not address the question of what, then, would have happened once Shays's men were installed in a building that could easily enough be surrounded and burned down over their heads. Nor does it give Shays's men credit for their patriotic refusal to actually wage war against the country whose liberty they had already

bought with blood. On the flip side, historians portray Shays as naïve for failing to execute a military assault on the arsenal, or else they see this as a failure of nerve or tactics. I believe that Shays was cornered at this point, and the march to the arsenal was a last-ditch attempt to demonstrate his people's innocence to the countryside, through martyrdom if necessary. It does seem likely that the people's disgust with the murders contributed to Bowdoin's land-slide defeat in the April elections.

42. For a firsthand account from the government side, see David Hoyt Jr.'s letter to his father, Pocumtuck Valley Memorial Association, Deerfield, Massachusetts.

43. Richards, *Shays's Rebellion*, 109.

44. Condon, *Shays' Rebellion*, 89.

45. Richards, *Shays's Rebellion*, 29.

46. Holland, *History of Western Massachusetts*, 301.

47. Robert Taylor takes up the question of Shays's retreat and finds, "No one has been able to explain satisfactorily why Shays's men, many of them seasoned veterans of the Revolution, showed so little spirit and fled without firing a single shot." *Western Massachusetts*, 160. The dominant historical narrative, that "Shays's Rebellion" was the unrest that led to the Consti-tution, did not, apparently, allow for dignified, nonviolent protest.

48. Crane, "Shays' Rebellion," 94.

49. Lockwood says that "the rank and file were eager to make an attempt to carry it by storm, but the leaders were too wary and prudent to permit such a rash course, appreciating the general inferiority of their adherents." *Western Massachusetts*, 133.

CHAPTER TEN: RETREAT INTO THE COLD

1. "To the Honorable Major General Lincoln, . . . Daniel Shays, Wilbraham, January 25th, 1787," *Worcester Magazine* 44, vol. 2 (February 1787): 534-535.

2. Lockwood, *Western Massachusetts*, 163.

3. Starkey, *Little Rebellion*, 133.

4. Any land they thought they might still settle, of course, was already inhabited, and there were further tragedies in the violence that cleared them for resettlement, but that is a story for another telling.

5. Crane, "Shays' Rebellion," 95.

6. Thomas Egleston, *The Life of John Paterson: Major General in the Revolutionary Army* (New York: Knickerbocker Press, 1894; repr. Kessinger Publishing, 2010), 179.

7. Brown, "Shays's Rebellion," 607.

8. "To Gen'l Shepherd of the Commanding Officer in Springfield, . . . Daniel Shays Capt, [Jan. 26, 1787], *Worcester Magazine* 45, vol. 2 (1787): 544; Capt. Shays to Gen. Shepard, Jan. 27th, 1787, *Hampshire Gazette*, Feb. 14, 1787, Memorial Libraries, Deerfield, MA.

9. Feer suggests that Lincoln's memory of being besieged and defeated in South Carolina kept him from keeping his forces in Springfield for long. For more details about Lincoln's decision to leave Springfield quickly, see *Shays's Rebellion*, 372.

10. Szatmary, "Shays' Rebellion in Springfield," 19.

11. Stearns, *Shays's Rebellion*, 49; Trumbull, *History of Northampton*, 507; Starkey, *Little Re-bellion*, 137-138.

12. Trumbull, *History of Northampton*, 507.

13. Stearns, *Shays' Rebellion*, 51; Szatmary, *Shays' Rebellion*, 103.

14. Lockwood, *Western Massachusetts*, 170-171.

15. Crane, "Shays' Rebellion," 95-96; Trumbull, *History of Northampton*, 509.

16. There is a legend in Hampshire County that Shays and his men sheltered at the Horse Caves on Mount Norwottuck. I have not found any evidence of this and suspect that it is a nineteenth-century invention to bolster the region's mythology of independence or to burnish the region's historical appeal for tourists after the Quabbin reservoir dissolved half of Pelham and four other towns, which had largely backed the Regulators. It is not impossible that

Shays and his men were still cold after trudging up a long steep hill and sought out the cliffs as a site where the steep exposed rocks would double the warmth of their fires by reflecting it back, giving them an island of warmth in the January night. But the caves are so far out of the way from any path between South Hadley and East Amherst that this story seems to be a legend invented later. The countryside around Amherst was mostly supportive of the farmers' cause. Shays and his men would not have needed to "hide out" in the Horse Caves.

17. Starkey, *Little Rebellion*, 138.
18. Lockwood, *Western Massachusetts*, 266.
19. Richards, *Shays's Rebellion*, 29.
20. Starkey, *Little Rebellion*, 130.
21. Lockwood, *Western Massachusetts*, 266.
22. Feer, *Shays's Rebellion*, 390.
23. Trumbull, *History of Northampton*, 508; Lockwood, *Western Massachusetts*, 170.
24. Trumbull, *History of Northampton*, 510.
25. Colton, "Conflict," 17.
26. Starkey, *Little Rebellion*, 143.
27. Parmenter, *History of Pelham*, 379.
28. Ibid., 381.
29. Ibid., 379.
30. See Smail, *Family of Daniel Shays*, 11, for the whole letter.
31. Parmenter, *History of Pelham*, 380.
32. Ibid., 381; Minot, *History of the Insurrections*, 129ff.
33. Parmenter, *History of Pelham*, 381.
34. Lockwood, *Western Massachusetts*, 174.
35. Ibid., 174.
36. Szatmary, *Shays' Rebellion*, 102.
37. Starkey, *Little Rebellion*, 153; Minot, *History of the Insurrections*, 152-153.
38. Trumbull, *History of Northampton*, 511.
39. Parmenter, *History of Pelham*, 378, 382.
40. Szatmary, *Shays' Rebellion*, 104.
41. Crane, "Shays' Rebellion," 97.
42. Parmenter, *History of Pelham*, 383.
43. Condon, *Shays' Rebellion*, 95; Richards, *Shays's Rebellion*, 31.
44. Stearns, *Shays's Rebellion*, 52.
45. Ibid.
46. Starkey, *Little Rebellion*, 143.
47. Stearns, *Shays's Rebellion*, 53.
48. Starkey, *Little Rebellion*, 133.
49. Richards casts doubt on this number, since "not a single officer was captured, and only a handful of privates were jailed." *Shays's Rebellion*, 31.
50. For a detailed discussion of Lincoln's strategy in levying punishments that were neither too severe nor too lenient, see Feer, *Shays's Rebellion*, 395ff.
51. Coolidge, *History of Petersham*, 119.

CHAPTER ELEVEN: THE FORCE DISSOLVES

1. Crane, "Shays' Rebellion," 99.
2. Condon, *Shays' Rebellion*, 100.
3. Glazier, *History of Gardner*, 81.
4. Szatmary, *Shays' Rebellion*, 106.
5. Trumbull, *History of Northampton*, 512.
6. Richards, *Shays's Rebellion*, 120.
7. While I have constructed the narrative around the farmers' point of view, I do still need to say that the "wilderness" of the woods they passed through—the forests' state of wild nature—

was itself a sign that the previous civilization had been driven to collapse—by many of the same bankers, financiers, land speculators, and settlers who were arguing over taxes and representation behind them in Massachusetts. For centuries, the Natives had maintained the forests through burning, to create open, parklike woods free of tangling undergrowth. When the colonists arrived, the fires stopped, and the forests returned to a state of 'wild nature,' without any sign of human management. For more on this, see Tom Wessels, *Reading the Forested Landscape: A Natural History of New England* (Woodstock, VT: Countryman, 1997), as well as Mann, *1491*.

8. Szatmary, *Shays' Rebellion*, 107. This part of Shays's experience is hardly documented. I find this date—four days after the surprise at Petersham—improbable without horses or sleighs, but there are accounts that place the men on foot, so readers will have to come to their own conclusions about this journey.

9. Szatmary, *Shays' Rebellion*, 108.

10. Richards, *Shays's Rebellion*, 120.

11. Szatmary, *Shays' Rebellion*, 107.

12. Stearns, *Shays's Rebellion*, 54.

13. Brown, "Shays's Rebellion," 609.

14. Crane, "Shays' Rebellion," 100.

15. Ibid.

16. Starkey, *Little Rebellion*, 159.

17. Ibid., 165.

18. Richards, *Shays's Rebellion*, 32.

19. Smail, *Family of Daniel Shays*, 12.

20. Starkey, *Little Rebellion*, 157.

21. Lockwood, *Western Massachusetts*, 160.

22. Szatmary, *Shays' Rebellion*, 112.

23. Richards, *Shays's Rebellion*, 33, 38. Feer adds that it was not long until the government also demanded that all tavern keepers take an oath to discourage "traiterous" talk. *Shays's Rebellion*, 388.

24. Holland, *History of Western Massachusetts*, 274.

25. Zinn, *People's History*, 94; Szatmary, *Shays' Rebellion*, 107; Starkey, *Little Rebellion*, 168.

26. Wehtje, "Boston's Response," 63.

27. Condon, *Shays' Rebellion*, 105.

28. Richards, *Shays's Rebellion*, 38.

29. Szatmary, *Shays' Rebellion*, 108.

30. Starkey, *Little Rebellion*, 166.

31. Smail, *Family of Daniel Shays*, 12; Szatmary, *Shays' Rebellion*, 108; Crane, "Shays' Rebellion," 104.

32. Starkey, *Little Rebellion*, 166.

33. None of my sources list a first name for Cornell.

34. Richards, *Shays's Rebellion*, 120.

35. Szatmary, *Shays' Rebellion*, 117.

36. Richards, *Shays's Rebellion*, 122.

37. Starkey, *Little Rebellion*, 164.

38. Paul David Nelson, *General Sir Guy Carleton, Lord Dorchester: Soldier-Statesman of Early British Canada* (Madison, NJ: Fairleigh Dickinson Press, Associated University Presses, 2000), 170.

39. Szatmary, *Shays' Rebellion*, 118.

40. Richards mentions the possibility that Dorchester had wanted to help the Regulators through an "Indian ally," but Canadian Foreign Minister Joseph Sidney quashed the plan. In any event, no help was forthcoming, and neither was Shays arrested in Quebec. Richards, *Shays's Rebellion*, 34. See also Szatmary, *Shays' Rebellion*, 118.

41. Starkey, *Little Rebellion*, 167.

42. Richards, *Shays's Rebellion*, 35.

43. Ibid.; Szatmary, *Shays' Rebellion*, 109; Starkey, *Little Rebellion*, 176.

44. Szatmary, *Shays' Rebellion*, 110-111; Condon, *Shays' Rebellion*, 103.

45. Charles Taylor, *History of Great Barrington, Massachusetts* (Great Barrington, MA: Clark W. Bryan, 1888), 315.

46. Ibid., 304ff; Richards, *Shays's Rebellion*, 35; Szatmary, *Shays' Rebellion*, 110.

47. Richards, *Shays's Rebellion*, 35; Starkey, *Little Rebellion*, 177.

48. Richards, *Shays's Rebellion*, 36; Brom & Bett vs. J. Ashley Esq., *Court Records, Inferior Court of Common Pleas*, vol. 4A, p. 55, no. 1, May 28, 1781, Berkshire County Courthouse, Great Barrington, Massachusetts, court records.

49. Szatmary, *Shays' Rebellion*, 110.

50. Taylor, *History of Great Barrington*, 313.

51. Ibid., 311.

52. Richards, *Shays's Rebellion*, 36.

53. Ibid., 113; Szatmary, *Shays' Rebellion*, 113-114.

54. Richards, *Shays's Rebellion*, 120; Starkey, *Little Rebellion*, 134.

55. Szatmary, *Shays' Rebellion*, 103.

56. Wehtje, "Boston's Response," 63.

57. Randall Conrad, "'A Captain with the Insurgents': Jason Parmenter of Bernardston," in Kaufman, *Shays' Rebellion*, 72; Condon, *Shays' Rebellion*, 99. This is likely the story that was told in petitions to free Parmenter from his death sentence, but it is consistent enough that I include it here. Some sources have Parmenter shooting it out with government men, but this cannot be verified either.

58. Many farmers carried debts to their kinsmen, neighbors, and townsmen. They were bound by webs of multilateral debts. Surely Shays was owed money in turn, but he was not in a position to file suits with the courts so the historical record only emphasizes Shays's' debts without any larger context. Smail, *Family of Daniel Shays*, 12; Richards, *Shays's Rebellion*, 54, 60-62.

59. Starkey, *Little Rebellion*, 249.

60. Starkey, *Little Rebellion*, 249.

61. Szatmary, *Shays' Rebellion*, 111, 112.

62. Ibid., 112; Taylor, *Western Massachusetts*, 112.

CHAPTER TWELVE: REFUGEES AND SETTLERS

1. Crockett, Walter Hill, *Vermont: The Green Mountain State* (New York: Century History, 1923). Vol. II, 420.

2. Stephen Butz. *Shays' Settlement in Vermont: A Story of Revolt and Archaeology*. (Stroud, UK: History Press, 2017), 114.

3. Stephen Butz, archeologist of the ruins known as the Shays Settlement in Sandgate, advances the theory that "Egg Mountain" is a more recent name for the hill Shays and his people settled. The settlement they started lasted into the early 1800s, but it was ultimately burned to the ground when illness killed a number of residents. His theory is that Ague Mountain became Egg Mountain over time. I have not been able to identify a contemporary name for the hill where Shays and his people settled. See Butz, *Shays' Settlement*, 152.

4. The Native Land website provides a fascinating tool that will show you the Native territories underlying current North American boundaries. Accessed January 24, 2021, https://native-land.ca/. For the history of using fire to maintain forests, see Wessels, *Reading*, 34.

5. Butz, *Shays' Settlement*, 123.

6. See Eric Sloane, *An Age of Barns* (New York: Funk & Wagnalls, 1967) and Eric Sloane, *A Museum of Early Tools* (New York: Funk & Wagnalls, 1964) for graphic descriptions of the tools and construction techniques Shays's men might have used.

7. Richards, *Shays's Rebellion*, 64.
8. Condon, *Shays' Rebellion*, 109.
9. Richards, *Shays's Rebellion*, 39.
10. Parmenter, *History of Pelham*, 385; Keyes, "Who Were the Pelham Shaysites?," 40.
11. Manuel and Manuel, *James Bowdoin*, 231.
12. Charles Bolton, *Bolton's American Armory* (Boston: F. W. Faxon, 1927), 75.
13. Feer, *Shays's Rebellion*, 449.
14. Szatmary, *Shays' Rebellion*, 112.
15. Condon, *Shays' Rebellion*, 110. For a detailed discussion of the government's strategy of administering lenient punishments, see Feer, *Shays's Rebellion*, 425ff.
16. Richards, *Shays's Rebellion*, 39. For more on the trials and evidence brought against the Regulators, see John Noble, "A Few Notes on the Shays Rebellion," *American Antiquarian Society* (October, 1902). For a complete list of punishments, see Crane, "Shays' Rebellion," 100ff.
17. Starkey, *Little Rebellion*, 80.
18. Ibid., 201.
19. Ibid., 212.
20. Richards, *Shays's Rebellion*, 97.
21. Ibid., 40; Crane, "Shays' Rebellion," 109.

CHAPTER THIRTEEN: STARTING ANEW

1. Kershaw, *James Bowdoin II*, 260; Richards, *Shays's Rebellion*, 38; Pole, "Shays' Rebellion," 454; Szatmary, *Shays' Rebellion*, 114.
2. Nobles, "Promise of the Revolution," 229.
3. Butz, *Shays' Settlement*, 123.
4. Conrad, "Captain with the Insurgents," 74; Condon, *Shays' Rebellion*, 112.
5. Richards, *Shays's Rebellion*, 58; Szatmary, *Shays' Rebellion*, 113.
6. Zinn, *People's History*, 94; Szatmary, *Shays' Rebellion*, 107; Starkey, *Little Rebellion*, 168.
7. Wehtje, "Boston's Response," 63.
8. Butz, *Shays' Settlement*, 112.
9. Pliny White, *Jonas Galusha: Vermont's Fifth Governor* (Montpelier: E. P. Walton, 1866), 10-11. See also Walter Hill Crockett, *Vermont: The Green Mountain State*, vol. 2 (New York: Century History, 1923), 420.
10. Manuel and Manuel, *Patriot Philosophers*, 229.
11. Szatmary, *Shays' Rebellion*, 116.
12. Crane, "Shays' Rebellion," 107.
13. Starkey, *Little Rebellion*, 80.
14. Richards, *Shays's Rebellion*, 95; Starkey, *Little Rebellion*, 205.
15. Richards, *Shays's Rebellion*, 119.
16. Starkey, *Little Rebellion*, 231; Richards, *Shays's Rebellion*, 119.
17. Stearns, *Shays's Rebellion*, 229.
18. Ibid., 57; Taylor, *Western Massachusetts*, 166.
19. Holton, "From the Labours," 297.
20. Marion Starkey points out that the season of protests led to a boom of babies named for Daniel Shays and other prominent figures in the protests, including Jacob Walker and Benjamin Lincoln. *Little Rebellion*, 236.
21. Starkey, *Little Rebellion*, 229, 249.
22. Richards, *Shays's Rebellion*, 144. Feer notes that Hancock's margin of victory was comparable to his earlier and subsequent margins of victory. *Shays's Rebellion*, 452. He argues that neither Hancock's victory nor the changes in the General Court indicate a landslide so much as a reversion to a political norm. Ibid., 448-461. He also notes that "political apathy returned" fairly quickly, and that in its next session, of the 150 representatives then sitting,

the General Court saw "not more than eight or ten" representatives from "either the County of Hampshire or Berkshire." Ibid., 466.

23. Condon, *Shays' Rebellion*, 114; Starkey, *Little Rebellion*, 187.
24. Trumbull, *History of Northampton*, 515.
25. Ibid., 515; Starkey, *Little Rebellion*, 218.
26. Trumbull, *History of Northampton*, 515-516.
27. Crane, "Shays' Rebellion," 107.
28. Trumbull, *History of Northampton*, 515-516.
29. Ibid., 516.

CHAPTER FOURTEEN: NEW LIFE, OLD LIFE

1. Starkey, *Little Rebellion*, 241.
2. Richards, *Shays's Rebellion*, 68-69.
3. *Records of the Governor and Council of the State of Vermont: Record of the Governor and Council, 1804-1813*, (Montpelier, VT: Steam Press of J. & J. M. Poland, 1877), appendix C, 423.
4. Richards, *Shays's Rebellion*, 41.
5. Ibid., 124.

EPILOGUE: REVERBERATIONS AND ECHOES

1. Szatmary, *Shays' Rebellion*, 115.
2. For the tradition history of Shays and the Constitution, see Richards, *Shays's Rebellion*, 139; Szatmary, *Shays' Rebellion*, 120; Starkey, *Little Rebellion*, 240; and Condon, *Shays' Rebellion*, 121ff.
3. In "Shays' Rebellion and the Constitution: A Study in Causation," *New England Quarterly* 42, no. 3 (September 1969), 388-410, and in *Shays's Rebellion*, Robert Feer shows that the common narrative, that "Shays's Rebellion" was the unrest that led to the Constitution, is without merit or foundation in fact. Feer points out that people like Stephen Higginson, who had originally drawn the link between the anti-austerity protests and the Constitution, had been advocating for a stronger federal government since as early as April 1784 ("Shays' Rebellion and the Constitution," 406), and that George Washington had been predicting the collapse of the republic for a decade (ibid., 396). Feer concludes that "there is no evidence that [the protests] changed in any significant way the thinking of the people who drew up and ratified the Constitution" (ibid., 410). Brynner's dissertation takes the opposite approach, showing in detail how the hysteria created around "Shays's Rebellion" was determinative in drawing Washington out of retirement, which gave the nationalists the symbolic momentum they needed to push for reforms that had failed in earlier conventions. *"Fire Beneath Our Feet,"* 185-217. Both Feer and Brynner agree that the reality of the protests did not in any way correlate with the panic that surrounded them.
4. Holton, "From the Labours," 295.
5. For a detailed discussion of the ratification debate in Massachusetts, see Richards, *Shays's Rebellion*, 139ff.
6. Szatmary, *Shays' Rebellion*, 133.
7. There are reports that Shays spent time in the debtor's prison in Bennington, but these reports are contested, and I could not find verification. It seems to me that this anecdote aligns a little too neatly with the stock narratives by which the people's leaders are caricatured as drunks or degenerates or otherwise demonized and diminished for their advocacy.
8. Smail, *Family of Daniel Shays*, 14.
9. Noel B. Gerson, *Statue in Search of a Pedestal: A Biography of the Marquis de La Fayette* (New York: Dodd, Mead, 1976), 78-83.
10. William Hogeland. *The Whiskey Rebellion: George Washington, Alexander Hamilton, and the Frontier Rebels Who Challenged America's Newfound Sovereignty* (New York: Scribner, 2006), 60ff.

11. Ibid., 59-69. See also Joseph Ellis, *Founding Brothers: The Revolutionary Generation* (New York: Knopf, 2000), 64.

12. Ellis, *Founding Brothers*, 48ff.

13. Hogeland, *Whiskey Rebellion*, 59-64.

14. Ibid., 67.

15. Richards, *Shays's Rebellion*, 159.

16. Feer says Shays may have returned to Massachusetts to pursue a legal action to collect a debt of nine pounds in 1792, but he may have simply been represented by a lawyer. *Shays's Rebellion*, 423.

17. Hogeland, *Whiskey Rebellion*, 20, 143.

18. Ibid., 153ff.

19. Ibid., 197ff.

20. It needs to be said, again, that the westward migration did not purge the state's injustice in new beginnings. Hogeland reports that the (speculative) value of George Washington's far western lands "increased by 50 percent." *Whiskey Rebellion*, 240. This increase in value drove further speculation and settlement, which only created new genocides and new contentions over speculators' valuations and common people's improvements. As I have stated above, a full account of America's obligations, in light of this history, is always waiting to be made.

21. Smail, *Family of Daniel Shays*, 15; Butz, *Shays' Settlement*, 142.

22. Smail, *Family of Daniel Shays*, 17, 18, 24-25.

23. Ibid., 16.

24. See Stetson Kennedy, *After Appomattox: How the South Won the Civil War* (Gainesville: University Press of Florida, 1995), for an account of Southerners' resistance to federal law from 1865 to 1877.

25. In *To Hell on a Fast Horse: Billy the Kid, Pat Garrett, and the Epic Chase to Justice in the Old West* (New York: William Morrow, 2009), Mark Lee Gardner states that the Regulators' exploits were food for a literary media marketplace that spawned countless articles and books. See 4ff, 180ff in particular.

26. This is a complex legacy relative to the resistance campaign Daniel Shays's people had staged. Clearly the specter of violence always haunted the Regulators, and their failure to either win a victory by taking arms or to allow themselves to be martyred by government men relegates them to an ambiguous obscurity in a country Richard Slotkin describes as the "Gunfighter Nation." Shays remains an enigmatic figure who has been claimed by libertarians and tax resisters, patriot militias and anticorporate activists alike. The absence of detail about his life has created a permeable character whose appearance can be tailored to any number of causes, but the facts about his nonviolent anti-austerity campaign are not so malleable that they can be accurately described as a rebellion.

Bibliography

Acts and Resolves of Massachusetts, 1786–87. Boston: Secretary of the Commonwealth, 1893. Accessed June 28, 2021. https://archive.org/details/actsresolvespass178687mass.

Alexander, John K. *Samuel Adams: America's Revolutionary Politician*. Lanham, MD: Rowman & Littlefield, 2002.

Anderson, Fred. *Crucible of War: The Seven Years' War and the Fate of Empire in British North America, 1754–1766*. New York: Vintage, 2000.

———. *The War That Made America: A Short History of the French and Indian War*. New York: Penguin, 2006.

Bartlett, Joseph Gardner. *Gregory Stone Genealogy: Ancestry and Descendants of Dea. Gregory Stone of Cambridge, Mass., 1320–1917*. Stone Family Association. Repr., Nabu Press, June 8, 2010.

Bassett, John Spencer. *The Regulators of North Carolina (1765–1771)*. Electronic edition. Chapel Hill: Academic Affairs Library, University of North Carolina at Chapel Hill, 2002. Accessed June 2, 2021. https://docsouth.unc.edu/nc/bassett95/bassett95.html.

Bell, Charles Henry. *History of the Town of Exeter, New Hampshire*. Boston: J. E. Farwell, 1888.

Bellamy, Edward. *The Duke of Stockbridge: A Romance of Shay's Rebellion*. New York, Boston: Silver, Burdett, 1900.

Bielinski, Stefan. *An American Loyalist: The Ordeal of Frederick Philipse III*. Albany: New York State Education Department, 1976.

Bolton, Charles Knowles. *Bolton's American Armory*. Boston: F. W. Faxon, 1927.

Bouton, Terry. *Taming Democracy: "The People," the Founders, and the Troubled Ending of the American Revolution*. New York: Oxford University Press, 2009.

Bowdoin, James. *The Bowdoin and Temple Papers*, Vol. 2. Boston: Massachusetts Historical Society, 1907.

Breen, Timothy H. *American Insurgents, American Patriots: The Revolution of the People*. New York: Hill and Wang, 2011.

Brom & Bett vs. J. Ashley Esq. *Court Records, Inferior Court of Common Pleas.* Vol. 4A, p. 55, no. 1. May 28, 1781. Berkshire County Courthouse, Great Barrington, Massachusetts. Accessed June 28, 2021. https://elizabethfreeman.mumbet.com/who-is-mumbet/mumbet-court-records/.

Brooke, John L. "To the Quiet of the People: Revolutionary Settlements and Civil Unrest in Western Massachusetts, 1774–1789." *William & Mary Quarterly* 46, no. 3 (July 1989): 425-462.

Brookhiser, Richard. "Want a Revolution?" *American History* 51, no. 2 (June 2016): 16-18.

Brown, Richard D. "Shays's Rebellion and Its Aftermath: A View from Springfield, Massachusetts, 1787." *William & Mary Quarterly* 40, no. 4 (October 1983): 598-615.

Brown, Richard Maxwell. *The South Carolina Regulators.* Cambridge, MA: Belknap Press of Harvard University Press, 1963.

Brynner, Rock. *"Fire Beneath Our Feet": Shays' Rebellion and its Constitutional Impact.* Ann Arbor, MI: University Microfilm International Dissertation Services, 1983.

Buffington, Samuel. Deposition. Springfield Technical Community College Daniel Shays website. Document from Forbes Library Special Collections, Northampton, MA. Accessed June 28, 2021. http://shaysrebellion.stcc.edu/shaysapp/artifactPage.do?shortName=deposition_sb1feb87&page=p002.

Butler, Caleb. *History of the town of Groton, including Pepperell and Shirley, from the first grant of Groton plantation in 1655.* Boston: Press of T. R. Marvin, 1848.

Butz, Stephen. *Shays' Settlement in Vermont: A Story of Revolt and Archaeology.* Stroud, UK: History Press, 2017.

Canny, Nicholas P. "The Ideology of English Colonization: From Ireland to America." *William and Mary Quarterly* 30, no. 4 (October, 1973): 575-598.

Chandler, Abby. "'Unawed by the Laws of their Country': Local and Imperial Legitimacy in North Carolina's Regulator Rebellion." *North Carolina Historical Review* 93, no. 2 (April 2016): 119-146.

Colton, Richard. "Conflict and Ambivalence in Shays's Rebellion." Springfield Armory National Historic Site. Unpublished paper, 2007.

Coolidge, Mabel Cook. *The history of Petersham, Massachusetts, incorporated April 20, 1754: Volunteerstown or Voluntown, 1730–1733, Nichewaug, 1733–1754.* Petersham, MA: Petersham Historical Society, 1948. Accessed June 28, 2021. Available for download, https://archive.org/details/historyofpetersh00cool.

Condon, Sean. *Shays's Rebellion: Authority and Distress in Post-Revolutionary America.* Baltimore: Johns Hopkins University Press, 2015.

Copeland, Alfred Minot. *Our County and Its People: A History of Hampden County, Massachusetts.* Boston: Century Memorial Publishing, 1902.

Crane, Ellery. "Shays' Rebellion." *Collections of the Worcester Society of Antiquity.* Vol. 1. Worcester, MA: Published by the Society. 1892. Proceedings for the Year 1881, 60ff. Digitized by Google. Accessed June 28, 2021. Available for download, https://archive.org/stream/collectionsworc04masgoog#page/n6/mode/2up.

Crockett, Walter Hill. *Vermont: The Green Mountain State.* Vol. 2. New York: Century History, 1923.

Cronon, William. *Changes in the Land: Indians, Colonists, and the Ecology of New England.* New York: Hill and Wang, 1983.

Culver, David M. "Shays' Rebellion and the Issue of Liberty and Power in a Free Society." *New England Social Studies Bulletin* 44, no. 2 (1987): 8-13.

Cutler, R. J., dir. "Ten Days That Unexpectedly Changed America: Shays' Rebellion—America's First Civil War." Video, 2006. History Channel.

Davis, David Brion, and Steven Mintz, eds. *The Boisterous Sea of Liberty: A Documentary History of America from Discovery through the Civil War.* New York: Oxford University Press, 2000.

Demos, John Putnam. *The Unredeemed Captive: A Family Story from Early America.* New York: Vintage, 2011.

Earle, Alice Morse. *Home Life in Colonial Days.* Stockbridge, MA: Berkshire House, 1993.

Egleston, Thomas. *The Life of John Paterson: Major General in the Revolutionary Army.* New York: Knickerbocker Press, 1894. Repr. Kessinger Publishing, 2010.

Ellis, Joseph. *Founding Brothers: The Revolutionary Generation.* New York: Knopf, 2000.

Feer, Robert. *Shays's Rebellion.* New York: Garland, 1988.

———. "Shays' Rebellion and the Constitution: A Study in Causation." *New England Quarterly* 42, no. 3 (September 1969): 388-410.

Fiske, Jeffrey. *The Battle of New Braintree: A Village in Shays' Rebellion.* New Braintree, MA: Towtaid, 1996.

Fitch, William Edward, MD. *Some Neglected History of North Carolina.* New York: Self-published, 1914. Accessed June 28, 2021. Available for download, https://archive.org/stream/someneglectedhis00fitc#page/n11/mode/2up/search/Tryon.

Flood, Charles Bracelen. *Rise, and Fight Again: Perilous Times along the Road to Independence.* New York: Dodd, Mead, 1976.

Fort Gilbert. West Brookfield MA—Massachusetts Historical Markers. Waymarking.com. Accessed June 28, 2021. http://www.waymarking.com/waymarks/WM C0XB_Fort_Gilbert_West_Brookfield_MA.

Fowler, William M., Jr. *The Baron of Beacon Hill: A Biography of John Hancock.* Boston: Houghton Mifflin, 1980.

———. *Samuel Adams: Radical Puritan.* New York: Longman, 1997.

Gardner. Mark Lee. *To Hell on a Fast Horse: Billy the Kid, Pat Garrett, and the Epic Chase to Justice in the Old West.* New York: William Morrow, 2009.

Genealogical Register of the Descendants in the Male Line of Robert Day of Hartford, Connecticut. 2nd ed. Northampton, MA: J & L Metcalf, 1848.

Gerson, Noel B. *Statue in Search of a Pedestal: A Biography of the Marquis de La Fayette.* New York: Dodd, Mead, 1976.

Gilbert, Abigail. Gentle Family Genealogy. Accessed June 28, 2021. http://www.pdgentle.com/pdgfamily/getperson.php?personID=P1328&tree=tree1.

Glazier, Lewis. *History of Gardner, Massachusetts: From Its Earliest Settlement to 1860.* Worcester, MA: Charles Hamilton, 1860. Accessed June 28, 2021. Available for download, https://archive.org/stream/historyofgardner00inglaz#page/n7/mode/2up.

Goldscheider, Tom. "Shays' Rebellion: Reclaiming the Revolution." *Historical Journal of Massachusetts* 43, no. 1 (Winter 2015): 62-93.

Goldstone, Lawrence. *Dark Bargain: Slavery, Profits and the Struggle for the Constitution.* New York: Bloomsbury, 2009.

Green, Mason A. *Springfield 1636–1886: History of Town and City.* Springfield, MA: C. A. Nichols, 1888.

Green, Samuel Abbott. *An Historical Sketch of Groton, Massachusetts, 1655–1890.* Groton, MA: Town of Groton, 1894.

Gross, Robert A., ed. *In Debt to Shays: The Bicentennial of an Agrarian Rebellion.* Charlottesville: University Press of Virginia, 1993.

———. "A Yankee Rebellion?: The Regulators, New England, and the New Nation." *New England Quarterly* 82, no. 1 (March 2009): 112-135.

Hale, Richard W., Jr. "The American Revolution in Western Massachusetts." *New England Historical & Genealogical Register* 129 (October 1975): 325-334.

Hall, Van Beck. *Politics Without Parties: Massachusetts 1780–1791.* Pittsburgh: University of Pittsburgh Press, 1972.

Hardesty, Jared. *Black Lives, Native Lands, White Worlds: A History of Slavery in New England.* Amherst, MA: Bright Leaf, 2019.

Herrick, William Dodge. *History of the town of Gardner, Worcester County, Mass., from the incorporation, June 27, 1785, to the present time.* Gardner, MA: Printed by A. G. Bushnell at the offices of the Gardner News, 1878.

Hogeland, William. *The Whiskey Rebellion: George Washington, Alexander Hamilton, and the Frontier Rebels Who Challenged America's Newfound Sovereignty.* New York: Scribner, 2006.

Holland, Josiah Gilbert. *History of Western Massachusetts: The Counties of Hampden, Hampshire, Franklin and Berkshire.* Springfield, MA: Samuel Bowles, 1855.

Holton, Woody. "'From the Labours of Others': The War Bonds Controversy and the Origins of the Constitution in Massachusetts." *William & Mary Quarterly* 61, no. 2 (April 2004): 271-316.

———. *Unruly Americans and the Origins of the Constitution.* New York: Hill & Wang, 2007.

Hoyt, David, Jr. *Letter to his Father.* Pocumtuck Valley Memorial Association, Deerfield, MA. Accessed June 28, 2021. http://shaysrebellion.stcc.edu/shaysapp/artifact.do?shortName= letter_dh26jan87.

Jefferson, Thomas. *Political Writings.* Edited by Joyce Appleby. Cambridge: Cambridge University Press, 1999.

Johnston, Henry Phelps. *The Yorktown Campaign and the Surrender of Cornwallis, 1781*. New York: Harper & Brothers, 1881.

Kaufman, Martin, ed. *Shays' Rebellion: Selected Essays*. Westfield, MA: Institute for Massachusetts Studies, 1987.

Kazar, John D. "No Early Pardon for Traitors: Rebellion in Massachusetts in 1787." *Historical Journal of Massachusetts* 33, no. 2 (October 2005): 109-138.

Kershaw, Gordon E. *James Bowdoin II: Patriot and Man of the Enlightenment*. Lanham, MD: University Press of America, 1991.

Keyes, Robert Lord. "Who Were the Pelham Shaysites?" *Historical Journal of Massachusetts* 28, no. 1 (Winter 2000): 23-55.

Kierner, Cynthia A. *Revolutionary America, 1750–1815: Sources and Interpretation*. Upper Saddle River, NJ: Prentice Hall, 2003.

———. *Traders and Gentlefolk: The Livingstons of New York, 1675–1790*. Ithaca, NY: Cornell University Press, 1986.

King, Moses. *King's Handbook of Springfield, MA: A Series of Monographs*. Springfield, MA: James D. Gill, 1884.

King, Nathan. *The International Encyclopedia of Revolution and Protest, 1500 to the Present*. Edited by Immanuel Ness. Malden, MA: Wiley-Blackwell, 2009.

Klarman, Michael. *The Framers' Coup: The Making of the United States Constitution*. New York: Oxford University Press, 2016.

Klein, Rachel N. "Ordering the Backcountry: The South Carolina Regulation." *William and Mary Quarterly* 38, no. 4 (October 1981): 661-680.

Lincoln, William. *History of Worcester, Massachusetts: From Its Earliest Settlement to September, 1836; With Various Notices Relating to the History of Worcester County*. Worcester, MA: Moses D. Phillips, 1837.

Lockwood, John H. *Western Massachusetts: A History: 1636–1925*. Vol. 1. New York: Lewis Historical Publishing, 1926.

Maier, Pauline. "Coming to Terms with Samuel Adams." *American Historical Review* 81, no. 1 (February 1976): 12-37.

———. *From Resistance to Revolution; Colonial Radicals and the Development of American Opposition to Britain, 1765–1776*. New York: W. W. Norton, 1991.

———. *The Old Revolutionaries: Political Lives in the Age of Samuel Adams*. New York: Knopf, 1980.

———. "Popular Uprisings and Civil Authority in Eighteenth-Century America." *William & Mary Quarterly* 27, no. 1 (January 1970): 3-35.

Mann, Charles. *1491: New Revelations of the Americas before Columbus*. New York: Vintage, 2006.

———. *1493: Uncovering the New World Columbus Created*. New York: Vintage, 2011.

Manuel, Frank E., and Fritzie P. Manuel. *James Bowdoin and the Patriot Philosophers*. Memoirs of the American Philosophical Society held at Philadelphia for Promoting Useful Knowledge. Vol. 247. Philadelphia: American Philosophical Society, 2004.

Mark, Irving. "Agrarian Revolt in Colonial New York, 1766." *American Journal of Economics and Sociology* 1, no. 2 (January 1942): 111-142.

Marsella, Paul D. "Propaganda Trends in the Essex Journal and the New Hampshire Packet, 1787–1788." *Essex Institute Historical Collections* 114, no. 3 (1978): 161-178.

Mattern, David B. *Benjamin Lincoln and the American Revolution.* Columbia: University of South Carolina Press, 1995.

Meeks, Harold. *Time and Change in Vermont: A Human Geography.* Chester, CT: Globe Pequot Press, 1986.

Middleton, Lamar. *Revolt U.S.A.* Freeport, NY: Books for Libraries Press, 1968.

Minot, George Richards. *History of the Insurrections in Massachusetts in 1786 and of the Rebellion Consequent Thereon.* New York: Da Capo, 1971.

Morris, Richard B. *America in Crisis: Fourteen Crucial Episodes in American History.* Edited by Daniel Aaron. New York: Knopf, 1952.

Mros, Richard. "Shays' Rebellion in Taunton." In *Shays' Rebellion: Selected Essays,* edited by Martin Kaufman. Westfield, MA: Institute for Massachusetts Studies, 1987.

Muir, Robert. *The Sprig of Hemlock: A Novel about Shays' Rebellion.* New York: Longmans, Green, 1957.

Nash, Gary. *The Unknown American Revolution: The Unruly Birth of Democracy and the Struggle to Create America.* New York: Viking, 2005.

Nelson, Paul David. *General Sir Guy Carleton, Lord Dorchester: Soldier-Statesman of Early British Canada.* Madison, NJ: Fairleigh Dickinson Press, Associated University Presses, 2000.

Neumann, George, and Frank Kravic. *Collector's Illustrated Encyclopedia of the American Revolution.* Texarkana, TX: Rebel Publishing, 1975.

Noble, John. "A Few Notes on the Shays Rebellion." *American Antiquarian Society* (October 1902). PDF file accessed June 28, 2021. Available for download, www.americanantiquarian.org/proceedings/44806459.pdf.

Nobles, Gregory. "The Promise of the Revolution. 'Satan, Smith, Shattuck, and Shays': The People's Leaders in the Massachusetts Regulation of 1786." In *Revolutionary Founders: Rebels, Radicals, and Reformers in the Making of the Nation,* edited by Alfred F. Young, 215-232. New York: Knopf, 2011.

O'Reilly, Kevin. "Was Shays' Rebellion an Important Cause of the Constitution? Evaluating Cause and Effect Reasoning." *New England Social Studies Bulletin* 44, no. 1 (1986): 43-48.

Parmenter, Charles. *The History of Pelham, from 1738 to 1898 including the Early History of Prescott.* Amherst, MA: Press of Carpenter & Morehouse, 1898. Accessed June 28, 2021. Available for download, https://archive.org/details/historyofpelhamm1738parm.

Paulin, Michael. *The Ballad of Daniel Shays.* Athol, MA: Transcript Press, 1986.

Pencak, William. "The Humorous Side of Shays' Rebellion." *Historical Journal of Massachusetts* 17, no. 2 (October 1989): 160-176.

———. "Samuel Adams and Shays' Rebellion." *New England Quarterly* 62, no. 1 (March 1989): 63-74.

Philbrick, Nathaniel. *Valiant Ambition: George Washington, Benedict Arnold, and the Fate of the American Revolution*. New York: Penguin, 2016.

Pole, J. R. "Shays' Rebellion and the Problem of Opposition Politics." In *Major Problems in the Era of the American Revolution, 1760–1791: Documents and Essays*, edited by Richard Brown, 3rd ed., 447-455. Boston: Houghton Mifflin, Cengage Learning, 2000.

Putnam, Rufus. *The Memoirs of Rufus Putnam and Certain Official Papers and Correspondence*. Boston and New York: Houghton, Mifflin, 1903.

Quinn, David B. *Ireland and America: Their Early Associations, 1500–1640*. Liverpool, UK: Liverpool University Press, 1991.

Rakove, Jack. *Revolutionaries: A New History of the Invention of America*. Boston: Houghton Mifflin Harcourt, 2010.

Randall, Willard Sterne. *Ethan Allen: His Life and Times*. New York: W.W. Norton, 2011.

Raphael, Ray. *Founding Myths: The Stories That Hide Our Patriotic Past*. New York: New Press, 2004.

———. *A People's History of the American Revolution: How Common People Shaped the Fight for Independence*. New York: New Press, 2016.

Raphael, Ray, and Marie Raphael. *The Spirit of '74: How the American Revolution Began*. New York: New Press, 2015.

Richards, Leonard. *Shays's Rebellion: The American Revolution's Final Battle*. Philadelphia: University of Pennsylvania Press, 2002.

Riley, Stephen T. "Dr. William Whiting and Shays Rebellion." *American Antiquarian Society* (October 1956): 119-166. PDF file accessed June 28, 2021. Available for download, www.americanantiquarian.org/proceedings/44539282.pdf.

Royster, Charles. *A Revolutionary People at War: The Continental Army and American Character, 1775–1783*. New York: W. W. Norton, 1979.

Schellhammer, Michael. "Mutiny of the New Jersey Line." *Journal of the American Revolution* (March 19, 2014). Accessed June 28, 2021. https://allthings liberty.com/2014/03/mutiny-of-the-new-jersey-line/.

Shattuck, Gary. *Artful and Designing Men: The Trials of Job Shattuck and the Regulation of 1786-1787*. Mustang, OK: Tate, 2013.

Shays, Daniel. "To the Honorable Major General Lincoln, . . . Daniel Shays, Wilbraham, January 25th, 1787," *Worcester Magazine* 44, vol. 2, February, 1787.

Sloane, Eric. *An Age of Barns*. New York: Funk & Wagnalls, 1967.

———. *Almanack and Weather Forecaster*. New York: Hawthorn/Dutton Books, 1955.

———. *A Museum of Early Tools*. New York: Funk & Wagnalls, 1964.

Smail, Elmer S. *The Family of Daniel Shays: From Descendants of Daniel Shays.* Edited by Mary Ann Nicholson. November 1934; Boston: New England Historic Genealogical Society, 1987.

Springfield Technical Community College. "Shays Rebellion and the Making of a Nation." 2008. Accessed June 28, 2021. http://shaysrebellion.stcc.edu/.

Starkey, Marion L. *A Little Rebellion.* New York: Knopf, 1955.

Stearns, Munroe. *Shays' Rebellion: 1786–7: Americans Take Up Arms against Unjust Laws.* New York: Franklin Watts, 1968.

Swift, Esther M. *West Springfield Massachusetts: A Town History.* Springfield, MA: West Springfield Heritage Association, 1969.

Szatmary, David P. *Shays' Rebellion: The Making of an Agrarian Insurrection.* Amherst: University of Massachusetts Press, 1980.

———. "Shays' Rebellion in Springfield," in *Shays' Rebellion: Selected Essays.* Martin Kaufman, ed. Westfield, MA: Institute for Massachusetts Studies, 1987.

Taylor, Charles. *History of Great Barrington, Massachusetts.* Great Barrington, MA: Clark W. Bryan, 1888.

Taylor, Robert F. *Western Massachusetts in the Revolution.* Providence, RI: Brown University Press, 1954.

Temple, J. H. *History of North Brookfield, Massachusetts. Preceded by an account of old Quabaug, Indian and English occupation, 1647–1676.* Published by the town, 1887. Accessed June 28 2021. Available for download, https://archive.org/details/historyofnorthbr00temp.

Trumbull, James Russell, and Seth Pomeroy. *History of Northampton, Massachusetts, from its settlement in 1654.* Northampton, MA: Press of Gazette Printing, 1898. Accessed June 28, 2021. Available for download, https://archive.org/details/historyofnortham02trum.

Unger, Harlow Giles. *John Hancock: Merchant King and American Patriot.* New York: Wiley & Sons, 2000.

Van Doren, Carl. *Mutiny in January.* New York: Viking, 1943.

Vaughan, Alden T. "The 'Horrid and Unnatural Rebellion' of Daniel Shays." *American Heritage* 7, no. 4 (June 1966): 50-81.

Vermont General Assembly. Legislative Sessions, 1778–1808. Accessed June 28, 2021. http://www.leg.state.vt.us/HouseClerk/Legislative%20Process.htm.

Vidal, Gore. *Homage to Daniel Shays: Collected Essays, 1952–1972.* New York: Random House, 1972.

Walton, E. P., ed. *Records of the Governor and Council of the State of Vermont.* Vol. 3. Montpelier, VT: Steam Press of J. and J. M. Poland, 1875.

Washington, George. *The Writings of George Washington: pt. III. Private letters from the time Washington resigned his commission as commander-in-chief of the Army to that of his inauguration as president of the United States: December, 1783–April, 1789.* Edited by Jared Sparks. Boston: Russell, Odiorne, and Metcalf, 1835.

Wehtje, Myron F. "Boston's Response to Disorder in the Commonwealth, 1783–1787." *Historical Journal of Massachusetts* 12, no. 1 (April 1984): 19-27.

———. "Boston's Response to Disorder in the Commonwealth, 1783–1787," in *Shays' Rebellion: Selected Essays*. Martin Kaufman, ed. Westfield, MA: Institute for Massachusetts Studies, 1987.

Wessels, Tom. *Reading the Forested Landscape: A Natural History of New England*. Woodstock, VT: Countryman, 1997.

White, Pliny. *Jonas Galusha: Vermont's Fifth Governor*. Montpelier, VT: E. P. Walton, 1866.

Wilds, Mary. *Mumbet: The Life and Times of Elizabeth Freeman: The True Story of a Slave Who Won Her Freedom*. Greensboro, NC: Avisson, 1999.

Williams, Glenn. *Year of the Hangman: George Washington's Campaign against the Iroquois*. Yardley, PA: Westholme, 2005.

Worcester Bank and Trust Company. *Historic Events of Worcester: A Brief Account of Some of the Most Interesting Events Which Have Occurred in Worcester during the Past Two Hundred Years*. Worcester, MA: Worcester Bank and Trust Company, 1922. Accessed June 28, 2021. Available for download, https://archive.org/stream/historiceventsof00worc_0#page/n1/mode/2up.

Worcester Magazine: From the Fourth Week of March to the First Week of October, 1787. Vol. 3. Worcester, MA: Isaiah Thomas, Printer, 1787.

Worcester Society of Antiquity. "Old-Time Taverns of Worcester." *Proceedings of the Worcester Society of Antiquity* 19, no. 2 (1903): 80.

Zinn, Howard. *A People's History of the United States*. New York: Harper & Row, 1980.

Acknowledgments

D ANIEL SHAYS AND THE STORY OF THE PROTESTS OF 1786 has been a cottage industry in western Massachusetts, and in American political studies generally. I could not have written this book without the excellent works that excavated the details from archives and records and from the horrors of eighteenth-century handwriting. I started with Leonard Richards, David Szatmary, and Robert Taylor's books, which were essential, as was Ray and Mary Raphael's *The Spirit of '74*, all of which ultimately helped me build a broad enough sense of the story to appreciate Rock Brynner's and Robert Feer's brilliant dissertations, and articles by Woody Holton and Pauline Maier, which shed light on the long histories that created conditions for protests. Key insights came from numerous other places, ranging from Esther Smail and the genealogists who published Daniel and Abigail Shays's family trees to Eric Sloane's research on eighteenth-century tools to Tom Wessels's history of the western Massachusetts landscape.

I was fortunate, early on in my research, to meet Richard Colton, now retired from his position as historian for the Springfield Armory National Historic Site. His deep knowledge and appreciation for Shays's and other regional histories was incredibly useful. Likewise were Peggie Hepler and Bruce Klotz, from the Pelham Historical Society, and Bill Budde, Curator of the Russell Vermontiana Collection at the Martha Canfield Library, all generous with their expertise on Daniel Shays and the Regulators, the period, and the geography.

I thank Cliff Read and his colleagues at the Massachusetts Department of Conservation and Recreation, for the tour of the Shays's home site in the Quabbin Reservoir, and the Pelham Historical Society, again, for continuing to run day trips to the site.

Early drafts of this book were aired at the Northampton Forbes Library's "Local History, Local Writers" series—thanks Susan Stinson—and at a private reading at Jean Zimmer's house some years ago, now.

I've been grateful to a number of people in media who have invited me to tell this story to their audiences. I've enjoyed speaking with Bill Newman, head of the Western Massachusetts ACLU, and human rights lawyer Buz Eisenberg, on the *Bill Newman Radio Show*, and also with Paki Wieland, Carolyn Oppenheim, Don Ogden, Bob Gardner, and Joel Saxe at Valley Free Radio. Thanks also to the *Valley Advocate* for their interest in Shays, back in March 2019, and to Danny New and WWLP, for including me in their Memorial Day coverage that May.

It was a real pleasure to contribute to John Biewen and Scene on Radio's Democracy in America series, and I thank Susan Ashman, Scott Gausen, and Alex MacKenzie for bringing me into the Armory's education and programming schedules, through the annual Shays lecture, and then through the first annual Shays Symposium, launched in 2019. Cliff McCarthy and the Pioneer Valley History Conference also gave me a warm welcome, and I look forward to more of their programs.

I'm going to limit my personal thanks to these people who looked at the manuscript and gave me feedback on it, because if I start to thank the good friends who've simply helped me keep going, I would have to write a memoir, and I would still inevitably fail to include someone. So I extend my thanks to the friends who endured long discussions about the Regulators' strategies and experiences as I tried to puzzle out the hidden contents of this history, and whose friendship made it possible to survive in a world that is not always amenable to the writing of books.

This book was vastly enriched by probing questions and thoughtful objections from Connie Congdon, who has been working on a Daniel Shays stage play, and from novelist Rilla Askew, whose novels set a towering and rich example, particularly *Fire in Beulah*, on the 1921 Tulsa race massacre.

This book also benefitted by painstaking commentary and insight from Jay Frost, Rob Bullis, Neil Forbes, and Taryn Puleo, who each deserve thanks from my readers, for helping excavate the narrative from the poetry that sometimes threatened to engulf it.

Peter Jones, Shane Book, Emmy Adasiewicz, and Scott Brown helped see me through some low moments when the book almost didn't happen—the fact that this book exists is a testament to their faith, encouragement, and creative literary problem solving, also to Lindsay Glazier's patience when my stubborn insistence on writing delayed our plans, or when detours to Shays sites took over our road trips.

This manuscript passed through crucial developmental stages at the hands of editor and dramaturge Nina Mankin and agents Roger Williams and Claire Gerus, who each helped hoist the book toward the shape it inhabits today. Historians Ray Raphael, Keith Krawczynski, and Stuart Leibiger made huge contributions with their review letters, which substantially broadened and deepened the narrative, in addition to honing its accuracy. I'm grateful as well to agent Susan Lee Cohen for her help in translating the story into a treatment for film.

I am especially grateful to my publisher, Bruce H. Franklin, for seeing and appreciating my unique approach to this story, and for the Westholme Publishing team, editor Ron Silverman, designer Trudi Gershenov, and intern Clara Dandy, for cleaning the manuscript up and introducing it to the world. Thanks also to photographer Laura Mason, for working with me and the afternoon light to snap the author photo.

Meaghan McDonnell was in the car with me on Route 202, the "Daniel Shays Highway," when I first asked "who's this Shays fellow?" Her incisive comments triggered at least two transformations that made the manuscript readable. It will give me the greatest satisfaction to put a copy of this book in her hands, and also in the hands of Dick Schappach and Terry D'Andrea, whose craftsmanship and joy and love and support were an inspiration even before I had ever started to write.

I'll end by expressing gratitude to all the people who are keeping the struggle for justice alive, and replenishing the well of solidarity, trust, and pride from which Daniel Shays and his people and so many others have enriched our country's history.

Index